Contemporary Research in Sports Economics

Political Economics
Competition and Regulation

Edited by
Udo Müller, Oliver Budzinski, Yücel Calbay,
Jörg Jasper and Torsten Sundmacher

Volume 14

PL ACADEMIC RESEARCH

Oliver Budzinski
Arne Feddersen (eds.)

Contemporary Research in Sports Economics

Proceedings of the 5th ESEA Conference

PL ACADEMIC RESEARCH

Bibliographic Information published by the Deutsche Nationalbibliothek
The Deutsche Nationalbibliothek lists this publication in the Deutsche Nationalbibliografie; detailed bibliographic data is available in the internet at http://dnb.d-nb.de.

Library of Congress Cataloging-in-Publication Data

ESEA European Conference in Sports Economics (5th : 2013 : Esbjerg, Denmark)
Contemporary research in sports economics : proceedings of the 5th ESEA Conference / Oliver Budzinski, Arne Feddersen (eds.).
pages cm. -- (Political economics. Competition and regulation, ISSN 1439-7528 ; volume 14)
ISBN 978-3-631-64657-1 -- ISBN 978-3-653-04103-3 (E-Book)
1. Sports--Economic aspects--Congresses. 2. Soccer--Economic aspects--Congresses. 3. Union of European Football Associations--Congresses. I. Budzinski, Oliver, 1970- author, editor of compilation. II. Feddersen, Arne, 1974- editor of compilation. III. Title.
GV716.E74 2014
338.4'7796--dc23
2014018923

ISSN 1439-7528
ISBN 978-3-631-64657-1 (Print)
E-ISBN 978-3-653-04103-3 (E-Book)
DOI 10.3726/978-3-653-04103-3

PL Academic Research is an Imprint of Peter Lang GmbH.

Peter Lang – Frankfurt am Main · Bern · Bruxelles · New York · Oxford · Warszawa · Wien

This publication has been peer reviewed.

www.peterlang.com

Contents

Prolog

Introduction

Oliver Budzinski, Arne Feddersen

The 5th ESEA Conference, organized by the University of Southern Denmark (SDU) and co-organized by the Ilmenau University of Technology (Germany), was celebrated on the 19th and 20th of September 2013 in Esbjerg, Denmark. The Blue Water Arena – home of the local first division football club Esbjerg fB – appeared to be an appropriate venue to hold a conference on sports economics. The conference was opened by the Vice Major of Esbjerg Jakob Lose, SDU Pro-Vice-Chancellor Bjarne G. Sørensen, ESEA President Stefan Szymanski and the local organizers Oliver Budzinski (Ilmenau University of Technology) and Arne Feddersen (University of Southern Denmark). More than 100 participants were present in Esbjerg representing 21 different countries. While the majority of participants naturally came from European counties, participants from three non-European countries (USA, Australia, Chile) have been welcome. Overall, 78 presentations were included in parallel sessions throughout the two days of the conference. A number of authors have decided to submit their papers to be published in this collected volume, which represents a compilation of the presentations and discussions at the conference.

During the almost six decades since *Simon Rottenberg*'s (1956) seminal contribution kicked off the economic analysis of sports markets and industries, sports economics has developed to become a serious, important and vital field of economics. Along with the proceeding commercialization of (professional) sports, understanding the economics of sport has both become more and more important and enjoyed an increasing popularity among researchers around the world. In doing so, theoretical rigor and empirical excellence of the discipline meets the standards of other branches of economics as witnessed by an increasing number of sports economics publications in the best economics journals. Notwithstanding, conceptual contributions remain important driving-forces of sports economics research. Starting with a strong North-American focus and concentrating on the American major leagues as well as on European-style football, the process of broadening the scope to include other sports disciplines and event as well as to mitigate the neglect of other geographical areas is still ongoing, offering a rich variety of open research questions and problems.

The establishment of the European Conference on Sports Economics – by now the largest annual sports economics conference in the world – initiated by

Wladimir Andreff in Paris in 2009 and the subsequent foundation of the European Sports Economics Association in Cologne in 2010 have already contributed to this process in a considerable way. This is evidenced by the closing chapter of this volume in which *Daam van Reeth* (chapter 16) presents an overview and an analysis of the first five annual conferences of ESEA. It shows an impressive variety of topics and documents the growth of the conference.

It is probably not surprising, though, that European-style football (sometimes labeled as soccer) has been at the heart of the conferences and scored the highest share among the research contributions. This was the same at the Esbjerg conference and is consequently also reflected in this conference volume. Probably the hottest topic in current football economics – in science as well in (sports) politics and public discussion – is the UEFA financial fair play regulation. With it, the Union of European Football Associations seeks to avoid bankruptcies and insolvencies of clubs by implementing and enforcing rules regulating financial behavior and investment decisions of clubs. Following an impressive keynote presentation by *Egon Franck* (University of Zürich) at the Esbjerg conference, an intensive and controversial discussion on the merits and pitfalls of the regulation fascinated and alerted the participating researchers.[1] This volume resumes this fruitful discussion with a special section on financial fair play (FFP) comprising five papers on the pros and cons of UEFA's strategy to regulate financial behavior of football clubs. *Thomas Peeters* and *Stefan Szymanski* (chapter 2) analyze the impact of FFP's break-even rule on individual teams in England, Spain, Italy and France. In a counterfactual analysis they show which teams would be gaining and losing on the field and in financial terms – and, thus, the effect on the sportive competition. *Sean Hamil* (chapter 3) highlights the reasons for and the advantages of FFP using the example of the English Football League. He argues that European football is facing an unprecedented financial crisis and that the implementation of the FFP regime is an entirely reasonable and logical response to this crisis. The next two contributions represent a more critical view on FFP. From an American perspective, *Joel Maxcy* (chapter 4) compares FFP to salary caps in U.S. professional sports leagues. He concludes a revenue-shift away from players as well as considerable costs of regulation because he expects that FPP compliance will be investigated and enforced neither equitably nor efficiently. Eventually, he raises doubts that FFP will benefit

---

1 A written version of this keynote presentation will be published in the ESEA conference special issue of the International Journal of Sport Finance (*Franck* 2014). See also the objection by *Stefan Szymanski* (2014) in the same special issue.

football fans, who would prefer better matches and lower prices. Against the background of European competition policy, *Oliver Budzinski* (chapter 5) provides an economic analysis of the competition effects of FFP. He concludes that the restrictive effects of FFP cannot be justified by a legitimate objective defense because systemic overinvestment problems are not inherent to European football. Eventually, *Thomas Könecke* and *Mathias Schubert* (chapter 6) take up the notion of 'financial doping' and provide a positive analysis on how once legitimate (financial) enhancement turns into something that is deemed to represent illegal doping. Thus, the authors provide important insights into the socio-economic genesis of regulations like FFP.

Next to the controversial discussion about the economics of FFP, the following part of this volume includes three papers on other performance and competition issues of contemporary football. *Nikolaus Beck* and *Mark Meyer* (chapter 7) analyze the performance effects of within-season coach turnover. Based upon parametric econometric models, the authors identify a significant long term restoration of home advantage under the new coaches. Consequently, they cannot support the common 'ritual scapegoating' interpretation of coach dismissals. *Tim Pawlowski* and *Oliver Budzinski* (chapter 8) contribute theoretically and empirically to a better understanding of possible reasons for deviations between statistically-measured and perceived competitive balance by focusing on so-called attention level effects from behavioural economics. The study by *Peter Ochieng* (chapter 9) empirically analyzes the influence of investments into football facilities and events on future success in international competitions in Asia.

The economic analysis of sports events then forms the core of the next part of this volume. *Waldimir Andreff* (chapter 10) presents a comprehensive analysis of the winner's curse phenomenon in sports. Such deficient overbidding occurs in bids for hosting a mega-sporting event, when several cities compete to host a team franchise, TV channels bid for a league's broadcasting rights, or teams overbid for recruiting a same free agent or superstar player. *José Baños*, *Levi Pérez*, *Victor Puente* and *Plácido Rodríguez* (chapter 11) analyze the impact of broadcasts of live sport events on television audience sizes, using the example of a Spanish public regional TV channel. Eventually, *Christopher M. Keshock*, *Brooke Forester* and *Shelley Holden* (chapter 12) tell a striking political economy story about government subsidization of amateur sports contests. The authors show how politicians use exaggerated monetary values to garner community support of the events they propagandize.

The final part of this volume (before the epilogue closes) focuses on the economic analysis of individual sports. *Daam van Reeth* and *Wim Lagae* (chapter 13) empirically analyze the opinion of people on doping in cycling. In general, their study shows a strong disapproval of doping use, however, with statistically significant differences among population groups. For instance, cycling fans tend to be less negative towards doping in cycling than non-cycling fans. Furthermore, the authors observe some clear gender-based and age-based differences in opinion: women and older people are much more opposed to doping than men and younger people. *Grzegorz Kwiatkowski* and *Ove Oklevik* (chapter 14) analyze the socio-demographic, psychographic and trip-related factors that determine sport event visitors' expenditure behavior. The empirical analysis is based on primary data collected by questionnaires at three FIS Ski Jumping World Cup events staged in Norway in 2013. Eventually, *Anika Müller* and *Oliver Budzinski* (chapter 15) provide a conceptual analysis of the market for motorsport centers. The theory of platform competition (also labeled as two-sided or multisided markets) is employed in order to understand the specific characteristics of this market.

In summary, this volume presents an excellent overview on current topics of sports economics analysis. It combines the controversial discussion on a hot policy issue like financial fair play in European football with state-of-the-art theoretical, empirical and conceptual analyses of relevant economic phenomena in sports. As such it perfectly represents the outcomes of the 5th ESEA Conference and supplements the related special issue of the association's outlet International Journal of Sports Finance (volume 9, issue 3).[2]

As the local organizers of the Esbjerg conference we thank the *Municipality of Esbjerg* and the *Faculty of Business and Social Science* at the University of Southern Denmark for their financial and *Inspiring Denmark*, *VisitEsbjerg*, *Jesper Strandskov*, *Eva Roth*, *Ulla H. Oehlenschläger*, *Christian R.M. Jensen*, and *Grzegorz Kwiatkowski* for their administrative, organizational, and/or general support. Furthermore, we would like to thank ESEA for the opportunity to organize the conference in Esbjerg. Finally, it would not have been possible to stage the conference without the voluntary help and support of the ESEA board members and the members of the Scientific Committee. This conference volume would not have been possible without the enormous editorial work of *Ina Fredersdorf* and *Nadine Neute* that we appreciate very much and are very thankful. Furthermore, we thank the *Chair for Economic Theory* at *Ilmenau University of Technology* who provided the resources for realizing this book project.

2 This special issue consists of *Cabane* (2014), *Coates* et al. (2014), *Franck* (2014), *Paul & Weinbach* (2014), and *Szymanski* (2014).

References

Cabane, C. (2014): Unemployment Duration and Sport Participation, in: International Journal of Sports Finance, Vol. 9, 3, forthcoming.

Coates, D., Wicker, P., Feiler, S. & Breuer, C. (2014): A Bivariate Probit Examination of Financial and Volunteer Problems of Non-profit Sport Clubs, in: International Journal of Sports Finance, Vol. 9, 3, forthcoming.

Franck, E. (2014): Financial Fair Play in European Club Football – What is it all about?, in: International Journal of Sports Finance, Vol. 9, 3, forthcoming.

Paul, R. & *Weinbach*, A. (2014): The Impact of Atmospheric Conditions on the Baseball Totals Market, International Journal of Sports Finance, Vol. 9, 3, forthcoming.

Rottenberg, S. (1956): The Baseball Player's Labour Market, in: Journal of Political Economy, Vol. 64, 3, pp. 242–258.

Szymanski, S. (2014): Fair Is Foul: A Critical Analysis of UEFA Financial Fair Play, in: International Journal of Sports Finance, Vol. 9, 3, forthcoming.

Financial Fair Play in European Football

Financial Fair Play: Winners and Losers on and off the Pitch

Thomas Peeters, Stefan Szymanski

Abstract

In this chapter we analyze the impact of the break-even rule embedded in Financial Fair Play on individual teams in England, Spain, Italy and France. In a counterfactual analysis we show which teams would be gaining and losing on the field and in financial terms. We also compare these results to the findings of the theoretical literature on Financial Fair Play.

Keywords

Financial Fair Play, break-even rule, European football

1. Introduction

In this chapter we look at the effects of the introduction of the break-even rule embedded in UEFA's Financial Fair Play regulations (*UEFA 2012*). The break-even rule forbids clubs to spend more in "relevant" costs than they earn in "relevant" revenues with some leeway in the form of an "acceptable deviation". In practice relevant costs include transfer costs (which is not the same as net transfer spending), player and manager salaries and other operating costs, but the term excludes investments in certain assets such as stadium facilities and youth academies. Relevant revenues are mainly comprised of match-day, media and sponsorship income. Crucially this excludes direct investments by team owners to fund operational losses. The rule is gradually going into effect in four phases, where UEFA is planning to decrease the acceptable deviation over time. Starting in 2014 teams are allowed to lose €45m over the past three seasons. This declines to €30m in 2016 and then further to an unspecified amount in 2019. In the long run UEFA wants to arrive at an acceptable deviation of €5m over three seasons. We analyze four regimes of the break-even rule, where we follow UEFA's targets for the acceptable deviation, i.e.:

- €15m: teams are allowed an average loss of €15m over three years
- €10m: teams are allowed an average loss of €10m over three years
- €5m: teams are allowed an average loss of €5m over three years
- final: teams are allowed a total loss of €5m over three years.

For the analysis in this chapter we rely on the model developed in *Peeters* and *Szymanski* (2014) to simulate counterfactual results for 4 leagues, the English Premier League (EPL), the Spanish Primera Division (La Liga), the Italian Serie A and the French Ligue 1. In this contribution we specifically focus on the results at the club level. For each league we first examine the financial consequences of the break-even rule. Which teams would see their costs decline, and by how much? Which teams could witness significant improvements in profitability? Then we examine what the effects on the field of play would be. How big could the impact of the break-even rule be on team's points total? What does this imply for the championship races in each of these leagues? Which teams could drop out and which would become competitive?

In the following section we briefly explain the mechanics of the modelling approach set out in *Peeters* and *Szymanski* (2014). We revisit the most crucial assumptions underlying the model and offer some intuition for the working of the counterfactual and its basic results. We then turn to a detailed discussion of our results in terms of wage to turnover ratios (wtto) and sports competition at the individual team level. The next section compares our results with those predicted by several theoretical models in the literature. In the final section we formulate a couple of concluding remarks and reflect on future extensions of this research agenda.

2. A Model to Simulate the Break-Even Rule

Figure 1 depicts a graphical representation of the model we develop in *Peeters* and *Szymanski* (2014) with just 2 teams. The model starts with the club owner, who derives utility both from winning games and from earning money on his investment in the team. Given his personal preferences for winning versus financial gains, each owner chooses a budget constraint which is either a negative amount he is willing to invest (i.e. finance the team's losses) or a positive amount he hopes to obtain (in the form of profits).

The second agent in our model is the manager of the club, whose task consists of winning as many points as possible given the budget constraint set by the owner. We assume that each game between teams i and j is a contest in which investments in talented players improve a team's chances of winning. This implies that a manager can raise the expected points his team obtains over the course of the season by increasing the total wage bill of the team. Additionally, we assume that home teams are more likely to win games and that each team has a specific individual productivity in the contest. The manager treats these two variables as given when deciding on the level of payroll he sets.

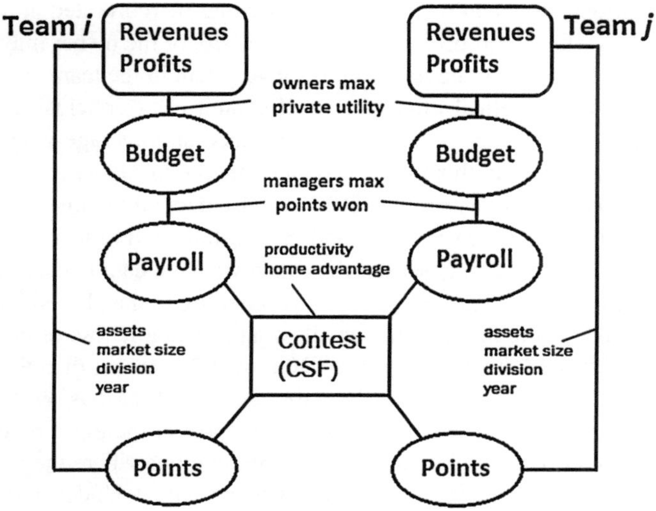

Fig. 1: Graphical representation of the model for 2 teams

Based on the probabilities of winning each individual game, we get the expected points won by the team over the course of the season. The model assumes that these are a major driver of the revenues the teams generate. Revenues further depend on the value of tangible fixed assets (mainly its stadium) and league-, season- and club-specific factors (such as the TV contract and local market characteristics). We assume that in the short run the manager can only influence revenues through the expected points total. Finally, each club also incurs costs other than payroll, e.g. maintenance of its infrastructure, which the manager minimizes in order to drive up the spending on player salaries. This leads us to define the profits of the team as the difference between revenues and the sum of payroll and other costs. We show in *Peeters* and *Szymanski* (2014) that the manager's decision problem boils down to selecting the maximum amount of payroll which allows the club profits (or losses) to be equal to the owner's budget constraint.

It is straightforward to introduce the break-even rule in this model by assuming that it will restrict owners who are willing to tolerate overly large financial losses. For those owners the rule pushes up the budget constraint, i.e. it has to become less negative and losses have to shrink. The manager can only respond by cutting back on salaries, which leads the team to win less games. This in turn has an effect on all other teams, who can now win more games with the same level of payroll. As a consequence they also obtain more revenues for each level of payroll they set. This additional financial wiggle room may either be reinvested in the playing squad, which is what a win-oriented owner would do, or the owner may decide to increase profits, improving the return on his investment in the team.

Given that the theoretical model by itself cannot offer conclusive results on interesting dimensions such as competitive balance and average wage bills, we estimate the parameters in this model and simulate the introduction of the break-even rule. In *Peeters* and *Szymanski* (2014) we use data on the financial accounts of clubs in 4 European countries (England, Spain, Italy and France) and simulate the break-even rule in the final season for which we have data in each league. We look at 4 regimes of the break-even rule corresponding to the phased introduction of the regulation. In the first regime we allow an acceptable loss of €45m over 3 seasons, in the second this is reduced to €30m over 3 seasons, then €15m over 3 seasons and in the "final" regime we allow for €5m over 3 seasons. We present two scenarios in each case, i.e. one where all owners pocket the extra revenues they get after FFP is introduced (the "profit" scenario) and one where they all reinvest those proceeds in their playing squad (the "win" scenario). Under both scenarios and in all leagues our results indicate that:

- average team payroll drops significantly and stronger in more stringent regimes,
- average wtto decreases drastically, again stronger in more stringent regimes,
- competitive balance may increase or decrease, but decreases as regimes get more stringent.

This leads us to conclude that the players (and those whose incomes depend on them) are going to be the primary losers when the break-even rule comes into effect. They would see a significant part of their economic rents shifted to the clubs, who could use this windfall to pay higher dividends. The tax authorities are an obvious second loser, since taxes on player wages are usually higher and easier to collect than taxes on capital gains of (often foreign) owners. Finally, and probably most importantly, we find little to no gains for consumers in the introduction of the break-even rule. First, in as far as competitive balance matters to European football fans, there seems to be little improvement in that area. The break-even rule would surely make it harder for the small teams to get financial backing to challenge the traditional top clubs. Second, financial stability of the clubs may be a worthy cause, but this is achieved mostly through other aspects of the FFP rules. Finally, it is clear that the break-even rule would do nothing to spur economic competition for consumers between teams.

3. Simulation Results

In the previous section we described the results in *Peeters* and *Szymanski* (2014) concerning the effects of the break-even rule in terms of league averages. We have not yet discussed however which individual teams would gain in financial and sports terms. In this section we therefore take a closer look at the individual team results in four league-seasons, i.e. the 2010 season for the Premier League and the 2011 season for the Primera Division, Serie A and Ligue 1. All reported simulation results in this section refer to the "Olley-Pakes" methodology outlined in *Peeters* and *Szymanski* (2014).

English Premier League

A first thing to note in relation to table 1 is that the results for Portsmouth should be disregarded as we have no data on their financial accounts for the 2010 season. In the simulation we use 2009 numbers and assume that the break-even rule has no impact on the club.

*Table 1: Simulated wtto for 2010 Premier League teams, * indicates team is constrained*

Club	real no FFP		€15m		€10m		€5m		final	
			Win %	Profit %	Win %	Profit %	Win %	Profit %	Win %	Profit %
Manchester Utd.	46.0	45.5	44.0*	43.4*	42.5*	42.0*	41.2*	40.6*	40.3*	39.6*
Arsenal	49.7	53.5	53.9	53.0	54.0	52.9	54.1	52.7	54.3	52.6
Chelsea	82.4	75.7	53.6*	53.7*	51.8*	51.9*	50.0*	50.1*	48.9*	48.9*
Liverpool	65.6	63.3	56.3*	56.2*	54.1*	54.0*	52.0*	51.9*	50.6*	50.4*
Manchester City	106.6	124.6	59.7*	59.8*	55.4*	55.5*	51.1*	51.3*	48.3*	48.5*
Aston Villa	88.0	85.9	65.7*	65.7*	61.0*	61.1*	56.3*	56.4*	53.2*	53.3*
Tottenham	56.0	53.0	53.7	52.3	53.9	52.2	54.2	51.9	54.4	51.6
~~Portsmouth~~		~~93.4~~	~~92.3~~	~~92.1~~	~~91.9~~	~~91.7~~	~~91.4~~	~~91.2~~	~~91.0~~	~~90.7~~
Everton	68.7	73.2	73.6	72.2	73.7	71.9	73.8	71.5	74.0	71.1
Fulham	63.9	79.9	80.2	78.8	79.6*	77.9*	73.0*	71.7*	68.5*	67.5*
Stoke	76.0	117.5	117.2	115.8	117.1	115.3	117.0	114.6	113.4*	110.7*
Sunderland	82.1	64.1	54.7*	54.8*	49.1*	49.3*	43.4*	43.6*	39.5*	39.8*
West Ham	74.4	63.9	46.1*	46.3*	39.8*	40.0*	32.7*	33.2*	27.1*	27.9*
Blackburn	82.0	75.4	75.8	74.4	75.9	74.0	76.1	73.5	76.3	73.1
Bolton	86.1	78.5	68.8*	68.8*	61.3*	61.4*	53.5*	53.7*	48.2*	48.4*
Birmingham	65.1	59.7	60.4	58.8	60.6	58.5	58.9*	56.5*	54.3*	52.4*

Club	real	no FFP	€15m		€10m		€5m		final	
			Win %	Profit %	Win %	Profit %	Win %	Profit %	Win %	Profit %
Hull	80.6	76.8	77.2	75.7	77.4	75.3	75.5*	73.1*	70.1*	68.0*
Wigan	90.5	111.2	111.1	109.5	111.0	108.9	102.9	101.2	95.4	94.1
Wolverhampton	49.1	42.7	43.9	42.0	44.3	41.8	44.9*	41.5*	45.4*	41.2*
Burnley	48.8	63.0	63.8	61.9	64.1	61.6	64.5	61.0	64.9	60.5

Looking at the state of affairs in the "real" and estimated "no FFP" scenarios reveals that, without the break-even rule, wtto ratios differ significantly among Premier League clubs. We find financially sustainable ratios in the 40%-60% range at the traditional large market teams (Arsenal, Manchester United and Tottenham) and at the bottom of the league with currently relegated sides Burnley and Wolverhampton. At the other end of the spectrum a good amount of teams are paying over 80% of their revenues in wages. Here, sugar daddy backed Manchester City leads the way boosting a payroll well above its annual income to sustain its competitiveness at the top. Several of the smaller market teams (e.g. Wigan, Aston Villa and Bolton) are also investing almost their entire turnover, probably in an attempt to safeguard themselves from relegation. As such, we find large financial burdens at the top and bottom of the league, but specifically at teams who are seemingly trying to achieve a level of sporting success, which has historically been above their reach.

The working of the break-even rule should be assessed by comparing the simulated regimes with the "no FFP" column. In the "profit"-scenario the effect on wtto is straightforward, as it leads to a decrease for all teams. Naturally, constrained teams, which are marked by a star, witness the most important profitability improvements. For sugar daddy owned Manchester City and Chelsea the gains may add up to 70% and 25% of revenues respectively. For smaller market teams such as West Ham, Aston Villa and Bolton, we see comparable percentage improvement, especially in the more stringent regimes. Unconstrained teams, such as Tottenham and Arsenal, see a small decline in wtto under the "profit"-scenario, as they save up the extra revenue they obtain. In the "win"-scenario they experience a slight deterioration of their wtto as a consequence of increased investments in their playing squad. It appears therefore that the largest part of the financial gains FFP could bring to the Premier League, would flow to sugar daddy owners and small market teams. They appear to be the financial winners of the introduction of the break-even rule.

Table 2 depicts the simulated points table of the 2010 EPL season. Comparing the simulated outcomes under the break-even rule to the "no FFP" case reveals that teams with a healthy wtto in the original regime see the largest point gains. Examples in this category are Arsenal (+3 to +6 points), Tottenham (+3 to +7 points), Everton (+3 to +7 points), Wolverhampton (+3 to +7 points) and Burnley (+2 to +5 points). Furthermore, we see large points losses for teams which experience some of the largest financial gains. At the bottom of the table this implies that West Ham (-6 to -17 points) and Bolton (-1 to -7 points) could be in serious danger of relegation. At the top Manchester City (-15 to -19 points) and Chelsea (-5 to -6 points) would find it a lot more difficult to challenge the traditional top teams Manchester United and Arsenal. A couple of teams seem to be able to win big both financially and on the playing field. Liverpool for example gains 10% to 15% in wtto and easily beats its direct competitors Manchester City and Chelsea in the points table.

Table 2: Simulated points table 2010 Premier League

Club	**real**	**no FFP**	**€15m**		**€10m**		**€5m**		**final**	
			win	**profit**	**win**	**profit**	**win**	**profit**	**win**	**profit**
Manchester Utd.	85	83.0	84.8	84.8	84.7	84.8	85.0	85.0	85.3	85.4
Arsenal	75	76.8	79.6	79.5	80.3	80.2	81.4	81.2	82.3	82.0
Chelsea	86	76.5	70.7	71.1	70.6	71.0	70.8	71.4	71.3	71.9
Liverpool	63	75.9	75.7	76.0	75.5	75.9	75.6	76.0	75.9	76.4
Manchester City	67	75.8	59.5	59.9	58.3	58.8	57.4	58.0	57.0	57.7
Aston Villa	64	62.7	58.3	58.6	57.1	57.6	56.2	56.8	55.9	56.5
Tottenham	70	53.8	56.8	56.5	57.7	57.3	59.1	58.5	60.4	59.6
~~Portsmouth~~		~~50.0~~	~~52.4~~	~~52.7~~	~~53.1~~	~~53.5~~	~~54.2~~	~~54.7~~	~~55.3~~	~~55.9~~
Everton	61	49.9	52.7	52.5	53.6	53.3	54.9	54.6	56.2	55.7
Fulham	46	46.4	49.1	48.9	49.7	49.6	48.6	48.7	48.2	48.4
Stoke	47	44.8	47.3	47.3	48.1	48.1	49.4	49.3	49.8	49.7
Sunderland	44	44.6	42.8	43.2	40.8	41.3	38.8	39.5	37.6	38.4
West Ham	35	44.1	37.8	38.3	34.8	35.4	31.1	32.0	27.8	29.0
Blackburn	50	43.1	45.7	45.6	46.6	46.4	48.0	47.6	49.3	48.7
Bolton	39	42.7	41.7	42.0	39.4	39.9	37.1	37.8	35.7	36.4
Birmingham	50	39.2	41.9	41.6	42.9	42.4	43.4	42.8	42.5	42.1
Hull	30	36.7	39.2	39.0	40.0	39.8	40.7	40.4	40.0	39.8
Wigan	36	35.8	38.1	38.0	38.9	38.8	38.2	38.3	37.4	37.7
Wolverhampton	38	35.5	38.5	37.7	39.6	38.5	41.2	39.7	42.8	40.8
Burnley	30	27.6	29.9	29.5	30.7	30.2	32.2	31.3	33.5	32.3

Spanish Primera Division

Table 3 shows that the financial health of Spanish first division teams, as measured by their wtto, is not dramatically different from the situation in England. As in England we see a diverse picture. Several small and large market teams contain payroll costs around or below 60% of turnover, while others (most notably Malaga) boost payrolls well above 90% of revenues. Contrary to popular belief, Real Madrid has a reasonable wtto and would not be restricted by the break-even rule in any of the regimes, while Barcelona would be restricted even in the "€15m" -scenario.

Table 3: Simulated wtto for 2011 Primera Division teams, indicates team is constrained*

Club	real no FFP		€15m		€10m		€5m		final	
			Win %	Profit %	Win %	Profit %	Win %	Profit %	Win %	Profit %
Real Madrid	60.2	63.4	63.5	63.4	63.5	63.3	63.6	63.1	63.7	62.9
Barcelona	79.6	87.4	82.4*	82.4*	80.6*	80.6*	78.8*	78.7*	77.7*	77.3*
Valencia	49.0	51.1	51.1	51.0	47.8*	47.9*	43.5*	43.5*	40.6*	40.6*
Atlético Madrid	71.0	71.0	71.1	71.0	67.3*	67.2*	61.6*	61.6*	58.0*	57.8*
Athletic Club	79.2	80.2	80.2	80.1	80.3	79.9	80.4	79.4	80.5	78.9
Villarreal	90.9	95.7	95.8	95.6	95.8	95.4	90.1*	89.7*	83.6*	83.1*
Málaga	169.3	157.3	157.2	157.1	146.1*	146.1*	129.7*	129.6*	118.6*	118.4*
Espanyol	71.9	68.7	68.8	68.7	68.9	68.5	68.5*	67.6*	61.0*	60.4*
Sevilla	93.5	97.2	97.2	97.1	97.2	96.8	97.2	96.2	97.2	95.6
Getafe	102.9	98.5	98.5	98.3	98.5	98.1	98.5	97.4	92.8*	91.6*
Dep. La Coruna	38.4	36.5	36.6	36.5	36.9	36.4	37.4	36.1	37.9	35.9
Real Sociedad	68.6	67.1	67.2	67.0	67.3	66.9	67.5	66.4	67.8	65.9
Real Zaragoza	89.6	88.3	72.5*	72.5*	58.0*	58.0*	42.4*	42.5*	30.8*	31.0*
Osasuna	81.9	82.4	82.4	82.3	82.5	82.0	82.6	81.5	82.7	80.8
Sporting Gijón	53.3	54.5	54.5	54.4	54.7	54.2	55.0	53.8	55.4	53.4
Hércules	76.1	69.2	69.2	69.1	63.2*	63.3*	43.4*	43.5*	28.0*	28.2*
Levante	54.9	55.7	55.8	55.6	55.9	55.4	56.3	55.0	56.7	54.6
Racing Santander	85.9	88.2	88.2	88.1	87.2*	86.9*	65.3*	65.3*	49.7*	49.8*
Mallorca	60.6	62.6	62.7	62.5	62.8	62.3	63.1	61.8	63.5	61.3
Almería	67.2	61.2	61.3	61.1	61.4	60.9	61.8	60.4	62.2	59.8

Unlike in England, almost all small market teams escape the effects of the break-even rule in the less stringent regimes, because their financial clout is too small to make €45m in losses over three seasons. Consequently only Zaragoza and

Barcelona are restricted in the "€15m"-scenario with more small market teams being affected as the regime becomes stricter. In the "final" regime we find large improvements in the profitability for a whole range of small market teams, such as Zaragoza (57%), Hercules (41%), Malaga (39%) and Racing Santander (39%). We also see a couple of restricted large market teams making significant gains in the 10%-15% range, i.e. Atletico Madrid, Valencia and Barcelona.

Looking at the points tables presented in table 4 reveals that significant point shifts should only be expected in Spain under the more stringent regimes. In the "final" regime we see large points losses for some restricted small market teams such as Zaragoza (-10 points) Hercules (-7 points) and Santander (-4 points). These teams seem to pay a price for their increased profitability in terms of competitiveness on the pitch. Other big financial winners, most notably Barcelona, Atletico, Valencia and Malaga barely see any effect on their points total. They could clearly be qualified as prime beneficiaries of the introduction of FFP. Most unrestricted teams witness small increases in their on-field performance, but these are never above 2 points.

Table 4: Simulated points table 2011 Primera Division teams

Club	**real no FFP**		**€15m**		**€10m**		**€5m**		**final**	
			win	**profit**	**win**	**profit**	**win**	**profit**	**win**	**profit**
Real Madrid	92	81.3	81.4	81.4	81.7	81.7	82.3	82.3	83.0	83.0
Barcelona	96	77.1	76.6	76.6	76.6	76.7	77.1	77.2	77.6	77.8
Valencia	71	64.4	64.6	64.6	64.1	64.2	63.8	63.9	63.8	64.0
Atlético Madrid	58	57.8	58.0	58.0	57.6	57.7	57.4	57.5	57.6	57.7
Athletic Club	58	56.4	56.5	56.5	56.9	56.9	57.7	57.7	58.6	58.5
Villarreal	62	54.9	55.0	55.0	55.3	55.3	55.4	55.5	55.4	55.5
Málaga	46	54.7	54.8	54.8	54.3	54.3	53.7	53.8	53.5	53.7
Espanyol	49	54.3	54.5	54.5	54.8	54.8	55.6	55.5	55.1	55.1
Sevilla	58	52.9	53.1	53.1	53.4	53.4	54.2	54.2	55.1	55.1
Getafe	44	48.8	48.9	49.0	49.3	49.3	50.1	50.1	50.3	50.3
Deportivo La Coruna	43	48.4	48.6	48.5	48.9	48.8	49.9	49.7	51.0	50.5
Real Sociedad	45	47.3	47.5	47.5	47.8	47.8	48.7	48.6	49.6	49.5
Real Zaragoza	45	46.6	44.4	44.4	42.1	42.2	39.3	39.5	36.6	36.9
Osasuna	47	46.3	46.4	46.4	46.8	46.8	47.6	47.5	48.5	48.4
Sporting Gijón	47	44.7	44.9	44.9	45.2	45.2	46.1	46.0	47.1	46.9
Hércules	35	43.8	44.0	44.0	43.2	43.3	39.7	39.9	35.7	36.0
Levante	45	43.5	43.7	43.7	44.0	44.0	44.9	44.8	45.9	45.7
Racing Santander	46	43.3	43.5	43.5	43.6	43.6	41.1	41.2	38.9	39.1

Club	real no FFP		€15m		€10m		€5m		final	
			win	profit	win	profit	win	profit	win	profit
Mallorca	44	40.7	40.9	40.9	41.2	41.2	42.1	41.9	43.0	42.8
Almería	30	37.3	37.4	37.4	37.8	37.7	38.6	38.5	39.6	39.4

Italian Serie A

Table 5 presents the wtto results for the Italian Serie A teams. As in the case of Portsmouth, we should also disregard the results for Bari because of missing 2011 data. Apart from Bari however, the vast majority of Italian clubs appear to control their payroll quite well in the "no FFP" scenario. In sharp contrast to Spain and England, just one team (Sampdoria) has an observed wtto above 80%. Especially teams in the bottom half of the table have a significantly lower wtto than their British and Spanish counterparts, with most teams staying well below the 60% mark. Most large market teams, in particular Internazionale, Milan and Roma, have relatively high wtto figures compared to the rest of the league.

This state of affairs is also reflected in the simulation results for the break-even rule. In the mildest regimes we find that only the top clubs are restricted. As in Spain, part of the explanation is that Italy's small market teams lack the economic clout to have consistent losses above €15m per season, but surely their better financial health also plays to their advantage. Surprisingly given their reasonable wtto, the effect on some of the top teams is quite strong. Internazionale for example improves its wtto by as much as 37% to 43% depending on the regime, while Milan and Juventus also save 13% to 17% and 7% to 13% respectively. Looking further down the table we find that significant payroll reductions only set in in the "final" regime for most clubs. A couple of clubs see significant profitability improvements in this scenario, most notably Sampdoria (30%), Lecce (16%) and Bologna (15%).

*Table 5: Simulated wtto for 2011 Serie A teams, * indicates team is constrained*

Club	real no FFP		€15m		€10m		€5m		final	
			Win %	Profit %	Win %	Profit %	Win %	Profit %	Win %	Profit %
Internazionale	70.0	69.6	32.6*	32.8*	30.2*	30.4*	27.9*	28.1*	26.5*	26.8*
Milan	63.5	65.8	52.4*	52.5*	50.7*	50.7*	49.0*	49.1*	48.0*	48.1*
Roma	64.0	62.5	60.8*	60.4*	57.6*	57.6*	54.6*	54.5*	52.6*	52.5*
Juventus	52.8	52.7	45.0*	45.1*	42.8*	43.0*	40.8*	41.0*	39.7*	39.9*
Napoli	44.2	48.5	48.9	48.2	49.0	48.0	49.3	47.8	49.6	47.5
Fiorentina	56.0	54.2	54.6	53.9	51.8*	51.5*	46.3*	46.3*	42.6*	42.8*
Genoa	70.0	68.3	68.5	67.8	68.6	67.7	67.6*	66.3*	63.2*	62.1*
Lazio	29.1	32.1	32.7	31.8	32.9	31.8	33.4	31.6	34.0	31.4
~~Bari~~		~~102.3~~	~~101.7~~	~~101.5~~	~~101.5~~	~~101.3~~	~~101.0~~	~~100.7~~	~~100.4~~	~~100.0~~
Palermo	41.9	44.1	44.5	43.7	44.7	43.6	45.1	43.4	45.5	43.1
Parma	57.8	56.3	56.6	55.9	56.8	55.7	57.0	55.4	53.7*	52.2*
Sampdoria	84.4	74.2	74.4	73.6	63.9*	64.0*	52.1*	52.3*	43.6*	44.0*
Bologna	56.6	56.1	56.4	55.7	56.6	55.5	49.0*	49.0*	41.2*	41.5*
Lecce	57.7	55.0	55.4	54.6	55.5	54.5	49.1*	49.0*	38.6*	39.0*
Udinese	50.9	60.0	60.3	59.6	60.5	59.4	60.7	59.1	61.1	58.6
Cagliari	40.0	40.9	41.5	40.6	41.7	40.5	42.2	40.2	42.7	39.9
Chievo	46.1	49.4	49.8	49.0	50.0	48.8	50.4	48.5	47.8*	46.0*
Cesena	51.5	53.6	54.0	53.2	54.2	53.0	54.5	52.7	55.0	52.2
Catania	37.2	39.9	40.5	39.6	40.7	39.5	41.3	39.2	41.9	38.9
Brescia	51.2	48.0	48.5	47.6	48.7	47.4	49.1	47.1	49.7	46.7

To gain insight into the effects of the break-even rule on the pitch, we calculate the simulated points table for the 2011 Serie A season in table 6. A first observation is that Internazionale suffers a significant decline in its on-field performance, i.e. up to around -13 points. The other restricted large market teams, Roma, Milan and Juventus manage to keep up their sports performance, suffering mild point declines if any. The projected points difference between both Milan clubs would grow significantly, meaning that Inter would be dropping out of contention for the league title. This seems intuitive, as Inter's payroll reduction would be far more severe than that of its direct competitors. The prime winner at the top appears to be Napoli. Our results project them to challenge Juventus for a top four finish, which leads to Champions League qualification.

In the bottom half of the table most teams enjoy small increases in their on-field performance, particularly in the mildest regimes. Once the break-even rule becomes stricter, the points total decline for some of the restricted teams, such as Sampdoria (-6 points), Lecce and Bologna (both -3 points). These could lead to relatively large falls along the final ranking, as almost all teams around these clubs see moderate additions to their points tally. Looking at the combined results on and off the pitch, we argue that Roma and Milan are the clear winners under the break-even rule regimes. They both obtain significant cost reductions, which do not hamper their ability to perform on the pitch.

Table 6: Simulated points table 2011 Serie A teams

Club	**real no FFP**		**€15m**		**€10m**		**€5m**		**final**	
			win	**profit**	**win**	**profit**	**win**	**profit**	**win**	**profit**
Internazionale	76	77.2	65.5	65.7	64.4	64.8	63.7	64.2	63.6	64.2
Milan	82	75.3	72.5	72.7	72.3	72.5	72.3	72.7	72.7	73.2
Roma	63	66.5	66.9	67.0	66.3	66.6	66.0	66.3	66.2	66.6
Juventus	58	58.3	56.2	56.5	55.7	56.0	55.5	55.9	55.8	56.4
Napoli	70	56.5	57.4	57.4	57.8	57.7	58.6	58.4	59.5	59.2
Fiorentina	51	55.0	56.0	56.0	55.4	55.5	54.0	54.4	53.3	53.9
Genoa	51	54.1	54.9	55.0	55.3	55.3	55.7	55.7	55.3	55.4
Lazio	66	52.4	53.6	53.3	54.0	53.6	55.0	54.3	56.1	55.1
~~Bari~~		~~49.7~~	~~50.4~~	~~50.5~~	~~50.6~~	~~50.9~~	~~51.2~~	~~51.5~~	~~51.9~~	~~52.4~~
Palermo	56	49.7	50.6	50.5	51.0	50.9	51.8	51.5	52.9	52.3
Parma	46	48.9	49.8	49.8	50.2	50.1	50.9	50.8	50.7	50.6
Sampdoria	36	48.7	49.5	49.5	47.1	47.4	44.1	44.5	41.7	42.3
Bologna	45	46.0	46.8	46.8	47.2	47.1	45.2	45.6	42.9	43.6
Lecce	41	45.8	46.6	46.6	47.0	46.9	45.4	45.7	41.9	42.6
Udinese	66	44.8	45.6	45.6	45.9	45.9	46.7	46.5	47.6	47.4
Cagliari	45	42.6	43.6	43.4	44.0	43.7	44.8	44.4	45.9	45.2
Chievo	46	39.2	40.0	39.9	40.3	40.2	41.1	40.8	41.0	40.8
Cesena	43	39.1	39.9	39.8	40.2	40.1	41.0	40.8	42.0	41.5
Catania	46	39.1	40.0	39.8	40.4	40.1	41.3	40.7	42.4	41.5
Brescia	32	37.2	38.0	37.9	38.4	38.2	39.2	38.8	40.2	39.6

French Ligue 1

Table 7 gives an overview of the team wtto for the French Ligue 1 clubs. In line with England and Spain, a significant group of French clubs have a wtto well above 80%. Among these, Lille stands out with a wtto close to 100%, followed by smaller teams such as Valenciennes, Lorient and Auxerre. Most other teams, show a wtto in between 60% and 80%. The only exception appears to be the tiny Arles, which was relegated after just one season in the league. An important remark in relation to table 7 is however that in 2011 both Monaco and Paris St Germain were not yet owned by their current benefactor owners. It is conceivable that these teams' recent investments in several superstar players have severely deteriorated their wtto. We are therefore cautious in using table 7 to assess the current financial health of the Ligue 1 teams.

With Ligue 1 being the smallest league in our sample in terms of economic size, it is not a big surprise that the milder regimes of the break-even rule do not restrict the French small market teams. Indeed, for both the "€15m" and "€10m" scenarios, the only restricted teams are the traditional large market teams Lyon and Paris St Germain. We project that the break-even rule reduces their wtto by about 5% to 20% depending on the FFP regime. Once the more stringent regimes set in, several small market teams could also witness significant improvements, e.g. for the "final" regime Valenciennes (-18%), Monaco (-16%), Nancy (-12%) and Lens (-12%). Most unconstrained teams experience very modest changes in wtto, which rarely surpass 1%.

Table 7: Simulated wtto for 2011 Ligue 1 teams, indicates team is constrained*

Club	real no FFP		€15m		€10m		€5m		final	
			Win %	Profit %	Win %	Profit %	Win %	Profit %	Win %	Profit %
Marseille	81.2	79.2	79.2	79.1	79.2	79.0	79.3	78.8	79.4	78.5
Lyon	72.0	69.9	60.6*	60.6*	56.8*	56.8*	52.9*	53.0*	50.5*	50.5*
Paris St Germain	74.4	70.9	65.6*	65.6*	60.1*	60.1*	54.5*	54.5*	50.8*	50.9*
Lille	99.0	105.1	105.1	105.0	105.1	104.9	105.1	104.6	101.0*	100.5*
Bordeaux	71.5	69.3	69.4	69.2	69.4	69.2	69.5	69.0	69.7	68.6
Auxerre	84.5	82.3	82.3	82.1	82.3	82.0	82.4	81.8	75.2*	75.1*
Montpellier	79.1	76.1	76.1	75.9	76.1	75.9	76.2	75.6	76.3	75.2
Rennes	76.8	79.1	79.2	79.0	79.2	78.9	79.3	78.7	79.4	78.2
Monaco	81.2	76.7	76.7	76.6	76.7	76.5	67.9*	67.9*	60.4*	60.5*
Toulouse	76.1	76.3	76.4	76.2	76.4	76.1	76.5	75.9	76.6	75.4
Sochaux	64.6	69.7	69.7	69.6	69.7	69.5	69.9	69.2	68.0*	67.2*
Lorient	85.6	87.5	87.5	87.3	87.5	87.2	87.6	86.9	87.6	86.4
Nancy	80.6	81.9	81.9	81.7	81.9	81.6	80.3*	80.0*	69.7*	69.7*
Saint Etienne	60.0	61.5	61.6	61.5	61.7	61.4	61.8	61.2	62.1	60.8
Lens	71.7	65.3	65.4	65.2	65.4	65.1	59.9*	60.0*	53.9*	53.9*
Nice	78.3	80.0	80.0	79.8	80.0	79.7	80.1	79.5	80.2	78.9

Club	real no FFP		€15m		€10m		€5m		final	
			Win %	Profit %	Win %	Profit %	Win %	Profit %	Win %	Profit %
Brest	62.7	64.2	64.3	64.1	64.3	64.0	64.5	63.8	64.7	63.4
Valenciennes	86.0	89.8	89.9	89.7	89.9	89.6	84.1*	84.1*	71.8*	71.9*
Caen	68.0	70.2	70.2	70.1	70.3	70.0	70.4	69.7	70.6	69.3
Arles	57.7	46.6	46.7	46.5	46.7	46.4	47.0	46.2	47.6	45.9

Table 8 holds the resulting points tables for the break-even rule simulations in the Ligue 1. In all regimes we find the largest declines in points totals, -3 to -5 points, for Paris St Germain and Lyon. Lille would be the main beneficiary of this, as it gets an opportunity to compete for the top 3 places. As in Italy, we project smaller point differences further down the table. Both Valenciennes and Monaco would only lose around 3 points despite a fall of more than 15% in wtto. Given that most of their direct competitors would see small gains however, they might lose a couple of places in the final ranking.

Table 8: Simulated points table 2011 Serie A teams

Club	real no FFP		€15m		€10m		€5m		final	
			win	profit	win	profit	win	profit	win	profit
Marseille	68	72.6	72.8	72.8	73.0	73.0	73.4	73.4	74.1	74.1
Lyon	64	69.1	66.5	66.5	65.4	65.4	64.4	64.5	64.2	64.5
Paris St Germain	60	68.1	66.8	66.8	65.2	65.3	63.7	63.8	63.0	63.3
Lille	76	65.1	65.3	65.3	65.5	65.5	65.9	65.9	65.9	66.0
Bordeaux	51	55.2	55.4	55.4	55.5	55.5	56.0	56.0	56.8	56.7
Auxerre	49	52.5	52.7	52.7	52.8	52.8	53.3	53.3	52.2	52.4
Montpellier	47	52.0	52.2	52.2	52.4	52.4	52.8	52.8	53.7	53.6
Rennes	56	51.8	52.0	52.0	52.1	52.1	52.6	52.6	53.4	53.3
Monaco	44	51.1	51.3	51.3	51.4	51.4	49.3	49.5	47.7	48.0
Toulouse	50	49.6	49.8	49.8	49.9	49.9	50.4	50.4	51.3	51.1
Sochaux	58	47.7	47.9	47.9	48.0	48.0	48.5	48.4	48.8	48.7
Lorient	49	46.3	46.5	46.5	46.6	46.6	47.1	47.1	47.9	47.8
Nancy	48	46.1	46.3	46.3	46.4	46.4	46.4	46.5	44.3	44.6
Saint Etienne	49	46.0	46.2	46.1	46.3	46.3	46.8	46.7	47.6	47.4
Lens	35	44.6	44.8	44.8	44.9	44.9	43.6	43.8	42.3	42.5
Nice	46	43.6	43.8	43.8	43.9	43.9	44.4	44.4	45.2	45.1
Brest	46	43.2	43.4	43.4	43.5	43.5	44.0	43.9	44.9	44.7

Club	real no FFP		€15m		€10m		€5m		final	
			win	profit	win	profit	win	profit	win	profit
Valenciennes	48	42.9	43.0	43.0	43.2	43.2	42.2	42.4	39.9	40.1
Caen	46	42.5	42.6	42.6	42.8	42.8	43.2	43.2	44.1	43.9
Arles	20	34.8	35.0	35.0	35.2	35.1	35.7	35.5	36.7	36.2

4. Comparison to the Theoretical Literature

In recent years a growing body of literature has emerged, which analyzes the effects of Financial Fair Play on European football. Several contributions look into the ethical and legal aspects of the FFP regulation, e.g. *Müller* et al. (2011), or at the effects on managerial incentives, e.g. *Franck* and *Lang* (2012). We do not directly discuss these issues, but our results may be useful to inform a debate on the desirability of FFP.

A further set of papers offers an economic assessment of the break-even rule using theoretical modelling. A first paper along these lines is *Madden* (2012), who looks explicitly at the welfare effects of the break-even rule. *Madden* (2012) assumes that fans have a taste for absolute playing quality in the league. With the break-even rule in place talent investment decreases, which leads to welfare losses for the fans. Our empirical results certainly confirm that a drop in talent investments (measured as the payrolls of the clubs) is to be expected. However, the odds of players dropping out of football in favor of alternative employment seem slim even with reduced salaries under FFP. It is therefore unlikely that the total talent pool in football will shrink considerably. Migration to less affected (Germany?) or unaffected leagues (outside Europe) is a more serious option. Whether or not FFP leads to a welfare loss for consumers in a particular country depends therefore on the international mobility of players (which is generally high) and the severity of the salary reductions in the league vis-à-vis other leagues.

A second paper by *Lang* et al. (2011) focuses more on the competitive balance effect of sugar daddy owners. This topic is directly related to our study, because one of the most important effects of the break-even rule we uncover is the dwindling influence of benefactor owners. *Lang* et al. (2011) infer that sugar daddies may decrease or increase competitive balance depending on whether the benefactors invest in small or large market clubs. Our results seem to confirm this assertion. In the Premier League for example we find that Chelsea and Manchester City could drop out of the title race, leading to reduced tension. A further group of small market teams would see significant decreases in its on-field performance, which could further reduce the pressure on traditional top teams, such as Arsenal and

Manchester United. Likewise, we see that in Spain the traditional top teams would strengthen their dominance. In the Serie A and Ligue 1 on the other hand, we find that most of the reduction in points would fall on some of the traditional top teams. This could be beneficial to the tension on the field.

Two further papers by *Sass* (2012) and *Vöpel* (2013), emphasize the dynamic effect the break-even rule may have on competitive balance. The reasoning goes that small teams need outside investment to challenge top teams on the pitch. Such an investment consequently allows them to grow their revenue potential, which renders them profitable in the long run. Without the possibility of outside funding however, these challenges disappear and the traditional top teams may consolidate their dominance. Our results are not derived from a dynamic model, which takes these effects into account, so we cannot simulate this effect directly. If we examine a couple of clubs, which are in the process of making investments of this kind, e.g. Manchester City and Chelsea, we see that the break-even rule would indeed hamper their chances of success on the field. It definitely seems conceivable therefore that the break-even rule reduces the scope of challenges to the traditional large market teams.

5. Concluding Remarks

In this chapter we have taken a closer look at the effects of the break-even rule on the performance of individual clubs on and off the pitch. We may conclude that FFP is likely to increase the profitability of European football clubs in general, and those restricted by the rule in particular. On the field of play several teams could see a serious decline in performance, while others manage to cut costs without suffering significant points losses. Our results confirm several effects predicted in the theoretical literature on FFP, which has taken shape over the last couple of years.

Our empirical model invites additional research on several dimensions. First, it seems evident that significant new insights could be obtained from a dynamic version of this model, which would allow for teams to enlarge their revenue potential through investment in on-field performance. Second, our model could be used to look at a whole host of policy issues relating to sports leagues. In *Peeters* and *Szymanski* (2014) for example, we simulate several versions of a US style salary cap, but a host of other options are available as well. Finally, it should be noted that our choice to model just four leagues is completely due to a lack of data on the financial records of other European leagues. An extension of our analysis to other leagues could greatly help to complete the economic assessment of the FFP regulations.

References

Franck, E. & Lang, M. (2012): What is Wrong with Sugar Daddies in Football? A Theoretical Analysis of the Influence of Money Injections on Risk-Taking, Working paper No. 160, Zurich: University of Zurich.

Lang, M., Grossman, M. & Theiler, P. (2011): The Sugar Daddy's Game: How Wealthy Investors Change Competition in Professional Team Sports, in: Journal of Institutional and Theoretical Economics, Vol. 167, 4, pp. 557–577.

Madden, P. (2012): Welfare Economics of "Financial Fair Play" in a Sports League With Benefactor Owners, Discussion Paper No. EDP-1221, Manchester: The University of Manchester.

Müller, C. J., Lammert, J. & Hovemann, G. (2011): The Financial Fair Play Regulations of UEFA: An Adequate Concept to Ensure the Long-term Viability and Sustainability of European Club Football?, in: International Journal of Sport Finance, Vol. 7, 2, pp. 117–140.

Peeters, T. & Szymanski, S. (2014): Financial Fair Play in European Football, in: Economic Policy, forthcoming.

Sass, M. (2012): Long Term Competitive Balance under UEFA Financial Fair Play Regulations, Working Paper No. 2012-5, Magdeburg: Universität Magdeburg.

UEFA (2012): UEFA Club Licensing and Financial Fair Play Regulations, edition 2012, http://www.uefa.org/MultimediaFiles/Download/Tech/uefaorg/General/01/80/54/10/1805410_DOWNLOAD.pdf (accessed 2014-2-04).

Vöpel, H. (2013): Is Financial Fair Play Really Justified? An Economic and Legal Assessment of UEFA's Financial Fair Play Rules, Research Paper No. 2013-79, Hamburg: Hamburgisches Weltwirtschaftsinstitut.

Financial Fair Play – Why Loss-Making Is a Problem: The Example of the English Football League

Sean Hamil

Abstract

Drawing on case material from the English Football League, this paper argues that (1) consistent loss-making is always a problem, even in the football industry, (2) European football is facing an unprecedented financial crisis, and (3) the implementation of the Financial Fair Play regime is an entirely reasonable and logical response to this crisis.

Keywords

benefactor, loss-making, bankruptcy, tax, financial fair play.

1. Introduction

It has long been the view of the author that it was simply impossible for the football industry to defy the laws of economic gravity and continue to make losses year after year without any long term consequences[1]. In England, there has never been a season since the foundation of the Premier League in 1992 when either the combined clubs in the Premier League (level 1) and the Football League (levels 2–4) made a pre-tax profit – substantial losses are the norm. For example, figures from the *Deloitte* Annual Review of Football Finance indicate that in the 2011/2012 season the 20 clubs in the Premier League lost £245m and the 72 clubs in the Football League lost £224m (*Deloitte* 2013: 29). The consequence of this wholesale loss-making has been a very high level of bankruptcy in English football, 57 separate bankruptcy events between 1992 and 2013 in the top four divisions, out of a total of 92 clubs. On every occasion an extended group of creditors, from Her Majesty's Revenue & Customs (the UK tax authority) to small business suppliers have gone unpaid. This in fact amounts to an indirect public and private "soft" subsidy to the football industry, a subsidy which, in the view of the author, at some point, as the losses ballooned, those on the receiving end were eventually going to call a halt to.

Many academic commentators, have argued that Financial Fair Play is an entirely unnecessary regulatory intervention in a system whose member clubs

1 For a wider discussion of this analysis see *Hamil* and *Walters* (2010).

demonstrate an extraordinarily high level of historical durability despite the numerous bankruptcies[2], with only a handful of clubs not re-emerging from the financial administration process to retain their place in the English professional leagues. However, it is the author's contention that, in fact, the scale of losses in English football's Football League reached such a pitch in the period 2009–2012 that maintaining the traditional laissez-faire position on financial regulation, whereby clubs were allowed to go bankrupt with the expectation that they would be bought out of the financial administration re-structuring process by new benefactor-owners without exiting the league, became untenable. This is because the tolerance of unpaid creditors, notably the UK tax authorities, for unpaid bills became exhausted, just as the supply of benefactor owners showed signs of becoming finite, opening up the real possibility that many clubs might actually collapse into liquidation. It was these factors that drove the English Football League to introduce the Financial Fair Play regulations in April 2012, following a vote in favour by its member clubs. Far from being an over-reaction, this was in fact an inevitable and entirely necessary response, to a genuine financial crisis in the English Football League, of a scale never previously experienced in its long history.

Drawing on macro data on the financial performance of Football League clubs, and three detailed case-studies of clubs who faced significant financial difficulties over the 2011–2013 period, this paper seeks to illustrate that in the case of the English Football League (1) consistent loss-making is always a problem, even for football, (2) the Football League is facing a financial crisis of unprecedented proportions, and (3) the implementation of a Financial Fair Play regime is an entirely reasonable and logical response to this crisis.

2. Why Financial Fair Play? Some Context

From the late 1990s it began to become apparent that, following the introduction of pay-per-view television in Europe and the consequent competition by broadcasters to purchase sport properties, whilst European football was benefiting from dramatically higher revenues largely driven by a dramatic increase in broadcasting income, these higher revenues did not translate into profitability for clubs. Rather these revenues were largely been spent on a form of playing talent "arms race" which saw elite players dramatically increase their salaries; leading to a

2 Professor *Stefan Szymanski* is a leading exponent of this argument. For example, see *Szymanski* (2010: 28–40).

concern that elite leagues across Europe would become a race between club owners with the greatest financial resources, so undermining the sporting integrity of the competitions.

The incentive for clubs to over-spend to achieve sporting success is widely recognized given that there is at least a correlation between expenditure on player salaries and transfers and sporting success[3]. The data from Deloitte on club player expenditure, demonstrates that club owners appear to believe that the increased expenditure does result in increased success, and this explains the hyper-inflation in both player salaries and transfer payments across European football.

At the same many clubs began to make significant losses which could only be sustained through subsidies from public bodies (e.g. local authorities through the provision of subsidized stadia for example) or private investors, or increasingly through clubs going bankrupt and leaving unpaid a wide range of creditors, for example other members of the football "family" (such as other clubs), and also the tax authorities. Famously, in March 2004, the then Chief Executive of UEFA, Lars Christer Olsson, referred to the practice of debt-led player acquisition and salary payment to achieve sporting success as "financial doping" (*UEFA* 2004) and the phrase has now entered into the mainstream sport business vocabulary. In short, UEFA were setting out a clear policy position: that the whole European football financial system would become unstable due to chronic loss-making unless counterbalancing action was taken. As we shall see, this is a contested diagnosis, but the diagnosis forms the philosophical foundation for the introduction of the Financial Fair Play system.

UEFA's initial policy mechanism to address the perceived problem was the UEFA Club Licensing System. Writing in the official UEFA Champions League magazine *Champions* in March 2004 CEO Olsson warned clubs that UEFA was entitled to exclude clubs from its competitions if they did not fulfil the requirements of the new Europe-wide Club Licensing System. Specifically he observed:

> "Too many sides are not planning for the long-term future of the club and think only about the very immediate outlook…There are clubs who have, in the past, indulged in what you could almost call financial doping – they've bought players but not paid their debts or even, in some cases, their players' salaries…Under our new club-licensing system, clubs will have to prove to their national associations that they have sound finances

3 For a discussion of this relationship see *Deloitte* (2013: 38–51 and, in particular, charts 3.2 and 3.4), *Szymanski* (2010: 29–32) and *Franck* (2014: 7–9).

> if they are going to play in European competition. We are determined to be firm about this...In future, clubs will not be allowed to have significant debts to other clubs, players or related parties and they will have to have an independent audited statement to show that. We can ask an external auditor to intervene if we suspect that a club is not fulfilling the requirements. After that, we have the authority to expel clubs from our competitions" (*UEFA* 2004a).

The licensing system evolved in two stages; UEFA introduced the UEFA Club Licensing system in 2004, and then the UEFA Financial Fair Play system in 2009. Both concepts set down minimum management and sporting criteria that clubs had to meet if they wished to compete in UEFA club competitions. The UEFA Club Licensing system incorporated some financial criteria, and also incorporated some punitive element: between the 2004/2005 and 2008/2009 seasons 16 teams (*UEFA* 2013b: 26) that had qualified for UEFA club competitions were denied admittance for failing to meet licensing criteria, some of which were financial. The introduction of the Financial Fair Play system in 2009 represented a significant step change in terms of the financial criteria that clubs wishing to compete in UEFA club competitions would have to meet.

3. Financial Fair Play: What Does It Entail?

The specific requirements of Financial Fair Play are outlined in the *UEFA Club Licensing and Financial Fair Play Regulations* (*UEFA* 2012a). Central to these regulations is the requirement that clubs wishing to meet the criteria necessary to be awarded a UEFA Club License must meet the Break-Even requirement[4].

In essence the Break-Even requirement operates as follows: *Relevant Expenses* (cost of sales, employee benefits expenses, other operating expenses, player transfer amortisation or expenses, finance costs) must not exceed *Relevant Income* (gate receipts, broadcasting rights, sponsorship & advertising, commercial activities, other operating income, player transfer profit or income, finance income, excess proceeds on disposal of tangible fixed assets. However, it is critical to note that there is *no limit* on expenditure on: infrastructure costs, youth development activities, and community development activities. This is to provide an incentive to clubs to develop their football business activity so that higher revenues will be balanced against expenditure.

4 For a short summary of the key elements of Financial Fair Play see *BBC Sport* (2011).

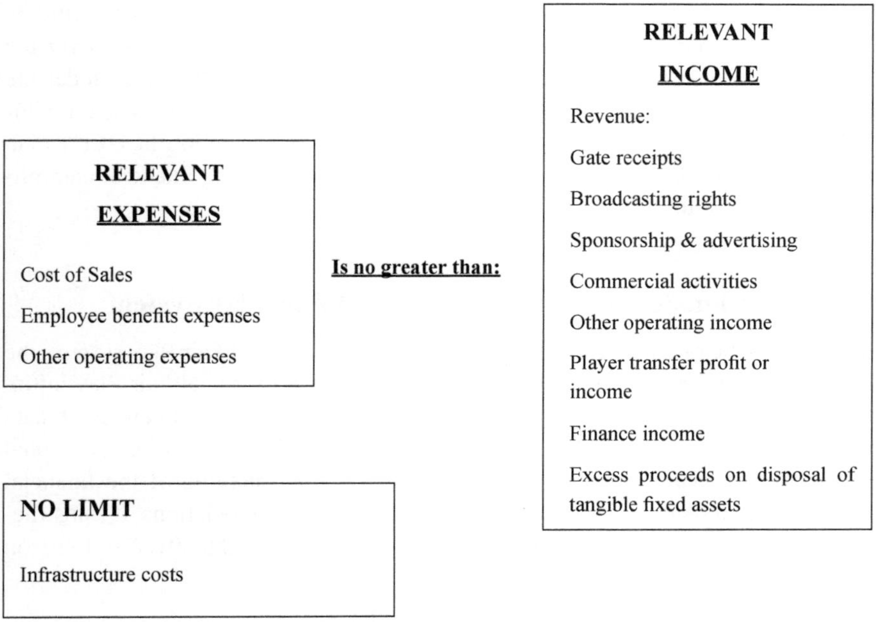

Fig. 1: The Break-Even Calculation

Franck (2014: 4) summarises the operating philosophy of Financial Fair Play very succinctly as follows:

> "… limiting 'external' money injections through FFP does not simply translate into 'less money for football payrolls' but rather into *'restoring efficient managerial incentives'*" [italics added by author].

In summary, the essence of how the Financial Fair Play regulations have been implemented is as follows. UEFA started monitoring clubs in 2013/2014, taking into account losses in the previous two years – 2011/2012 and 2012/2013. Thereafter, losses are to be calculated over a three year period. Over these two financial years owners will be allowed to lose €45m, as long as they are prepared to cover these losses with equity/share investments. Thereafter, the acceptable loss will reduce over time. The purpose of calculating losses over a three year period is so that a club is not unfairly penalised on the basis of one challenging financial year, where perhaps it failed to qualify for UEFA club competition and suffering a corresponding fall in revenues resulting in a substantial loss. The first sanctions for clubs not fulfilling the break-even requirement can be taken during the 2013/2014 season and the first possible exclusions relating to break-even breaches would be for the UEFA competition season 2014/2015 (*UEFA* 2012b). However over the 2011–2013 period UEFA was already penalising (*UEFA* 2013a) clubs under the regulations who were behind in their payments to other clubs, on occasion withholding prize money owed to these clubs via their participation in UEFA club competitions until such time as they had met their outstanding financial commitments to other clubs.

4. The Rationale for the UEFA Financial Fair Play System

To return to the rationale for the introduction of the Financial Fair Play system, the central assumption underlying UEFA's adoption of the Financial Fair Play initiative is that there is a serious financial crisis in European football. Drawing on data gathered through the UEFA Club Licensing process UEFA publishes an annual *Club Benchmarking Report* which presents a detailed pictured of the financial health of top division football across UEFA's 54 member associations. It is instructive to view the headline (*UEFA* 2013b; 2013c) figures for the 2010/2011 season published in 2013:

- A 3% increase in top division income over the 2009/2010 season making a total of €13.2bn. So in revenue terms European elite club football is performing exceptionally well, far outstripping the annual rate of economic growth in the European Union over the same period.
- Fixed asset investment by the 237 clubs competing in UEFA club competitions equalled €4.8bn, but €6.9bn was spent on player transfers and €5bn on player wages and associated costs. In other words, Europe's clubs are much more likely to spend increased revenues on players than on developing fixed assets such as stadia which might assist them to increase revenues and develop more sustainable business models.
- Between 2007 and 2011 top division salaries and related costs increased by 38% but revenues only increased by 24%. Player cost inflation significantly outstripped revenue implying a financially unsustainable model where club owner/benefactors are not prepared to subsidise losses.
- Combined employee and net transfer costs were 71% of revenues, an extremely high ratio.
- €1.7 billion 'bottom-line' (pre-tax) net losses reported by top division clubs. This is an extremely high level of loss-making.

This data would tend to indicate that European football is the embodiment of the old business saying "revenue is vanity, profit is sanity". European football has an extremely attractive product which has seen revenues increase dramatically and consistently, but hyper wage and transfer spending has meant that the industry is chronically loss-making. As in the English case briefly outlined above, these losses are either covered by owner-benefactors, through soft public subsidy (through direct subsidy, or indirectly through non-payment of taxes), or laundered through the bankruptcy process as clubs across Europe collapse under the weight of their debts. As is discussed below, football would appear to be subject to a "soft budget"[5] constraint, both public and private.

5. Is Financial Fair Play Necessary?

Many academic commentators have dismissed Financial Fair Play as unnecessary and an over-reaction. *Vöpel* (2011: 54–60) articulates the views of many when he observes:

> "Empirically, insolvency has not been shown to be a serious problem in professional football and, moreover, there is no obvious systemic risk resulting from the insolvency of a single club that would justify tighter regulation" (*Vöpel* 2011: 59).

Szymanski (2010: 28–40), whilst acknowledging that football clubs are historically loss-making, makes the point that that only a tiny proportion ever go out of existence; and typically, when they become bankrupt, simply re-enter their respective competitions with new owners. This, he argues, is evidence of a natural, economic, self-righting process within the industry which precludes the necessity for any expensive (and by definition very complex and challenging) regulatory intervention as proposed through the application of the Financial Fair Play regulations.[6]

However, the critics of the need for financial regulatory intervention in the football industry overlook one significant factor; the depth of the financial crisis in European football is of *unprecedented* proportions. As the data from the UEFA *Club Benchmarking Reports* makes clear, the scale of losses being experienced by clubs, and the size of "investment" being demanded of

---

5 For a detailed explanation of the operation of the "soft budget" constraint in football see *Franck* (2014: 6–8) and *Storm & Nielsen* (2012).

6 As an aside, this assessment places little importance on the need to protect the interests of the creditors of bankrupt clubs who are paid only a fraction of what they are owed when clubs collapse.

benefactor owners is of a scale never before seen in European football. It is this that is driving demands for some form of "financial fair play", as the following illustration from the English Football League demonstrates. It is the fear that the football industry may actually be about to reach the point where the supply of benefactor-owners prepared to shoulder losses is becoming finite, and the willingness of public authorities to tolerate unpaid taxes and generally offer a soft public subsidy has reached its limit, which has raised the real possibility of clubs going into bankruptcy only to be followed by liquidation; it is this fear that is driving the demand for the introduction of Financial Fair Play regimes, and not any "politically" informed agenda to initiate regulatory intervention for its own sake.

5.1 The Football League Takes Action

Top level English professional football is structured as a pyramid of four divisions consisting of the Premier League (level 1) and the Football League (levels 2–4, consisting of the Championship, Division 1 and Division 2) with promotion and relegation between each division and from Division Two (level 4) to the Football Conference (levels 5 and 6).

Historically, the ownership model of English football might be characterised as the "benefactor" model. This involves a single private business owner taking responsibility for running the club and underwriting its losses. As the Football League itself outlined in its evidence (*House of Commons Culture Media & Sport Committee* 2011a) to the 2011 Football Governance enquiry by the House of Commons Culture, Media & Sport Committee (see detail below), there is virtually no expectation that an owner might generate a normal profit from their investment in a Football League club:

> "It should be noted that the lack of economic value created by Football League clubs means the capital markets are often closed to them. For example, only two Championship clubs made an operating profit in 2009. As a result, clubs are becoming more reliant on an operational model that requires benefactors or entrepreneurs with a high risk tolerance" (*House of Commons Culture Media & Sport Committee* 2011a).

Although perhaps a more accurate characterisation might be that clubs require benefactors or entrepreneurs who have a high financial "loss" tolerance.

There has never been a season since the foundation of the Premier League in 1992 when either the combined clubs in the Premier League and the Football League made a pre-tax profit – substantial losses have been the norm. For example, as was mentioned in the introduction, figures from the Deloitte *Annual*

Review of Football Finance indicate that in the 2011/2012 season the 20 clubs in the Premier League lost £245m and the 72 clubs in the Football League lost £224m (*Deloitte* 2013: 29), The scale of financial losses sustained by English Football League clubs is extremely high. For example, in the 2011/2012 season clubs in the Football League Championship (level 2 of English professional football) recorded a total pre-tax loss of £158m on turnover of £476m (the respective figures in 2010/2011 were a pre-tax loss of £189m on turnover of £423m). The losses amongst League 1 clubs (level 3) in 2011/2012 were £58m, on turnover of £120m. This is loss-making on a truly extraordinary scale which would simply not be tolerated in any mainstream industry.

Between 1992 and 2013, a period of exponential revenue growth at the 72 football league clubs, there were 56 club bankruptcy occasions (*Deloitte* 2013: 69), clear evidence that the majority of clubs, at one time or another, were simply unable to meet their obligations to their creditors and had to seek protection through the bankruptcy financial administration process. That these bankruptcies happen so regularly is hardly surprising given the scale of debt that Football League clubs take on, largely to finance player transfers and wages. For example, the total debt of the 24 (with estimates being made for the debt of two clubs, the accounts of Coventry and Portsmouth not being available perhaps connected with the fact that both clubs had gone bankrupt, in 2013 and 2012 respectively) clubs in the Football League Championship in the summer of 2012 was £972m (*Deloitte* 2013), implying a debt-to-turnover ratio of 223%.

There is also evidence that in the past some clubs were able to use the bankruptcy process to shed debt and then re-emerge financially stronger and able to compete more aggressively in the player labour market achieving an unfair financial advantage in the process over those clubs who stayed solvent and paid their creditors. The success of Leicester City in winning promotion to the Premier League from the Football League at the end of the 2001/2002 season led the Football League clubs to vote to implement a ten point sporting penalty for all clubs entering administration, to act as a disincentive to any clubs seeking to use the financial administration process following bankruptcy to secure a sporting advantage, a rule that remains in place (*BBC Sport* 2003).

On every bankruptcy occasion an extended group of creditors, from Her Majesty's Revenue & Customs (the UK tax authority) to small business suppliers have gone unpaid. This in fact amounts to an indirect public and private "soft" subsidy to the football industry, a subsidy which at some point, as the scale of losses increased exponentially as the cost of competing for labour in the English leagues exploded, those unpaid creditors were eventually going to call a halt to. The collapse into bankruptcy of Portsmouth FC (*BBC Sport* 2010a) in 2010, the first club to go bankrupt whilst in the Premier League[7], with multi-million pound losses, in retrospect was a turning point. In May 2010 its total debts were estimated at £135m (*BBC Sport* 2010b). The report by the administrator of the bankruptcy laid bare the very wide range of creditors who would have to accept only a very small percentage of the monies owing to them (*PKF* 2012). In an article commenting on the affair in *The Guardian* newspaper prominent sport business journalist *David Conn* (2010) summarised the wider impact of the bankruptcy, drawing on data listing the details of creditors in the Portsmouth bankruptcy administration report likely to receive only a tiny percentage of the money owing to them:

> "The list of unsecured 'ordinary' creditors, who must take a hit, is a painful litany of the inexcusably unpaid. Here is the South Central ambulance service, owed £19,535.39, Portsmouth city council, £28,690 down in rates [local taxes], Portsmouth Students' Union, owed £2,955. A number of schools are owed significant sums, apparently for the hire of sports facilities, including Cowplain Community School in Waterlooville, with £14,743.54 outstanding, the Priory Community Sports Centre in Southsea, owed £11,000, and King Edward School in Southampton, who will have to accept a fraction of a £41,714.01 bill the Premier League club ran up with them."

The scale of English football's debts, and its inability to pay them, in particular debt to the tax authorities, became a major source of debate amongst British parliamentarians during the House of Commons Culture, Media & Sport Committee enquiry into the Governance of English Football in the Spring of 2011 (*House of Commons Culture, Media & Sport Committee* 2011b).[8] It is worth noting that this enquiry had itself been initiated by the Sport Minister Hugh Robertson MP, who in January 2011 offered the view that "football is the worst governed sport in this country" (*Winter* 2011), hardly an endorsement of the quality of the financial administration of the industry. Despite its successes there were many aspects of English football as it entered the second decade of the 21st century that were a cause of public disquiet.

One of these sources of public disquiet was English football clubs' often cavalier attitude to the payment of taxes. From the beginning of the global financial crisis in 2008 the UK tax authority, Her Majesty's Revenue & Customs (HMRC),

7 Though it is important to note that many of the clubs that collapsed into bankruptcy in the Football League did so after failed attempts to stay in the Premier League resulted in relegation, and as a result of failed attempts to achieve promotion to the Premier League.

8 For full details see *Sportbusinesscentre* (2011).

had become increasingly impatient with football clubs' non-payment of tax. In fact, the non-payment of taxes of English football clubs had become something of a national scandal. By way of illustration, the City of London corporate law firm Olswang commented in their evidence to the House of Commons enquiry that:

> "... the practice of using cash set aside for HMRC [to pay tax] as working capital for the club [was widespread]. In any other industry, this is an incredibly serious offence that typically leads quickly to a winding up petition and personal consequences for those involved... this seems to be a relatively widespread practice in football ... the fact that this practice was widespread in football is evidence of the *parallel universe* [italics added by author] that has long surrounded the operation of a football club in this country. Many clubs appear to operate outside the accepted commercial and legal boundaries that other businesses must adhere to" (*House of Commons Culture Media & Sport Committee* 2011c).

Post the 2008 financial crisis and this practice became unsustainable. Both the Football League (*House of Commons Culture Media & Sport Committee* 2011a) and the *Premier League* (2013) introduced new reporting requirements for their clubs. The Football League informed the House of Commons enquiry:

> "In August 2010, [Football League] clubs agreed to additional financial reporting requirements for Championship clubs, in line with Premier League regulations. These include the provision of 'future' financial information relating to the subsequent season and the need for clubs to demonstrate no overdue transfer fees, compensation fees, key employee wages or PAYE/NIC. Clubs in default, or clubs with business plans that cast doubt on their ability to fulfill fixtures or meet their ongoing obligations, will be required to submit to budget constraints, including the possibility of a registration embargo" (*House of Commons Culture Media & Sport Committee* 2011a).

In effect both the Football League and Premier League were demanding that their members keep the leagues informed that their tax payments were up-to-date, or face a transfer embargo or other financial constraints, confirmation that non-payment of tax had been a serious problem.

On the 25th April 2012 the English Football League announced that it was introducing a version of the UEFA Financial Fair Play system in the three divisions of English football below the level of the Premier League (*Football League* 2012). This was a dramatic initiative because it illustrated the depth of concerns that the Football League had about the financial health of many of its clubs. The regulations were designed to force clubs to operate on a financially sustainable basis and set limits to the level of losses they could make without sanction. Their introduction followed a strategic review by the Football League Board. They drew their inspiration from the "Financial Fair Play" initiative first approved by the governing body of European football, UEFA, in September 2009, and briefly outlined above, whereby over a phased period (2012–2015) clubs wishing to participate in UEFA competitions would have to meet robust financial sustainability criteria (*UEFA* 2014).

In an interview with *BBC Sport* in April 2012 (*BBC Sport* 2012c) Football League CEO Greg Clarke (a former CEO of London Stock Exchange-quoted telecoms company Cable & Wireless) explained the rationale for the Financial Fair Play regulations, in the starkest possible terms. He observed that the Football League had been heading for a *financial train wreck* with total debt forecast to balloon to between £1.5 and £2bn unless controls were introduced, with the likelihood that 5–7 clubs a season would collapse into financial administration per season going forward leaving much of this debt unpaid; for this reason the introduction of some form of *Financial Fair Play* regulations was critical to save the league from financial disaster. Given the scale of the losses of Football League clubs, and their enormous debts, the bleak assessment of the scenario presented by Greg Clarke, although unprecedented, appeared entirely realistic, the necessity for urgent action be taken to curb reckless spending by Football League clubs absolutely clear.

To explain how Greg Clarke's comments translate from the macro picture presented for the entire 72 clubs in the league's three divisions to the micro operating environment of individual clubs business management it is instructive to view some case-studies which illustrate a pattern of managerial decision-making and associated financial difficulty which is entirely typical of football clubs in the English Football League: the cases of Bury FC, Swindon Town FC, and Coventry City FC.

5.2 Bury FC

On the 24th December 2012 (*BBC Sport* 2012a) the Football League Division 1 (the third tier of English professional football) club Bury FC was placed under a player transfer embargo. This followed receipt by the club of a short-term loan from the Professional Footballers Association (PFA) (such loans are normally made where a club is having difficulty paying its player wages.). But a spokesman for the club stated that taking the loan did not mean that the club was in difficulties:

> "All businesses experience cash-flow problems and we're no different to anyone else," [the club's] commercial director… told BBC Radio Manchester "December is traditionally not a brilliant month for attendances…" (*BBC Sport* 2012a).

Just over three months later, on the 10th April 2013 *BBC Sport* reported that Bury needed £1m of external funding to survive. A club statement read:

> "Bury FC has been experiencing financial difficulties all season and we are currently in a transfer embargo imposed by the Football League because of our [2nd] short term loan from the PFA. At this moment in time the situation is now critical. *We are quickly running out of money by trying short-term fixes* [italics added by author] that are not working long term" (*BBC Sport* 2013c).

The BBC reported that the club were forced to allow defender Joe Skarz to leave the club and join Rotherham on transfer deadline day in an attempt to save money on wages, while manager Kevin Blackwell was unable to select a full complement of seven substitutes for many of their previous League One games. After the second transfer embargo was imposed, Blackwell revealed (*BBC Sport* 2013b) that "three or four" of his players were appearing for the club without pay.

Clearly the club had been in financial difficulties for some time. The best that could be said of the incumbent business management was that they suffered from excessive optimism. However a more critical question is: why were Bury trying to buy players when they are chronically indebted and unable to meet their existing player wage obligations without recourse to an emergency loan from the players' union? Surely a player transfer is the ultimate "short-term fix"?

On the 29th May 2013 it was announced that a new consortium had taken over Bury after the club was relegated to Division 2 (level 4 of English football) and had sold 16 players leaving only 8 first team members. Six months later, in an interview with *BBC Sport* on the 27th November 2013 (*BBC Sport* 2013n) new Bury chairman Stewart Day disclosed that more than £1.5m had been invested in the club since the takeover when the club had been close to financial collapse. The investment was required to stabilise the club's finances:

> "That's gone in to pay off the debts and move things forward and there's more coming… When we took over, the club was over their overdraft facility by quite a significant amount, so we don't have an overdraft facility at the football club any more. We live within our means… It's a difficult period… We're still paying for people who aren't at the football club – whether that's commercial staff, staff behind the scenes or playing staff. That's unfortunately part of the football world at the moment" (*BBC Sport* 2013n).

The amount required to be invested to stabilise the club had been greater than anticipated. Earlier, in a *BBC Sport* interview in August 2013 the team manager Kevin Blackwell had disclosed that:

> "The fact the club couldn't afford a lawyer to transfer the deeds from the old regime to the new regime shows how desperately short of money we were" (*BBC Sport* 2013a).

The Bury story perfectly encapsulates the reality of the financing of football in the English Football League, with its pattern of extraordinary risk taking as clubs take on high player salary fixed costs having spent aggressively in the player transfer market in order to gamble on promotion to a higher division which only three clubs in a division can actually achieve in any one season, followed by the inevitable retrenchment and frequently bankruptcy. The case puts into micro level context the macro commentary of Football League CEO Greg Clarke on the state of the League clubs' finances in 2012.

5.3 Swindon Town FC

On the 6th October 2012 English Football League (FL) Division 1 club Swindon Town FC announced that it was the subject of a transfer embargo under the Football League's Financial Fair Play regulations. The club was found to be in breach of the requirement within the regulations that their expenditure on wages and related fees was not in excess of 65% of turnover (*BBC Sport* 2012d). The transfer ban did not please Swindon manager Paolo Di Canio, who for the following month proceeded to regularly express his frustration with the situation in the media, publicly challenging his club board as to whether they shared his sporting ambition for the team, specifically to achieve a second promotion in two years. On the 6th November the transfer ban was lifted following additional equity investment (*BBC Sport* 2013p). *De facto* Di Canio's message regarding the strategic objective of a football club was as follows: the job of the owners was to sustain financial losses so that the manager could buy players of sufficient calibre to get the team promoted. And if the owners didn't do that then the manager would publicly criticise his employers for not "sharing his ambition" until they did. This in fact is the business "model" that has characterised English football for generations; although it is a model in which owners were more often than not willing accomplices as they prioritised chasing the glory of sporting success (and the reflected glory and prestige that it brought) over profit, with bankruptcy often being the outcome as in fact had been the case at Swindon Town in 2002 (*Deloitte* 2013: Appendix 13).

On the 30th January 2013 it was announced that Swindon had been sold to new investors by owner Andrew Black who had decided he was no longer prepared to "invest" in the club; although this is perhaps stretching the definition of the term "investment" beyond its normal incorporation of an expectation of a "return on investment" to mean that he was in fact no longer prepared to subsidise the club's losses; the alternative to a sale was for the club to be put in financial administration, as the club was reported to be on the verge of bankruptcy (*BBC Sport* 2013o).

The news threw into stark relief just how dire Swindon Town's finances were, and why the Football League's ban on the club engaging in transfer activity made absolute financial sense; for clearly there was a major question mark over the club's ability to pay the costs of these transfers going forward, and to allow such transfers might have tipped the club into bankruptcy.

In March 2013 a second transfer embargo imposed by the Football League two months earlier was lifted following the paying off of historical debt by the new owners (*BBC Sport* 2013q). In the meantime Paolo Di Canio had resigned as manager on the 18th February accusing the club of "broken promises" (*BBC Sport* 2013k). In a press interview on the 7th January 2013 De Canio had offered to spend £30,000 of his own money to keep loan players in contract at Swindon (*BBC Sport* 2013j), a drop in the ocean given that the club's debts were in the £ millions. In reality his reason for leaving appeared much more prosaic – when a combination of the application of the Football League Financial Fair Play rules and successive owners' unwillingness to continue to shoulder significant financial losses manifested themselves in strict controls on player transfer and wage expenditure Paolo Di Canio opted to leave Swindon Town FC.

In December 2013, following a year of cost-cutting which saw the club's losses fall from £3.6m to £1.2m, the ownership of the club again changed hands, with new owner, former professional player and player's agent Lee Power, committing to underwrite ongoing losses (*BBC Sport* 2013r). In a press interview (*BBC Sport* 2013i) Mr Power observed:

> "We've made considerable cuts to the budget, which has been well-documented… We've got no debt at the moment and any money that is being haemorrhaged by the club, I'm personally putting in to cover. The Football League has looked through our books and we have proof we can get through to the end of the season. Instead of accumulating more debt, I'm injecting money to keep it debt free" (*BBC Sport* 2013i).

In effect Swindon was operating according to the established principles of the benefactor model of ownership, whereby a private owner subsidised the club's losses in order to ensure its competitiveness on the field of play. Were the benefactor to withdraw support, and a new owner-benefactor not be found, then clearly the outlook for financial survival of the club would be bleak. The club was not financially sustainable on the basis of its own revenues.

5.4 Coventry City FC

On the 2nd March 2012 former Premier League club Coventry City FC was placed under a temporary transfer embargo for failing to file their accounts in time (*BBC*

Sport 2012b). However, the club's board insisted that the situation was not serious, with the CEO commenting on the club's website:

> "As part of the accounts submission process we have to be able to show committed funding out for the next financial year… We could not do this as we are still in the process of agreeing and negotiating budgets with the owner… There is *nothing untoward about this and it is perfectly normal to be negotiating funding with the owner* [italics added by author]. We would hope to secure funding commitments in the very next few weeks… The owner has previously funded the club for a period of more than four years and, is currently reviewing our budget proposal for the coming year… We totally understand and appreciate that supporters might be concerned, but while the situation is far from ideal, we are confident it will be resolved very soon" (*BBC Sport* 2012b).

The player transfer embargo was lifted in June 2012.

However, during the following 2012/2013 season it became clear the club *was* in serious financial difficulties. In a press interview on the 1st March 2013 the club CEO commented:

> "We are under unbelievable external pressure… The real challenge is actually accessing revenues to be able to put a reasonable team on the pitch next season… Frankly, if we don't get those revenues the club will go into a downward spiral… we talk to our insolvency practitioner every day and they are deeply concerned… Next season [2013/2014] we will be under a transfer embargo… We are way in excess of the salary cap that we would be applying on the revenues we have today and which are projected for next season" (*BBC Sport* 2013g).

This was the third season in a row that Coventry City had had a transfer ban imposed for late filing of their financial accounts, resulting in transfer embargoes.

Later that month Coventry City FC was deducted 10 points by the Football League (*BBC Sport* 2013d) following its collapse into administration. It followed an administration order from their Ricoh Arena stadium landlords, Arena Coventry Ltd, over a year's unpaid rent of £1.3m.

With the dispute over the level of rental payments with the owner of their stadium in the city of Coventry, the Ricoh Arena, unresolved, Coventry FC started the 2013/2014 season in the First Division of the Football League (level 3 of English football) playing 34 miles away at Northampton Town's ground to dramatically reduced crowds as a result of fans' boycott. The club had started the season with the ten point penalty (*BBC Sport* 2013f) for entering financial administration in the previous season (*BBC Sport* 2013m, 2013h). Controversially, the Football League allowed ownership of the football club to pass to an investment group associated with the previous owners of the club when it had gone into administration. The decision, and the one to allow Coventry FC to play at Northampton Town, was defended by the Football League's CEO Greg Clarke:

> "We were faced with choices... One of the choices was to say 'no' which would have meant Coventry City wouldn't have been able to complete their fixtures at the start of the season and wouldn't have been eligible for the Football League. They would have been gone... We would have promoted one more club from the Conference at the end of the season and gone back to 72 clubs without Coventry City... I really think people need to understand the dangers the club faces, and how hard the Football League is working to make sure the principle objective of keeping the club alive is served" (*BBC Sport* 2013e).

Clearly, in the Football League's assessment, Coventry City FC, were very close to going into liquidation. Their business model allowed their survival only by the League allowing maximum flexibility in allowing the club to play at a geographical location far removed from their home base which was deeply unpopular with its own supporters.

In February 2014 Coventry FC continued to play in Northampton, and the stand-off with the owners of their old ground in the city of Coventry regarding a potential return, with the owners of the club seeking to buy the ground at a knockdown price, also continued (*Conn* 2013). The Coventry FC situation again illustrated the familiar pattern of significant risk-taking followed by financial collapse, leaving the club weaker and the quality and integrity of the League undermined also.

6. The Curse of the "Sugar Daddy" Benefactor

The advent of a new benefactor "sugar daddy" owner in English Football League clubs is normally a celebrated event. The new owner initially brings some form of financial stability, as in the cases of Bury and Swindon above, and also hope for the future. However, in a high insightful analysis of the self-defeating nature of the existing business of European football Professor *Egon Franck* (2014: 19) illustrates that, without a systemic reform of a system that incentivises reckless financial risk-taking, and then seeks to socialise the consequences of that unsuccessful risk-taking through non-payment of debt to creditors, then the result is chronic financial instability. It is worth quoting at length his analysis (*Franck* 2014: 19):

> "Obviously, those clubs that do not have soft budget constraints find themselves victims of the 'salary bubble' produced by the clubs with soft budget constraints. Trying to maintain their existing level of playing strength by keeping their share of 'star players' would require spending significantly more in the player market. At first sight this could generate

a strong incentive to further increase efficiency through 'better management' in order to remain competitive on the pitch.

However, if the margin to further increase efficiency through 'better management' becomes too small compared to the 'buying power' originating from money injections of benefactors at their competitors, these clubs will have to accept sporting decline or to change sides and start gambling on success by investing more aggressively. Since there is no doubt at all that sporting decline generates disutility for decision-makers and fans of the club alike, the soft budget constraints of some clubs clearly intensify the incentives for other clubs to overspend as soon as the external money injections have reached a magnitude that makes all reasonable efforts to increase efficiency through 'better management' look ridiculous. In this sense 'unlimited' money injections and 'really' soft budget constraints have a tendency to crowd out incentives for 'good management' and to propagate throughout the entire league.

In the end managerial moral hazard and rent-seeking tend to become infinitely repeated games in a league where the expectation of being bailed out has become part of collective experience. The potential arms race mutates into a zombie race, where an entire league operates on the verge of insolvency, chronically expending more than its earnings, but being systematically rescued by external money injections year after year."

By the Football League's own admission, its decision to introduce Financial Fair Play regulations in April 2012 might in large part been informed by a fear that many of its clubs were on the verge of mutating into participants in just such a *zombie race*.

7. Conclusion

In February 2013, the English Premier League announced it was introducing its own version of the Financial Fair Play regulations. West Ham United co-owner David Gold told *BBC Sport* regarding the decision of a majority of Premier League clubs to introduce "Financial Fair Play":

> "... it's a restraint on over-spending. If clubs increase their revenues then they can increase their spending... We have got restraint, that's the important thing. What's driving the whole thing is we've got to avoid another Portsmouth... " (*BBC Sport* 2013s).

The decision of the Premier League clubs simply demonstrated what had already been clearly signposted by the decision-making of the Football League, that English football did face a genuine financial crisis, and one that could not be resolved in the traditional laissez-faire fashion. A more direct interventionist approach was required, and the instrument of that approach was Financial Fair Play.

The Minister for Sport, Hugh Robertson MP, understandably, welcomed the move:

> "I am pleased that Premier League clubs have agreed further financial regulations that will help ensure they are run on a more sustainable basis. The Government has been clear that we want clubs to be on a secure financial footing for the long-term health of the game. This is a welcome and positive move" (*BBC Sport* 2013l).

Such sustainability would of course lead to an end to losses having to be subsidised indirectly by public and private creditors who by now were doubtless complaining, entirely understandably, to their public representatives about an industry where such practices could be tolerated.

Financial Fair Play constitutes a form of soft salary cap. But of course, as David Gold points out, if clubs can grow their business revenues they can still grow their player expenditures. "Financial Fair Play" regimes are designed to encourage sustainable businesses through encouraging clubs to build revenues whilst being constrained from spending more than they can afford on player salaries and transfers, often at the expense of their creditors. In the context of English football the application of Financial Fair Play regulations does require a cultural shift in thinking away from the kind of "parallel universe" alluded to in the evidence of City of London law firm Olswang to the House of Commons Culture, Media & Sport Committee enquiry to one where an acceptance of the need to apply normal business disciplines and not rely on indirect subsidies becomes the norm. However, in reality neither English, or indeed European, football has much choice in the matter. As *Franck* (2014: 4) observes:

> "…The time for repeated managerial moral hazard and rent-seeking games in European football is over, if FFP comes into action. Football managers will have to concentrate on productive efforts to develop the football business as a whole and in a sustainable way instead of focusing on 'payroll gambling' in a sort of 'football casino'."

Despite what Paolo Di Canio may appear to believe, you cannot defy economic gravity forever. Europe is in the middle of the worst economic recession since the 1930's and neither government agencies, private creditors, or investors are any more prepared to accept the losses served up to them by the old football model. The football industry is different, but it is not that different!

References

BBC Sport (2003): League to Punish Stricken Clubs, http://news.bbc.co.uk/sport1/hi/football/3136404.stm (accessed 2014-02-25).

BBC Sport (2010a): Pompey become first top flight club in administration, http://news.bbc.co.uk/sport1/hi/football/teams/p/portsmouth/8538457.stm (accessed 2014-02-25).

BBC Sport (2010b): Portsmouth debt goes up to £135m, http://news.bbc.co.uk/sport1/hi/football/teams/p/portsmouth/8665753.stm (accessed 2014-02-25).

BBC Sport (2011): UEFA's Plans for Balanced Budgets and Level Playing Fields, http://www.bbc.com/sport/0/football/14482429 (accessed 2014-02-25).

BBC Sport (2012a): Bury placed under transfer embargo by Football League, http://www.bbc.co.uk/sport/0/football/20664209?print=true (accessed 2013-04-9).

BBC Sport (2012b): Coventry City hit by transfer embargo, http://www.bbc.co.uk/sport/0/football/17232219 (accessed 2013-02-25).

BBC Sport (2012c): Football League Chief Greg Clarke Backs Financial Fair Play, http://www.bbc.co.uk/sport/0/football/17848620 (accessed 2013-04-09).

BBC Sport (2012d): Paolo Di Canio Confirms Transfer Embargo, http://www.bbc.co.uk/sport/0/football/19857015 (accessed 2014-04-09).

BBC Sport (2013a): Bury FC: Kevin Blackwell's side looking up after surviving 'oblivion', http://www.bbc.co.uk/sport/0/football/23591995?print=true (accessed 2014-02-25).

BBC Sport (2013b): Bury takeover finally completed and embargo lifted, http://www.bbc.co.uk/sport/0/football/22701080 (accessed 2013-06-10).

BBC Sport (2013c): Bury: League One strugglers 'need £1m to survive', http://www.bbc.co.uk/sport/0/football/22095559?print=true (accessed 2013-06-10).

BBC Sport (2013d): Coventry City deducted 10 points by the Football League, http://www.bbc.co.uk/sport/0/football/21970140 (accessed 2014-02-25).

BBC Sport (2013e): Coventry City: Football League chief Greg Clarke feared for club, http://www.bbc.co.uk/sport/0/football/23718996 (accessed 2014-02-25).

BBC Sport (2013f): Coventry City: Football League docks Sky Blues ten points, http://www.bbc.co.uk/sport/0/football/23548760 (accessed 2014-02-25).

BBC Sport (2013g): Coventry City: Jordan Stewart signs before transfer embargo, http://www.bbc.co.uk/sport/0/football/21629194 (accessed 2014-02-25).

BBC Sport (2013h): Coventry City: The Sky Blues unhappy anniversary, http://www.bbc.co.uk/sport/0/football/23686822 (accessed 2014-02-25).

BBC Sport (2013i): Lee Power: Swindon Town owner moves to allay money fears, http://www.bbc.co.uk/sport/0/football/25217953 (accessed 2014-02-25).

BBC Sport (2013j): Paolo Di Canio offers own money to keep players at Swindon, http://www.bbc.co.uk/sport/0/football/20928212 (accessed 2014-02-25).

BBC Sport (2013k): Paolo Di Canio quits as manager of Swindon Town, http://www.bbc.co.uk/sport/0/football/21499926 (accessed 2013-04-09).

BBC Sport (2013l): Premier League agree new financial regulations, http://www.bbc.co.uk/sport/0/football/21374699 (accessed 2013-03-25).

BBC Sport (2013m): Ricoh return would be 'crazy' without full control, http://www.bbc.co.uk/sport/0/football/24287505 (accessed 2014-02-25).

BBC Sport (2013n): Stewart Day: Bury chairman reveals initial £1.5m investment, http://www.bbc.co.uk/sport/0/football/25105961?print=true (accessed 2014-02-25).

BBC Sport (2013o): Swindon Town sold to Jed McCrory's consortium, http://www.bbc.co.uk/sport/0/football/21258477 (accessed 2013-04-09).

BBC Sport (2013p): Swindon Town transfer embargo lifted, says Sir William Patey, http://www.bbc.co.uk/sport/0/football/20229134 (accessed 2013-04-09).

BBC Sport (2013q): Swindon Town: Transfer embargo lifted at League One club, http://www.bbc.co.uk/sport/0/football/21967892 (accessed 2013-04-09).

BBC Sport (2013r): Swindon Town's finances 'healthy' despite £1.2m deficit, http://www.bbc.co.uk/sport/0/football/25347029 (accessed 2013-02-25).

BBC Sport (2013s): *BBC Sport* (2013t): Premier League agrees new financial regulations, http://www.bbc.com/sport/0/football/21374699 (accessed 2014-04-05).

Conn, D. (2010): Portsmouth save their money for millionaires whilst paupers go unpaid, http://www.theguardian.com/football/blog/2010/apr/22/portsmouth-football-creditors-money-millionaires (accessed 2014-02-25).

Conn, D. (2013): Coventry City owners lead Coventry to Northampton and towards the abyss, http://www.theguardian.com/football/blog/2013/dec/02/coventry-city-owners-northampton-league-one-sisu/print (accessed 2014-02-25).

Deloitte (2013): Annual Review of Football Finance, München: Deloitte.

Football League (2012): Financial Fair Play in the Football League, http://www.football-league.co.uk/page/FLExplainedDetail/0,,10794~2748246,00.html (accessed 2014-02-25).

Franck, E. P. (2014): Financial Fair Play in European Club Football – What is it all about?, Working Paper No. 328, Zürich: University of Zurich.

Hamil, S. & Walters, G. (2010): Financial Performance in English Professional Football: an 'Inconvenient Truth', in: Soccer & Society, Vol. 11, 4, pp. 354–372.

House of Commons Culture Media & Sport Committee (2011a): Written Evidence submitted by Football League, http://www.publications.parliament.uk/pa/cm201012/cmselect/cmcumeds/792/792we11.htm (accessed 2014-02-25).

House of Commons Culture Media & Sport Committee (2011b): Culture, Media and Sport Committee – Seventh Report, Football Governance, http://www.publications.parliament.uk/pa/cm201012/cmselect/cmcumeds/792/79202.htm (accessed 2013-04-09).

House of Commons Culture Media & Sport Committee (2011c): Football Governance – Culture, Media and Sport Committee Contents, Written evidence submitted by Olswang, http://www.publications.parliament.uk/pa/cm201012/cmselect/cmcumeds/792/792vw47.htm (accessed 2014-03-27).

PKF (2012): Portsmouth 2010 Ltd: In Administration – Joint Administrator's Proposals, http://static.bdo.uk.com/assets/documents/2013/05/PKF_Portsmouth_Proposals.pdf (accessed 2014-02-25).

Premier League (2013): Background to introduction of new financial rules, http://www.premierleague.com/en-gb/news/news/2012-13/feb/background-to-introduction-of-new-financial-rules.html (accessed 2014-02-25).

Sportbusinesscentre (2011): Birkbeck Sport Business Centre staff are frequently asked to provide evidence or advice to parliamentary inquiries, http://www.sportbusinesscentre.com/research/government-enquiries/ (accessed 2013-04-09).

Storm, R. K. & Nielsen, K. (2012): Soft budget constraints in professional football, in: European Sport Management Quarterly, Vol. 12, 2, pp. 183–201.

Szymanski, S. (2010): The Financial Crisis and English Football: The Dog That Will Not Bark, in: International Journal of Sport Finance, Vol. 5, 1, pp. 28–40.

UEFA (2004): Club Licensing Is Vital Says Olsson, http://www.uefa.com/uefa/footballfirst/protectingthegame/clublicensing/news/newsid=157594.html (accessed 2012-10-01).

UEFA (2012a): Club Licensing and Financial Fair Play Regulations, http://www.uefa.org/MultimediaFiles/Download/Tech/uefaorg/General/01/80/54/10/1805410_DOWNLOAD.pdf (accessed 2014-02-25).

UEFA (2012b): Financial Fair Play – Media Information, http://www.financialfairplay.co.uk/resources/FFP%20Press%20Kit%20EN_FINAL_en%20_1_.pdf (accessed 2012-10-28).

UEFA (2013a): Six clubs sanctioned for overdue payables http://www.uefa.org/disciplinary/news/newsid=2039939.html (accessed 2014-03-02).

UEFA (2013b): UEFA Club Licensing Benchmarking Report Financial Year 2011, http://www.uefa.org/MultimediaFiles/Download/Tech/uefaorg/General/01/91/61/84/1916184_DOWNLOAD.pdf (accessed 2014-02-25).

UEFA (2013c): UEFA Club Licensing Benchmarking Report Financial Year 2011–11 Selected Findings, http://www.uefa.org/MultimediaFiles/Download/Tech/uefaorg/General/01/91/62/73/1916273_DOWNLOAD.pdf (accessed 2014-02-25).

UEFA (2014): Financial Fair Play, http://www.uefa.org/protecting-the-game/club-licensing-and-financial-fair-play/index.html (accessed 2014-04-07).

Vöpel, H. (2011): Do We Really Need Financial Fair Play in European Club Football? An Economic Analysis, in: CESifo DICE Report, Vol. 9, 3, pp. 54–60.

Winter, H. (2011): Hugh Robertson: Football is the worst governed sport in Britain, http://www.telegraph.co.uk/sport/football/teams/england/8272697/Hugh-Robertson-football-is-the-worst-governed-sport-in-Britain.html (accessed 2014-02-25).

The American View on Financial Fair Play

Joel Maxcy

Abstract

Financial Fair Play (FFP) regulations restrict the total spending by football clubs on salaries and other expenses. The policy resembles the restraints on players' compensation imposed by American sports leagues. FFP is expected to reduce the number of player transfers, and the bidding for their services, lowering the players' share of the revenues. These outcomes are similar to salary cap results in American sports. Moreover, experience from American college sports suggests that that effective policing and enforcement of FFP regulations will be more costly than desired, thus FPP compliance will be investigated and enforced neither equitably nor efficiently. Last, there is nothing to suggest that FFP will benefit football fans, who would prefer better matches and lower prices.

Keywords

Financial Regulation, Football Economics, Labor Markets, Financial Fair Play

1. Introduction

The Union of European Football Association's (UEFA) Financial Fair Play (FFP) regulations, the stated intent of which is to restrain excessive spending on the part of European football clubs, bear resemblance to the mandated restraints on players' compensation imposed by American sports leagues. In contrast to American sports, which have an extensive history of imposing spending restraints, FFP rules are just proceeding, having been introduced in 2010. FFP requires that UEFA member football clubs "break even" financially. Essentially, the new rules require that total spending on player salaries and other expenses does not exceed the club's generated revenues (*Peeters & Szymanski* 2013). Clubs found in violation of the rules face UEFA's punitive measures, which can include exclusion from competition. UEFA began to monitor all club finances in 2011. Disciplinary action will be taken for the first time in 2013–14 with exclusions from competition, if warranted, to take effect the following season.

Analysis of American approaches and outcomes may inform European expectations, given the more than two decades worth of experience with explicit salary and payroll caps in the professional team-sport leagues. There are important distinctions in relating UEFA to the major American professional sports leagues, by which a cursory assessment would render the comparison tangential. However, a thorough examination suggests that despite important differences, including the acknowledged objectives and methods of the spending checks, the real drivers of the restraints are quite comparable. Those are restrictions on payments to players, which increase club profits and preservation of control by the present owners and governing body officials. Parallel outcomes may be expected. Limits on compensation in college sports have also long been set in place by the National Collegiate Athletic Association (NCAA). The comparison to amateur, but highly commercial, American college sports is also appropriate, because organizationally they are more similar to UEFA than American professional leagues.

The NCAA functions as a sovereign governing body performing a similar function to UEFA. College sports, like football leagues, are divided into divisions based on the level of competition. The more than 1000 NCAA members compete at one of three levels for most sports, and at one of four in American football, based on the university's investment in athletics. NCAA divisions are subdivided into regional conferences of typically eight to sixteen members, and are similar in many ways to the national football leagues. The university teams compete for both conference and NCAA (national) championships in a variety of sports. The conference championships are most often based on a regular season round-robin schedule. The NCAA's national level competitions consist of a same-year post season tournament with entry and seeding based on regular season results. Schools with aspirations can and do move to higher levels of competition, and the top division is growing without a formal promotion and relegation system. College sports likewise are not designed for profit, but rather fit into their university's overall objectives. Football and basketball at the most competitive levels compare to professional sports in fan interest and revenue generation. Yet, as with UEFA football clubs, few programs are profitable and even with compensation for athletes limited to an in-kind exchange for educational services, the call for spending restraints is common (*Knight Commission* 2009). The NCAA's punitive measures at the most extreme may exclude the offenders from competition.

Certainly FFP will reduce the number of player transfers, the bidding for services, lower the players' share of the spoils and increase profits. Additionally, as others have indicated, the balance of power will more acutely center on the traditionally wealthy clubs as capital injections to upstart clubs from outside benefactors will become more difficult (*Peeters & Szymanski* 2013). It is also likely, based on the American college sports experience, that effective policing and enforcement of FFP regulations will be more costly than desired. Therefore FPP compliance will be investigated and enforced neither equitably or efficiently. Last, while taxpayers may benefit if public subsidies are curtailed, no particular benefit is apparent for football fans/consumers, who would be expected to prefer better matches at lower prices. There is nothing to suggest that FFP will make any improvements along these lines.

2. Defining "Fair"

The stated motivation for restraints by league and governing body officials on both sides of the Atlantic is a conception of fairness. For American professional sport leagues that issue is wrapped in the cloth of competitive balance; while UEFA's declared objective of fair revolves around club finances, solvency, and the requisite of self-sufficiency for all. The NCAA's Eligibility Information web page heightens the word fairness on its banner (*NCAA* 2013). Fair by this notion implies that all college athletes are held to the same amateurism (no pay) and academic standards. In the NCAA's world, it's fair to take fifty-point drubbing from a team comprised of fellow "student athletes", but not to play a competitive game with one that has lost its amateur purity.

Fair in the American sense reflects a collectivist ideal in that expenditures on talent are evenly balanced, no matter the disparity in resources or the club's capacities to generate revenue. Theoretically, spending restraints level the allocation of talent across clubs, therefore matches are more competitive and more interesting for fans. This increases consumer welfare and conceivably helps derive revenues league wide, although the earnings of larger market clubs may be impeded. As the leagues would have us believe, the restraint on players' salaries is just an agreeable side effect of the objective of leveling the playing field.

Conversely, the European version of fair implies a market based efficiency, implicitly holding that disproportionate spending on talent is appropriate. Fair in this context suggests that clubs must not extract additional advantages by spending beyond their means, and that those means do not include the subsidy of a benefactor...public or private. Evidently what is perceived as particularly unfair in this context is a capital injection from a wealthy private benefactor or sugar daddy, the term used in football to describe such individuals who inject large amounts of capital into clubs to primarily to acquire talent (*Peeters & Szymanski* 2013: 3).

Economic analysis of political markets suggests that the primary consequence of the imposition of any regulation is a redistribution of income or wealth (*Downs* 1957; *Buchanan & Tullock* 1962). League or organization spending mandates, whether enacted in the name of competitive balance or financial responsibility, by intention redistribute income. The principal outcome, experienced in America and expected for UEFA clubs, all predicated on a notion of "fair", is that rents are shifted away from the athletes and toward the owners and other stakeholders.

Nevertheless, the division of revenue between players and club owners, to those on the outside, should matter only as to how a reallocation may change the quality of competition and other aspects of overall wellbeing.

The American experience shows that payroll and player-salary restraints have at best a marginal effect on competitive balance, and although these leagues are comparatively well balanced, other factors are more important to that issue. NCAA regulations stress that equitable competition is predicated on all participants adhering to the rules, and not necessarily competitive matches and games. The broad spending restraints of FFP are actually likely to acerbate competitive imbalance[1], restrict the chances of underdogs to improve their lot, and generally make football leagues more predictable (less interesting?). Moreover, FFP directly discourages investment in football clubs and leagues so the overall result is likely a reduction in consumer welfare.

3. Labor Relations, Antitrust and Competition Law

Organizational distinctions between American leagues and European football are important. Policy in American professional leagues is formulated jointly as a negotiation between ownership and the players' unions, while sport specific governing bodies oversee European leagues. American professional leagues are responsible only to themselves, and governing bodies in European sports set policy for all levels of the sport within their jurisdictions. The rise of player unions in American sports leagues threatens owners control and their seat at the bargaining table reflects as much.

American players have organized as labor unions since the 1960s and the relevant league policy is now fully set through the collective bargaining process, as determined by American labor law. The subsequent collective bargaining agreements (CBAs) are immune from antitrust law through a non-statutory exemption (*Weiler* et al. 2010). Ironically, owners have used a provision of labor law to their advantage in negotiating salary restraints. For American sports, the labor exemption to antitrust appears to be settled and the owners, providing they preserve negotiating leverage, can maintain or even augment spending restraints. European football is bound by the mandated regulations of UEFA. However, the matter of the legality of spending restraints is not settled and UEFA is banking on FFP rules being granted autonomy from EU competition law. The European Commission (EC) on competition offered preliminary support for FFP.

---

1 *Peeters & Szymanski's* simulation shows greater imbalance when FFP is in full force.

However, FFP faces a court challenge and whether it violates completion law remains to be decided.[2]

The timing of the actions implementing spending restraints in both instances correlates with court ordered labor market freedom for players. Labor market mobility rights for players replaced highly restrictive systems, whereby transfers of clubs and the bidding for services were completely controlled by club owners – the player reservation system and the retain and transfer rules for American and European sports, respectively. Each of these methods, which were slightly different means to the same end, significantly restrained player compensation. For the first three quarters of the twentieth century American sport leagues operated under the reservation system, which in its most restrictive form allowed for player transfers between teams only at the club's discretion. In other words, the clubs owned the property right to each player's labor service (*Rottenberg* 1956). Free agency in American sports was ordered by arbitration (MLB) or court antitrust cases in the mid and late 1970s (*Weiler* et al. 2010).

Player salaries, the most significant cost in professional sports, exploded in the aftermath of mobility rights (*Quirk & Fort* 1992). The NBA, citing extreme financial strife shortly after losing an antirust challenge mandating players' free agent rights in 1978 (*Robertson* versus NBA 1978) and the National Basketball Players Association (the union) agreed to professional sports' first modern era payroll cap in 1984. More restrictive payroll caps in the NFL and NHL, both of which were longer able to fend off true free agency, followed in the 1990s and 2000s.[3] Yet, American professional leagues explicitly limit spending controls to player salaries. Salary caps contrary to expectations are not immune from antitrust law because competitive balance improvements have a procompetitive result that exceeds the anticompetitive salary restraints. Rather the restraints are protected because they are enacted through collective bargaining. This antitrust exemption has fostered a position that has enabled owners in the NBA, NFL, and NHL to use labor law to their advantage and increase the owners' shares of the spoils under cap rules.

American professional leagues have used the lockout, which is a work stoppage motivated by the owners, to reduce the players' income share under salary cap rules. The spirit of the labor law provision authorizing lockouts is that it gives management a tool to balance the union's right to strike. Logically, the side with

---

2 Player agent Daniel Striani has brought a complaint with the European Commission in 2013 that FFP anti-competitive and will negatively impact on his ability to generate income. Legal experts are skeptical that FFP falls within the limits of competition law (*Geey* 2013).

3 MLB has not imposed a limit on payrolls but has placed a luxury tax on payrolls exceeding a threshold since 1997 (*Maxcy* 2011).

the most leverage to shift the terms of the CBA in their favor will initiate a stoppage. Modern day American sport club ownership is much better suited to weather the storm of a stoppage; compared to players they are wealthier, more diversified, and with long-term contracts for broadcast rights, luxury suites, and sponsorships, they are less dependent than in the past on game specific revenue. There have been, in the past fifteen years, three lockouts in the NHL, two for the NBA, and one in the NFL, including one for each league since 2011. The owners have each time gained a new CBA that is more favorable to their interests. Notably, the players' designated share of revenue in each league has fallen from more than 60% to less than 50% in the past three years.

Likewise, FFP appears largely to be a response to the Bosman ruling of 1995 which fully dismantled the retain and transfer system, and set off a salary explosion. Free agency in Europe, with no union-negotiated restrictions, is actually a purer form than the American versions and that is most likely to the players' benefit. Moreover, European football has a long history of well documented financial struggles. However these financial problems for European football clubs long precede the Bosman ruling (*Szymanski & Zimbalist* 2005), and never before has there been such an effort to regulate spending. Unlike in the American closed leagues, profit is not clearly an objective. *Peeters & Szymanski* (2013) report that in the most recent survey, nearly two-thirds of UEFA top division clubs reported operating losses. Nonetheless, the escalation of player wealth post Bosman, along with sugar daddy investment, has garnered great public attention and this combination, more than financial transparency and solvency, is conceivably the true motivation for governing bodies to do something, and with FFP they have indeed.

FFP restrictions may exceed what is legal under EC competition law, and the results of a challenge already filed will tell. The EC has offered support for FFP on the grounds that it is proportional, meaning the anti-competitive repercussions, i.e. restricting incomes of players and their agents, are balanced by the prevention of club bankruptcies (*Slater* 2013). Bosman lawyer Jean-Louis Dupont has presented the initial legal challenge. His complaint filed on behalf of Mr. Striani in 2013, however, may take as many as five years to settle (*Geey* 2013). In the meantime, the regulations and potential sanctions for violations are effective. Accordingly, while American salary and payroll restraints have a significant history and are on solid legal ground, FFP portends much uncertainty on both grounds. American sports benefit from court rulings that allow labor law to trump antitrust law in the case of conflict between the two. Moreover, American labor law is federal and therefore uniform across all states. Competition law falls under the EC jurisdiction; however European labor law varies by country making uniform interpretations difficult. It is more likely that EC competition law would hold in the case of a conflict. Beyond the legal issues, the closed league system, underscores the quest for competitive balance in the American system.

4. Closed Leagues and Competitive Balance

The closed league system, as opposed to an open system of club formation and entry, also differentiates the American system from European football (*Noll* 2002). Closed leagues limit membership so that new clubs and owners enter only at the invitation of current members. In contrast to the open leagues, there is no promotion and relegation system and membership is fixed year-to-year regardless of club performance. Moreover, the new owners of existing clubs must be approved by the current members. Closed league objectives are plainly financial (*Szymanski and Zimbalist* 2005), and the economic characterization of clubs as profit maximizers cannot be denied. The closed system creates significant market power. A single dominant league has emerged in all major American team sports, establishing a monopoly. Attempts to form rival leagues have either failed, or when successful have been absorbed in whole or part by the dominant league. Moreover, the monopoly league is able to provide each member club a local monopoly by granting each exclusive market rights to their territory, which limits competition in each local market.

A consequence of the local monopolies formed by closed league territorial rights is that the range of club's market sizes and revenue potential is greatly disparate. Major leagues in America are made up of thirty or thirty-two clubs and there is typically only one franchise per sport in each city or metropolitan area. The exceptions are the two largest metros, New York and Los Angeles, which typically have one additional club in each major league.[4] Clubs' market sizes are thus unequal; the largest having metropolitan populations greater than the smallest by factors of ten or more. Contrast this with an open system where free entry and the lack of territorial restrictions naturally level market size as more clubs share large metropolitan regions. For example, metropolitan London is home to a several EPL clubs each season, and more than ten clubs in all divisions of the English Football League. Several other English cities, Manchester for instance, support at least two Football League clubs (*Noll* 2002). The great disparity of market size, combined with the American tradition of tying clubs to cities, leads to greater public scrutiny

4 Chicago also has two MLB (baseball) clubs, and inclusion of northern New Jersey in the New York City metro area gives that area three National Hockey League (NHL) teams. Some metropolitan areas also support an additional minor league club in baseball or hockey.

of competitive balance. Goliaths like the New York and Los Angeles clubs have a great market size advantage over the Davids such as Kansas City, Nashville, and Green Bay; there is significant hype to make or keep a level playing field.

Regulations put forward under the auspices of leveling the playing field so that large market clubs do not dominate the talent market are widely held among the sports media and fan bases as appropriate. Such rules serve the profit and control motives of owners in two ways. First is the presumption that greater competitive balance is achieved and with that comes greater fan interest and more customers (*Neale* 1964). Notwithstanding, the most direct effect on profits is that the labor market restrictions lower the single greatest expense of sports clubs, player compensation.

Consequently, even if revenues are not increased by better balance, the lower labor costs give rise to greater profits.

Financial considerations, especially for small market clubs, are actually at the heart of spending restraints in American professional leagues. The most recent work stoppages in American Sports, the National Football League (NFL) and National Basketball Association (NBA) in 2011, National Hockey League (NHL) in 2012, were each motivated by owners' desire for greater restrictions on spending—by means of more restrictive payroll caps. In each case the claim was made that the small market franchises were on the verge of bankruptcy. For instance, the NBA put forth that operating losses totaled $300 million for each of the three seasons preceding the lockout, with twenty of thirty teams in the red (*Thompson* 2011). The NHL made similar claims of distress. Small market financial issues and competitive balance are plausibly two sides of the same coin. More restrictive limits on salaries doubtless improve the bottom line for all clubs, but the effect on competitive balance is not clear.

5. Effects of Payroll Restraints

Noll (2002) submits that the European open system, with promotion and relegation, will theoretically result in better competitive balance than the closed American systems. That is not the case in practice; *Peeters* and *Szymanski*, 2013 explain why. Moreover they suggest and show with simulation that even though better competitive balance is not an explicit goal of the policy, FFP actually increases imbalance in some cases, and this should be a concern. Furthermore, they show that an American style salary cap reliably promotes better balance than FFP.

In theory salary caps level the distribution of talent, e.g. *Fort & Quirk* (1995), *Vrooman* (1995), *Késenne* (2000). On this basis *Peeters* and *Szymanski*, 2013 simulate talent markets for a pure salary cap system in contrast to FFP rules on revenue-based spending for several top European football leagues. They show that cap systems do provide better balance compared to what would be the case for FFP. The actual effect of spending restraints on balance is ambiguous in American leagues. Salary caps systems are not pure, meaning they have been distorted by exceptions, e.g. the NBA's soft cap, described below; they are intertwined with other league policies affecting balance, such as revenue sharing; and they do not proscribe investment in other resources that promote winning, such as coaches' pay or facility upgrades. Notwithstanding, there is a salary cap history in American leagues and the effect of salary restraints can be evaluated empirically, as is done here.

For this analysis, competitive balance before and after the imposition of a major spending restraint is checked for each of the four major team-sport leagues, MLB, the NBA, the NFL and the NHL. In the NFL a hard salary cap, that is one with no exceptions, was compulsory to begin the 1994 season and has remained in place since then. The NBA employed a "soft" cap since the 1980s, meaning clubs could exceed the cap limit when renegotiating the contracts of their current players. However following the 1998–99 lockout, the resultant CBA applied a radically new system; that being a cap on individual player's salaries with upward adjustments based only on the player's years of experience. Although the soft cap remained and allowed exceptions on clubs' total payrolls, that CBA also included a luxury tax to be levied for all teams exceeding the cap threshold. The NHL instituted an NFL style hard salary cap to begin 2005–06, following a lockout that had cancelled the entire 2004–05 season. MLB has no salary cap; however a luxury tax on payrolls is levied. Termed the competitive balance tax, it penalizes all teams exceeding a defined payroll threshold and took its present form in 2003.

The results showing competitive balance, before and after the restraint rule for each league, are reported in Table 1. The timing of imposed restraints is of course different for each league, and for the sake of consistency we evaluate an even number of years before and after the restraint took effect in each league.[5] Competitive balance is measured using the standard Noll-Scully ratio of actual to ideal standard deviation of winning percent (RSD). Data were collected from *Rodney Fort's* (2013) Sports Business Data collection.[6] A statistically significant improvement in balance is found after imposition of the spending restraint in both the NBA and NHL. The effect is strongest in the NBA, but also important in the NHL. RSD averages also fall in MLB, but the difference is not significant at the 0.1 level. The

5 The comparison years are equal within but not across leagues. Other combinations of years surrounding the restraint were tested and provided similar results in each case. The balancing of the number of years on either side of the restraint makes for the cleanest and most consistent presentation.

6 Fort calculated the RSD for annually for each sport.

NFL's RSD results are nearly identical for the selection of seasons before and after implementation of their salary cap.

Table 1: American Major Leagues: Competitive Balance (RSD) Before and After Imposition of Spending Restraints

NBA			
Year PRE	**RSD**	**Year POST**	**RSD**
1984–85	2.649	1999–2000	2.916
1985–86	2.602	2000–01	2.846
1986–87	2.797	2001–02	2.495
1987–88	2.852	2002–03	2.612
1988–89	2.936	2003–04	2.465
1989–90	3.151	2004–05	2.803
1990–91	2.863	2005–06	2.469
1991–92	2.888	2006–07	2.396
1992–93	2.865	2007–08	3.056
1993–94	3.210	2008–09	3.117
1994–95	2.921	2009–10	2.951
1995–96	3.102	2010–11	2.910
1996–97	3.458	2011–12	2.537
1997–98	3.431	2012–13	2.811
1984–98	**2.980**	**1999–2013**	**2.742**
St.Dv.	0.250		0.241
P t-test			0.009***

NHL			
Year PRE	**RSD**	**Year POST**	**RSD**
1996–97	1.411	2005–06	1.9789
1997–98	1.742	2006–07	1.852
1998–99	1.752	2007–08	1.193
1999–2000	1.880	2008–09	1.586
2000–01	1.950	2009–10	1.543
2001–02	1.658	2010–11	1.532
2002–03	1.693	2011–12	1.449
2003–04	1.729	2012–13	1.510
1996–2004	**1.727**	**2005–13**	**1.581**
St.Dv.	0.150		0.226
P t-test			**0.088***

MLB			
Year PRE	**RSD**	**Year POST**	**RSD**
1993	2.374	2003	1.782
1994	1.536	2004	2.200
1995	1.448	2005	1.388
1996	1.422	2006	1.265
1997	1.488	2007	1.238
1998	2.239	2008	1.738
1999	2.013	2009	1.701
2000	1.764	2010	1.696
2001	1.649	2011	1.851
2002	2.056	2012	2.038
1993–2002	**1.799**	**2003–12**	**1.690**
St.Dv.	0.330		0.299
P t-test			0.236

NFL			
Year PRE	**RSD**	**Year POST**	**RSD**
1975	1.877	1994	1.401
1976	1.882	1995	1.225
1977	1.704	1996	1.474
1978	1.379	1997	1.455
1979	1.394	1998	1.712
1980	1.495	1999	1.494
1981	1.389	2000	1.576
1982	1.281	2001	1.628
1983	1.396	2002	1.321
1984	1.682	2003	1.535
1985	1.644	2004	1.540
1986	1.670	2005	1.694
1987	1.353	2006	1.447
1988	1.346	2007	1.661
1989	1.442	2008	1.658
1990	1.622	2009	1.611
1991	1.743	2010	1.498
1992	1.655	2011	1.637
1993	1.284	2012	1.549
1975–93	**1.539**	**1994–2012**	**1.532**
St.Dv.	0.193	SD	0.128
P t-test			0.453

It is interesting that the NBA's balance, which has far and away the worst RSD measures over time, was improved the most by salary restraint. Yet, the salary cap had no statistically verifiable effect in NFL, which has consistently measured the best RSD. The NBA's 1999 changes limiting individual player's salaries were emphatic. Prior to the rule Michael Jordan's $33.14 million personal annual salary under the soft cap exceeded the team payroll threshold of $26.9 million in 1997–98.[7] NBA revenues have more than doubled over the following sixteen years, but no player has reached Jordan's record annual salary since; the Laker's Kobe Bryant is, in 2013–14, the highest salaried NBA player, earning just over $25 million.

An implication, when comparing the NBA and NHL results to the NFL, is that when competitive balance levels are poor imposing a policy designed to improve the outcome cannot help but be effective. However, when the level of balance is suitable and contingent on other factors, enforcing a restraint may not matter. In the case of European football, whose national leagues tend to have comparatively low levels of competitive balance, payroll restraints may in reality follow the simulations of *Peeters* and *Szymanski*, 2013 and improve competitive balance... but it is not clear that anyone cares. Perhaps for UEFA stakeholders it is better to have complete control of a poorly balanced league than to part with control of a better balanced one.

6. The Cost of Enforcing the Rules

Rules are enacted to modify behavior and naturally there is an incentive to skirt those rules to retain the desired activities. American professional leagues, with restrictions limited to player salaries and payrolls, transparent reporting as mandated by both club and union interests, and only about thirty clubs to monitor, reveal no particular difficulties in policing their regulations. Nonetheless, players' agents in partnership with willing clubs have found ways to circumvent the system, and these actions have brought further refinement to the restraint rules, which are actually quite complex. For example, after a clever move by free throw specialist Chris Dudley and the New York Knicks to manipulate the soft cap exceptions, the NBA was forced to adjust for sign and trade situations (*Wise* 1997). The NFL modified cap regulations, so as to prorate bonus payments to annual values counting toward the cap limit, after the Dallas Cowboys manipulated the rules by signing fashionable cornerback Deion Sanders to a contract with a small base salary and

7 Jordan's Bulls paid out a of $61.33 million total payroll in 1997–98 more than double that season's team cap value. Derived from *Fort*'s (2013) data collection.

large back loaded (to be paid later) bonus (*Hemmer* 1997). However the problems associated with policing and compliance for UEFA are more likely similar to the colossal issues in this regard confronted by the NCAA.

The NCAA must police its very restrictive amateur rules that prohibit payments to athletes beyond an athletic scholarship that provides the athlete's tuition, books and supplies, and basic living expenses. Additionally, NCAA athletes are not permitted to use their reputation as an athlete to earn income from any other source; hence amateur status is forfeited and athletes are declared ineligible for NCAA competitions. Comparable to professional sports in revenue generation, and with likewise high returns to winning, basketball and football players in particular, are worth far more to their schools than the payment they receive.

The competition to recruit star players is great and so is the incentive to cheat the rules. Moreover, NCAA athletes must retain academic eligibility in addition to meeting and maintaining amateur status. Specifically, they must be full time students making progress toward a college degree. Consequently, there are rules on compensation, recruiting, and academic eligibility to be monitored and enforced. The NCAA's has a book of bylaws for each division that delineates these rules; it is 450 pages long just for the top division (*NCAA* 2012a). Policing and enforcing the rules effectively is expensive, and absorbing the cost by reduction in redistribution payments, is not particularly in the interest of the membership… unless one is feeling directly victimized by a rival's cheating. The NCAA returns more than three-fourths of its more than $800 million in annual revenue to member schools (*NCAA* 2012b). According to *Richard Justice* (2011) the NCAA had only 38 full-time investigators to cover 120 schools playing Division 1A football and the 335 competing in Division 1 basketball. All top level schools maintain at least one compliance officer within their athletic department and each school is encouraged to self-report violations, which of course is a conflict of interest. If a school wants to cheat, and there is plenty of incentive to do so, they can likely get away with it. Each year brings several high profile scandals revealing violations of either the amateur rules—players receive improper benefits—or academic standards. Observers find the NCAA enforcement process to be an appealing combination of unfair and inept (*Miller* 2012).

UEFA's enforcement scenario is similar to the NCAA's in that they must police a large and diverse membership, many who will have strong incentives to break the rules. Likewise, because the rules are multifaceted, covering all aspects of revenue generation and spending, the process if done correctly promises to be more expensive than the organization's membership are willing to spend. UEFA, like the NCAA, will employ a bare bones staff of regulators, a reported 15 accountants to monitor 630 clubs (*Gibson* 2013). However the issues facing UEFA are different, as the value and disbursement of sponsorship funds rather than amateurisms takes center stage.

Already sponsorship deals are being accused of sidestepping FFP rules. Recent contracts are alleged to be sugar daddy injections rather than market-value transactions, which are permitted as a legitimate source of revenue. Most notorious is the French League's Paris Saint-Germain's sponsorship deal, announced in 2013, with the Qatar Tourism Authority, whereby PSG will earn up to €200million per-year from the four-year deal (*Ogden* 2013). Previously a 2011 contract to pay £35million per-year over 10 years to EPL's Manchester City by Etihad Airways of Abu Dhabi and £57per year from Chevrolet to EPL league-mate Manchester United were considered excessive sponsorship deals (*Ogden* 2013). The problem for UEFA, in addition to monitoring and evaluating a plethora of financial information regarding all actual revenues and expenses, is that they must be the arbitrators of what constitutes fair "market-value"; then determine and enforce sanctions for violators. UEFA's warnings to Manchester City and PPG (*Gibson* 2013) that cheating will not be tolerated suggest that, as enforcement goes, maintaining control of top leagues, where financial solvency is not generally a problem, will take precedence over punishing little guys who fall into the red.

7. Ownership Restrictions

Regulating the capital injections of sugar daddies is the second of the four implied FFP objectives listed by *Peeters* and *Szymanski*, 2013. Limiting the financial influence of wealthy foreigners may appear to be fair to domestic clubs, but from an American perspective this restriction is more likely one to facilitate maintained control. The influx of foreign investment, especially noteworthy are the oil rich benefactors from the Middle East and Russia, challenges the traditional football powers like Real Madrid and FC Barcelona in Spain's top division, La Liga, and Arsenal and Manchester United in the English Premier League (EPL).

Manchester City won the EPL in 2012 following the major investment from the Abu Dhabi investors. The EPL's Chelsea FC is underwritten by Russian oilman Roman Abramovich, and after anguishing as an also ran for years, the club has been prominent and highly competitive since Abramovich's 2003 investment. The success of these clubs, and their challenge to the old guard, doubtless makes the football leagues competitions exciting, but the sugar daddies' contributions spark concern. Most recently, PSG's €2 Billion per year deal with Qatar's Tourism

Authority is being scrutinized as an underhanded attempt to buy the Champions League title. These sponsorships will be deemed to breach FFP regulations if the value exceeds the market rate for sponsorships as determined by UEFA accountants. The difference between the payment and the determined market value will be subtracted from club's reported revenues, potentially leaving the high spending clubs in violation of the FFP solvency rules and subject to sanctions, including expulsion.

The FFP restrictions limiting sugar daddy investment appear to be a backdoor method to accomplish what American closed leagues can directly regulate. Ownership in closed leagues is by definition at invitation only. All leagues have regulations as to who may own a team, and they also place some restrictions on the activities in which the owners may engage. The NFL, for example, enforces the most severe restrictions on ownership. They ban large publicly traded corporations from retaining teams. This policy allows the league to be comprised of only individual owners, creating a relatively homogeneous group. The NFL also proscribes majority owners from also holding a MLB, NBA or NHL team located in NFL home cities. New owners of existing franchises in American leagues typically require a super majority vote of the current owners, for instance 75% approval in MLB. Those desiring to buy teams are sometimes famously denied. For example, outspoken entrepreneur Mark Cuban, who owns the NBA's Dallas Mavericks, has been rejected by MLB despite submitting the highest bids for clubs on at least three occasions (Dallas Morning News 2013). *Peeters* and *Szymanski,* 2013 in fact suggest that FFP moves European football nearer the closed league model and the implicit push out of foreign benefactors supports their conjecture.

8. Conclusion

FFP, which will require football clubs to maintain fiscal responsibility, may appear on the surface to be quite different from salary caps and other restraints on player compensation in American sports. There are fundamental structural differences, such as open versus closed league systems and the external legal environments to be negotiated, for sure. However, as revealed here, the driving forces of profit and control are very similar and the same may be expected of the outcomes.

By and large the motivation of the masters, the owners and stake holders, of the respective leagues and organizations, for spending regulations is to insure the profits by maintaining or retaking control of policy and the associated revenue streams. Control was partially ceded to the players' unions in American professional sports leagues over thirty years ago. However, using labor law to improve their negotiating has gradually tilted the scale back toward owners. The imposition of increasingly restrictive payroll restraints is proof. The NCAA meanwhile aggressively contests any changes that would provide athletes any say in matters, and so far with much courtroom success, though perhaps their legal standing is becoming less stable.

Open league football has encountered perhaps more pressing control problems. Existing stakeholders in European football leagues face two challenges. The situation with the athletes, though not unionized, is similar to American professional sports, where court ordered mobility rights have shifted much income and control toward players. Importantly distinct though, is that open leagues cannot easily control membership, as do closed leagues, and sugar daddies have found investment in football lucrative. FFP appears to be as much about insuring control of football and its profit streams for its traditional masters as it is about securing widespread fiscal health.

UEFA and American sports leagues count on stirring public insecurity over what could be described as non-existent problems. Americans believe that competitive balance is always under threat and sports will be dominated by the large market clubs. Europeans are concerned about the financial viability of their football clubs and therefore football as they know it. Policies that promise to rectify these issues are bound for public support and the masters of the games take advantage. The real motivation for regulation, maintaining control and greater profits for the rich, would garner far less public support. Notwithstanding, the consequences of spending regulations, especially FFP, promise few benefits to the fans and consumers.

Improved competitive balance, the assurance on which American regulations are based, is not conclusively shown to result. FFP could actually worsen balance, especially when the break-even condition strictly applied, which is not an amenable outcome for football fans. Furthermore, the forced belt tightening purports to only correct a problem that is one more of perception than reality. Football has long reported financial difficulties yet survived, if not thrived. If anything FFP mandated disinvestment will detract from the consumers' experience. All the same, this is sports and regardless of policy changes on either side of the Atlantic, fans will greatly appreciate the products, which are the great games. It is after all entertainment, and as has been said of another hedonistic activity; when it's good it's fantastic and when bad… it's still pretty good.

References

Buchanan, J.M. & *Tullock, G.* (1962): The Calculus of Consent. Ann Arbor: University of Michigan Press.

Dallas Morning News (2013): Mavericks' Mark Cuban on not owning a baseball team: Major League Baseball is run more like the mafia than it is a business, http://www.dallasnews.com/sports/dallas-mavericks/headlines/20130824-mark-cuban-on-not-owning-a-baseball-team-major-league-baseball-is-run-more-like-the-mafia-than-it-is-a-business.ece (accessed 2013-11-27).

Downs, A. (1957): An Economic Theory of Democracy. Cambridge: York: Cambridge University Press.

Fort, R. (2013): Rodney Fort's Sports Business Data, https://sites.google.com/site/rodswebpages/codes (accessed 2013-11-02).

Fort, R., & *Quirk, J.* (1995): Cross-Subsidization, Incentives, and Outcomes in Professional Team Sports Leagues, in: Journal of Economic Literature, Vol. 33, 3, pp. 1265–1299.

Geey, D. (2013): The Financial Fair Play Challenge to UEFA, http://www.danielgeey.com/the-financial-fair-play-challenge-to-uefa (accessed 2013-11-27).

Gibson, O. (2013). Manchester City and PSG cannot 'cheat' financial fair play, UEFA warns. The Guardian, http://www.theguardian.com/football/2013/feb/04/manchester-city-financial-fair-play (accessed 2013-11-27).

Hemmer, A. (1997): Prime Time Rewrote the Rules, in: Cincinnati Business Journal, May 9., http://www.bizjournals.com/cincinnati/stories/1997/09/08/newscolumn3.html?page=all (accessed 2013-11-27).

Justice, R. (2011): College sports is out of control, and there's no way the NCAA can police all of it, http://blog.chron.com/sportsjustice/2011/08/is-the-miami-scandal-worse-than-smus/ (accessed 2013-11-27).

Késenne, S. (2000): The Impact of Salary Caps in Professional Team Sports, in: Scottish Journal of Political Economy, Vol. 47, 4, pp. 422–430.

Knight Commission on Intercollegiate Athletics (2009): College Sports 101: A primer on money, athletics and higher education in the 21st century, http://www.knightcommission.org/collegesports101/table-of-contents (accessed 2013-11-27).

Maxcy, J. (2011): The Effect on Player Transfers of a Luxury Tax on Club Payrolls: The Case of Major League Baseball, in *Andreff, W.* (ed.): Sports Economics: Participation, Events, and Professional Team Sports, Cheltenham, UK and Northampton, MA, US: Edward Elgar. pp. 80–92.

Miller, S. (2012): The NCAA Needs to Let Someone Else Enforce Its Rules. The Atlantic, October 23, http://www.theatlantic.com/entertainment/archive/2012/10/the-ncaa-needs-to-let-someone-else-enforce-its-rules/264012/, http://blog.chron.com/sportsjustice/2011/08/is-the-miami-scandal-worse-than-smus/ (accessed 2013-11-27).

NCAA (2013): Eligibility: Fairness. Academics. Equitable Competition, http://www.ncaa.org/wps/wcm/connect/public/NCAA/Eligibility/ (accessed 2013-12-01).

NCAA (2012a): 2012–13 Division I Manual, http://www.ncaapublications.com/productdownloads/D113.pdf (accessed 2013-11-27).

NCAA (2012b): Consolidated Financial Statements, 2011–12., http://www.ncaa.org/wps/wcm/connect/public/NCAA/Finances/NCAA+consolidated+financial+statements (accessed 2013-11-27).

Neale, W. C. (1964): The peculiar economics of professional sports: A contribution to the theory of the firm in sporting competition and in market competition, in: The Quarterly Journal of Economics, Vol. 78, 1, pp. 1–14.

Noll, R. (2002): The economics of promotion and relegation in sports leagues: the case of English football, in: Journal of Sports Economics, Vol. 3, 2, pp. 169–203.

Ogden, M. (2013): Paris Saint-Germain sponsorship deal eclipses all rivals but opens questions about Financial Fair Play regulations. The Telegraph, November 12, http://www.telegraph.co.uk/sport/football/european/10443730/Paris-Saint-Germain-sponsorship-deal-eclipses-all-rivals-but-opens-questions-about (accessed 2013-11-27).

Peeters, T. & Szymanski, S. (2013): Financial Fair Play in European Football. Working paper, Antwerp: University of Antwerp Faculty of Applied Economics.

Quirk, J. P., & Fort, R. (1992) : Pay dirt: The business of professional team sports. Princeton, NJ: Princeton University Press.

Robertson vs. National Basketball Association (1978): 369 Federal Supplemental. 867.

Rottenberg, S. (1956): The baseball players' labor market, in: Journal of Political Economy, Vol. 64, 3, pp. 242–258.

Slater, M. (2013): Fighting financial fair play. BBC, October 1, http://m.bbc.com/sport/football/24333604 (accessed 2013-11-27).

Szymanski, S. & Zimbalist, A. (2005): National Pastime: How Americans Play Baseball and the Rest of the World Plays Soccer. Washington D.C.: Brookings Institution Press.

Thompson, D. (2011): The NBA Lockout: Here's What You Need to Know. The Atlantic, June 30, http://www.theatlantic.com/business/archive/2011/06/the-nba-lockout-heres-what-you-need-to-know/241251/ (accessed 2013-11-27).

Vrooman, J. (1995): A General Theory of Professional Sports Leagues., in: Southern Economic Journal, Vol. 61, 4, pp. 971–990.

Weiler, P. C., Roberts, G. R., Abrams, R. I. & Ross, S. F. (2010): Sports and the Law: Text, Cases and Problems, 4th Ed. Minneapolis MN: West.

Wise, M. (1997): Dudley Wins His Bid to Sign With the Knicks. New York Times, September 8, http://www.nytimes.com/1997/09/08/sports/dudley-wins-his-bid-to-sign-with-the-knicks.html (accessed 2013-11-27).

The Competition Economics of Financial Fair Play

Oliver Budzinski

Abstract

This paper provides an economic analysis of the competition effects of UEFA's financial fair play regulations. It concludes that the restrictive effects of the break-even rule cannot be justified by a legitimate objective defense (according to European competition policy) because significant financial problems due to overinvestment are not inherent to European football.

Keywords

financial fair play, sports economics, competition economics, European competition policy, football, soccer, overinvestment, rat race

1. Introduction

Professional sports – and European-style football[1] in particular – is a serious commercial business with considerable turnovers and revenues. As a consequence, powerful market participants experience incentives to reap supracompetitive rents by restricting the beneficial forces of competition at the expense of customers or suppliers. At first sight, however, such powerful or dominant players do not seem to exist in professional sports. In contrast to ordinary goods markets, professional sports requires the existence of a sufficient number of competitors in order to produce the product at all (*Rottenberg* 1956; *Neale* 1964): a monopoly football club would obviously not be able to provide a marketable good. Thus, there is typically no worry of *single-club dominance* in this sense. However, sports competition also requires the definition, implementation and enforcement of sporting rules. This is typically the role of sports associations who govern and regulate the sports competition. Sports associations usually are private companies (sometimes non-for-profit companies) and, in football, membership associations with the members being lower-level sports associations and, at the bottom of the pyramid, the clubs who provide football teams on all levels. For instance, the *UEFA* (Union of European Football Associations) consists of national football associations as members such as the *DFB* (Deutscher Fußball-Bund; Germany), the *FA* (The Football Association; England) or the *RFEF* (Real Federación Española de Fútbol; Spain). The national associations

1 Throughout this paper, the term *football* will refer to European-style football (sometimes also labeled *soccer*) – and not to American football.

then consist of regional associations and the regional associations have all the clubs playing football within their region as members – including professional clubs as well as grassroots clubs. Along this pyramidal structure, all these football associations enjoy a monopoly position within their region. The resulting market power is rather modest on the bottom levels of the pyramid since being a member of the higher level association implies the duty to stay in line with the higher level associations while, at the same time, the influence on the higher level association is often rather limited due to the large number of voting members. Furthermore, the lowest level associations usually do not govern a professional league; instead, they are dealing with amateur and grassroots leagues and competitions. The market power on the top level of the pyramid, however, is significant since this is the level where the most valuable competitions take place (the *UEFA Champions League* and the *UEFA Europa League*) and a large number of member associations imply substantial scope for independent action. While it may be debatable how independent from the national associations UEFA can act, it appears to be rather obvious that the influence of the clubs participating in UEFA's competitions is rather indirect – either through the chain of associations along the pyramidal structure or through lobbyism.[2]

In summary, it does not seem to be far-stretched to ascribe a significantly powerful position to UEFA. In economic terms, UEFA is a market-internal regulatory agency enjoying a monopoly position. Now, how are the activities of a sports association relevant to the professional sports market, i.e. to the commercial side of sports? Firstly, UEFA (like most associations governing commercialized sports competitions) engages not only in setting and enforcing sporting rules, but also in commercial activities, namely the bundling and sale of broadcasting rights for the UEFA competitions as well as the marketing of the brands of these competitions. Secondly, the setting and enforcing of sporting rules itself entails a business element that is difficult to disentangle. Sporting rules may well be shaped with the purpose of increasing the attractiveness of sports and, thus, turnovers and revenues. And, sporting rules may well be shaped with the effect of reducing competition intensity in order to reap supracompetitive rents from customers or suppliers.[3] Therefore, rule-making activities by UEFA constitute a commercial strategy by a dominant entity – and, as such, scrutiny regarding the effects on competition is justified.

---

2 *Budzinski & Szymanski* (2014) provide a discussion whether UEFA may be viewed as a horizontal cartel of football clubs or an independent player with a monopoly position in the market for competition organizing services, representing a bottleneck along the vertical supply chain of professional football.

3 Consequently, the European Court of Justice ruled in its landmark Meca-Medina case that sporting rules are subject to competition policy and must comply with competition law. See Case C-519/04P, *Meca Medina v. Commission*, ECR 2006, I-6991.

Consequently, the so-called *financial fair play regulations* (FFP) implemented by UEFA may raise competition concerns since they regulate the investment behavior of clubs participating in UEFA club competitions – an intervention that appears to be potentially restrictive from the outset on. And, indeed, in 2013, the Belgium player agent *Daniel Striani* launched a complaint with the European Commission as well as a proceeding at the European Court of Justice against FFP (inter alia) on competition law grounds.[4] According to the sports-specific competition policy practices of the European Commission (following the Meca-Medina judgment of the European Court of Justice), rules enacted by sports associations do not violate European competition law if

(a) they pursue legitimate objectives (*legitimacy*),
(b) their restrictive effects are inherent to these objectives (*inherence*), and
(c) proportional to the benefits (*proportionality*).[5]

In this paper, I argue from a competition economics perspective that UEFA's financial fair play regulations in its current shape violate the principles of inherence and proportionality and, thus, deserve a critical review by competition policy authorities. After summarizing the main features as well as outlining the possible anticompetitive effects of FFP (section 2), I review the three principles legitimacy, inherence and proportionality against the background of economic theory (section 3). Eventually, I reflect upon the results including possible alternatives (section 4). Sticking to an economic analysis, neither do I dwell upon legal questions and theories, nor do I predict outcomes of legal procedures. Instead, I provide hints about an economic assessment of FFP within the current competition policy framework in Europe.

2. Possible Restrictive Effects of Financial Fair Play

The *UEFA* (2012, 2014) introduced FFP in September 2009 as a part of revised licensing regulations, coming into full force with the 2013/2014 season.[6] Every club that wants to enter one of UEFA club competitions (*UEFA Champions League* and *UEFA*

---

4 See http://www.financialfairplay.co.uk/latest-news/legal-challenge-to-uefa-ffp-rules-by-bosman-lawyer and http://www.financialfairplay.co.uk/latest-news/further-legal-challenge-to-ffp-by-striani-and-dupont (both accessed 2014-02-15, 16.38)

5 See representing the view of the European Commission *Kienapfel & Stein* (2007), providing a legal analysis *Weatherill* (2006), and providing an economic analysis *Budzinski* (2012).

6 See for economic-based analyses of FFP *Vöpel* (2011), *Madden* (2012), *Müller* et al. (2012), *Peeters & Szymanski* (2012, 2014a, 2014b), *Preuss* et al. (2012), *Sass* (2012), *Franck* (2013), *Hamil* (2014), *Maxcy* (2014), *Szymanski* (2014) as well as *Lindholm* (2010) and *Long* (2012) for legal sciences-based analyses and *Könecke & Schubert* (2014) for a social sciences-based analysis.

Europa League) must obtain an UEFA license (next to the sporting qualification via the national leagues) and, thus, comply with the financial fair play regulations.

The FFP regulations consist, in substance, of two rules:

- the no overdue payables rule: overdue payables are understood to be all outstanding payments (towards employees, social and tax authorities or other clubs) that have not been paid by the contractually agreed deadline, and
- the break-even rule: *relevant* expenses must be paid out of *relevant* income or, in other words, *relevant* expenses must not exceed *relevant* income (see table 1); an aggregate deviation of up to € 5 million (over three financial years) is acceptable.

Violations of these rules trigger a series of sanctions, ranging from reprimands to the exclusion of the non-complying club from the European club competitions.

Table 1: The Break-Even Rule

RELEVANT INCOME		RELEVANT EXPENSES
– gate revenues – revenues from sponsorship and advertising – revenues from broadcasting rights – commercial activities revenues (merchandising, food and beverages sales, conferencing, lotteries, etc.) – other operating income (including non-football income related to the club) – finance income (interest revenue)	≥	– costs of sales and materials – wages and salaries (including related expenses such as social security contributions or medical care) – other operating expenses (e.g. match expenses, administration and overhead expenses) – finance costs and dividends
NON-RELEVANT INCOME		NON-RELEVANT EXPENSES
– Income transactions above fair value[7] – donations and assumptions of debt by a third person – income from non-football operations not related to the club – income from non-monetary credits (e.g. revaluations of assets and inventories)		– expense transactions below fair value[7] – youth development – community development activities (e.g. promoting participation in sports or advancing social development in education, health, amateur sports, etc.) – non-monetary debits and charges – finance costs of tangible fixed assets – non-football operations not related to the club – income taxes

Source: own compilation from UEFA (2012: 72–82).

7 The UEFA determines the fair value of relevant transactions according to conventional business practices. If the estimated fair value differs from the recorded value, then an adjustment must be made. In the case of income, however, no upward adjustment is possible, in the case of expenses, no downward adjustment is possible (*UEFA* 2012: 75, 78).

While the no overdue payables rule relates to issues of payment behavior and solvency, the break-even rule interferes with the investment behavior of the clubs. It effectively caps the investment of the competitors on the market for match playing services (the clubs) because it restricts the maximum expenses for the competition team (= relevant expenses) to the volume of the defined *relevant* income. As such, it represents a *relative budget cap*. This has two important implications:

1. The cap is uneven among competitors in the sense that clubs with higher relevant income are allowed to spend more than clubs with lower relevant income. In this sense, FFP represents a discriminatory cap.
2. The definition of relevant income excludes some types of sources for financing investment into the competition team. Notably, financial injections by so-called benefactors (sometimes also labeled *sugar daddies*; e.g. *Lang* et al. 2011; *Franck & Lang* 2013; *Franck* 2013) do not present relevant income and, thus, cannot serve to break even expenses. Somewhat simplifying, the concept of relevant income requires the clubs to live on their football related (*earned*) incomes and revenues. Note, however, that for a transitional period, injections that increase the equity of a club (injections by shareholders) increase the acceptable deviation between relevant incomes and relevant expenses. The acceptable volume is decreasing over time with the goal of diminishing it (*UEFA* 2012: 36).[8]

The no overdue payables rule does not appear to cause considerable restrictive effects, whereas the break-even rule comes along with several anticompetitive concerns, namely (i) the salary reduction effect, (ii) the incumbent protection effect, (iii) the consolidation effect, and (iv) the investment security effect.

The *salary reduction effect* refers to the effects of the break-even rule on the market for talent, i.e. the players market, as well as on the related market for consulting services for players (the players' agents market). Expenses on player salaries as well as on transfer activities represent the dominant part of the relevant expenses of professional football clubs. If the break-even rule caps expenses due to the limitation to relevant income as a source of financing expenses, then it is very likely that a downward trend in players' salaries as well as in transfer payments will result.[9] The deflatory effect on the level of players' salaries will

8 The starting volume is € 45 million and is reduced to € 30 million until 2018. After that "a lower amount as decided in due course by the UEFA Executive Committee" (*UEFA* 2012: 36) will come into force.

9 Indeed, economic simulation models provide support for the dampening effect on player salaries (*Peeters & Szymanski* 2014a, 2014b).

cause an accompanying deflatory effect on the revenues of players' agents. In summary, the investment level reduction induced by FFP comes at the expense of the earning possibilities of players and players' agents. Thus, rents are shifted away from these groups to the clubs and/or UEFA, which represents a restrictive effect towards upstream suppliers.[10]

The *incumbent protection effect* refers to the above explained implications of the relative character of the cap. Basically, the break-even rule implies that clubs need to adjust their investment (into talent) to the level of their revenues. If a club enjoys high revenues, then it is able to spend accordingly. If a club suffers from low revenues, then it needs to keep its expenses on a low level as well. This means that clubs who enjoy high revenues right now can maintain their competitive advantage by high investments. However, clubs who do not enjoy high revenues right now cannot freely invest into becoming more competitive. Instead, FFP forces them to maintain their lower competitive level by capping their investments. In other words, the break-even rule frustrates catching-up investments. This favors the incumbents on the top level of European football who enjoy high revenues because of recent success and valuable brands (because of more historical success). It disadvantages clubs who are not on that top level yet but who want to challenge the incumbents. In summary, FFP cements the market structure on the top level of European football (*Vöpel* 2011; *Drut & Raballand* 2012; *Sass* 2012; *Szymanski* 2014) and protects the incumbents from new challenges by upward-pressuring upstarts, newcomers and maverick competitors. Thus, the competition for participating in (and entering) the top leagues may be significantly impeded by FFP (creating a barrier to entry). While this restrictive effect is a general one, it may be particularly directed towards upstarts that are financed by wealthy private persons (e.g. FC Chelsea, Manchester City, Paris St. Germain) or by company ownership (e.g. the engagement of Red Bull) who are increasingly challenging the established big clubs. Restricting these money injections may be particularly welfare-reducing (*Madden* 2012).

The related *consolidation effect* refers to a decreasing volatility of changes in competitive advantages and disadvantages. FFP may be viewed to be an agreement that clubs seeking to improve themselves must do so in a slow and measured fashion that is less likely to create losses but, by the same token, also is less likely to create upsets. As a consequence, changes in competitiveness happen slower than

10 See the reasoning of *Dupont* (2013) who, as the lawyer of *Striani*, is advocating the antitrust complaint against FFP. He views FFP to be the action of a cartel among the clubs (transmitted via the UEFA as an association of clubs) in order to exploit the (upstream) players' and players' agent markets.

fans want – and would be willing to pay for if the investments were successful (see *Coates* et al. 2014 on the importance of upsets for consumer welfare in professional sports).

Eventually, the *investment security effect* points to an anticompetitive exclusion of entrepreneurial risk. FFP via its break-even rule is likely to lessen the risk of bad investments (e.g. into talent) since both the volume of investment and the magnitude of competitiveness consequences are deflated.

In total, FFP – or the break-even rule, in particular – may lessen competition intensity at the expense of the fans. Negative effects on consumer welfare may arise through two channels. Firstly, the deflating effect on salaries and transfer payments is likely to lead to a reduction of the level of talent quality. Top European players looking for their best earning options may decide to leave the European market and top foreign talent may be more reluctant to enter the European market. Since it is part of fans' welfare to witness outstanding talent (economics of superstars) a reduction of talent quality ceteris paribus goes along with a reduction in consumer welfare – in particular if the talent reduction is not associated with a price reduction[11]. Secondly, the lower competition intensity due to the incumbent protection effect and the consolidation effect may lead to decreasing competitive efforts by the clubs which harms the performance level. Being protected against new challengers combined with an ossifying effect on the relative competitiveness of the participants enables both the UEFA and the incumbent competitors to extract supracompetitive rents at the expense of fans[12], in particular, if there are no close substitutes to premier level European football.

3. Are the Restrictive Effects Defendable?

The anticompetitive stories outlined in the preceding section show that FFP causes restrictive effects that have the potential to infringe either the European anti-cartel

---

11 Since it is money from private investors that is deterred by FFP, whereas all revenue sources that are paid for by the fans remain unchanged (or even increase in importance since money injections from wealthy owners are restricted), a deflatory effect on prices (tickets, broadcasting rights, etc.) cannot be expected in the short run. In the midterm, however, the reduction in absolute talent quality may lead to a sinking willingness-to-pay, in particular for broadcasting rights. Still, this effect may well be mitigated by the lack of close substitutes to top level professional football.

12 See *Budzinski* and *Szymanski* (2014) for a reasoning how UEFA itself may benefit from restricting access to top European leagues to the incumbent superstar clubs and from deterring new challengers.

rules (Article 101 (1) TFEU) or the rules against an abuse of dominance (Article 102 TFEU) – depending on whether FFP is viewed to constitute a cartel among football clubs organized by UEFA as an association of undertakings or UEFA is viewed to be a dominant undertaking (*Budzinski & Szymanski* 2014). However, the restrictive effects may be justified – and thus fail to infringe European competition rules – if they are inherent and proportional to legitimate objectives (*European Commission* 2007; *Budzinski* 2012). The next sections discuss whether FFP meets these three conditions from an economic perspective.

3.1 Legitimacy: The Objectives of Financial Fair Play

According to the *European Commission* (2007: 68), legitimate objectives are usually those that relate to the proper organization and conduct of competitive sport. This may include objectives like ensuring fair sport competitions with equal chances for all teams, ensuring the uncertainty of results by the absence of match-fixing, the protection of the athletes' health, protecting the safety of the spectators, the encouragement of training of young athletes, ensuring of financial stability of sport clubs and teams, the rules of the game (ensuring uniform and consistent exercise of a given sport), etc. (*European Commission* 2007; *Kienapfel & Stein* 2007). Thus, the financial stability of the sporting competitors is explicitly quoted as a legitimate objective. According to UEFA (2012: 2), the objectives of the financial fair play regulations are

- to improve the economic and financial capability of the clubs, increasing their transparency and credibility,
- to place the necessary importance on the protection of creditors and to ensure that clubs settle their liabilities with players, social/tax authorities and other clubs punctually,
- to introduce more discipline and rationality in club football finances,
- to encourage clubs to operate on the basis of their own revenues,
- to encourage responsible spending for the long-term benefit of football, and
- to protect the long-term viability and sustainability of European club football.

These objectives appear to be comfortably in line with the Commission's concept of legitimate objectives, perhaps with the only exception of the objective to encourage clubs to operate on the basis of their own revenues. It may be debatable whether it represents a legitimate objective to limit the sources of financing business investment as long as these sources do not involve taxpayer money. Why should non-revenue based financial means represent an illegitimate source of financing investments? Increases of equity or borrowed capital do represent very usual instruments of financing investments in 'ordinary' business.

Naturally, the listed objectives are the *stated* objectives of UEFA and in competition policy analyses it is common to look beyond the stated objectives because smart companies will obviously not state anticompetitive (or here: illegitimate) objectives in public. However, I do not want to speculate on UEFA's hidden agendas here and, therefore, I will assume that the criterion of legitimate objective is generally fulfilled.[13]

3.2 Inherence: Systematic Market Failure in Football?

3.2.1 Financial Crisis in Football

From an economic perspective, the concept of inherence requires to demonstrate that economic competition among professional football clubs without a regulation of investment behavior would *systematically* fail. Instead, football clubs would systematically engage in irrational, irresponsible and unsustainable (over-)spending. It is important to emphasize that inherence requires systematic market failure and not just individual bad financial management of some clubs. In other words, the restrictive effects of FFP are inherent to the pursued objectives if otherwise the football market would display systematic overinvestment. If unrestricted investment inevitably leads to unsustainable overinvestment, then a restriction of investment behavior can be called inherent.

The recent sports economics literature includes a long and controversial discussion about losses and debts in football (inter alia, *Frick & Prinz* 2006; *Lago* et al. 2006; *Andreff* 2007; *Dietl & Franck* 2007; *Barajas & Rodríguez* 2010, 2014; *Haugen & Solberg* 2010; *Szymanski* 2010; *Drut & Raballand* 2012; *Hamil* 2014). Some of the contributions as well as general press and media articles list impressive debt figures of single clubs and even accumulated figures for overall leagues.[14] However, the interpretation of these figures is often rather unclear. In particular the general media discussion (but also some of the more scientific treatments) often lacks a relation of debt figures to asset values of the football clubs, ignoring the rationale behind the usual business practice of working with a certain share of borrowed capital (in particular when a company or a business is growing in commercial terms – as is the football business). The relatively low number and frequency of insolvencies in premier level football leagues does not necessarily support systematic market failure, in particular, since only in very few cases, the

---

13 However, see the contrary assessment by *Long* (2012: 91–92).

14 The *UEFA* (2011) itself published a so-called benchmarking report stating that more than 50 per cent of the top 650 football clubs in Europe were producing losses, accumulating in 2011 to a sum of € 1700 million.

football clubs were forced to leave the market (*Vöpel* 2011). In most of the cases, the losses are eventually covered by private investors. Be it fans or wealthy individuals – as long as losses are covered without injecting taxpayer money, it is hard to see a serious problem from an economic point of view.[15] In summary, the empirical picture is not as conclusive as it may appear at first sight.

So, what about potential reasons for *systematic* market failure, in this case systematic overinvestment to an extend that endangers the existence of so many competing clubs that the league itself is in jeopardy. The literature offers quite a number of characteristics and mechanisms of commercial football markets that may cause overinvestment. Some theories serve to explain why single clubs fail to produce a viable investment strategy. For instance, management incompetence due to a preference for hiring former sports stars over business experts (*Frick & Prinz* 2006: 72–73), negative shocks due to unexpected failures of revenue sources (*Szymanski* 2012) or negative externalities from insolvent clubs on other clubs due to financial interrelations in consequence of mutual transfer transactions (*Müller* et al. 2012: 121–122) are discussed. While all of these explanations have their merits, they cannot explain systematic failure, i.e. inevitable deficiency of the league competition. Financial failures of single competitors (in particular because of mismanagement) are a normal phenomenon and do not constitute market failure.

Furthermore, the sports economics literature offers some theories that are more suited to explain systematic market failure. Firstly, systematic overinvestment may be caused by football clubs behaving as win maximizers instead of profit maximizers (inter alia, *Késenne* 1996, 2006; *Vöpel* 2011; *Storm* 2012). Models of league competition show that, in equilibrium, win maximizing teams invest more into talent than profit maximizing teams and, if the profit maximization equilibrium is defined as the paragon, in this sense win maximizing teams overinvest. Due to the special characteristics of European football, win-maximizing behavior is generally accepted (empirically and in theory) to better describe European football markets than profit-maximizing behavior (which is generally viewed to be a good

15 There have been cases where taxpayer money has been used to save a famous football club from insolvency (for instance, the controversial 2001 Real Madrid case; *Gröteke* 2004). This represents a competitive concern – one that, however, falls under the state aid control policy. In December 2013, the European Commission started three new in-depth investigations into cases of public funding of several Spanish football clubs (with Real Madrid and Barcelona CF being among them) on the background of a possible violation of state aid rules (*European Commission* 2013). The questionable public support measures include tax privileges, state guarantees for bank loans, and real estate transactions at unusual conditions.

description of American professional sports leagues). If no profits are extracted from the clubs (non-for-profit character, the goal of maximizing wins), then it is plausible that investment into sporting success is higher than in profit-oriented organizations. However, it is questionable whether this explanation suffices to explain non-viable overinvestment creating a systematic debt-accumulating and insolvency-producing market failure. Even if wins are maximized and, thus, higher investment levels are realized than in the profit maximizing equilibrium, this does not automatically imply that win maximization is pursued unconditionally (in an irrational and irresponsible way). Rational win maximizers will attempt to maximize sporting success under the condition of financial viability. Not maximizing profits is hardly the same as unconditional overinvestment until bankruptcy. In summary, win maximizing behavior alone does not explain systematic market failure; additional factors must be considered.

3.2.2 A Rat Race?

Secondly, several authors have characterized competition among football clubs as a deficient rat race and, thereby, emphasized the systematic character of the market failure (in particular *Müller* et al. 2012; also *Vöpel* 2011; *Sass* 2012).[16] The fundamental idea of the rat race is that competitors compete for a fixed and indivisible reward. Since only the best competitor (the fastest rat) gets the reward (the cheese), the effort levels of all competitors increase without an increase of the output (which is fixed), thus reducing efficiency (*Akerlof* 1976: 603–606).[17] Some authors emphasize that competition among football clubs resembles such a rat race because of what they call (strict) positional competition: "there is only one champion and a team's ranking can fall regardless of how well it plays in absolute terms. 'Positional' competition of this kind is similar to a 'rat race'" (*Vöpel* 2011: 55). "Unlike most common competitive processes, in a rat race additional input – despite being carefully considered within the framework of maximizing individual objectives – is not rewarded in overall terms. This is due

16 *Franck* (2013: 9) uses the term *zombie race*.

17 *Akerlof* (1976) applies the rat race concept to a "surrealistic" (603) labor market where workers compete for a fixed wage by providing a fixed amount of output with different speeds. It is crucial for the model results that a higher speed of providing the output does not entail any benefits – otherwise the induced race would not reduce efficiency! The aim of the paper is to provide examples where social structures and perceptions matter for the equilibrium outcome of a market (*Akerlof* 1976: 617) – in the case of the rat race example the social structure is the workers' "desire to have an equilibrium with all workers of the same class" (604; referring to classes of abilities).

to sport leagues exhibiting a remorseless ranking arithmetic, as better positions in the table cannot be shared and clubs are stringently banished to inferior ranks" (*Müller* et al. 2012: 121). This theory indeed provides a reasoning involving systematic market failure: if the aspiration levels of the teams do not match the available ranking positions (i.e. more than one teams wants to win the championship, etc.), the strict positional competition necessarily leads (i) to efforts exceeding the rewards (systematic overinvestment) and (ii) to an increasing mismatch between investment and reward in the course of time (systemic debt accumulation) as the teams stick to a risk-friendly gambling for success (*Whitney* 1993; *Dietl & Franck* 2007).

However, the crucial question is whether the necessary conditions for a rat race are suitable assumptions for commercial football competition. The two conditions are:

- a constant reward that cannot be increased by the absolute level of efforts (thus, it is a matter of allocation – who will get the reward – and not of growth) and
- the increasing efforts are waste, i.e. they do not entail any benefit (other than the fixed reward).

The first condition requires that the revenues of a football club strictly depend on the position it achieves in the final league ranking. Furthermore, a higher position in the ranking is strictly associated with a higher reward (revenue). Only relative effort (compared to the competitors) matters for the achieved revenue level and not absolute efforts. These are the characteristics of the rat race-resembling strict positional competition. In order to discuss the accuracy of these characteristics for competition among football clubs, a look at the revenue sources (for instance, UEFA's relevant revenues, see table 1) is helpful.

- Gate revenues depend on stadium attendance figures, which are certainly related to sporting success but also depend on other factors like popularity of the club, attractiveness of the team (e.g. offensive play), (home) market size, advertising activities of the club, pricing strategies, etc. Thus, this revenue type does not strictly depend on the ranking position. It is well possible – and empirically supported – that lower ranking clubs realize higher ticket revenues than higher ranking clubs.
- Revenues from sponsorship and advertising also do not strictly depend on ranking positions. Sporting success certainly helps but other factors like negotiation skills, popularity of the club, size of the local industry, etc., are of significant relevance as well. Again, lower ranking clubs can – and do quite frequently – enjoy higher revenues of this type than higher ranking clubs.

- Revenues from broadcasting rights represent the revenue type where the strict relation of ranking position and revenue volume is best fulfilled – at least in systems of centralized marketing of broadcasting rights. In these systems (like in Germany, England or on the UEFA level), the league as whole collects the individual broadcasting rights from the teams, bundles them and sells them out of one hand to the media. Then, the revenues are allocated among the league members according to a collectively agreed upon allocation mechanism. Typically, this allocation mechanism provides money according to ranking positions, so that teams' rewards indeed strictly increase with their ranking position. Furthermore, the allocation mechanisms usually include considerable discontinuities, i.e. one position better is associated with an over-proportional increase in reward (e.g. winning the championship or qualifying for a European competition; in the negative sense, relegation implies an over-proportional loss of revenues). In summary, this type of revenues indeed fits the concept of strict positional competition – under the condition of centralized marketing[18].
- Commercial activities' revenues, again, do not depend strictly on ranking positions.
- Other operating income and finance income do not depend strictly on ranking positions as well.

Among all of UEFA's relevant revenue sources merely one single revenue source, revenues from collectively sold broadcasting rights, mirrors the necessary condition of a rat race-styled positional competition. According to recent figures from the German Bundesliga (*DFL* 2014: 7–10), revenues from the collective sale of broadcasting rights sum up to 28.53 per cent of total revenues. Sponsorship and advertising revenues yield 26.64 per cent of total revenues and gate plus hospitality revenues amount to 21.6 per cent, transfer income to 7.12 per cent, merchandising revenues to 5.54 per cent and the remaining commercial activities to 10.55 per cent. Consequently, less than a third of all revenues resembles a positional competition structure and more than two-thirds of the revenues do not strictly depend on the position reached in the league ranking.

Extending the discussion to monetary injections from benefactors and other "non-relevant" (according to FFP) sources further loosens the dependence of

18 In systems of individual marketing of broadcasting rights, there is no strict relation between ranking position and revenues since other factors (popularity, attractiveness, size of the local market, fan base, etc.) come into play.

income on the reached position in the final league standings.[19] Without any doubt, success helps to create higher revenues, however, this is a normal (and beneficial) element of economic competition. Decisively, the total reward is not fixed at all. Next to sporting success, there are various ways how clubs can increase their different types of revenues. Thus, the first condition for a rat race-deficiency is clearly not met.

Note that the only revenue type that fits into the logic of positional competition only does so because UEFA (and some of the national football associations) designed the mechanism to allocate the money from the collectively sold broadcasting rights (which constitutes a cartel raising anticompetitive concerns[20]) in exactly such a way! In other words, the only element of systematic overinvestment incentives does not originate from market competition but is introduced *against the market forces* by the market-internal regulatory agency itself. From this perspective, ceteris paribus, overinvestment does not appear to be *inherent* to football competition – instead it appears to be *inherent* to other UEFA regulations.

A brief look on the second condition for a deficient rat race-type of competition indicates that it is probably not met either. The increase in effort of all teams increases the quality of talent and play and, thus, creates benefits for fans and players (salaries). In contrast to the reasoning of the rat race advocates, the increasing effort does not produce the same output (and thus reduce efficiency). Instead, it produces a higher quality output (*Szymanski* 2014: 5). In turn, this should increase the willingness-to-pay of fans and (consequently) media which draws a connection to the "fixed" reward that, then, is not fixed in a dynamic notion. And, indeed, revenues from all types, but especially from broadcasting rights, have been growing considerably in recent years.

While the conditions of a systematically-deficient rat race are not given in football markets, there is some controversy whether the contest character of sports competition inherently entails incentives for irresponsible and unsustainable overinvestment (pro: *Dietl* et al. 2008; *Franck* 2013; contra: *Madden* 2012; *Peeters & Szymanski* 2012, 2014a, 2014b; *Szymanski* 2014).

3.2.3 Systematic Bail-outs?

Thirdly, there is a stream of the literature that views systematic market failure rooted in so-called *soft budget constraints* (*Andreff* 2007; *Storm* 2012; *Storm*

---

19 In other words, by excluding these revenue types from the break even condition, UEFA's FFP regulations may actually strengthen the rat race elements instead of combating them. However, the effect would probably not be very relevant in its magnitude.

20 See e.g. *European Commission* (2003), *Massey* (2007) and *Budzinski* (2012).

& *Nielsen* 2012; *Franck* 2013). The core idea is that there is a systematic bail-out for insolvent football clubs, so that their managers – in anticipation of the bail-out – systematically fail to consider the budget constraint when deciding on expenses. This represents a type of a moral hazard problem that is caused by a mismatch of decision competency and liability for the decision's consequences. As a result, the soft budget constraint syndrome causes systematic and non-viable overinvestment. In analogy to the *too-big-to-fail* phenomenon in 'ordinary' markets (and, in particular, in banks markets), it could be claimed that football clubs are *too-prominent-to-fail* (*Budzinski* & *Müller* 2013) and can rely on being rescued.

Notwithstanding the justified criticism that football markets do not resemble post-socialist transformation markets (to which the soft budget constraint syndrome originally applied) to a sufficient degree to apply this theory (*Szymanski* 2014: 5), the underlying argument may still have some merit. A crucial issue is the identity of the bail-out providers. In order to classify bail-outs as systematic market failure, there must be some systematic (and not just incidental) bail-out activity. *Franck* (2013: 11–19) names the state and private benefactors as *supporting organizations* providing the bail-outs. With respect to the injection of taxpayer money, *Franck* (2013: 12–14) refers to unpaid overdue taxes and social security contributions by Spanish football clubs as evidence. While he is absolutely right in his criticism of the lax enforcement practice of Spanish authorities and the resulting moral hazard problems, it is difficult to see how this represents a market failure (and not a regulation failure) – in particular beyond the special case of Spain.[21] Furthermore, it does not justify the break-even rule of FFP in the sense of the inherence concept. The no overdue payables rule of FFP suffices to take care of this specific problem.

A much more sophisticated problem is political-economic reasoning that local politicians experience incentives to support 'their' clubs in order to please voters or reap locational benefits of having a famous and successful football club (*Franck* 2013: 15–17). If the existing state aid rules fail to deal with this problem (which would need to be analyzed first – and the European Commission is currently investigating the Spanish cases), this may present a justification for limiting the relevant income by excluding monetary or non-monetary injections financed by taxpayers. Still, the break-even rule goes significantly beyond doing this.

---

21 Indeed, as mentioned earlier, the European Commission has recently started an in-depth investigation in these cases, investigating whether European state aid rules got violated (*European Commission* 2013; for an early economic analyses of the general problem see *Gröteke* 2004).

And this relates to the second group viewed to be responsible for bail-outs – the private benefactors or sugar daddies (*Lang* et al. 2011; *Franck* & *Lang* 2013; *Franck* 2013: 17–19). However, from a competition economics perspective, it is difficult to argue against voluntary equity injections by private investors. The individual decision where and when to place an investment represents a cornerstone of the efficiency advantages of market competition. If financial distress is the concern, then financial injections into equity – strengthening the financial fundament of the clubs in question – actually alleviates the problem. Not surprisingly, *Madden* (2012) derives positive welfare effects of benefactors' money injections in a theoretical model (see with different modeling also *Peeters* & *Szymanski* 2012, 2014a). From an economic point of view, it seems difficult to discriminate between (promoted) sponsorship money and (unwanted) equity money. In effect, both represent financial means provided by private actors because of expected utility increases worth the money. Discriminating between commercial and personal motives is difficult and often arbitrary, does not alter the effects – and becomes eventually blurry when considering the engagement of Red Bull buying into clubs like RB Salzburg (formerly Austria Salzburg) and R(asen)B(allsport) Leipzig (formerly SSV Markranstädt).

In summary, the too-prominent-to-fail issue may represent a concern for the functioning of competition among professional football clubs. However, more research is needed into how systematic this phenomenon is: are all clubs too prominent to fail? Or does it affect just specific ones? And is there really a problem beyond enforcing state aid rules in order to discipline the use of taxpayer money? Altogether, from an economics perspective, there is little support for FFP – and, in particular, the discriminatory investment restrictions of the break-even rule – being inherent to the objectives of rational, responsible and viable financial behavior.

3.3 Proportionality: Are There Less Restrictive Alternatives?

Even if – for the sake of the argument – inherence was accepted, the restrictive effects of the financial fair play rules would need to be *proportional* to the legitimate objectives. Establishing proportionality would require two things. Firstly, the objectives must be important enough to justify the restrictive effects. If competition among football clubs without investment restrictions was necessarily causing irresponsible and non-viable financial behavior with an inherent market failure (which is doubtful, see section 3.2.), then the objectives of restoring rational, responsible and sustainable investment strategies may be important enough to justify the restrictive effects. Proportionality is certainly unproblematic in regard to the no overdue payables rule since the restrictive effects of this element of FFP are marginal if existing at all. The more difficult assessment relates to the break-even rule, discriminating between different types of revenues and monetary injections. Its effects of protecting incumbents, cementing the market structure and shifting rents from players to clubs (see section 2) are considerably restrictive so that justifying them in terms of proportionality would require substantial objectives, for instance, relating to the fundamental functioning of the market. The weak link, however, remains the inconclusive empirical evidence for and the questionable theoretical reasoning of a systematic market failure (see section 3).

Secondly, the restrictive effects can only be called proportional to the objectives if there does not exist any less restrictive alternative to achieve the same goals. In the context of FFP, this would ask for regulatory alternatives for combating overinvestment without restrictive effects on players' salaries, market access, competition intensity and, at the end of the day, consumer welfare. According to *Dietl* et al. (2008) overinvestment becomes more probable if

- the correlation between talent investment and winning probability tightens,
- simultaneous investments dominate consecutive investments,
- the league has an open structure with promotion and relegation (in contrast to an American-style closed league), and
- revenue differentials both within a league and between hierarchical leagues increase.

Note, however, that overinvestment here relates to the paragon of a profit-maximizing equilibrium and does not necessarily represent unsustainable and irresponsible (non-viable) overinvestment (and thus does not necessarily imply systematic market failure). Notwithstanding this qualification, the results reveal alternative avenues to limit overinvestment incentives. While the first three factors may be difficult to shape via regulation (or entail even more restrictive effects than FFP), the fourth factor – the magnitude of the revenue differentials – provides a particularly interesting starting point from a competition economics perspective. The reason is that revenue differentials within UEFA club competitions and between the UEFA leagues and the national leagues that result from the distribution of broadcasting rights revenues are by and large not the result of market processes in the current institutional framework of European football. Instead, these revenue differentials are defined and implemented by UEFA (and the national football associations) as a part of its centralized marketing strategy (the cartel for selling broadcasting rights). At the same time, revenue differentials from the allocation of broadcasting revenues represent a significant part of total revenue differentials. Moreover, it is exactly this type of revenue where a strict relation between ranking position and revenue volume applies (see section 3.2.2.). So, there is the interesting situation that one of the main factors setting incentives for overinvestment is rooted in UEFA's regulation and policy itself. A change in the revenue sharing policy, thus, is likely to alleviate overinvestment incentives and provide an avenue to achieving the legitimate objectives without (additional[22]) restrictive effects (*Schokkaert* 2013). Other potentially less restrictive instruments that were suggested in the literature include changes in the competition format, equal and non-discriminatory budget caps, reduction of compensation packages, transfer payment caps, and so-called luxury taxes (*Lindholm* 2010: 208–211; *Schokkaert* 2013).[23]

However, the FFP regulations themselves may offer routes for less restrictive interventions achieving similar objectives. Perhaps, the no overdue payables rule alone would already suffice to achieve the legitimate objectives of FFP – without causing the restrictive effects of the break even rule. And even the break even rule can be changed in a way that most of the competition concerns would probably be resolved. The unlimited inclusion of equity-increasing injections as relevant income into the FFP scheme (see table 1 of section 2) might already suffice to alleviate the competition concerns to an extent that the remaining, less severe restrictive effects may qualify to be proportional to legitimate objectives motivated by too-prominent-to-fail problems.

In summary, it will be difficult to reason that the FFP regulations in its current shape are not excessive when compared to alternative instruments achieving the same legitimate objectives. This criticism does not encounter all elements of FFP. The no overdue payables rule is likely to be completely unproblematic in competition terms. While the break even rule is much more crucial in this regard, it is particularly the – according to the economic analysis unnecessary – restrictive and selective character of the revenue sources that are *relevant* in UEFA's diction that causes most of the concerns.

4. Reflection and Conclusion

Even if the FFP regulations fail to meet the conditions of inherence and proportionality of its restrictive effects to the legitimate objectives, then there remains the

---

22 The broadcasting rights cartel itself comes along with restrictive effects on competition. However, the *European Commission* (2003) cleared it under conditions and obligations (critical discussion: *Massey* 2007; *Budzinski* 2012). Since it exists anyway (as a consequence), it may solve the overinvestment problem as well without additional intervention.

23 It would require a comparative economic analysis for each of these suggested instruments in order to determine whether they are indeed less restrictive.

possibility to accommodate them under the conditions of Article 101 (3) TFEU[24]. If FFP enhances allocative and dynamic efficiency, provides a fair share of these benefits to consumers and if the benefits are specific to the agreement and competition is not significantly impeded, then the European Commission may allow the agreement in total or under conditions and obligations. Whether FFP meets the conditions of Article 101 (3) TFEU has been subject to analysis in the competition law literature with pessimistic conclusions about its suitability for such an antitrust exemption (*Lindholm* 2010: 211; *Long* 2012: 96–100). This view is supported by the economic perspective in this paper, pointing to considerable anticompetitive effects for consumers and competition (violating the consumer benefits and no impediment of competition criteria) as well as emphasizing the existence of less restrictive alternatives (violating the cartel specificity criterion). Furthermore, the questionable market failure reasoning (section 3) casts doubt upon the probability of efficiency-enhancing benefits of FFP (*Szymanski* 2014).

Altogether, it appears to be doubtful that UEFA's financial fair play regulations (in their current shape) stand in full compliance with European competition rules – at least from an economic perspective. Against this background, it appears to be a bit surprising that EU Competition Commissioner Joaquín Almunia publicly sided with UEFA president Michel Platini in praising the FFP initiative (*Almunia* 2012; *Almunia & Platini* 2012). However, at a closer look, the statements explicitly merely mention FFP's compliance with state aid law (*Long* 2012: 84–86). The concerns, however, address the laws against private restraints of competition (anti-cartel rules and abuse control). Given the complaint and the court proceeding initiated by player agent Daniel Striani, the Commission is forced to take a closer look at the competition law compliance of FFP and it will be interesting to see the outcome. From the perspective taken in this paper, a modification of FFP broadening the relevant income concept of FFP's break even rule represents sort of a minimum requirement for alleviating the most important anticompetitive concerns (incumbent protection effect and consolidation effect; partly also salary reduction effect). A commitment along these lines then may be enough to appease a Commission that does appear to be taking a sympathetic stance towards the fundamental ideas of FFP.[25] Whether such a minimum modification of FFP would represent an optimal outcome from a competition economics perspective is more difficult to say and in particular depends

---

24 This requires to classify FFP as an agreement among undertakings and/or associations of undertakings. See for a discussion *Budzinski* and *Szymanski* (2014).

25 Furthermore, the Commission has recently put focus on reaching mutual agreements with the parties to a case instead of more unilaterally enforcing competition rules (*Budzinski & Kuchinke* 2012).

on the comparative assessment of alternatives like (i) reliance on the FFP element no overdue payables rule alone in order to combat imminent insolvency risks, (ii) modifying the allocation mechanism of broadcasting rights revenues in order to reduce revenue differentials (and thus overinvestment incentives), or (iii) the implementation of other instruments (luxury tax, non-discriminatory budget cap, etc.).

References

Akerlof, G. (1976): The Economics of Caste and of the Rat Race and other Woeful Tales, in: The Quarterly Journal of Economics, Vol. 90, 4, pp. 599–617.

Almunia, J. & Platini, M. (2012): Joint Statement, http://ec.europa.eu/competition/sectors/sports/joint_statement_en.pdf (accessed 2014-03-28).

Almunia, J. (2012): Letter to Michel Platini, http://ec.europa.eu/competition/sectors/sports/letter_almunia_en.pdf (accessed 2014-03-28).

Andreff, W. (2007): French Football – A Financial Crisis Rooted in Weak Governance, in: Journal of Sports Economics, Vol. 8, 6, pp. 652–661.

Barajas, Á. & Rodríguez, P. (2010): Spanish Football Clubs' Finances: Crisis and Player Salaries, in: International Journal of Sport Finance, Vol. 5, 1, pp. 52–66.

Barajas, Á. & Rodríguez, P. (2014): Spanish Football in Need of Financial Therapy: Cut Expenses and Inject Capital, in: International Journal of Sport Finance, Vol. 9, 1, pp. 73–90.

Budzinski, O. (2012): The Institutional Framework for Doing Sports Business: Principles of EU Competition Policy in Sports Markets, in: International Journal of Sport Management and Marketing, Vol. 11, 1–2, pp. 44–72.

Budzinski, O. & Kuchinke, B. A. (2012): Deal or no Deal: Consensual Arrangements as an Instrument of European Competition Policy?, in: Review of Economics, Vol. 63, 3, pp. 265–292.

Budzinski, O. & Müller, A. (2013): Finanzregulierung und internationale Wettbewerbsfähigkeit: Der Fall Deutsche Bundesliga, in: *Dewenter, R., Haucap, J. & Kehder, C.* (eds.): Wettbewerb und Regulierung in Medien, Politik und Märkten, Nomos: Baden-Baden 2013, pp. 261–290.

Budzinski, O. & Szymanski, S. (2014): Are Restrictions of Competition by Sports Associations Horizontal or Vertical in Nature?, Ilmenau Economics Discussion Papers, Vol. 19 (86).

Coates, D., Humphreys, B. R. & Zhou, L. (2014): Outcome Uncertainty, Reference-dependent Preferences and Live Game Attendance, in: Economic Inquiry (forthcoming).

DFL (2014): Bundesliga Report 2014 – Die wirtschaftliche Situation im Lizenzfußball, Frankfurt a.M.: DFL.

Dietl, H. M., Franck, E. & Lang, M. (2008): Overinvestment in Team Sports Leagues: A Contest Theory Model, in: Scottish Journal of Political Economy, Vol. 55, pp. 353–368.

Dietl, H. M. & Franck, E. (2007): Governance Failure and Financial Crisis in German Football, in: Journal of Sports Economics, Vol. 8, 6, pp. 662–669.

Drut, B. & Raballand, G. (2012): Why Does Financial Regulation Matter for European Professional Football Clubs?, in: International Journal of Sport Management and Marketing, Vol. 11, 1, pp. 73–88.

Dupont, J. – L. (2013): Football's Anticompetitive Streak, in: The Wall Street Journal, http://online.wsj.com/news/articles/SB10001424127887324077704578357992271428024 (accessed 2014-03-04).

European Commission (2003): COMP/C.2-37.398 – Joint Selling of the Commercial Rights of the UEFA Champions League, Commission Decision, 2003/778/EC, Brussels.

European Commission (2007): The EU and Sport: Background and Context, Commission Staff Working paper accompanying the White paper on Sport, SEC(2007)935, Brussels.

European Commission (2013): State Aid: Commission Opens In-depth Investigation into Public Funding of Certain Spanish Professional Football Clubs, Press Release IP/13/1287, 18/12/2013.

Franck, E. (2013): Financial Fair Play in European Club Football – What is it all about?, UZH Business Paper Working Series No. 328, Zurich: University of Zurich.

Franck E. & Lang, M. (2013): A Theoretical Analysis of the Influence of Money Injections on Risk Taking in Football Clubs, Working Paper No. 0160, Zurich: University of Zurich, Institute for Strategy and Business Economics.

Frick, B. & Prinz, J. (2006): Crisis? What Crisis? Football in Germany, in: Journal of Sports Economics, Vol. 7, pp. 60–75.

Gröteke, F. (2004): Zur Frage der Behandlung von Regulierungen in der Beihilfenkontrolle und mögliche Konsequenzen des Grundstücksverkaufs von Real Madrid, in: Finanzreform, Vol. 1, 11, pp. 146–159.

Hamil, S. (2014): Financial Fair Play – Why Loss-Making Is a Problem: The Example of the English Football League, in: *Budzinski, O. & Feddersen, A.* (eds.): Contemporary Research in Sports Economics: Proceedings of the 5th ESEA Conference, Frankfurt a.M.: Lang, forthcoming.

Haugen, K. H. & Solberg, H. A. (2010): The Financial Crisis in European Football: A Game Theoretic Approach, in: European Sport Management Quarterly, Vol. 10, 5, pp. 553–567.

Késenne, S. (1996): League Management in Professional Team Sports with Win Maximizing Clubs, in: European Journal for Sports Management, Vol. 2, pp. 14–22.

Késenne, S. (2006): The Objective Function of a Team, in: *Andreff, W. & Szymanski, S.* (eds.): Handbook of the Economics of Sport, Cheltenham, UK: Edward Elgar Publishing, pp. 601–609.

Kienapfel, P. & Stein, A. (2007): The Application of Articles 81 and 82 EC in the Sport Sector, in: Competition Policy Newsletter, Vol. 3, pp. 6–14.

Könecke, T. & Schubert, M. (2014): Socio-economic Doping and Enhancement in Sport: A Case-based Analysis of Dynamics and Structural Similarities, in: *Budzinski O. & Feddersen, A.* (eds.): Contemporary Research in Sports Economics: Proceedings of the 5th ESEA Conference, Frankfurt a.M.: Lang, forthcoming.

Lago, U., Simmons, R. & Szymanski, S. (2006): The Financial Crisis in European Football, in: Journal of Sports Economics, Vol. 7, pp. 3–12.

Lang, M., Grossman, M. & Theiler, P. (2011): The Sugar Daddy's Game: How Wealthy Investors Change Competition in Professional Team Sports, in: Journal of Institutional and Theoretical Economics, Vol. 167, 4, pp. 557–577.

Lindholm, J. (2010): The Problem with Salary Caps under European Union Law: The Case against Financial Fair Play, in: Texas Review of Entertainment & Sports Law, Vol. 12, 2, pp. 189–213.

Long, C. R. (2012): Promoting Competition or Preventing it? A Competition Law Analysis of UEFA's Financial Fair Play Rules, in: Marquette Sports Law Review, Vol. 23, 1, pp. 75–101.

Madden, P. (2012): Welfare Consequences of "Financial Fair Play" in a Sports League with Benefactor Club Owners, in: Journal of Sports Economics, online first, doi:10.1177/1527002512465759.

Massey, P. (2007): Are Sports Cartels Different?, in: World Competition, Vol. 30, 1, pp. 87–106.

Maxcy, J. (2014): The American View on Financial Fair Play, in: *Budzinski, O. & Feddersen, A.* (eds.): Contemporary Research in Sports Economics: Proceedings of the 5th ESEA Conference, Frankfurt a.M.: Lang, forthcoming.

Müller, J. C., Lammert, J. & Hovemann, G. (2012): The Financial Fair Play Regulations of UEFA: An Adequate Concept to Ensure the Long-Term Viability and Sustainability of European Club Football?, in: International Journal of Sports Finance, Vol. 7, pp. 117–140.

Neale, W. C. (1964): The Peculiar Economics of Professional Sports, in: The Quarterly Journal of Economics, Vol. 78, 1, pp. 1–14.

Peeters T. & Szymanski, S. (2012): Vertical Restraints in Soccer: Financial Fair Play and the English Premier League, Working Paper No. 2012028, Antwerp: University of Antwerp, Faculty of Applied Economics.

Peeters, T. & Szymanski, S. (2014a): Financial Fair Play in European Football, in: Economic Policy, forthcoming.

Peeters, T. & Szymanski, S. (2014b): Financial Fair Play: Winners and Losers on and off the Pitch, in: *Budzinski, O. & Feddersen, A.* (eds.): Contemporary Research in Sports Economics: Proceedings of the 5th ESEA Conference, Frankfurt a.M.: Lang, forthcoming.

Preuss, H., Haugen, K. & Schubert, M. (2012): UEFA Financial Fair Play: The Curse of Regulation, Working Paper No. 7, Mainz: Institute of Sport Science.

Rottenberg, S. (1956): The Baseball Player's Labor Market, in: Journal of Political Economy, Vol. 64, 3, pp. 242–258.

Sass, M. (2012): Long-term Competitive Balance under UEFA Financial Fair Play Regulations, Working Paper No. 5/2012, Marburg: University of Marburg.

Schokkaert, J. (2013): Financial Fair Play, Alternative Instruments and Competitive Balance, http://footballperspectives.org/financial-fair-play-alternative-instruments-and-competitive-balance (accessed 2014-03-04).

Storm, R. K. & Nielsen, K. (2012): Soft Budget Constraints in Professional Football, in: European Sport Management Quarterly, Vol. 12, pp. 183–201.

Storm, R. K. (2012): The Need of Regulating Professional Soccer in Europe: A Soft Budget Constraint Argument, in: Sport, Business and Management: An International Journal, Vol. 2, pp. 21–38.

Szymanski, S. (2010): The Financial Crisis and English Football: The Dog that will not Bark, in: International Journal of Sports Finance, Vol. 5, 1, pp. 28–40.

Szymanski, S. (2012): Insolvency in English Professional Football: Irrational Exuberance or Negative Shocks? Working Paper No. 12–02, October, Michigan: University of Michigan, Department of Kinesiology.

Szymanski, S. (2014): Fair Is Foul: A Critical Analysis of UEFA Financial Fair Play, in: International Journal of Sports Finance, Vol. 9 (3), forthcoming.

UEFA (2011): The European Club Licensing Benchmarking Report, Nyon: UEFA.

UEFA (2012): UEFA Club Licensing and Financial Fair Play Regulations, Edition 2012, Nyon: UEFA.

UEFA (2014): Procedural Rules Governing the UEFA Club Financial Control Body, Edition 2014, Nyon: UEFA.

Vöpel, H. (2011): Do We Really Need Financial Fair Play in European Club Football? An Economic Analysis, in: CESifo DICE Report, Vol. 9, 3, pp. 54–60.

Weatherill, S. (2006): Anti-doping Revisited – the Demise of the Rule of 'Purely Sporting Interest'?, in: European Competition Law Review, Vol. 27, pp. 645 ff.

Whitney, J. D. (1993): Bidding till Bankrupt: Destructive Competition in Professional Team Sports, in: Economic Inquiry, Vol. 31, 1, pp. 100–115.

Socio-economic Doping and Enhancement in Sport: A Case-based Analysis of Dynamics and Structural Similarities[1]

Thomas Könecke, Mathias Schubert

Abstract

The term 'doping' usually serves the purpose to hint at or denounce a development or a practice that is illegal or deemed illegitimate. Yet, the question remains as to how exactly the term could be defined in a more general context than just physiological doping. Such a definition is provided in this article by focusing on the underlying structures and processes that transform legitimate enhancement into illegal doping.

Keywords

doping, enhancement, financial doping, socio economic doping, governance, financial fair play

1. Introduction

During the last years the trend is observable that the term doping is increasingly used beyond its common understanding (*Asmuth* 2010: 15) – often with the intention of denigrating behaviour or circumstances deemed unfair. *Bette* and *Schimank* (2006: 24–35) highlight that doping in elite sport is a frequently recurring theme in mass media – the scandals in cycling prove that, at times, doping even seems to be better covered than the actual sport event. A prominent example is the case of *Oscar Pistorius*, who regularly faced accusations of 'techno-doping' due to the Cheetah devices he uses. In the context of the high investments of wealthy club owners or other benefactors in European club football in recent years the term 'financial doping' has become an issue (*Wilson* 2009). Also outside sports the term can be found as is for instance the case when cognitive enhancement is referred to as 'brain doping' (*Dietz* 2011; *Dresler* et al. 2013).

Since the term is applied to an increasing number of contexts in sport, a reflection of the doping phenomenon as a metaphor for the dissolution of boundaries and fraud (*Geipel* 2006) seems to be more topical than ever. While *Feiden* and

1 The theoretic approach used in this article was first established by the authors elsewhere (*Könecke & Schubert* 2013; *Schubert & Könecke* 2014). Therefore, parts of this paper (mainly chapters 1–3) draw from the initial publication *Schubert & Könecke* (2014).

Blasius (2002: 1) note that the term doping may also be apprehended in a positive way, in most cases it is used to describe circumstances which, in the eye of the speaker, provide an illegitimate advantage (*Franck* 1999). *Schetsche* (1996: 65) explains that the intention behind such remarks is to scandalize a specific issue in public discourse. Such processes may eventually result in a pressure for action on sports authorities and decision makers. In the case of the above-mentioned financial doping, the public debate on excessive cash injections into clubs can be considered one of the reasons why UEFA eventually tried to call a halt to this behaviour through the policy of Financial Fair Play. Critically, similar to other forms of 'doping', the type of – in this case financial – enhancement that is to be forbidden has been common practice for a rather long time.

Against this background, the major aim of the article at hand is to point out similarities that accompany discussions concerning different types of medical and socio-economic enhancement in sport. Given that it is usually these discussions and the dynamics they cause that trigger processes eventually leading to anti-doping regulations, *Bette* and *Schimank* (2006: 10) note that the doping phenomenon is – against common opinion – more a sociological, i.e., a social, than a medical or legal topic. Methodologically, a case-based approach will be used, analysing different examples of doping and enhancement in sport. Throughout the process, a general, classification of enhancement and doping subject to legality and perceived legitimacy will be gradually applied (*Könecke & Schubert* 2013; *Schubert & Könecke* 2014). The research presented hereafter can thus be classified as positive economics since the aim of the analysis is to illustrate and classify certain processes and dynamics as well as the corresponding perceptions without looking further into the underlying motivations of the relevant actors.

The article is structured as follows: First, a critical discussion of the core values of sport as the central arguments for anti-doping is provided. Afterwards, 'classical' doping and its 'career as a social problem'[2] (*Schetsche* 1996) are outlined, with reference to the notion of doping being characterised as a social construct as well as the corresponding backgrounds of the policy of anti-doping. Based on these results, a categorisation of doping (and enhancement) in sport subject to the dimensions legality and legitimacy is provided. Subsequently, further insights concerning 'classical' doping are transferred to socio-economic practices of

---

2 *Schetsche's* (1996) book is entitled 'Die Karriere sozialer Probleme' (*Engl: 'The career of social problems', transl. by authors*) and has been published in German language only. He also published a book on the empirical analysis of social problems (*Schetsche* 2008).

performance enhancement in sport. Financial doping and its origins are delineated, with reference to UEFA's Financial Fair Play regime. The article continues with an analysis, to what extent other contexts and circumstances may be identified which justify the label 'socio-economic doping'. Afterwards, the amateurism-regulations concerning 'professionalism' of athletes that were in effect in Olympic competition until the 1980s are looked at to further broaden the understanding of socio-economic doping and enhancement. In this context, the Doping-Matrix as general classification will be used to illustrate the different stages of the introduction and abolishment of the corresponding rules. The last chapter concludes this article and highlights the relevance of the results by relating them to a wider context.

2. Sport-intrinsic Values and Doping

In general, most authors agree on the following four values of sport as central to anti-doping policy: the health of the athletes, the principle of fairness and equal opportunities, the naturalness of sporting performance as well as the exemplary function of sport and its athletes (*Bette & Schimank* 2006; *Habermas* 2001; *Houlihan* 2002; *Ljungqvist* 2002; *Preston & Szymanski* 2003). Nevertheless, there is also a consensus in literature concerning the inconsistency of these arguments (*Houlihan* 2002; *Preston & Szymanski* 2003; *Lopez* 2012). *Asmuth* (2010: 93–95) highlights the problematic nature of the aspects by identifying the criteria 'health', 'fairness/equal opportunities' and 'naturalness' in the context of doping as aporiae – that is, arguments which mutually inhibit one another.

The principle of fairness and equal opportunity raises complications as well: 'The unfair-advantage argument is also slippery when pressed. The nature of sport is that some participants have advantages over others, many arising from natural ability' (*Preston & Szymanski* 2003: 616). Furthermore, often due to socio-economic factors, athletes do not have equal opportunities. This refers to, for example, access to facilities and support which athletes in rich countries in the West have enjoyed for years and which have not been available to athletes from poor countries.[3] In reference to *Connor* (2009), *Mazanov & Connor* (2010: 51) conclude, that 'notions of fairness in Olympic competition are rendered obsolete by financial, social, political and genetic inequalities seen across elite sport.'

---

3 Not surprisingly, several studies have already shown that GDP is one of the best indicators of Olympic success (*Rathke & Woitek* 2008 for Olympic Summer Games, and *Emrich* et al. 2012: 1898, for Winter Games).

The naturalness of sporting performance, the third core value, is also problematic. Many authors have stressed the 'arbitrariness of the natural/artificial divide in the anti-doping literature and the contradictions and inconsistencies it has brought with it' (*López* 2012: 58; *Dimeo* 2007; *Houlihan* 2002; *Møller* 2010). Furthermore, many kinds of sport nowadays are heavily dependent on high-technology aid. Modern pieces of sport equipment, for example used in motor sport or sailing as well as in winter sports, usually are high-tech products and necessary for success sometimes even on very low levels of competition.

Finally, the complex exemplary function of sport remains. As *Lenk* points out, '[t]he most important functions of sport are not just sport. They are and remain educational, social and philosophical' (2000: 155). However, by looking at the three arguments previously discussed, which considerably contribute to the role-model aspect, it is fairly obvious that it is also weakened by a number of inconsistencies (*Houlihan* 2002).

3. 'Classical' Doping and its 'Career as a Social Problem'

Doping is considered to be a massive threat for modern high-performance sport and the consumption of performance-enhancing substances in leisure and recreational sport is also increasingly becoming an issue (*Feiden & Blasius* 2002: 39; *Kläber* 2010). Their use, however, is not a new phenomenon but looks back on a long history (*Mazanov & McDermott:* 2009). Remarkably, it should be noted that doping has not been practiced for ages, but rather ancient practices became stigmatised as doping at a certain moment in time. This means that certain performance-enhancing practices nowadays are referred to with the negatively connoted term doping due to a corresponding historic and social context (*Dresen* 2010: 17–18).

It can be stated that the use of performance-enhancing substances and methods in sport becomes doping when respective prohibitions are issued. This happens because certain behaviour is considered to offend core values intrinsic to sport. All these values could, however, be questioned to some extent as has been pointed out above. This raises the question as to why these arguments are still considered so important that the policy of anti-doping enjoys a broad consensus. An approach to answering this question is offered by *Schetsche* (1996: 65) in claiming that for the public perception of a problem, conditions of life and subjective suffering are brought into a social context: Collective actors interpret these as socially caused and alterable circumstances which are inconsistent with their system of values. According to the author, a problem has obtained recognition when it is described and assessed in this way by a sufficient number of individuals.

Against this background the reason for the introduction of anti-doping policies by sport authorities in the 1960s has to be called into mind: Until the 1960s the use of performance enhancing substances in sport was not or only barely regulated (*Hoberman* 2001; *Mazanov & Connor* 2010). While there is evidence of substantial drug use in the eighteenth and nineteenth century (*Houlihan* 2002), in essence one can only speculate as to the actual extent of their use back then. The prohibition and sanctioning of the use of certain substances through sport associations was caused by a number of casualties allegedly caused by the abuse of these substances that created a very concerned public reaction (*Institut für Biochemie der DSHS Köln* 2008). In the aftermath, certain practices of performance-enhancement came to be 'recognised as a problem' (*Schetsche* 1996). In particular because sport claims to represent especially high moral standards, pressure on sport authorities arose and still exists. This pressure was even strengthened by a growing public concern about drugs in society: As *Waddington* and *Smith* (2009) vividly point out, the development of anti-doping policy in sport from the 1960s was intimately associated with (and contaminated by) the 'moral panic' about the 'abuse' of drugs in the wider society. Therefore, 'it is important to recognize how public attitudes and anxieties towards the use of controlled drugs in society generally have 'spilled over' into the sports arena and have influenced – and continue to influence – anti-doping policies in sport' (*Waddington & Smith* 2009: 43).

Although (elite) sport may not claim to perfectly adhere to the four core values as mentioned above of sport, they are commonly accepted as being elementary to sport in general. Thus, drugs in sport are still perceived by a sufficiently high number of individuals as a contradiction to this system of values, a situation which – though not referring to sport in particular – has been described by *Schetsche* (1996: 65). This forces the sport system to still succumb to the resulting pressure for action and maintain the policy of anti-doping. Hence, in the first place doping is more a social than a natural-scientific phenomenon, since the use of performance-enhancing substances and methods dates back way further than the discussion on what is considered legal/illegal and legitimate/illegitimate in the context of sport. Consequently, anti-doping regulation(s) can be considered the result(s) of one (or many) 'career(s) as a social problem' (*Schetsche* 1996) of formerly accepted enhancing means and methods, as is shown in Figure 1.

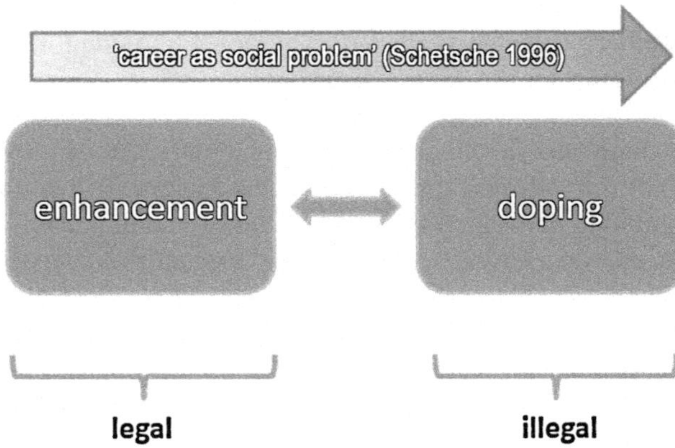

Fig. 1: From enhancement to doping: a career as a social problem

Due to the resulting activities of anti-doping authorities, prohibitions have become increasingly extensive since the 1960s. The aim to clearly and unambiguously define circumstances representing a sanctionable infringement of the rules (*Institut für Biochemie der DSHS Köln* 2008), however, caused new difficulties. The central problem of controllability, for example, manifests itself in the problematic nature concerning thresholds – that is the difficulty to define a quantitative threshold for some substances. The example of caffeine shows that thresholds, as well as the whole doping question, are a social construct and thus the result of negotiation processes (*Gugutzer* 2009: 12–13). The excessive ingestion of caffeine had once been part of the Prohibited List, which includes all means and methods that are considered offenses against anti-doping regulations by sport federations. After having been forbidden for some time, caffeine has been removed from the list in 2004. This happened mainly due to the different biological constitutions of athletes making the prosecution of the abuse according to thresholds impossible (*Müller* 2006: 94). Although it still seems to be broadly agreed that caffeine may enhance athletic performance, it was decided to not further prosecute its abuse. Thus it can be concluded, that the vast topic physiological doping does not have to be entirely resolved in all aspects for sport authorities to keep up the notion that they seriously struggle to maintain the core values intrinsic to sport.

4. Rethinking the Concept of Doping in Sport

As pointed out in the introduction, the major aim of this article is to point out similarities that accompany discussions concerning different types of medical and socio-economic enhancement in sport. For this purpose, a broadened systematisation of the performance-enhancing behaviour presented in Figure 1 that has been derived in other publications (*Könecke & Schubert* 2013; *Schubert & Könecke* 2014) will be applied hereafter. The resulting model comprises three forms of performance-enhancing behaviour which can be distinguished in terms of legality and legitimacy.[4] Legality in this context denotes lawfulness according to the rules in sport. Legitimacy is given when a practice is considered sufficiently compatible with the discussed values elementary to sport. Thus, the following options of categorisation result: legal and legitimate, that is, commonly accepted practices of performance enhancement (hereafter referred to as 'enhancement'), such as training, while the term 'practice' implies that automatic processes such as age-related length growth or other physical developments during adolescence are not included. The exact opposite is 'doping' as an illegal and illegitimate performance-enhancing behaviour.[5] Those legal forms of performance-enhancing behaviour considered illegitimate are classified as 'illegitimate enhancement'. The corresponding classification is depicted in Figure 2.

---

4 The distinction between legal and legitimate methods of performance enhancement is part of *Merton's* (1968) anomie theory and has been mentioned in pertinent literature on doping before. Furthermore, the processes of legitimisation and delegitimisation of social norms have been applied to doping in earlier studies (for example, *Anshel* 1991; *Emrich* et al. 1992; *Emrich* 2004).

5 It should be noted, however, that there is a distinction between doping on the one hand and infringements to the rules of the game: for example, when in football a striker uses his hand, this is both illegitimate and illegal and it increases the probability of success, while no-one would consider it to be doping. Thus, as we see it, doping is about improving performance while still adhering to the rules of competition on the pitch; which is not the case when a football player uses his hand to score a goal, as this action takes place within/during competition and is, therefore, to be regarded as cheating in the sense of infringements to the rules of the game or competition.

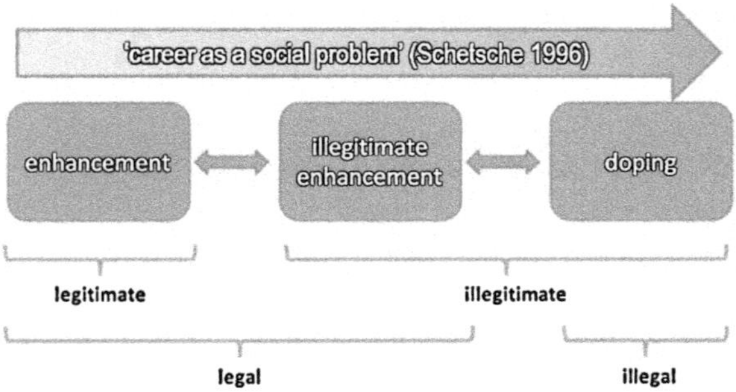

Fig. 2: Classification of enhancement and doping subject to legality and legitimacy (modified after Schubert and Könecke 2014)

Concerning classical doping (cf., Chapter 3), the classification applies as follows: Means and methods that had been used for decades (if not centuries or even millennia) caught public attention due to the tragic deaths of athletes linked to performance-enhancing substances. This led to a public debate resulting in a consensus deeming certain – at this point still legal – practices illegitimate. Due to this, sport authorities had to react and passed the first anti-doping regulations. As a result, the use of some – but not necessarily all – performance-enhancing substances that were considered illegitimate became illegal in sport (i.e., doping).

This example shows that formerly accepted performance-enhancing behaviour that has been forbidden due to its generally perceived illegitimacy can be classified as 'doping'. Or – the other way around – 'doping' denotes a performance-enhancing practice that has been declared unlawful due to its perceived illegitimacy.[6]

5. UEFA Financial Fair Play and a General Definition of Financial Doping in Sport

The ideas just described can also be applied to financial injections into football clubs and the UEFA Financial Fair Play-regulation (FFP). Concerning these, basically the same analysis can be performed. Investments into several European

6 *Franck* (1999: 524) states that from an ethical perspective the use of substances which are not yet ostracised but aim at an unphysiological performance enhancement already represents doping. However, this perspective will not be elaborated any further here.

football clubs by rich benefactors and an increasing over-indebtedness in European club football led to claims within UEFA that long-term stability of European football was at risk (*UEFA* 2011). This notion was shared by actors within football[7] and to some extent also in the public and political debate.[8] *Karl-Heinz Rummenigge*, for instance, in his double position as chief executive of Germany's FC Bayern Munich and chairman of the European Clubs Association (ECA) caught attention as a strict opponent of such investment models. In this aspect, the parallels between classical and financial doping seem to diverge, as in the latter the pressure for action emanates from actors within the system, while in the case of classical doping it was mainly due to public consternation. However, according to *Garcia* et al. (2011: 243), especially in 'England the tensions between globalisation and traditional football values seem to be particularly strong [...] and the English Premier League faces severe criticism over the proliferation of foreign owners'.

Summing up, it can be stated that investments not based on sporting performance or some kind of reasonable economic exchange – e.g., between a club and a sponsor – were deemed illegitimate. Eventually, this resulted in UEFA's Financial Fair Play-regulation in May 2010, while its basic principles had already been approved by the Executive Committee in September 2009 (*UEFA* 2009).[9] Consequently, another performance-enhancing practice that had undergone a career as a social problem had been forbidden – at least within European club football competitions – due to a debate regarding its legitimacy.

Against this background, a definition of 'financial doping' in sport in a rather broad sense can be derived: Financial doping is to be understood as external funding of a club or athlete, irrespective of the use of the money, that is deemed illegitimate by a sufficiently high number of actors – within or outside of sport – and declared illegal by the corresponding regulating body (*Schubert & Könecke* 2014).[10]

---

7 For example, Financial Fair Play is officially supported by the European Club Association (ECA), the European Professional Football Leagues (EPFL), as well as the player union FIFPro (*UEFA* 2009).

8 Public and political interest has recently manifested itself in European Commission Vice-president *Joaquín Almunia*'s claim that FFP would be supported politically (*European Commission* 2012).

9 A detailed analysis of FFP is provided elsewhere in this volume. For an extensive overview of the research on FFP, see, for example, *Preuss* et al. (2014).

10 At this point it should be noted that neither in UEFA's rules itself nor in other official reports of UEFA in relation to FFP the term financial doping is used.

A closer look at this definition reveals another parallel between financial doping in European club football and classical doping in sport: Not all substances that enhance athletic performance and violate the above-mentioned values intrinsic to sport are forbidden by the Prohibited List. The same is true of certain types of money injections into football clubs that are also exempt from the FFP-rules. In the assessment of the break-even result the funding of youth development and infrastructure through an external investor may be declared as non-relevant expenses under certain circumstances (*UEFA* 2012: Art. 58). However, such practices could easily be classified as 'enhancement' according to the classification presented in Figure 2. Since this kind of funding may remain allowed, it should – depending on the perceived legitimacy – be classified either as 'enhancement' or as 'illegitimate enhancement'.

This example shows that a definition is needed that indicates when money is to be considered 'good money' and when 'bad money'. The first kind of funds may be used within the clubs and the latter cannot without risking punishment. This consideration is interesting, as again it shows that in analogy to classical doping, all doping-regulations include exceptions and thresholds that open the door for circumventing the 'spirit of the rule'. Depending on the extent to which this is deemed indecent, other 'careers as a social problem' (*Schetsche* 1996) may result, which eventually could lead to an expansion of the rules, i.e. further prohibitions ('doping').

6. From Financial to Socio-economic Doping in Sport

The reaction of sport authorities to the delegitimation of a specific kind of performance-enhancement by a sufficiently high number of relevant actors seems to frequently take place in a stereotyped way, what manifests itself in the structural similarities of the policies issued. Interestingly, such a reaction – i.e., establishing specific anti-doping legislation – can also cause awareness and pressure for action in other fields of sport.

In the case of UEFA's fight against financial doping in European club football, it should be expected that at least other popular team sports might feel compelled to react. And indeed, in 2012 the introduction of Financial Fair Play in the Basketball Euroleague was announced (*Euroleague.net* 2012). Should, for instance, the league system in German basketball become subject to a regulative intervention such as FFP, developments as in the case of FC Bayern Munich's basketball-section may be deemed questionable. Due to massive support of the main branch of the club, the best men's team was able to get promoted to the highest division within a relatively short period of time. Already in the second division *Dirk Bauermann*, the German national coach at that time, had been signed into the team, beside several high-profile players (*Broker-Test.de* 2010). It can be assumed that for other basketball clubs such a conduct might not have been possible. By implication, in this case a transfer of socio-economic resources within the FC Bayern Munich sport club took place, which structurally resembles financial doping in professional football. The benefactor, however, was not a wealthy external investor but the main branch of the club, and thus partially also the most successful German football team. A public debate on the legitimacy of such a practice may probably lead to a classification as 'illegitimate enhancement' according to our model and eventually could also result in a prohibition ('doping'). The case of FC Bayern Munich is especially delicate, as chief executive *Karl-Heinz Rummenigge* heavily contributed to the 'recognition' (*Schetsche* 1996) of financial doping as a problem in European club football. This shows to what extent structurally similar practices can be assessed very differently depending on their perceived legitimacy by the respective person or group of people.[11]

It has to be brought to attention that not only types of direct financial enhancement but also further practices and circumstances in sport can be integrated into the model presented in Figure 2. In the case of FC Bayern Munich, this could be the benefit of the club's brand and its related social standing (mainly generated by the football team) being reflected on the basketball section. The section did not only profit from the club's direct financial capability that surpasses that of any other basketball team or club in Germany. It also had considerable further socio-economic advantages apart from direct financial support. The sponsorship of the Munich-based online broker Direkt Anlage Bank (DAB) is one example of this. DAB became the main sponsor of the basketball section in 2010 when the first men's team was still only a member of the 2nd highest division. When the sponsorship was announced, DAB's board member Markus Gunter was quoted with the following words: 'This is why we have chosen the partnership with the FC Bayern, the first and the best in German football – and soon positively also in basketball' (*Broker-Test.de* 2010).[12] A look at how the sponsorship was visually communicated underscores Mr. Gunter's words (Figure 3). The main club's emblem – that is widely related to the football team – dominates the rather small basketball and the word 'basketball'.

11 If the scope of observation is geographically expanded, the already mentioned correlation between the economic prosperity of a country and its sporting success may also imply a form of socio-economic performance-enhancement which is still commonly accepted. However, it is not difficult to imagine that demands from developing countries may necessitate a corresponding reassessment, as *Müller* et al.'s (2012: 139) statement concerning FFP shows: 'it is the task of the governing body of the competition to limit the sphere of action in a way that a level of equal opportunities which is accepted among the stakeholders can be assured'.

12 The original German quotation is: ‚Deshalb haben wir uns auch für die Partnerschaft mit dem FC Bayern entschieden, dem Ersten und Besten im deutschen Fußball – und bald sicher auch im Basketball.'

Fig. 3: *Visual presentation of DAB's sponsorship of FC Bayern Munich's basketball section (Source: http://www.tz-online.de/sport/fcb-basketball/wer-sitzt-gruenen-bank-1117318.html, November 24, 2013)*[13]

Performance-enhancing behaviour of this kind reaching beyond mere financial aspects, makes a labelling as 'socio-economic enhancement' appear logical. Depending on its perception as legitimate or illegitimate, it could consequently be classified according to our categorisation depicted in Figure 2. Since some other basketball clubs in the first division have already expressed their dissatisfaction with FC Bayern Munich's socio economic enhancement of its basketball section, it is very obvious that another career as a social problem could occur in this regard as well. The result could be another regulation declaring certain types of financial or socio-economic enhancement – even between different sections of the same club – illegal doping. Whether or not this will actually happen will largely depend on the perception of other high-profile clubs in German basketball concerning their own profit related to the new contestant. Right now it seems that the vast public interest generated by FC Bayern Munich's basketball section is considered an advantage for most relevant stakeholders. Therefore, it is unlikely that such enhancement will be forbidden in the near future.

7. Amateurism in the Olympics and the 'Doping-Matrix'

Based on the analysis conducted so far, it may appear that the problematisation of financial and/or socio-economic enhancement is a rather new phenomenon. Yet the ban of professional athletes from Olympic competition until the 1980s is one example that proves the opposite. The underlying discussion originated in

13 The words below the emblems translate as follows: 'Together first and best'.

the times when athletic competition was mainly a pastime of English gentlemen-athletes. They could afford to spend money on sport without earning anything with it. Athletes not belonging to the upper class could usually not do so (*Remijsen & Clarysse* 2012). As can be seen, banning socio-economic types of doping does not mainly have to serve the purpose to protect the underprivileged.

Also in the early years of modern Olympism it was agreed that athletes participating in the Olympic Games should be straight amateurs. I.e., any acceptance of monetary rewards or financial support for or because of sport and also many kinds of sponsorships led to an illegibility for participation in Olympic Games. That means that most kinds of financial support for athletes were forbidden and could thus be declared 'financial doping' – even though the term was obviously not used in this regard – in the categorization introduced above (Figure 2).

Several contestants fell victim to the amateurism-rule. The most famous one probably was *Jim Thorpe*. He won the pentathlon and the decathlon in 1912 in Stockholm and was greeted by the Swedish king with the words 'You, Sir, are the greatest athlete in the world!' (*Remijsen & Clarysse* 2012). But because he had accepted money for playing semi-professional baseball, the gold medalist was later disqualified and the medals were 'taken away from him' (*Remijsen & Clarysse* 2012).

In 1982 *Jim Thorpe* was posthumously reinstalled as an Olympic champion. Prior to this, the amateurism-regulations had gradually been lifted by the International Olympic Committee (IOC) beginning in the early 1970s. Finally, '[i]n 1986, professional athletes were given permission […] to compete in each sport of the Olympic Games' (*Olson* 2007). What had happened before could be called a 'reverse' career as a social problem of professionalism in Olympic sport. The IOC itself had become more and more professionalized and earned ever more money (*Trosien & Preuß* 1999: 217). Parallel to this, a consensus between a sufficiently high number of relevant actors within the Olympic family had agreed that professionalism in Olympic sport was not to be deemed illegitimate anymore. Consequently, the above-mentioned legislative measures were removed, finally resulting in a total legalization of financial support for Olympic athletes.

To include developments of this kind into our classification, it will be further adapted: Another category, 'legitimate doping', will be introduced to account for the process that took place before professionalism was legalized by the IOC (thus becoming 'legitimate enhancement'). The new classification, labelled 'Doping-Matrix', is depicted in Figure 4.

Regarding the example of professionalism in Olympic sport, the Doping-Matrix (Figure 4) can be clarified as follows. 'Enhancement' covers any type of financial support an athlete gets in order to enable him to become better at his sport.

When this practice is deemed illegitimate by a sufficiently high number of relevant actors, it becomes 'illegitimate enhancement'. As soon as regulations forbidding this demeanor result, it may be classified 'doping'. If – as was the case with professionalism in the Olympics – a 'reverse' career as a social problem occurs, the corresponding doping-practice loses the notion of being illegitimate. That means, that a sufficient amount of stakeholders now consider the practice legitimate, even though it is still illegal. As a result, pressure for action arose within the Olympic movement to legalize this kind of financial doping for athletes. After this occurred, it could be classified as regular 'enhancement'.

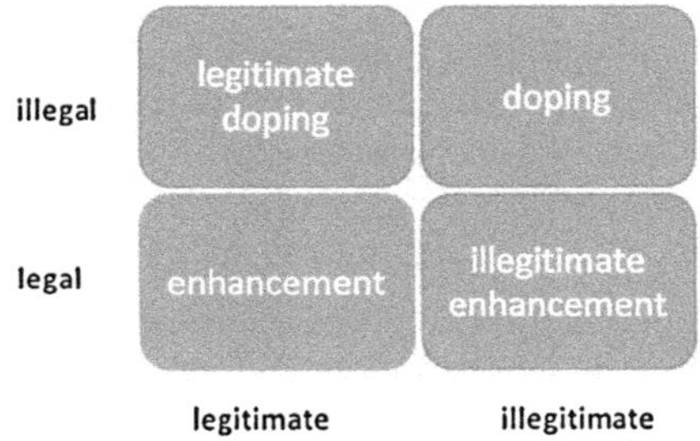

Fig. 4: Doping-Matrix: Final classification of doping and enhancement subject to legality and legitimacy (modified after Könecke & Schubert 2013; Schubert & Könecke 2014)

8. Summary and Conclusion

Relating to *Bette & Schimank* (2006) it has been pointed out that classical – i.e., physiological – doping is more of a social than a medical or legal phenomenon. That means a specific enhancement is not 'doping' per se. It becomes doping through negotiation in social discourse. That means that social processes determine if certain types of enhancement become generally considered illegitimate. If this happens, legislative measures and prohibitions can follow, i.e., the enhancement becomes (illegal) doping.

Against this backdrop, the following points have to be stressed:

1. Almost all enhancement is 'suitable' for a career as a social problem as defined by *Schetsche* (1996). Since notions of legitimacy can be influenced considerably, the perception of a certain enhancement as problematic can also be 'created'. Furthermore, general developments might influence the perception of certain measures that have formerly been considered impeccable. As mentioned before, this seemingly was the case with regular doping and could

also have been the case regarding the financial crisis in Europe and UEFA's Financial Fair Play.

2. Not every possible stakeholder has to share the notion that a specific type of enhancement is illegitimate. If a sufficiently high number of relevant actors does so, a career as social problem may result.
3. As indicated in the Doping-Matrix (Figure 4), a 'reverse' career as a social problem – a deproblematisation so to speak – may occur. This happens if a certain enhancement that is forbidden by the respective authorities ('doping'), loses its illegitimacy in general belief. As a result, it would be classified as 'legitimate doping' in the Doping-Matrix. In this case, the governing body might feel obliged to legalize the measure. Thus, it would become – legal and legitimate – enhancement.

The last remarks of this article are devoted to the public attention socio-economic enhancement and doping seem to attract nowadays. It will, for instance, be interesting to see how the advantage athletes from rich nations seem to have regarding success in the Olympic Games (*Rathke & Woitek* 2008 for Olympic Summer Games, and *Emrich* et al. 2012: 1898, for Winter Games) will be dealt with in the future. Concerning the athletic success of Britain's team in the London Games in 2012, an English journalist remarked that '[a] cynic might say Britain achieved this turnaround in Olympic sport through a massive programme of financial doping, via Lottery Funding, but this conceals the improvements in sports administration and the emergence of gifted athletes with winning mentalities' (*Hayward* 2012). As can easily be seen in this short passage, the discussion concerning financial doping in football seems to have spread to this field as well. The link to excessive financial support seems to strongly influence the perceived legitimacy of sporting successes as can be seen in the lines just cited.

Furthermore, the protests in Brazil surrounding the preparations for the Olympic Games in 2016 and above all the FIFA World Cup in 2014 seem to be linked to the notion that some actors – such as FIFA or the IOC and certain politicians – apparently profit much more from these events than the broad public. Furthermore, the opinion seems to be rather common that money spent on sport infrastructure should be better used for education or public facilities. The same could be true of the recent public ballot that was held in the Munich region concerning the application for the 2022 Winter Olympic Games. The inhabitants of four regional districts could vote either in favour of or against entering the bid. And, surprisingly for many – especially within the world of sport (*FAZ.net* 2013) – the voters in all four districts were against bidding for the Games (*Eichler* 2013).

Summing up, it can be concluded that socio-economic enhancement and doping will probably be one of the topics the sport world will have to deal with more seriously and on a much larger scale in the future. We hope that the Doping-Matrix will contribute to a better understanding of the structures and dynamics that underlie the corresponding discussions and processes.

References

Anshel, M. (1991): A Survey of Elite Athletes on the Perceived Causes of Using Banned Drugs in Sport, in: Journal of Sport Behaviour, Vol. 14, pp. 283–307.

Asmuth, C. (2010): Was ist Doping? Fakten und Probleme der aktuellen Diskussion, Bielefeld: Transcript Verlag.

Bette, K.-H. & Schimank, U. (2006.): Die Dopingfalle: Soziologische Betrachtungen, Bielefeld: Transcript Verlag.

Broker-Test.de (2010): DAB Bank wird Hauptsponsor des Basketball-Teams des FC Bayern: Neuer Trikot mit Logo des Online Brokers präsentiert, http://www.broker-test.de/dab-bank/nachrichten/dab-bank-wird-hauptsponsor-des-basketball-teams-des-fc-bayern-16750 (accessed 2013-11-24).

Connor, J.M. (2009): Towards a Sociology of Drugs in Sport, in: Sport in Society, Vol. 12, 3, pp. 327–328.

Dietz, P. (2011): Hirndoping durch Sport?: Das Phänomen „Cognitive Enhancement durch Sport“ ist noch wenig erforscht und bedarf weiterer wissenschaftlicher Aufbereitung, in: Doping, Vol. 4, pp. 192–195.

Dimeo, P. (2007): A History of Drug Use in Sport 1876–1976: Beyond Good and Evil, New York, London: Routledge.

Dresen, A. (2010): Doping im Spitzensport als soziales Problem: Ursachen und Folgen eines gesellschaftlichen Diskurses, Wiesbaden: VS Verlag für Sozialwissenschaften.

Dresler, M., Sandberg, A., Ohla, K., Bublitz, C., Trenado, C., Mroczko-Wąsowicz, A., Kühn, S. & Repantis, D. (2013): Non-pharmacological Cognitive Enhancement, in: Neuropharmacology, Vol. 64, pp. 529–543.

Eichler, C. (2013): Das Ende des Wintermärchens: Klares „Nein“ zu Olympia 2022 in München, http://www.faz.net/aktuell/sport/wintersport/klares-nein-zu-olympia-2022-in-muenchen-das-ende-des-wintermaerchens-12657703.html (accessed 2013-11-24).

Emrich, E. (2004): Doping im Sport aus soziologischer Sicht, in: *Messing, M., Müller, N. & Preuß, H.* (eds.): Olympischer Dreiklang: Werte – Geschichte – Zeitgeist, Kassel: AGON-Sportverlag, pp. 285–321.

Emrich, E., Papathanassiou, V., Pitsch, W. & Altemeyer, L. (1992): Abseits der Regeln: erfolgreiche Außenseiter: Überlegungen zum Doping und anderen Formen abweichenden Verhaltens im Sport aus soziologischer Sicht, in: Leistungssport, Vol. 22, 6, pp. 55–58.

Emrich, E., Klein, M., Pitsch, W. & Pierdzioch, C. (2012): On the Determinants of Sporting Success – A Note on the Olympic Games, in: Economics Bulletin, Vol. 32, 3, pp. 1890–1901.

Euroleague.net (2012): Euroleague Commercial Assets Board Approves Financial Fair Play for Euroleague, http://www.euroleague.net/euroleague-basketball/news/i/94796/6330/euroleague-commercial-assets-board-approves-financial-fair-play-for-euroleague (accessed 2013-09-04).

European Commission (2012): Joint Statement on UEFA's Financial Fair Play Rules and EU State Aid Policy, http://ec.europa.eu/competition/sectors/sports/joint_statement_en.pdf (accessed 2013-02-24).

FAZ.net (2013): „Olympia-Aus wird Gegnern irgendwann leidtun": Nach Münchner Bürgerentscheid, http://www.faz.net/aktuell/sport/sportpolitik/nach-muenchner-buergerentscheid-olympia-aus-wird-gegnern-irgendwann-leidtun-12658386.html (accessed 2013-11-24).

Feiden, K. & Blasius, H. (2002): Doping im Sport: Wer – womit – warum, Stuttgart: Wiss. Verl.-Ges.

Franck, E. (1999): Sportethische Kasuistik, in: *Korff, W.* (ed.): Ausgewählte Handlungsfelder, Gütersloh: Gütersloher Verl.-Haus, pp. 520–554.

Garcia, B., Niemann, A. & Grant, W. (2011): Conclusion: a Europeanised Game? in: *Niemann, A., Garcia, B. & Grant, W.* (eds.): The Transformation of European Football: Towards the Europeanisation of the National Game, Manchester: Univ. Press, pp. 239–261.

Geipel, I. (2006): Gut trainierte Scheinheiligkeit, Die Welt, http://www.welt.de/print-welt/article149462/Gut-trainierte-Scheinheiligkeit.html (accessed 2013-0401).

Gugutzer, R. (2009): Doping im Spitzensport der reflexiven Moderne, in: Sport und Gesellschaft – Sport and Society, Vol. 6, 1, pp. 3–29.

Habermas, J. (2001): Die Zukunft der menschlichen Natur. Auf dem Weg zu einer liberalen Eugenik? Frankfurt a. M.: Suhrkamp.

Hayward, P. (2012): Paralympics 2012: London Bids a Fiery and Emotional Farewell as Curtain Falls on this British Summer of Love, http://www.telegraph.co.uk/sport/olympics/paralympic-sport/9532453/Paralympics-2012-London-bids-a-fiery-and-emotional-farewell-as-curtain-falls-on-this-British-summer-of-love.html (accessed 2013-09-03).

Hoberman, J. M. (2001): Mortal Engines: The Science of Performance and the Dehumanization of Sport, Caldwell, N.J: Blackburn Press.

Houlihan, B. (2002): Dying to Win: Doping in Sport and the Development of Anti-doping Policy, 2nd ed., Strasbourg: Council of Europe Publ.

Institut für Biochemie der DSHS Köln (2008): Was ist Doping? http://www.dopinginfo.de/rubriken/01_doping/01.html (accessed 2013-03-07).

Kläber, M. (2010): Körper-Tuning. Medikamentenmissbrauch im Fitness-Studio: Body Tuning. Drug Abuse in the Fitness Studio, in: Sport und Gesellschaft – Sport and Society, Vol. 7, 3, pp. 213–235.

Könecke, T. & Schubert, M. (2013): Constellations of Socio-Economic Doping and Enhancement in the Olympics, in: *Preuß, H. & Bielons, G.* (eds.): 6th International Sport Business Symposium, Buenos Aires: Book of Abstracts, pp. 60–62.

Lenk, H. (2000): Blickpunkt Olympia: Entdeckungen Erkenntnisse Impulse. Towards a Philosophical Anthropology of the Olympic Athlete and/as Achieving Being. Petersham, NSW: Agon-Sportverl; Walla Walla Press.

Ljungqvist, A. (2002): Pharmakologische Manipulation der sportlichen Leistung – ist das Hase-Igel-Rennen unendlich? In: *Digel, H. & Dickhut, H.-H.* (eds.): Doping im Sport, Tübingen: Attempto-Verlag, pp. 77–86.

López, B. (2012): Doping as Technology: a Rereading of the History of Performance-enhancing Substance Use in the Light of Brian Winston's Interpretative Model for Technological Continuity and Change, in: International Journal of Sport Policy and Politics, Vol. 4, 1, pp. 55–71.

Mazanov, J. & Connor, J. (2010): Rethinking the Management of Drugs in Sport, in: International Journal of Sport Policy, Vol. 2, 1, pp. 49–63.

Mazanov, J. & McDermott, V. (2009): The Case for a Social Science of Drugs in Sport, in: Sport in Society, Vol. 12, 3, pp. 276–295.

Merton, R. K. (1968): Social Theory and Social Structure, New York: Free Press.

Møller, V. (2010): The Ethics of Doping and Anti-doping: Redeeming the Soul of Sport? London, New York: Routledge.

Müller, J. C., Lammert, J., & Hovemann, G. (2012): The Financial Fair Play Regulations of UEFA: An Adequate Concept to Ensure the Long-Term Viability and Sustainability of European Club Football?, in: International Journal of Sport Finance, Vol. 7, 2, pp. 117–140.

Müller, R. K. (2006): Die Grenzwertdiskussion, in: *Müller-Platz, C.* (ed.): Entwicklung in der Dopingforschung, Köln: Sportverlag Strauß, pp. 93–99.

Olson, E. (2007): Olympic Athletes: The Sponsorship behind the Athletes, http://www.infoplease.com/spot/olympic-athletes.html (accessed 2013-11-24).

Preston, I. & Szymanski, S. (2003): Cheating in Contests, in: Oxford Review of Economic Policy, Vol. 19, 4, pp. 612–624.

Preuss, H., Haugen, K. K. & Schubert, M. (2014): UEFA financial fair play – the curse of regulation. *European Journal of Sport Studies (online first version).* DOI: 10.12863/ejssax2x1-2014x1.

Rathke, A. & Woitek, U. (2008): Economics and the Summer Olympics: an Efficiency Analysis, in: Journal of Sport Economics, Vol. 9, 5, pp. 520–537.

Remijsen, S. & Clarysse, W. (2012): Amateurism, http://ancientolympics.arts.kuleuven.be/eng/TE016EN.html (accessed 2013-11-24).

Schetsche, M. (1996): Die Karriere sozialer Probleme: Soziologische Einführung, München: Oldenbourg.

Schetsche, M. (2008): Empirische Analyse sozialer Probleme, Wiesbaden: VS Verlag für Sozialwissenschaften.

Schubert, M. & Könecke, T. (2014): 'Classical' doping, financial doping and beyond: UEFA's Financial Fair Play as a policy of anti-doping. International Journal of Sport Policy and Politics, online first version: http://www.tandfonline.com/doi/full/10.1080/19406940.2013.854824#tabModule (accessed 2014-01-28).

Trosien, G. & Preuß, H. (1999): Sport – Fernsehen – Ökonomie: Zur Medienpräsenz von Sportleistungen, in: Trosien, G. (ed.): Die Sportbranche: Wachstum – Wettbewerb – Wirtschaftlichkeit, 2nd ed., Frankfurt: Campus-Verlag, pp. 209–235.

UEFA (2009): Green Light for Financial Fair Play, http://www.uefa.com/uefa/stakeholders/professionalfootballstrategycouncil/news/newsid=879610.html (accessed 2013-02-28).

UEFA (2011): Financial Fair Play Ensures Football's Stability, http://www.uefa.com/uefa/footballfirst/protectingthegame/financialfairplay/news/newsid=1585317.html (accessed 2013-05-06).

UEFA (2012): UEFA Club Licensing and Financial Fair Play Regulations (Edition 2012), http://www.uefa.com/MultimediaFiles/Download/Tech/uefaorg/General/01/80/54/10/1805410_DOWNLOAD.pdf (accessed 2013-04-22).

Waddington, I. & Smith, A. (2009): An Introduction to Drugs in Sport: Addicted to Winning? London, New York: Routledge.

Wilson, J. (2009): Arsene Wenger Accuses Manchester City and Real Madrid of 'Financial Doping', http://www.telegraph.co.uk/sport/football/teams/arsenal/5985204/Arsene-Wenger-accuses-Manchester-City-and-Real-Madrid-of-financial-doping.html (accessed 2013-03-07).

Performance and Competition in International Football

In Urgent Need of Change? Within-season Coach Dismissals, Regression-to-the-mean, and Performance of Football Teams

Nikolaus Beck, Mark Meyer[1]

Abstract

Based on a comprehensive German Soccer dataset, we estimate parametric econometric models of the performance consequences of coach substitutions. In doing so, we pay special attention to the inherent regression-to-the-mean problem and present a methodological suggestion to cope with this issue in match level based analyses. Moreover, we consider two dynamic conceptions from organization theory as well as the famous "scapegoating thesis". We identify a significant long term restoration of home advantage under the new coaches. Thus, the traditional "ritual scapegoating" interpretation of coach dismissals fails for our data. These findings are outstanding as they do contradict widely held beliefs.

Keywords

football, executive succession, parametric analysis, regression-to-the-mean

1. Introduction

The situation is well known. If an organizational unit (e.g. work team, department, division, or the whole firm) does not perform as aspired, the board or other responsible superiors are inclined to dismiss the respective executive and replace him or her with someone else. After all, the executive is responsible for the performance of the organizational unit. For boards, the dismissal of an executive is an effective way to show that actions have been taken and the problem of under-performance has been addressed. In fact, the literature maintains that poor performance is a major reason for executive succession (*Kesner & Sebora* 1994; *Giambatista* et al. 2005).

The pattern of failure induced executive change is especially visible in the team sports area where the position of the current coach is almost always put into question if his or her team performs poorly. Empirical results support the assumption that mainly poorly performing teams replace their coaches (*Beck* et al. 2008; *Frick*

1 We are grateful to the Thuringia ministry of education for the special research grant that allowed us to acquire the data we used in the present study.

et al. 2010). The high conspicuity of coach changes is due to the exceptional societal interest in team sports and the respective amount of media coverage. Sport teams have to face extremely strong pressures from several stakeholders with supporters and sponsors most important among them. Therefore, boards of sports teams might especially feel the need to react quickly and visibly by laying off the coach. However, the question remains whether such replacements actually have the ability to reintroduce team success. Although this question, which is, of course, also relevant for any other type of executive succession, is rather old and has been addressed many times, a clear answer is still not available.

Our study refers to ambiguous findings of the economics of football literature in this regard (*Audas* et al. 2002; *Bruinshoofd* & ter *Weel* 2003; *Koning* 2003; *de Dios Tena* & *Forrest* 2007; *Balduck* et al. 2010; *Hughes* et al. 2010; *ter Weel* 2011) and tries to offer an approach that is capable of reducing these ambiguities by taking the following aspects into account:

First, from a theoretical point of view, we want to stress that in contrast to the early studies on coach succession in sport teams the younger econometric analyses do hardly provide any comprehensive theoretical foundation. Accordingly, even though several studies took some sort of time horizon into account (*Audas* et al. 2002; *de Dios Tena* & *Forrest* 2007; *Hughes* et al. 2010; *ter Weel* 2011), we generally miss a consistent and theoretically justified conceptualization which discriminates short term effects of coach successions from long term effects (*Carroll* 1984; *Amburgey* et al. 1993; *Dowell* & *Swaminathan* 2000). Indeed, only *Hughes* et al. (2010) provide a detailed theoretical discussion of short- and long-term effects of coach succession. However, as will be shown on the following pages, their reasoning is not without alternatives.

Second, from a methodological point of view, we do think that many studies do not apply carefully elaborated controls for unobserved heterogeneity in teams' performance levels. Not taking the inherent strength of a team into account can lead to severe biases in the estimation of the effect of coach change since no distinction can be made between the effect of coach change on performance and the reverse influence. Moreover, without controlling for the strength of a team's *opponent* comparisons between pre-dismissal and post-dismissal performances (*Bruinshoofd* & *ter Weel* 2003; *Hughes* et al. 2010; *Wagener* et al. 2010; *ter Weel* 2011) might be subject to selection biases. Therefore a statistical analysis of within season coach replacements should incorporate the obvious fact that recent pre-dismissal matches were played against other opponents than the following post-dismissal matches.

Furthermore, even if the above criticism was met by incorporating adequate controls for team-inherent performance levels, the problem of the "regression-to-the-mean-phenomenon" (*Kahneman* & *Tversky* 1973; *Lee* & *Smith* 2002) would still remain: organizations with poor or deteriorating performance are more inclined to undertake radical changes (*Greve* 1998, 2000, 2003). Hence, they are most likely to sack managers or executives who are held responsible for the decline in performance. If bad performance really was an outlier then the probability of performance-increases would of course be quite high in the next periods. In the long run, performance simply should converge to its mean level (*Greve* 1999; *Notz* et al. 2001). Thus, an immediate increase in performance after coach succession as it was found in the studies of *de Dios Tena* and *Forrest* (2007) and *Hughes* et al. (2010) might be caused by the lack of control for regression-to-the-mean.

Our paper proceeds as follows. The next section introduces general considerations from organization theory from which hypotheses on short and long term effects of coach dismissal on team performance are derived. These annotations are supplemented by theoretical considerations on the noncausal "ritual scapegoating" hypothesis which is related to the methodological regression-to-the-mean-problem. We then provide an introductory account of our dataset, a comprehensive disaggregated panel covering results of all German Soccer „Bundesliga" matches between 1992 and 2004, develop our methodological framework and summarize our empirical results. Finally, we conclude with a discussion of our findings.

2. The Impact of Change on Performance – Insights from Organization Theory

2.1 Basic Theoretical Considerations

Studies on the replacement of sports team coaches have been among the first to empirically and theoretically capture the consequences of executive change. Seminal contributions by *Grusky* (1960, 1961, 1963) and *Gamson* and *Scotch* (1964) compiled three conflicting basic theories about the impacts of managerial change on team performance (*Rowe* et al. 2005):

- According to the "common sense" theory, new coaches actually are capable of motivating players, and of changing training and tactics successfully. Thus, there exists a direct causality from hiring a new coach to performance change on the pitch.
- On the other hand, the opposing "vicious circle" theory highlights the disruptive effects of managerial turnover. Consequently, the introduction of a new coach causes an immanent risk of deepening the initial performance dip which finally might bring about the decision of yet another (disruptive) coach replacement.

- Finally, the "ritual scapegoating" theory refuses any direct causality from coach dismissal to performance changes. Hence, as performance will not react to this kind of personal replacement, boards which sack their coaches actually just demonstrate their willingness to relieve increasing pressures by supporters and media.

While these theories did stimulate numerous empirical studies, their findings are not consistent. There exist several studies (*Grusky* 1963, 1964; *Brown* 1982; *Fizel & D'Itri* 1997; *Audas* et al. 2002; *Bruinshoofd & ter Weel* 2003) which indicate that changes in organizational leadership deteriorate the morale and motivation of organizational members, a result that is in accordance with the "vicious circle" thesis. Nevertheless, *Gamson* and *Scotch* (1964), *Fabianic* (1984; 1994), *Pfeffer* and *Davis-Blake* (1986), *McTeer* et al. (1995), *Koning* (2003), *Wagner* (2010) or *Balduck* et al. (2010) observed performance improvements after coach succession. These results support – on a first glance – the "common sense" theory. However, such a result does not rule out the "scapegoating" thesis since there might be no *causal* relationship between short term improvements and coach succession – even if performance increases shortly after a coach replacement. Such a scenario is widely known as the "regression-to-the-mean-phenomenon".

In the following subsections we want to discuss possible consequences of coach successions by drawing on these basic considerations from organizational theory and explicitly distinguishing between immediate and long term effects.

2.2 The Shock-and-recovery Argument

The first possible pattern of short- and long-term impact of executive change is very much related to the seminal contribution of *Hannan & Freeman* (1984) who look at organizational survival, which can be considered the strongest indicator of performance. They maintain that core change always has an immediate detrimental effect that leads to a sudden increase in the organizational death rate. This detrimental effect should occur because prior and well known internal routines are suspended and, concurrently, confidence of internal and external stakeholders in the new organizational structure declines immediately. As a consequence, organizations which have undergone an organizational core change resemble newly founded organizations (*Child & Kieser* 1981) which have to face the difficulties of not yet having established viable organizational routines and confidence of stakeholders (*Stinchcombe* 1965). However, *Hannan* and *Freeman* (1984) also argue that the immediate increase in the disbanding risk of organizations decreases (for the surviving organizations) with time since the change has taken place. Such a recovery happens because employees and external stakeholders get increasingly accustomed to the newly introduced routines and structures and develop confidence again. If the change leads to a better adaptation to environmental conditions, it is even possible that survival chances increase to a level that would not have been reached without the change.

For the specific case of executive succession, such a shock and recovery scenario can theoretically be developed by referring to the leadership literature, in which there is wide consensus that the replacement of an executive causes subsequent change (*Helmich & Brown* 1972; *Goodstein & Boeker* 1991; *Tushman & Romanelli* 1985; *Boeker* 1997). An executive succession is associated with change of routines and procedures since the arriving manager can be expected to apply his or her own, idiosyncratic concepts of how tasks should be organized and executed. And these concepts mostly differ from those of his or her predecessor (*Hughes* et al. 2010; *Gabarro* 1987). Especially routines that determine the shape of informal networks as well as the style of supervision can be supposed to be suddenly changed with the arrival of a new executive (*Grusky* 1963; *Hill* 2005). Employees are likely to face the new, unfamiliar situation with insecurity and scepticism. Moreover, the new executive often possesses rather little knowledge about the specific problems that an organization or a team that he or she is going to lead has to face (*Hambrick & Fukutomi* 1991). Thus, in most cases the new executive has no readily applicable strategy which is capable of coping with these specific problems (*Gabarro* 1987). All these factors lead to an immediate drop in performance.

In the long run a team or an organization can recover from the immediate disruption of performance that is caused by executive change. *Hughes* et al. (2010) maintain that new executives need time to learn about the internal and external circumstances and problems that are relevant for the organization or the team. This learning process helps to revise the executive's initial concepts of routines and structures and it helps to develop strategies that fit the idiosyncratic conditions of the organization or team (*Hambrick & Fukutomi* 1991). Moreover, the new executive can also be expected to be able to gain confidence from internal subordinates who get accustomed to his or her leadership style as well as from the external environment (*Hill* 2005). This establishment of confidence leads to a recovery of performance. Therefore, in terms of a combination of the "vicious circle" and the "common sense" theses, one can set up the following hypotheses:

Hypothesis 1a: Team performance decreases immediately after coach succession.

Hypothesis 1b: Team performance increases with time elapsed since a coach succession took place.

Carroll (1984) found – consistent with this scenario – an immediate detrimental effect of CEO-successions and a long term recovery. *Hill* (2005) found an immediate detrimental effect of successions by outsiders and a strong long term beneficial effect on performance.

With respect to the impact of coach change on the performance of football teams *Audas* et al. (2002) found an immediate deterioration of performance that remains significant until 16 matches after coach succession. On the other hand, *Hughes* et al. (2010) found almost the opposite result: shortly after coach succession the performance of football teams increases slightly, however insignificantly in comparison to the performance in the period of more than ten matches before a coach change took place. In the long run there is again a (significant) reduction in performance. These results correspond very much to the findings of *de Dios Tena* and *Forrest* (2007) who analysed coach succession in the Spanish Football League. They report that performance of teams that play at home increases significantly after a coach change. This positive effect decreases quite rapidly in size and significance with the number of home matches that a team plays after coach succession. For matches that are played on foreign ground a similar pattern can be observed which, however, lacks any significance. Thus, the results of these recent studies on coach change and performance of football clubs suggest that there might exist a pattern, which is completely contrary to the presented shock-and-recovery argument. The following section shows that theoretical arguments for such a "refreshment-and-decline-thesis" can again be borrowed from the organization theory literature.

2.3 The Refreshment-and-decline-thesis

Haveman et al. (2001) as well as *Virany* et al. (1992) argue that executive replacements in reaction to important environmental changes or turbulence have the quality to increase the performance of organizations. Executive replacement in such a situation should have immediate beneficial consequences for an organization because new persons in leading positions usually are able to abandon managerial inertia and facilitate the adaptation to new environmental conditions. Moreover, executive succession also signals to the relevant institutional environment the organization's readiness to restructure and revitalize itself. This seems to be especially important in the situation of within-season coach dismissal. Here turbulence in the environment most often means extensive coverage of the club's critical situation by the media. This can lead to enormous pressure on the board of a club to fire the current coach since very often, local and nonlocal newspapers as well as TV and radio programs already raise the question of how long the club can *afford* to keep the current coach in position. The turbulence which is created by supporters can be even stronger: they might no longer be willing to attend home games or they might express their displeasure in the stadium e.g. by showing off big posters with harsh criticism or by booing their own team. Under these circumstances the replacement of the coach might work as a relief to a situation which is becoming increasingly burdensome. Thus a positive reaction by the media and the supporters after coach replacement should clearly contribute to the uplift of a team's motivation and thus, increase the performance of the team.

Also internal conditions can contribute to an immediate rise in team performance. *Hambrick* and *Fukutomi* (1991) argue that in some cases, new executives can possess a high degree of power right from the beginning of their tenure, for example when a new executive was hired in a state of crisis and the former one had to step down. In these cases new managers are expected to make quick and deep changes. And they are given more power than usual in order to initiate those changes. In football it can be observed that new coaches that are hired within the current season to save a troubled club are allowed to immediately buy new players or to undertake deep changes in the amount and style of training or in the tactics applied on the pitch – things that otherwise would cause a lot of resistance by the club's board or the players.

According to this view, within season coach replacements are essentially intended to end an era of frustration by improving the human capital of the team as well as by introducing brilliant new ideas concerning training and tactics on the pitch. However, it is conceivable that such a sudden uplift in performance degrades over time. *Hughes* et al. (2010) explain their unexpected finding of a long term deterioration of team performance after coach replacement with the notion that the initial success of new coaches, i.e. the short period of temporary relief, makes them overlook greater weaknesses of the team. Thus new coaches might fall into a competency trap (*Levitt & March* 1988). Since their immediate changes obviously work (however basically because the morale of the players gets boosted), they stick to the newly introduced routines and procedures even if the underlying problems of the team still prevail. Therefore, e.g. deficiencies in players' abilities or in the communication and interaction within a team which might have been obscured during the period of rising hopes and motivation prevail again after moods have "normalized" (*Gamson & Scotch* 1964). Since it also takes time until a new coach acquires enough knowledge to implement long lasting and successful *strategic* change, e.g. the acquisition of players that really fit the team, it becomes evident that a team's performance worsens again after it has improved immediately after coach succession.

We therefore are also able to formulate the following hypotheses which represent an alternative combination of the "common sense" and the "vicious circle" theory:

Hypothesis 2a: Team performance increases immediately after a coach succession.

Hypothesis 2b: Team performance decreases with time elapsed since a coach succession took place.

Besides the results of *Hughes* et al. (2010) as well as *de Dios Tena* and *Forrest* (2007) which have already been presented, the findings of *Gamson* and *Scotch* (1964), *Fabianic* (1984, 1994) and *McTeer* et al. (1995) – tentatively – provide further support to these arguments as they found coach succession associated with short term, but not long term improvements of teams' performance.

3. The "Ritual Scapegoating" and "Self-Fulfilling Prophecy" Interpretation

In addition to the two sets of contradicting hypotheses which have been presented so far, there is a third line of argument which leads to the formulation of yet another set of alternative hypotheses. The classic study on the impact of coach succession by *Gamson* and *Scotch* (1964) revealed that, compared to the point of time of a coach's dismissal, teams achieved significantly better results in the period shortly after the replacement. Additionally, a distinct deterioration of teams' performance within the two weeks period before the replacement also became apparent. In the long run, however, coach replacements did not seem to pay off. Thus these findings are very similar to the results of *Hughes* et al. (2010).[2] Yet, *Gamson* and *Scotch* (1964) argue that the "slump" of results prior to firing a coach more or less inevitably forces an ensuing increase in performance. In other words, if teams were really *under*performing, they just could not always do as poorly as in the period shortly before the coach was fired. Thus, sacked coaches are just subject to "ritual scapegoating": when outcomes are severely below their targets,

2 Comparable to these finding are the results of *Brown* (1982) who distinguishes between the sub-season before a new coach came into power and the sub-season thereafter and looked at mean performance during these sub-seasons. He also found that teams deteriorate heavily before a coach replacement and that teams experience an increase in performance after coach replacement. However, due to the aggregate nature of the data used in the study of *Brown* (1982) no conclusions of a possible degrading over time of the impacts of coach dismissals can be made.

boards increasingly tend to sack their coaches in order to appease media and fans. But the very poor performance of this period might just represent an "outlier", i.e. a rarely occurring *random* deviation from mean performance. Therefore, new coaches actually just have to wait. Finally, they should explicitly benefit from the laws of probability.

This relationship between a "slump" effect and scapegoating is meanwhile better known as the "regression-to-the-mean-phenomenon" (*Lee* & *Smith* 2002): organizations with poor or deteriorating performance are more inclined to undertake radical changes (*Greve* 1998, 2000, 2003). Hence, they are most likely to sack managers or executives who are held responsible for the decline in performance. If bad performance really was an outlier then the probability of performance-increases would of course be quite high in the next periods. In the long run, performance simply should converge to its mean level (*Greve* 1999; *Notz* et al. 2001). Thus, an immediate increase in performance after coach succession as it was found in the studies of *de Dios Tena* and *Forrest* (2007) and *Hughes* et al. (2010) might be caused by the lack of control for regression-to-the-mean!

What is more, in the case of coach succession regression-to-the-mean has the quality to produce a "self fulfilling prophecy": as mentioned above, media and supporters often demand the replacement of an underperforming team's coach which eventually happens. Then performance in fact improves again which reinforces the attitude that the quest for coach dismissal was right and the new coach is the right person at the right time. Therefore support, which previously declined, should increase again and this might trigger the team's motivation which can help to improve performance in the longer run. Also poorly performing clubs which do *not* replace their coaches benefit from the regression-to-the-mean-phenomenon and experience a positive shift of performance after a period of unusually bad results. However, in most of these cases supporters might still be sceptical since the coach whom they make responsible for the previous mess is still in charge. Thus, it can be expected that support for previously underperforming teams which bounce back to normal performance without coach replacement is lower than for those teams which in fact have replaced their coach. This in turn should lead to performance disadvantages in the longer run for teams who dispense with coach replacement after a period of severe underperformance. These considerations suggest that if one is able to apply a suitable control for the regression-to-the-mean-phenomenon an immediate positive effect of coach succession should disappear, however a positive long term effect of coach change should be detectable. We formulate the following hypotheses as a combination of the scapegoating and common sense thesis:

Hypothesis 3a: Regression-to-the-mean causes the indications of immediate improvements in team performance after coach replacements. With appropriate control for the regression-to-the-mean-effect these short-run indications decrease or vanish.

Hypothesis 3b: In the long-run team performance improves after coach replacement. This improvement is detectable after controlling for regression-to-the-mean.

4. Data and Modelling Framework

4.1 Data and Descriptive Statistics

Our empirical study is based on a comprehensive dataset covering 12 Bundesliga seasons from August 1992 to May 2004. In each championship 18 different teams took part, each of them facing the others twice (once at home and once away). Consequently, a total of 306 matches per season were observed, giving a total of 3672 Bundesliga matches over 12 seasons. Due to the end-of-season relegation system which replaces the 3 worst performing teams by the 3 best performing teams of the lower division (Second Bundesliga), these 3672 matches were carried out by a total of 35 individual soccer clubs which joined the first division within this 12 years period. For each match, a complete record of sports statistics, including the name of the current team coach, has been provided by "Sport-Dienst-Agentur Merk", a commercial service agency which offers a wide variety of soccer data.[3] For home teams as well as for away teams the total number of matches managed by a successor (i.e., a coach which differed from the one at match day one) amounted to 590 in both cases. Overall, these observations have been triggered by 112 coach replacements.

Our study only takes within-season replacements into account since we are interested in the question whether attempts of "rescuing" a club by firing the current coach might be beneficial. Concerning the dynamic effects of coach replacements we restrict our observation samples to the end of each season (following findings of *Allen* et al. 1979). As coaches' contracts regularly run out at the end of a season, a distinction between coach dismissals as a rescue activity against a regular

3 We acquired the data for the period of 1992–2004, basically for the following reasons: We wanted to observe a homogeneous period with the same number of clubs in the Bundesliga. This was the case only after the transition season of 1991/1992 in which the East German clubs were integrated in the Bundesliga. Also the labor market for football coaches increased after reunification. We then acquired the data of as many seasons as our budget allowed. The 12 seasons provide enough observations for a rigorous and valid statistical analysis.

succession could not be made if we also considered between-seasons replacements. The between-season time interval is furthermore always used intensively for restructuring teams by purchasing and selling players because these transfer activities are highly restricted within a season. Hence, within the between-season episode teams' strengths might be varied significantly which – of course – influences a team's general performance to a high degree. We therefore think that it is almost impossible to trace the effects of coach successions beyond the end of season.

Tables 1 and 2 summarize some elementary descriptive statistics concerning clubs' ranking at the moment of a coach's dismissal. The figures seem to affirm our supposition that most replacements are indeed executed for inducing short term performance shifts: with the median ranking of clubs sacking their coaches corresponding to position 15, an overwhelming majority of these events obviously took part in severe danger of being relegated. (At the end of season table, rank 15 represents the worst positioning which still allows a team to remain in the Bundesliga.)

Table 1: Clubs' ranking at coach dismissal

	Observations	Minimum	Maximum	Mean	Median
Home	54	2	18	13.09	15
Away	58	2	18	13.69	15

Table 2 shows that most coach replacements were undertaken quite early in the second half of the season. In fact the median starting day of a new coach is the 22nd match in a season if he starts at home and at the 20th match if he takes over the new position in an away match. Thus boards obviously try to wait before they take action, but they also tend to react early enough in order to facilitate the (time consuming) implementation of new routines under the successor.

Table 2: Coach succession – new coach starts his job at match day

	Observations	Minimum	Maximum	Mean	Median
Home	54	4	34	20.67	22
Away	58	4	34	20	20.5

Additionally, the figures in table 2 reveal that we are analysing a suitably-balanced sample. Aiming at identifying the partial effect of coaches' substitutions, we would prefer to observe most dismissals in the middle of the seasons, i.e., we would favour observations where the number of matches with the former coach equals the number of matches with the later one. Our sample does not seem to depart too far from this ideal.

4.2 Modelling Framework

Most econometric studies of the performance effects of within-season coach dismissals have been applied within an ordered probit setup (*Audas* et al. 2002; *de Dios Tena & Forrest* 2007; *Hughes* et al. 2010) or by means of difference-in-difference estimators (*Bruinshoofd & ter Weel* 2003; *Wagner* 2010; *ter Weel* 2011). At a first glance the latter approach might seem to represent a self-evident technique to control for regression-to-the-mean as the performance consequences of coach dismissals are directly compared to performance tracks of similar teams which faced comparable performance dips but retained their coaches. However, apart from the fact that these estimates can consider subsample information only,[4] seemingly similar performance dips might be quite different for teams that differ in inherent strength and that have to face opponents of different strength. We are therefore convinced that any statistical analyses of football teams' performances always should try to control for the individual team strengths of the involved opponents. As will be shown, the incorporation of *Koning's* (2000) fixed-effects conceptualization (which has been recently discussed by *Balduck* et al. 2010) into ordered probit approaches offers a straightforward way to proceed.

5. A Refined Approach of Controlling for Regression-to-the-mean

5.1 The First Step: Defining the Statistical Model

Audas et al. (2002) estimate an ordered probit model which controls for individual teams' average historical win ratios up to 24 months before the current match. This inclusion of "general performance levels" controls for the assumption that clubs with a general poor performance are more inclined to replace coaches. As a consequence, the estimation of the influences of coach replacements is not affected by the reverse influence of a team's general performance on the probability of coach replacements. Furthermore, *Audas* et al. (2002) also control for the most recent match results (last 4 away matches, last 9 home matches) of both teams. Together with the win ratio variables, these recent match results are intended to control for mean-reversion effects. However, the strength of the opponents is not controlled for in their approach.

4 Usually, only the last four matches before a coach change and the next 4 games after a coach change are considered (*ter Weel* 2011; *Wagner* 2010; *Bruinshoofd & ter Weel* 2003). Accordingly, given an 18 teams division, it is only possible to analyse within-season dismissals after match day 4 and before match day 31.

We are convinced that their underlying idea to incorporate team quality together with mean-reversion controls represents a promising path for the analysis of football data. Nevertheless, given that we intend to carry out an analysis of the performance effects of *within-season* coach dismissals, some refinements appear necessary. *Audas* et al. (2002) employ a model specification which includes pre-season win ratios as team specific quality indicators. But professional football clubs regularly deploy the between-season time interval for intensive player transfer activities as these are highly restricted within a season which might change the inherent team quality considerably. We therefore opt for a methodological framework which enables us to employ full *ex post* information for the estimation of general team strength as well as season specific quality indicators. For this we fall back to *Koning* (2000) who introduced the following methodological framework: assume the outcome of an arbitrary match in an 18-team league as being determined by a latent random variable D_{ij}^* for which holds

$$D_{ij}^* = \alpha_i - \alpha_j + \varepsilon_{ij}, \quad \alpha_{18} = 0 \quad \varepsilon_{ij} \sim N(0,1), \quad i,j = 1,\ldots 18, i \neq j \tag{1}$$

The α's denote the fixed effects of the home (i) and the away (j) team at a certain match in a given season. Thus $\alpha_i - \alpha_j$ captures the effects of differences in all seasonally invariant factors like a club's budget, its "bundle of talents" and infrastructure (e.g. training facilities, stadiums, medical assistance, etc.) between home and away teams on match outcome (scaled to the omitted 18th club). For each season, we proceeded similar to *Koning* (2000) in that we generated 17 team specific variables which have a value of one if a certain team plays at home and minus one if it plays away (zero otherwise). Under the assumption that an observed match result D_{ij} can be attributed to the latent difference in strength as

$$D_{ij} = \begin{cases} 1 & \textit{for} \quad D_{ij}^* \leq c_1 \\ 2 & \textit{for} \quad c_1 < D_{ij}^* \leq c_2 \\ 3 & \textit{for} \quad c_2 < D_{ij}^* \end{cases} \tag{2}$$

with $D_{ij} = 1$ if the home team loses, $D_{ij} = 2$ in case of a draw and $D_{ij} = 3$ if the home team wins and the c's indicating the limit points, we are able to obtain a well-defined ordered probit model which can be estimated by standard maximum likelihood procedures. The introduction of additional vectors of covariates straightforwardly generalizes this approach to account for the additional impacts of team specific variables. In addition we also included a control for individual home advantages of clubs. Letting γ_i denote this season- und club-specific dummy variable with assigned values of one if team i plays at home and 0 otherwise, our estimated latent variable equation can thus be expressed as

$$D^*_{ij} = \alpha_i + \gamma_i - \alpha_j + \beta_H' \, x_i + \beta_A' \, x_j + \varepsilon_{ij} \tag{3}$$

with x_i ; x_j referring to the vectors of additional covariates for home and away teams and β_H ; β_A denoting their respective parameter vectors. For each season, 17 different strength parameters and 17 different home dummies have been estimated. Thus, each of our performance models includes a total set of 408 individual team specific parameters.

5.2 The Second Step: Controlling for Performance Deviations

While the α's control for the general performance of a team within a given season, they do not control for performance-deviations. Therefore the regression-to-the-mean problem has to be tackled by means of additional measures. We chose the current *rank* in the overall standings to exert such a control. The current rank indicates the *seasonal* performance of teams up to the actual match day as, e.g., a team moving to the bottom of the schedule most likely experienced a series of poor performances. Hence, similar to other studies, our model does also incorporate the most recent history of a given team. However, here we only rely on within-season information. As the α's control for the general seasonal performance of each individual club the current rank thus indicates *relative* deviations of actual from general performance. This is important. Only deviations from basic performance can be expected to cause a reaction by the club and not the current standing itself. If a climber from the second division found itself at rank ten in the overall standings, the club's board would certainly consider it a tremendous success. If Germanys leading club, Bayern Munich, was at rank ten in the overall standings, the club would consider it a catastrophe.

5.3 Independent Variables

In order to distinguish between immediate and long term effects of coach succession we followed the approach of modelling organizational change in the population ecology literature (*Carroll* 1984; *Amburgey* et al. 1993; *Dowell & Swaminathan* 2000) and included the following two covariates in the vectors x_i and x_j:

Coach change. This is a general coach replacement dummy which was constructed in the following way: for each of the 18 clubs of every season we investigated whether a substitution took place. If this was the case, the coach change dummy for home teams switched from 0 to 1 at the first home match of the new coach as well as for all subsequent home matches of the respective team until the end of season. Accordingly the coach change dummy for away teams switched from 0 to 1 for all away matches of the respective team until the end of season. These two variables should thus capture the immediate consequences of coach replacements, which are allowed to vary between home and away matches.

TSC (Time Since Change): This variable traces the dynamic effects of coach replacements. It indicates the accumulated (total) number of matches which a new coach of the team has already experienced at his current employment *before* the actual match day. Even if the new coach continued his work in the subsequent season this variable was just computed until the end of the current season. Again we distinguished between accumulated home and away matches since coach replacement. Such a distinction seems especially relevant since it is well known that teams get a different feedback from home crowds (*de Dios Tena & Forrest* 2007).

5.4 Further Control Variables[5]

Team heterogeneity: Based on six individual demographic player characteristics we built a heterogeneity index for each team in each match (see also *Beck & Meyer* 2012). The characteristics are: tenure in the team, age, nationality, number of Bundesliga matches and number of titles won by each player. According to *Gibson* and *Vermeulen* (2003) each of these individual players characteristics were compared with the corresponding characteristics of every teammate who was active in a given match. This comparison resulted in individual overlap indices between every pair of players. By using the following equation, measures between 0 and 1 could be achieved:

$$overlap_{i,j} = \frac{\min(x_i, x_j)}{\max(x_i, x_j)} - \frac{\min_{sample}}{\max_{sample}} \cdot \frac{1 - \frac{\min(x_i, x_j)}{\max(x_i, x_j)}}{1 - \frac{\min_{sample}}{\max_{sample}}} \quad (4)$$

In a next step, we summed up these individual comparisons over all six variables, yielding a team vector of pairwise overlap metrics. As the mean of this vector aggregates individual comparison data into a team-specific scalar-index, this mean is a measure of team homogeneity and its inverse is the measure of team heterogeneity at each round of each season.

5 We tried out many more control variables, however they did not yield significant effects and did not change the results of our regression analysis.

Match significance represents a standard control variable in econometric analyses of football results (*Audas* et al. 2002 or *Goddard & Asimakopoulos* 2004). We therefore constructed two dummy variables indicating whether a match was significant for home teams but not for away teams or, respectively, whether a match was significant for away teams but not for home teams. Matches were considered significant if it was still possible for a team to get relegated, to win the national championship and/or to qualify for the European Cup competitions (Champions League as well as UEFA cup). In order to assess this possibility it was assumed that all competitors for these achievements receive on average one point from the remaining matches.

Finally we want to point out that negative signs of the away effects represent an improvement for the respective team as the dependent variable has been defined from the perspective of the home team.

6. Results

Table 3 summarizes basic descriptive statistics and correlations of our dataset. Regression results are presented in Table 4.

Model 1 was estimated without the inclusion of the rank variables, i.e. without the variables that are supposed to control for regression-to-the-mean, while Model 2 refers to the complete model as illustrated above. Without a control for current ranking, coach replacements seem to be involved with significant immediate improvements in team performance which is in accordance with our hypothesis 2a. The improvement in performance is significant for home as well as for away matches. Interestingly, the long term effect of a new coach change (time since change) is insignificant but tentatively positive for home matches in Model 1.

Table 3: Descriptive statistics and correlations

	Mean	Stdv.	Match Result	Coach change – home team	Coach change – away team	Time since change – home team	Time since change – away team	Rank home team	Rank away team	Heterogeneity – home team	Heterogeneity – away team	Match significance – home team	Match significance – away team
Match Result	2,725	1,291	1,000	-0,018	0,052	-0,004	0,052	-0,144	0,147	0,053	-0,066	0,016	-0,021
Coach change – home team	0,166	0,372		1,000	0,072	0,744	0,075	0,270	0,001	-0,012	-0,057	-0,168	-0,124
Coach change – away team	0,166	0,372			1,000	0,085	0,738	-0,013	0,293	-0,051	-0,023	-0,116	-0,159
Time since Change – home team	1,403	4,232				1,000	0,084	0,161	0,006	-0,007	-0,054	-0,239	-0,157
Time since Change – away team	1,395	4,243					1,000	-0,024	0,169	-0,040	-0,017	-0,165	-0,212
Rank home team	9,658	5,197						1,000	-0,017	-0,239	0,012	-0,047	0,006
Rank away team	9,288	5,173							1,000	0,005	-0,245	-0,006	-0,060
Heterogeneity – home team	0,318	0,042								1,000	0,201	0,096	0,092
Heterogeneity – away team	0,317	0,042									1,000	0,090	0,106
Match significance – home team	0,928	0,258										1,000	0,536
Match significance – away team	0,928	0,259											1,000

Table 4: Ordered probit models of team performance

	Model 1		Model 2		Model 3	
	Coeff.	SD	Coeff.	SD	Coeff.	SD
Coach change – home team (C_H)	0.272***	0.097	0.108	0.099		
Coach change – away team (C_A)	-0.263***	0.100	-0.082	0.103		
Time since Change – home team (TSC_H)	0.008	0.008	0.018**	0.008	0.020***	0.007
Time since Change – away team (TSC_A)	0.003	0.009	-0.009	0.009	-0.013*	0.007
Rank home team (R_H)			0.060***	0.008	0.061***	0.008
Rank away team (R_A)			-0.066***	0.008	-0.068***	0.008
Heterogeneity- home team (HET_H)	-4.614***	1.189	-4.670***	1.199	-4.604***	1.188
Heterogeneity- away team (HET_A)	2.044*	1.195	1.890	1.205	1.959*	1.186
Significance of match for home team	0.097	0.105	0.139	0.105		
Significance of match for away team	-0.025	0.106	-0.069	0.105		
Limit "Draw"	-1.493***	0.499	-1.606***	0.522	-1.626***	0.517
Limit "Home Win"	-0.643	0.499	-0.735	0.521	-0.755	0.517
Log Likelihood	-3296.222		-3237.488		-3239.269	
Pseudo R^2	0.12		0.13		0.13	
Observations	3564		3564		3564	

* $p<0.10$ ** $p<0.05$ *** $p<0.001$

Models contain 408 additional variables (seasonal strength indicators and home dummies) which are not presented. Both models have only been estimated for the results of match days 2–34 as this allows a calculation of the rank variables. The dependent variable had been coded as home loss=1, draw=2, home win=3.

Yet, the pattern emerging from the results of Model 2 is notably different. It turns out that performance increases in a highly significant manner for home as well as for away teams with rising ranks. At a first glance this might appear surprising as high ranks correspond to rankings close to the bottom of the league standings. However, remember that we control for each team's general seasonal performance. Hence, teams that are deviating negatively from their general performance levels indeed can expect an increase in actual performance over the next periods. Therefore, we identify a significant positive correlation between team performance and team rank. This clearly indicates that regression-to-the-mean is existent! Moreover, with included rank variables the immediate effects of coach replacements vanish. This supports our hypothesis 3a. Apparently, negative deviations from general performance of a team increase the likelihood of a coach succession as well as the likelihood of success within the next matches. The new coach, however, does not have any immediate impact on the performance of the team! Moreover, with control for regression-to-the-mean the long term effect of coach successions increases and turns significant, but only for home matches. In Model 3 we dispensed with the variables that yielded insignificant effects in Model 2. Now the long term effect of coach change is also (slightly) significant for away teams but still smaller than for home teams. Thus hypothesis 3b is supported by our results: the performance of a team increases with tenure of a new coach who replaced his predecessor during the current season. It has to be mentioned though, that the sizes of the coefficients are not very large. Nonetheless, even if the size of the coefficient is rather small, the simple "ritual scapegoating" view does not seem fully sustainable.

By looking at the effects of the control variables it becomes evident that demographic heterogeneity of teams reduces performance (see also *Beck & Meyer* 2012). This effect is much stronger for home teams. The importance of a match, however, does not exert any significant influence on match outcome and is therefore no longer considered in Model 3.[6]

Findings of a "Rule-of-thumb" Simulation Exercise: finally, there remains one elementary question. How much, in terms of points, do teams that replace a coach during the season, actually benefit from a long-term increase in home performance? In order to answer this question we took the Model 3 estimates to derive some rough assessments as follows. First, for each match within our sample we modelled result probabilities in absence of any coach dismissals. The outcomes of this "no coach change" reference scenario were then compared to the results of 216 individual simulations, with each simulation assuming that one (and only one) of the 18 teams of a given season dismissed its coach at mid season, i.e. the last 17 matches of this team were played with a new coach. For each team and each season under consideration we then calculated the expected increase in points per match as:[7]

---

6 Admittedly, our decision to consider matches significant for each team which might still get relegated, win the national championship and/or qualify for the European Cup competitions (Champions League as well as UEFA cup) resulted in a situation where almost any match of our sample appeared to be significant. Thus, this result does not seem astonishing in our view.

7 Please bear in mind that a win in the Bundesliga is rewarded with 3 points and a draw with 1 point.

$$3*[\Pr(win)|\ \text{coach change} - \Pr(win)|\ \text{no coach change}] + \\ +1*[\Pr(draw)|\ \text{coach change} - \Pr(draw)|\ \text{no coach change}] \tag{5}$$

Please note that all calculations were based on deterministic simulations (i.e. random shocks were not modelled within these simulations). The underlying calculations might thus be illustrated with references to the Model 3 latent variable equation as follows: assuming two arbitrary teams i,j (with index i denoting the home team) and a given season under inspection (we omit any seasonal subsubscripts to ease our presentation), this equation is given as:

$$\begin{aligned} D_{ij}^{*} = {} & \hat{\alpha}_i + \hat{\gamma}_i - \hat{\alpha}_j + \hat{\beta}_{H,1}.TSC_i + \hat{\beta}_{H,2}.R_i + \hat{\beta}_{H,3}.HET_i \\ & + \hat{\beta}_{A,1}.TSC_j + \hat{\beta}_{A,2}.R_j + \hat{\beta}_{A,3}.HET_j \end{aligned} \tag{6}$$

Our supposed variations in covariate *TSC* have already been mentioned (always 0 in the reference scenario, 1 on matchdays 18 to 34 for the selective team of the alternative scenario under consideration). The appointment of constant numerical values to control variable *R* (team rank) in every scenario, i.e., the calculation of static simulations, eased our computations significantly. This variable therefore always equalled a numerical value of 9 for any team at any match of our simulation runs. As regards covariate *HET* (team heterogeneity), we decided to fix the values for home and away teams to their respective sample averages.

Under these assumptions and given the set of parameter estimates $\hat{\alpha}_i, \hat{\gamma}_i, \hat{\alpha}_j, \hat{\beta}_{H,1}, \hat{\beta}_{H,2}, \hat{\beta}_{H,3}, \hat{\beta}_{A,1}, \hat{\beta}_{A,2}, \hat{\beta}_{A,3}$ as outlined within table 4 the individual numerical values of $\hat{D}_{ij}^{*}$ can be straightforwardly derived for every match. Then, the limit point estimates c_1 and c_2 together with the tabulated values of the standard normal distribution Φ can be applied in order to map single $\hat{D}_{ij}^{*}$ estimates to individual result probabilities according to:

$$\begin{aligned} \Pr(D_{ij}) = 1 &= \Pr(\hat{D}_{ij}^{*} + \varepsilon_{ij} \le \hat{c}_1) = \Pr(\varepsilon_{ij} \le \hat{c}_1 - \hat{D}_{ij}^{*}) = \Phi(\hat{c}_1 - \hat{D}_{ij}^{*}) \\ \Pr(D_{ij}) = 1 &= \Pr(\hat{c}_1 - \hat{D}_{ij}^{*} < \varepsilon_{ij} \le \hat{c}_2 - \hat{D}_{ij}^{*}) = \Phi(\hat{c}_2 - \hat{D}_{ij}^{*}) - \Phi(\hat{c}_1 - \hat{D}_{ij}^{*}) \\ \Pr(D_{ij}) = 1 &= \Pr(\hat{c}_2 < \hat{D}_{ij}^{*} + \varepsilon_{ij}) = \Pr(\hat{c}_2 - \hat{D}_{ij}^{*} < \varepsilon_{ij}) = 1 - \Phi(\hat{c}_2 - \hat{D}_{ij}^{*}) \end{aligned} \tag{7}$$

In figure 1a and 1b our overall findings have been arranged separately for home and away teams. Since the coach change has taken place after the 17th round and the long term effect starts to unfold after the 1st match with the new coach, i.e. the

19th round, there are 16 rounds at which the long term effect of coach change can possibly have an impact on team success. Each dotted line corresponds to the effect at one of these 16 rounds, with the lowest line indicating the effect of the 1st round at which the effect unfolds (= round 19). The X-axis denotes the expected points that a team can gain *without* coach change. Thus, irregular distances between the dots mirror the diverse team strength constellations of the individual fixtures under inspection. It becomes evident that teams with a very high or a very low expected gain in points, i.e. with a very high or low winning probability, hardly profit from a coach change while mediocre teams for which winning is as likely as losing (with an expected value of about 1.5) benefit the most from it. Moreover the increase in points over the different rounds can also easily be detected: mediocre home teams at round 19 can be expected to gain only about 0.02 points at the current match from the coach change while mediocre home teams at round 34 can gain about 0.36 points at the current match. The range of points gained thanks to coach replacement for mediocre away teams ranges between 0.01 and 0.22.

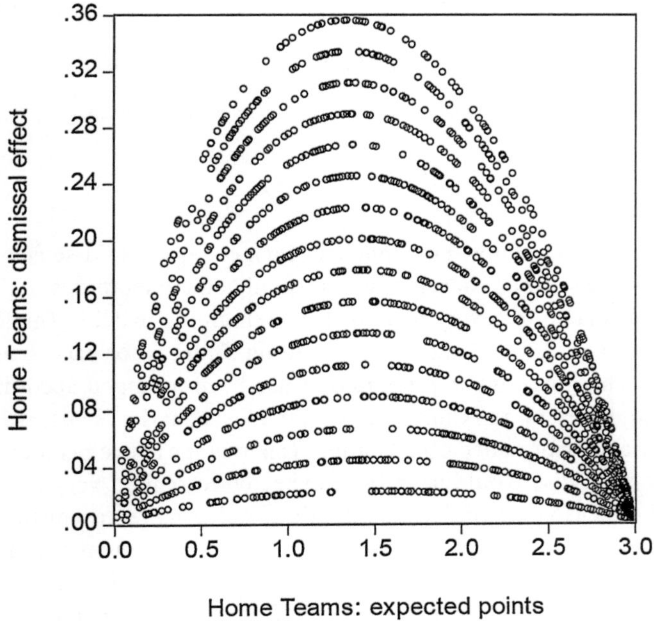

Fig. 1.a: Dismissal effect against originally expected points (home teams)

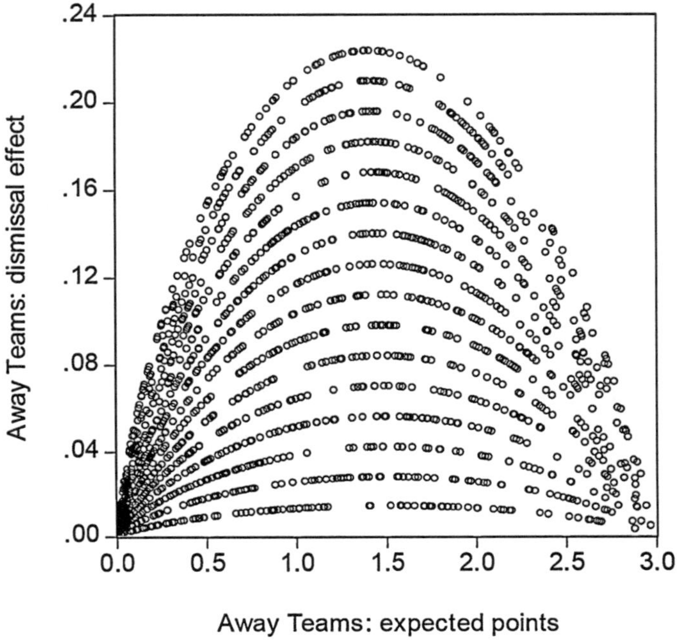

Fig. 1.b: Dismissal effect against originally expected points (away teams)

Finally we wanted to know how much a coach change at mid-seasons pays off at the end of the season. Therefore we accumulated the increases of the expected points per match for every team over its remaining matches (matchdays 19 to 34) per season. Table 5 shows the resulting findings for each season under inspection. This time, our representation has been arranged according to the implied end of season rankings of our reference scenario. Thus, we may now discuss which performance effects might (on average) have been expected for teams that otherwise would have been expected to rank at very low positions at the end of season schedule. The last three columns represent the summary of the findings, i.e. the mean, the maximum and the minimum accumulated increase in expected points within our 12 year sample period. The content of the last three columns is also depicted in figure 2. The volatile pattern of this graph corresponds to random variations in seasonal playing schedules. Please note that for a given season the implied long-run performance effects of a coach dismissal do obviously depend on the given playing schedule. If a weak team played all top teams at the end of season consecutively, we would expect to observe minor performance effects for this team compared to a situation where the team strengths of its end of season opponents altered considerably. Nevertheless, it seems unambiguous that our simulated increases in expected points are not too impressive: the maximum number of additional points that a team might generally expect after coach succession at mid-season is, according to our estimations, 2.33, the overall mean number of increases in expected points equals 1.7. It can also be seen that teams with medium rankings benefit most of a coach succession while clubs at the top benefit least. For them, the long term effect of coach succession hardly pays off as their pre-dismissal winning probabilities already tend to dominate within almost every match. Clubs at the bottom benefit also in a slightly weaker fashion as their respective winning probabilities appear too low in order to benefit from a marginal increase due to coach changes.

Table 5: Points gained thanks to the long term effect of coach succession. (Accumulated findings over matchdays 18 to 34)

Team Strength	92/93	93/94	94/95	95/96	96/97	97/98	98/99	99/00	00/01	01/02	02/03	03/04	Min	Mean	Max
1	1.211	1.702	1.036	1.069	1.183	1.029	0.971	0.989	1.205	1.116	1.089	1.234	0.971	1.153	1.702
2	1.338	1.507	1.332	1.577	0.952	1.474	1.689	1.256	1.779	1.119	1.464	1.183	0.952	1.389	1.779
3	1.473	1.468	1.334	2.059	1.340	1.770	1.284	1.523	1.695	1.221	2.031	1.775	1.221	1.581	2.059
4	1.543	1.755	1.660	2.132	1.505	1.691	1.495	1.837	1.790	1.202	1.709	1.698	1.202	1.668	2.132
5	1.422	2.139	1.862	2.332	1.414	1.694	1.637	1.964	2.015	1.482	1.401	1.519	1.401	1.740	2.332
6	2.021	1.730	1.603	2.208	1.336	2.223	1.970	1.440	1.770	1.625	1.961	1.395	1.336	1.773	2.223
7	1.557	2.201	1.809	2.236	1.980	2.087	1.947	1.915	2.007	1.466	1.866	1.660	1.466	1.894	2.236
8	1.678	1.696	1.684	2.073	2.116	1.835	1.995	2.087	2.088	1.882	2.089	1.441	1.441	1.889	2.116
9	1.928	2.068	1.900	2.204	1.807	1.905	1.903	1.940	1.727	1.777	2.013	1.644	1.644	1.901	2.204
10	1.804	2.066	1.749	2.144	2.118	2.009	2.176	1.882	1.809	1.798	1.762	1.740	1.740	1.921	2.176
11	2.070	1.977	1.701	2.019	2.045	2.132	2.194	1.986	2.018	2.217	1.955	1.330	1.330	1.970	2.217
12	1.723	2.048	1.938	2.100	1.912	1.878	1.852	1.829	1.954	1.548	1.830	1.793	1.548	1.867	2.100
13	1.836	1.931	1.711	2.042	1.950	2.038	1.855	1.507	1.820	1.587	2.103	1.658	1.507	1.836	2.103
14	1.662	1.679	1.566	1.910	1.774	1.966	1.746	1.722	1.713	1.825	1.824	1.912	1.566	1.775	1.966
15	1.525	1.693	1.571	2.106	1.828	2.008	1.939	1.707	1.546	1.423	1.805	1.721	1.423	1.739	2.106
16	1.539	1.553	1.615	1.942	1.742	2.043	1.980	1.407	1.388	1.498	1.650	1.804	1.388	1.680	2.043
17	1.565	1.396	1.190	1.916	1.418	1.368	1.939	1.377	1.687	1.385	1.611	1.363	1.190	1.518	1.939
18	1.530	1.143	0.895	1.399	1.398	1.787	1.477	1.197	1.217	1.476	1.422	0.965	0.895	1.325	1.787

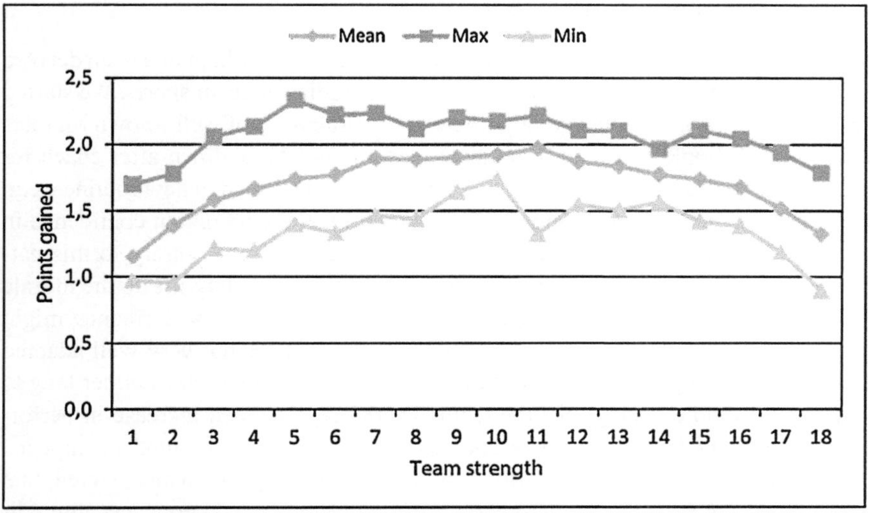

Fig. 2: Simulated accumulated effects of coach dismissals at round 17, seasons 1992/93–2003/04

Although our results show that teams benefit only to a limited extent from the long term effect of coach change (in terms of points), we want to maintain that even a small gain in points induced by a coach dismissal might indeed be very decisive: Even though in a majority of cases, the marginal achievements caused by coach succession might turn out insufficient for averting the risk of relegation or qualification for a European cup competition there are numerous examples in which a minimal difference in points determined the fate of a club.[8] Furthermore, we should recall that our underlying concerns focus on the *general* effects of within season coach dismissals. As a matter of fact, individual coaches do not have to induce homogenous successor-effects. Thus, it seems quite self-evident that the best performing coaches will show outstanding achievements. Nevertheless, as this paper was intended to introduce our suggested modelling framework to a general discussion within organizational sciences, this industry-specific detailed analysis of individual successor-effects has to remain for future research.

8 For example, at the end of the 1998/99 season the 1. FC Nürnberg was relegated just because this team had scored fewer goals than Eintracht Frankfurt. Apart from this, both teams had achieved 37 points and a goal difference of minus 10.

7. Discussion and Conclusion

This study tested hypotheses concerning coach succession which had been derived from dynamical organizational theory and prior studies on team sports. We started from the "shock-and-recovery" argument. The suspension of well-known routines and policies should cause an immediate performance breakdown after coach replacement. However, once the team members get accustomed to new routines, e.g. training methods or tactics, and supporters as well as media regain confidence in the club, the performance should gradually increase again. Contrary to this pattern was the notion that coach replacements might immediately lift up the morale of team members. However, such an extraordinary boost in performance might lead to the retention of newly introduced routines that are not very well adapted to the underlying problems of the team. Moreover it generally takes rather long to develop a suitable strategy for the team. Therefore, a sudden increase in performance should be followed by a gradual decline. Finally, we presented a composed "ritual scapegoating – self-fulfilling prophecy" assumption which stated that coach replacements in reaction to poor performance records do not cause immediate performance variations. Eventual sudden increases in performance thus should only be governed by regression-to-the-mean-effects. However, even regression-to-the-mean itself might indeed trigger a long-rung increase in performance as it reawakens support by the team's environment that often fiercely asked for such a coach replacement.

In our study of the impact of coach succession on the performance of German soccer teams we found strong regression-to-the-mean-effects: negative deviations from a team's general performance level determine a near-term reversion and they trigger the replacements of the coaches. Thus the reversion effect is not causally determined by coach replacements but simply by the laws of probability. Thus, the immediate "scapegoating" assumption as stated within hypothesis H3a was supported by our findings. Yet, there was also partial support for the dynamic "common-sense" hypothesis H3b as coach replacements indeed do seem to increase team performance in home matches over time.

How can such a result be explained? We think that the following scenario is rather likely: the supporters and the local media are often heavily demanding the replacement of the coach when a team gets into troubles. When those external stakeholders perceive that things are indeed getting better after coach replacement these actors obviously regain confidence in the team and the support increases again. Regression-to-the-mean is responsible for a self-fulfilling prophecy: the supporters ask for a coach change in order to improve the situation, the laws of probability cause indeed a performance increase after coach replacement and the supporters receive confirmation for their request and increasingly support the team again – not knowing that the new coach is probably not responsible for the improvement. This induces gradual improvements of the team's motivation and an incremental growth in output. Teams that do not replace the coach in times of crisis also benefit from regression-to-the-mean. However since their supposed request for coach change was not fulfilled they can be assumed to remain sceptical and may not develop the same level of new confidence as supporters of clubs that in fact changed the coaches in troublesome periods. Therefore a positive long term effect of coach change can be observed. However, the increasing support can unfold its influence more strongly at home matches. At away matches the team has to face an opposing crowd and support from supporters of the own team is considerably lower. – The team primarily rediscovers its home advantage which might have been lost in the paralysing bad-performance past (for a similar argument see *de Dios Tena & Forrest* 2007). In our opinion, these findings are outstanding as they do contradict widely held beliefs. In fact, although the study by *de Dios Tena & Forrest* (2007) supports the view that beneficial effects of a coach succession only occur at home matches, their study, in which no control for regression-to-the-mean was introduced, found an influence pattern of coach succession that is in line with hypotheses H2a and H2b. Actually, for these hypotheses we find no support at all.

Our findings have demonstrated the importance of including fixed effects and a suitable control for regression-to-the-mean in order to estimate the impact of executive succession correctly. This, we think, is not only relevant for studies in team sports but for any analysis in the field of organization theory, which focuses on the consequences of fundamental change on organizational performance.

References

Allen, M. P., Panian, S. K. & Lotz, R. E. (1979): Managerial Succession and Organizational Performance: a Recalcitrant Problem Revisited, in: Administrative Science Quarterly, Vol. 24, 2, pp. 167–180.

Amburgey, T. L., Kelly, D. & Barnett, W. P. (1993): Resetting the Clock: the Dynamics of Organizational Change and Failure, in: Administrative Science Quarterly, Vol. 38, 1, pp. 51–73.

Audas, R., Dobson, S. & Goddard, J. (2002): The Impact of Managerial Change on Team Performance in Professional Sports, in: Journal of Economics and Business, Vol. 54, 6, pp. 633–650.

Balduck, A.-L., Prinzie, A. & Buelens, M. (2010): The Effectiveness of Coach Turnover and the Effect on Home Team Advantage, Team Quality and Team Ranking, in: Journal of Applied Statistics, Vol. 37, 4, pp. 679–689.

Beck, N., Brüderl, J. & Woywode, M. (2008): Momentum or Deceleration? Theoretical and Methodological Reflections on the Analysis of Organizational Change, in: Academy of Management Journal, Vol. 51, 3, pp. 413–435.

Beck, N. & Meyer, M. (2012): Modeling Team Performance: Theoretical and Empirical Annotations on the Analysis of Football Data, in: Empirical Economics, Vol. 43, 1, pp. 335–356.

Boeker, W. (1997): Strategic Change: the Influence of Managerial Characteristics and Organizational Growth, in: Academy of Management Journal, Vol. 40, 1, pp. 152–170.

Brown, M. C. (1982): Administrative Succession and Organizational Performance: the Succession Effect, in: Administrative Science Quarterly, Vol. 27, 1, pp. 1–16.

Bruinshoofd, A. & ter Weel, B. (2003): Manager to Go? Performance Dips Reconsidered with Evidence from Dutch Football, in: European Journal of Operational Research, Vol. 148, 2, pp. 233–246.

Carroll, G. R. (1984): Dynamics of Publisher Succession in Newspaper Organizations, in: Administrative Science Quarterly, Vol. 29, 1, pp. 93–113.

Child, J. & Kieser, A. (1981): Development of Organizations over Time, in: *Nystrom, P. C. & Starbuck, W. H.* (eds.): Handbook of Organizational Design, New York: Oxford University Press, pp. 1928–1964.

De Dios Tena, J. & Forrest, D. (2007): Within-season Dismissal of Soccer Coaches: Statistical Analysis of Causes and Consequences, in: *European Journal of Operational Research*, Vol. 181, 1, pp. 362–373.

Dowell, G. & Swaminathan, A. (2000): Racing and Back-pedaling into the Future: New product Introduction and Organizational Mortality in the US Bicycle Industry 1880–1918, in: Organization Studies, Vol. 21, 2, pp. 405–431.

Fabianic, D. (1984): Organizational Effectiveness and Managerial Succession: an Update of an Old Problem, in: *Journal of Sport Behavior*, Vol. 7, 4, pp. 139–152.

Fabianic, D. (1994): Managerial Change and Organizational Effectiveness in Major League Baseball: Findings for the Eighties, in: Journal of Sport Behavior, Vol. 17, 3, pp. 135–147.

Fizel, J. L. & D'Itri, M. P. (1997): Managerial Efficiency, Managerial Succession and Organizational Performance, in: Managerial and Decision Economics, Vol. 18, 4, pp. 295–308.

Frick, B., Pestana Barros, C., & Prinz, J. (2010): Analysing Head Coach Dismissals in the German "Bundesliga" with a Mixed Logit Approach, in: European Journal of Operational Research, Vol. 200, 1, pp. 151–159.

Gabarro, J. J. (1987): The Dynamics of Taking Charge, Boston: Harvard Business School Press.

Gamson, W. A. & Scotch, N. A. (1964): Scapegoating in Baseball, in: American Journal of Sociology, Vol. 70, 1, pp. 69–72.

Giambatista, R. C., Rowe, W. G. & Riaz, S. (2005): Nothing Succeeds like Succession: a Critical Review of Leader Succession Literature since 1994, in: The Leadership Quarterly, Vol. 16, 6, pp. 963–991.

Gibson, C. & Vermeulen, F. (2003): A Healthy Divide: Subgroup Strength as a Stimulus for Team Learning Behavior, in: Administrative Science Quarterly, Vol. 48, 2, pp. 202–239.

Goddard, J. & Asimakopoulos, I. (2004): Forecasting Football Results and the Efficiency of Fixed-odds Betting, in: Journal of Forecasting, Vol. 23, 1, pp. 51–55.

Goodstein, J. & Boeker, W. (1991): Turbulence at the Top: a New Perspective on Governance Structure Changes and Strategic Change, in: Academy of Management Journal, Vol. 34, 2, pp. 306–320.

Greve, H. R. (1998): Performance, Aspirations, and Risky Organizational Change, in: Administrative Science Quarterly, Vol. 43, 1, pp. 58–86.

Greve, H. R. (1999): The Effect of Core Change on Performance: Inertia and Regression toward the Mean, in: Administrative Science Quarterly, Vol. 44, 3, pp. 590–614.

Greve, H. R. (2000): Performance, Aspirations, and Asset Growth in the Japanese Shipbuilding Industry, Working Paper, University of Tsukuba.
Greve, H. R. (2003): Organizational Learning from Performance Feedback. A Behavioral Perspective on Innovation and Change, Cambridge: Cambridge University Press.
Grusky, O. (1960): Administrative Succession in Formal Organizations, in: Social Forces, Vol. 39, 2, pp. 105–115.
Grusky, O. (1961): Corporate Size, Bureaucratization, and Managerial Succession, in: American Journal of Sociology, Vol. 67, 3, pp. 261–269.
Grusky, O. (1963): Managerial Succession and Organizational Effectiveness, in: American Journal of Sociology, Vol. 69, 1, pp. 21–31.
Grusky, O. (1964): Reply to Scapegoating in Baseball, in: American Journal of Sociology, Vol. 70, 1, pp. 72–76.
Hambrick, D. C. & Fukutomi, G. D. S. (1991): The Seasons of a CEO's Tenure, in: Academy of Management Review, Vol. 16, 4, pp. 719–742.
Hannan, M. T. & Freeman, J. (1984): Structural Inertia and Organizational Change, in: American Sociological Review, Vol. 49, 2, pp. 149–164.
Haveman, H. A., Russo, M. V. & Meyer, A. D. (2001): Organizational Environments in Flux: the Impact of Regulatory Punctuations on Organizational Domains, CEO Succession, and Performance, in: Organization Science, Vol. 12, 3, pp. 253–273.
Helmich, D.L. & Brown, W.B. (1972): Successor Type and Organizational Change in the Corporate Enterprise, in: Administrative Science Quarterly, Vol. 17, 3, pp. 371–380.
Hill, G. C. (2005): The Effects of Managerial Succession on Organizational Performance, in: Journal of Public Administration Research and Theory, Vol. 15, 4, pp. 585–597.
Hughes, M., Hughes H., Melahi, K. & Guermat, C. (2010): Short-term versus Long-term Impact of Managers: Evidence from the Football Industry, in: British Journal of Management, Vol. 21, 2, pp. 571–589.
Kahneman, D. & Tversky, A. (1973): On the Psychology of Prediction, in: Psychological Review, Vol. 80, 4, pp. 237–251.
Kesner, I. F. & Sebora, T.C. (1994): Executive Succession: Past, Present & Future, in: Journal of Management, Vol. 20, 2, pp. 327–372.
Koning, R. (2000): Balance in Competition in Dutch Soccer, in: The Statistician, Vol. 49, 3, pp. 419–431.
Koning, R. (2003): An Econometric Evaluation of the Effect of Firing a Coach on Team Performance, in: Applied Economics, Vol. 35, 5, pp. 555–564.
Lee, M. & Smith, G. (2002): Regression to the Mean and Soccer Wagers, in: Journal of Behavioural Decision Making, Vol. 15, pp. 329–342.
Levitt, B. & March, J. G. (1988): Organizational Learning, in: Annual Review of Sociology, Vol. 14, 1, pp. 319–340.
McTeer, W., White, P. G. & Persad, S. (1995): Manager/Coach Mid-season Replacement and Team Performance in Professional Team Sport, in: Journal of Sport Behavior, Vol. 18, 1, pp. 58–68.
Notz, W. W., Boschman, I. & Bruning, N.S. (2001): Punishment without Cause: Regression Effects of Leader Attribution Errors, in: Journal of Applied Social Psychology, Vol. 31, 11, pp. 2401–2416.
Pfeffer, J. & Davis-Blake, A. (1986): Administrative Succession and Organizational Performance: How Administrator Experience Mediates the Succession Effect, in: Academy of Management Journal, Vol. 29, 1, pp. 72–83.

Rowe, W. G., Cannella, A. Jr., Rankin, D. & Gorman, D. (2005): Leader Succession and Organizational Performance: Integrating the Common-sense, Ritual Scapegoating and Vicious-circle Succession Theories, in: Leadership Quarterly, Vol. 16, 2, pp. 197–220.

Stinchcombe, A. L. (1965): Social Structure and Organizations, in: *March*, J.G (ed.): Handbook of Organizations, Chicago: Rand McNally & Company, pp. 142–193.

Ter Weel, B. (2011): Does Manager Turnover Improve Firm Performance? Evidence from Dutch Soccer, 1986–2004, in: De Economist, Vol. 159, 3, pp. 279–303.

Tushman, M. L. & Romanelli, E. (1985): Organization Evolution: A Metamorphosis Model of Convergence and Reorientation, in: *Cummings, L. L. & Staw, B. M.* (eds.): CT Research in Organizational Behaviour, Greenwich: JAI Press, pp. 299–357.

Virany, B., Tushman, M.L. & Romanelli, E. (1992): Executive Succession and Organizational Outcomes in Turbulent Environments: an Organization Learning Approach, in: Organization Science, Vol. 3, 1, pp. 72–91.

Wagner, S. (2010): Managerial Succession and Organizational Performance – Evidence from the German Soccer League, in: Managerial and Decision Economics, Vol. 31, 6, pp. 415–430.

Competitive Balance and Attention Level Effects: Theoretical Considerations and Preliminary Evidence

Tim Pawlowski, Oliver Budzinski*

Abstract

We try to better understand possible reasons for deviations between statistically-measured competitive balance (CB) and perceived CB. Moreover, we suggest answers to the following questions: are there specific dimensions of CB that are perceived to be significantly less balanced in the Danish Superligaen compared to the other two leagues? Are there objective measures that "confirm" the fans' perception or does OCB in general deviate from PCB?

Keywords

competitive balance, sports economics, behavioural economics, mid-term outcome uncertainty, fan perception

1. Introduction

Following the uncertainty of outcome hypothesis (UOH) introduced by *Rottenberg* with his seminal work in 1956, competitive balance (CB) represents an important element of attractiveness of professional sports leagues. However, many studies correlating measures of competitive balance and success indicators such as attendance or viewer figures have not been successful in establishing clear evidence for the relevance of UOH in European professional football.

For instance, studies using the *Theil* (1967)-measure to analyse the impact of short-term (game) uncertainty on stadium attendance either found a non-significant (*Benz, Brandes & Franck* 2009) or negative (*Buraimo & Simmons* 2008) effect suggesting that some caution is required in the use of the UOH (*Szymanski* 2006). For instance, the negative effect may be explained with fans preferring to see either a favourite home team with the chance to win by clear margin (*Forrest* et al. 2005; *Coates & Humphreys* 2010) or a favourite away team which offers the chance to see an upset (*Coates, Humphreys & Zhou* 2014) or a strong brand with star players (*Pawlowski & Anders* 2012). Also, in the longer run there is not much support for the UOH. For instance, season-aggregate attendance has actually increased in some leagues (e.g. Germany and England), even as European leagues have become increasingly dominated by a

* The author gratefully acknowledges the financial support provided by an UEFA Research Grant.

small number of teams over the last decade (*Flores, Forrest & Tena* 2010; *Pawlowski, Breuer & Hovemann* 2010; *Pawlowski* 2013b: 2). This motivated further research into a completely new direction, which *Zimbalist* (2002: 112) already suggested in 2002 by stating, that "the best measure of competitive balance is the one to which fans show the greatest sensitivity". *Pawlowski* (2013a; b) as well as *Pawlowski & Budzinski* (2013) further developed this thought and measured the perception of competitive balance through the eyes of the fans by applying a stated preference approach. They found that the perceived competitive balance (PCB) indeed matters for fans.

However, an interesting puzzle occurs in their analysis as long-term PCB differs from long-term objectively measurable CB (OCB). Specifically, while the Danish Superligaen is perceived by the fans as being less balanced compared to the German Bundesliga and the Dutch Eredivisie, objective measures such as the competitive balance ratio (*Humphreys* 2002) suggest, that the Danish Superligaen is evenly or even more balanced than the other two leagues.

In this chapter, we try to better understand possible reasons for this gap between OCB and PCB. Moreover, we try to find answers to the following questions: are there specific dimensions of CB that are perceived to be significantly less balanced in the Danish Superligaen compared to the other two leagues? Are there objective measures that "confirm" the fans' perception or does OCB in general deviate from PCB?

The remainder of this chapter is organised as follows: First, we recapitulate the findings of our previous studies to demonstrate the arising puzzle (chapter 2). We then discuss possible (theoretical) reasons for this puzzle (chapter 3) as well as some new supportive evidence for attention level effects, i.e. fans' perception may just focus on specific parts of the (and not the overall) league competition (chapter 4). Finally, a summary and some conclusions for further research are provided (chapter 5).

2. Objective versus Perceived Competitive Balance: A Comparison

With the objective to better understand the fans' view on competitive balance, a written survey was distributed amongst soccer fans in three countries in a recent research project. Overall, n = 1,203 fans in Germany; n = 267 fans in Denmark, and n = 219 fans in the Netherlands were surveyed in the stadiums and in bars where football matches are regularly broadcast live before/during 14 matches in the first divisions of the respective leagues.[1]

An index of overall PCB was measured with two different approaches: First, it was asked:

1 For a detailed description of the research project and the employed methods please refer to *Pawlowski* (2013a; 2013b) as well as *Pawlowski & Budzinski* (2013).

*Thinking back to previous seasons: how would you rate the level of suspense/excitement ('*Spannung*') of the LEAGUE on a scale of 0–10 (0 ≡ not at all suspenseful/exciting ... 10 ≡ very suspenseful/exciting)?*[2]

Second, a (potentially oversimplified) scenario was tested to investigate the willingness-to-pay (WTP) of fans for CB:

*Imagine you could increase the level of suspense/excitement ('*Spannung*') in the LEAGUE by making a financial contribution! How much would you be willing to pay per stadium ticket per game?*

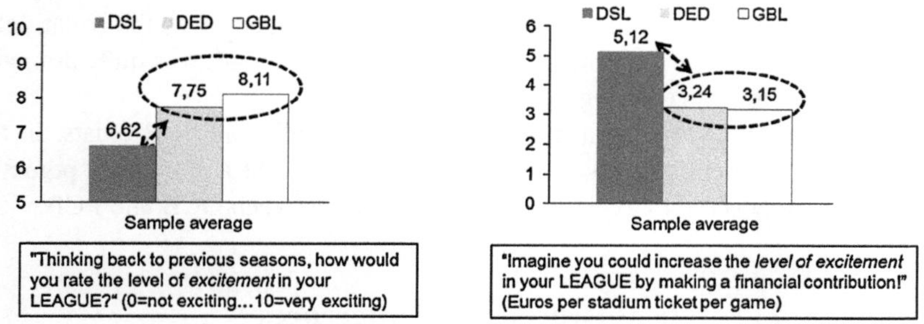

Fig. 1: Perceived level of excitement and willingness-to-pay to increase the current level of excitement in the Danish Superligaen (DSL), the Dutch Eredivisie (DED) and the German Bundesliga (GBL) (Pawlowski 2013a)

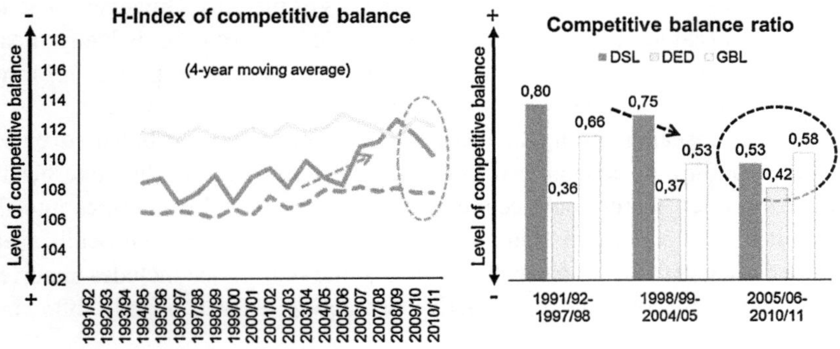

Fig. 2: Trends in competitive balance in the Danish Superligaen (DSL), the Dutch Eredivisie (DED) and the German Bundesliga (GBL) (Pawlowski 2013a)

---

2 As various regression and principal component analysis reveal (*Pawlowski* 2013a; 2013b) the overall index of PCB generated this way (is partly explained by and therefore) reflects the short-, mid- and long-term dimensions of CB as proposed in the literature (*Cairns, Jennett & Sloane* 1986).

The results suggest that the Danish Superligaen is perceived to be relatively less exciting as the level of PCB is on average 6.62 (compared to 7.75 for the Dutch Eredivisie and 8.11 for the German Bundesliga) and the Danish Fans are on average willing to pay around € 5.12 (compared to € 3.24 in the Netherlands and € 3.15 in Germany) per stadium ticket per game to increase the current level of excitement (see Figure 1).[3] For reasons of comparison, in addition to the PCB measures as described before, we analyzed the level of OCB based on two different measures. Interestingly, both, the H-Index of CB and the Competitive Balance Ratio (CBR)[4], indicate the Dutch Superligaen to be comparably less balanced. Moreover, for a long time the Danish Superligaen was the (relatively) most balanced league though the decrease of OCB in Denmark was quite dramatic during the recent years (see Figure 2).

These results suggest that a difference between OCB and PCB exists. In the next section we attempt to take a look behind this insight and explore potential theories that may serve to explain these differences between OCB and PCB.

3. Possible Theoretical Reasons for Differences between OCB and PCB

If fans would follow the model of the perfectly-rational *homo oeconomicus*, then there should be no difference between the statistically measured CB in European football leagues and the perceived CB in the eyes of the fans. However, to better understand possible effects of perception that deviate from statistically measured effects, we need to move away from simplistic notions of perfect information, perfectly rational behaviour and textbook-level microeconomics.

Economic research during the past five decades has contributed to enrich our understanding of economic behaviour by introducing branches like behavioural economics, institutional economics and experimental economics into the mainstream of economic thinking. Altogether they picture an empirically well-supported image of the rational-behaving economic subject that includes imperfect information, subjective and constructive perception as well as rule-following,

---

3 Further analysis reveals that PCB actually matters for fans as their consumption patterns might be affected (*Pawlowski* 2013a; 2013b; *Pawlowski & Budzinski* 2013).

4 The H-Index of CB is based on the sum of the quadratic share of points won by each club in a league adjusted for the number of teams (*Depken* 1999). The CBR is derived as the ratio of the average standard deviation of team points to the average SD of league points (*Humphreys* 2002).

heuristic behaviour. Cognitive resources are scarce and, consequently, individuals economize on these resources, which includes limiting information gathering (*Simon* 1955; *Stigler* 1961), economizing on the interpretative force of the brain by relying on mental models (*Kahneman & Tversky* 1979; *Denzau & North* 1994; *Kahneman* 2003a, 2003b) as well as focusing their scarce cognitive resources on those problems where their employment promises to yield extraordinary revenues and reverting to heuristics-following behaviour in ordinary situations (*Budzinski* 2003; *Vanberg* 2004).

This is a world where perception matters and plays a considerable role. Rational behaviour, then, does not so much describe 'right' behaviour in terms of statistical facts, but instead – less ambitiously – the consistency of mind and action. Drawing broadly on a body of economic thought that is enriched by these influences, three possible explanations for the (non-)divergence of OCB and PCB can be derived: framing effects (3.1), threshold effects (3.2), and attention level effects (3.3). These effects are discussed in the following.

3.1 Framing Effects

Framing effects imply that the context of a perception or a decision situation matters for interpretation and action: individuals are framed by past experiences as well as the environment of a situation and this influences how they perceive and interpret a given phenomenon. With respect to CB this means that fans are not influenced by a given CB-value in an isolated way. Instead, that CB-value is perceived in the context of the previous CB-values, which represent the framing of the fans and act as reference points for the individual, subjective valuation. As a consequence, changes in CB-values become more important than cardinal levels. If CB has been very low in a given league, then any improvement from that low level may be perceived as "high" CB because fans have been accustomed to low CB-levels and take the past imbalance as a reference point (anchoring effects). On the other hand, if CB-levels are high, a small deterioration of CB may already be perceived as "low" CB because fans have adjusted their reference point to the high level. The subjective assessment of CB is then driven by a mismatch of CB-expectation and actual CB: if CB is higher than expected, PCB will likely exceed OCB, whereas it will fall short of OCB if CB is lower than expected.[5] As

5 Next to past expressions of CB, expectations can additionally be driven by other influences. For instance, CB-expectation could be extraordinary high because of welcomed rule changes or an extraordinary influx of prominent (star) players (allocated to many teams), etc.

a consequence, it may happen that $OCB_{LEAGUE\_A} > OCB_{LEAGUE\_B} \wedge PCB_{LEAGUE\_A} < PCB_{LEAGUE\_B}$.[6]

Consider the following hypothetical example: country A, on the one hand, has a comparably imbalanced premier-level league say with CBR-levels oscillating around values of 0.3. Country B's fans, on the other hand, enjoy a premier-level league with CBR-levels around values of 0.7. Now, in the recent seasons, CBR of League A unexpectedly jumps to 0.45 whereas CBR level of League B unexpectedly drops to 0.55. While League B remains the more balanced one in OCB terms, framing effects may well drive PCB of (disappointed) League B-fans below the PCB of (positively surprised) League A-fans.

Indeed, in our study, we can find some support for this line of explanation (*Pawlowski & Budzinski* 2013). As can be seen in section 2, the decrease in OCB seems to influence perceptions in a stronger way than the level of OCB in the case of the Danish league. Note that the Danish league actually is characterized by a better OCB-value than the premier-level leagues in the Netherlands and in Germany in the first two periods and still better than the Dutch league in the third period (see figure 2). Yet, the decrease of CB is much more dramatic in Denmark than in the other two leagues. CBR for Denmark has decreased by around 34 per cent (from 0.8 to 0.53) from the first to third period, whereas for Germany it has decreased 'only' by around 12 per cent (from 0.66 to 0.58) and the Dutch one increased by around 14 per cent (from 0.36 to 0.42). So, generalizing over the three periods, we can – a bit simplifying – see that while for OCB levels $OCB_{Denmark} > OCB_{Germany} > OCB_{Netherlands}$ holds, PCB-levels are characterized by $PCB_{Denmark} < PCB_{Netherlands} < PCB_{Germany}$.

Thus, the difference between OCB- and PCB-levels may be explained by changes of CB (as a framing factor) being a stronger influence on fans' perception than CB-levels.

3.2 *Threshold Effects*

Threshold effects correspond to an important behavioural economics-qualification of the concept of optimality: instead of aspiring to an optimal level of satisfaction in regard to the consumption of any goods, individuals are typically less ambitious

6 *Coates, Humphreys & Zhou* (2014) employ a somewhat similar thought on a match level when they model individual consumer choice as depending on a utility function that, inter alia, includes the difference between the actual match outcome and the expected match outcome as a (positive or negative) utility source (surprise win by the supported team and surprise loss by the supported team respectively).

and settle for a "satisficing" level. Once a certain level of satisfaction is reached, no more further cognitive resources are spent on further optimizing the consumption in question. Instead, the scarce cognitive resources are focused on consumption areas where no satisfying level has yet been reached. In other words, (small) variations above the satisficing level do not matter. However, if the "satisficing" threshold is undercut, then a strong (demand) reaction is triggered (discontinuity effect).

While the empirical evidence for such effects differs among different types of wants and needs as well as among corresponding goods categories, fans' desideratum for balanced competition within the league may provide a fitting example. So far, sports economics research has struggled to identify any optimal level of CB; identification of optimum has neither theoretically, nor empirically been managed. It appears to be broadly accepted that this, inter alia, has to do with conflicting influences such as the attractiveness of close competition in terms of high uncertainty of outcome and unpredictability of results versus the attractiveness of superstar players and superstar teams that inevitably generate some minimum imbalance. Perfect CB would basically imply a random walk (without any favourites or underdogs) and most sports economists will agree that this is not optimal. An additional factor in question may well be that fans are not interested in any optimal CB, i.e. they do not have an (explicit or implicit) notion of an optimum regarding CB themselves. Instead, fans may rather be interested in a satisficing CB. In this case, a discontinuity effect emerges: CB changes above the satisficing level of CB are not perceived to be relevant for consumption behaviour whereas a drop of CB below the satisficing level may cause discontinuous, perhaps even extreme consumption reactions.

Again, we find preliminary supportive evidence that the relation between CB and fans' consumption includes a discontinuity in terms of some kind of a "tipping point" or threshold above which changes in CB are not very relevant for fans whereas fans' consumption behavior does change significantly once CB falls below that crucial threshold: while *Pawlowski* (2013a; 2013b) could detect that the PCB conditional demand curves are s-shaped (indicating an area of inelastic response for both, very high and very low values of PCB), the findings by *Pawlowski* and *Budzinski* (2013) suggest that changes in the fans' willingness-to-pay for improvements of CB are triggered by CB falling below a crucial threshold, i.e. WTP 'jumps' to a higher level as a reaction to this.

3.3 Attention Level Effects

In addition to the theoretical effects and their preliminary supportive evidence discussed above, a third effect might be relevant in this context as valuations of individuals depend on the degree of (their) attention that is drawn to a specific phenomenon. This attention level depends – next to the individual's preferences – on salience-related aspects like media intensity (presence in broadcasting, newspapers, internet, boulevard media, etc.) and relative importance of specific subparts of the overall phenomenon. In regard to the valuation of goods, a typical consequence is that valuations of those products that receive high attention levels outshine those of products with low attention levels in the perception of the consumer.

With respect to the competitive balance of premier-level football leagues, the effects of diverging attention levels may be particularly relevant since the relative importance of competition among teams differs significantly depending on the positions within the league's ranking that these teams are fighting for. Put drastically, competition for top positions is considerably more important than competition in the 'dull' midfield: while the close duel of two teams for championship fame will be associated with high attention levels, a close fight of three teams for position 10 in an 18- or 20-teams league will certainly receive significantly lower attention levels. The relative importance of the championship race is obviously higher than of the race for a midfield position[7] and, correspondingly, media intensity (regarding all dimensions) will be much higher for the former than for the latter.

However, the diverging attention levels can have an important influence on the perception of the competitive balance of the league. Consider the following two scenarios for an 18-teams league: A) the championship race between three teams is close until the last minute of the season; the three top teams are very evenly matched in terms of performance levels. However, the "race for position 10" is early decided because the differences in competitiveness are rather high among the midfield teams; B) The championship race is decided very early in the season due to the clear dominance of one team that is head and toes above the competition. However, the "race for position 10" is very intense among four teams that are very evenly matched.

7 Please note, that competition for midfield positions is relevant in some leagues (e.g. the German Bundesliga) because media revenues are (partly) redistributed based on the past season(s) positioning in the final league table(s). Therefore, different (midfield) positions go along with (slightly) different amounts of club-specific media revenues. However, without any doubt, competition for the top positions is considerably more important for (most of the) fans. Recent sports economics research provides evidence that the same is true for the participants of the league: effort levels for comparably less important midfield position races are lower than such for more important decisions like the race for the championship (*Feddersen, Humphreys & Soebbing* 2012).

It should not be surprising if the PCB of scenario A is significantly and considerably higher than the PCB of scenario B. However, the standard OCB measures, measuring the CB of the overall league, will not necessarily come to the same result because they do not distinguish between a close fight for position 1 and a close "fight for position 10". So, while statistically (OCB) every sub-competition within the league is associated with the same value, the fans (PCB) will value some sub-competitions higher than others – due to diverging attention levels. Differences between OCB and PCB may be rooted in the phenomenon that CB between (few) top teams may be more important for fan perception than the balance of the league in total.

Looking into typical European soccer premier-level leagues, we can indentify several sub-competitions that exceed the 'ordinary' fight for positions in the league ranking in terms of relative importance and media intensity, i.e. the championship race, the race for the qualification positions for the European-level competitions (UEFA Champions League; UEFA Europe League), the race against relegation[8], and qualification positions for play-off rounds (depending on the league's championship structure).

The consequent hypothesis is that PCB is more driven by the closeness of these comparatively important sub-competitions (i.e. by the CB among the contenders for the relevant positions in the league ranking) than by the CB of the overall league that typically determines the standard OCB measures. If this hypothesis can be supported, then the gap between PCB and OCB will disappear when OCB measures are employed that do not target the league as a whole but focus on the relevant sub-competitions (i.e. mid-term components of league competition). The next section provides some supportive evidence for this hypothesis.

4. Competitive Balance and Attention Level Effects: Preliminary Evidence

Jennett (1984) was the first who introduced the idea to measure the so-called mid-term components of UO who disentangle the overall CB measure by looking at match significance. His and other modified measures were employed in subsequent studies to test the relevance of mid-term UO for consumers objectively. The findings suggest a significant positive effect on stadium attendance if a team

8 European football leagues are typically open leagues in which the teams on the last positions in the ranking are relegated to a lower-level league and replaced by the top performers of these power level leagues.

still had a chance to contend for the championship (*Jennett* 1984; *Pawlowski & Anders* 2012) or to earn promotion (*Forrest & Simmons* 2002). Therefore, – and in contrast to the ambiguous findings with regard to the relevance of objectively measured short- and long-term UO – objectively measured *mid-term* UO seems to be of importance for fan behavior. Thus, it appears promising to look at whether OCB and PCB differ in this dimension.

In addition to the overall index of PCB generated by the instrument as described in chapter 2, 11 items reflecting the short-, mid- and long-term UO were evaluated within the project on a 4-point scale (1 ≡ I do not agree … 4 ≡ I agree completely) with the following type of question:

Thinking back to previous seasons, what is your opinion of the LEAGUE with regard to…?.

Figure 3 summarizes the mean values for the 4 items reflecting mid-term UO. Interestingly, in line with the findings for the overall index of PCB, the Danish Superligaen is perceived to be significantly less balanced also with regard to the mid-term UO. Specifically, the race for the championship appears to be less balanced as most of the Danish Fans disagree with the statement that the fight for the title remains exciting for a long time within a season.

These perceptions by the fans are confirmed by the available 'objective' data. Five years prior to the inquires (season 2006/07–2010/11) there have been four different champions in the German Bundesliga and the Dutch Eredivisie each while FC Copenhagen won all but one championship in Denmark. Furthermore, the "championship relevance" of games further strengthens this result. A game possesses championship relevance if at least one of two teams still has a (mathematical) chance of winning the championship. Significantly, in the season before the inquiry took place (2010/11) only 45% of the games in Denmark had such championship relevance while it was more than 60% of the games in Germany and the Netherlands.

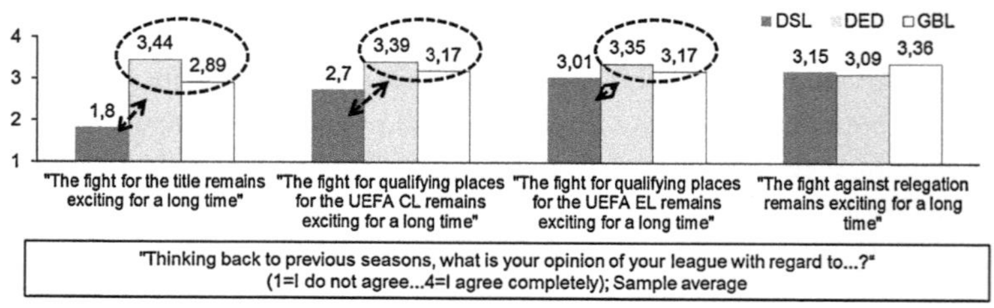

Fig. 3: Fans' evaluation of different dimensions of excitement in the Danish Superligaen (DSL), the Dutch Eredivisie (DED) and the German Bundesliga (GBL) (Pawlowski 2013a)

Figure 4 provides some descriptive evidence based on the average winning margin in three different leagues. While the champions in the Dutch Eredivisie and the German Bundesliga are on average 3.4 and respectively 5.2 points ahead, the champions in the Danish Superligaen are on average 12.4 points ahead of the team in second place. Significantly, in 2010/11 FC Copenhagen was 26 points ahead of the runner-up Odense BK.

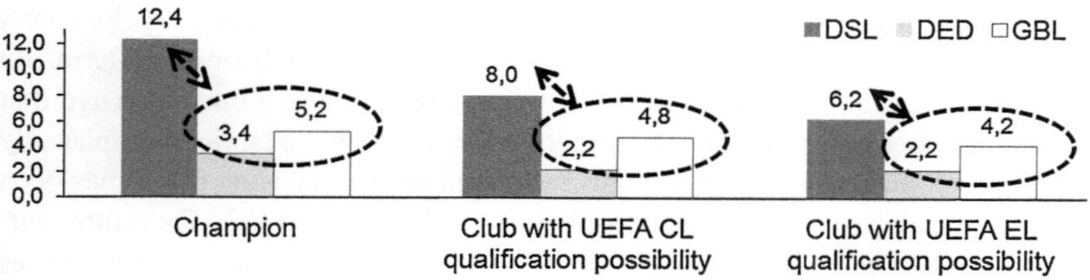

Fig. 4: Average number of points ahead in the Danish Superligaen, the Dutch Eredivisie and the German Bundesliga

In summary, the stronger imbalance of the Danish league can be found both in perceived and objective measures if mid-term measures are analyzed. For instance, mid-term PCB and mid-term OCB measures both reflect the comparatively strong imbalance of the Danish league when it comes to analysing championship relevance. While the ranking among the Dutch and the German league, which are rather close to each other, is not unambiguous, still the objective and subjective measures show exactly the same pattern, i.e. $OCB_{Denmark} < OCB_{Germany, Netherlands}$ and $PCB_{Denmark} < PCB_{Germany, Netherlands}$. This supports our hypothesis that PCB is more driven by the closeness of comparatively important sub-competitions (i.e. by the CB among the contenders for the relevant positions in the league ranking) than by the CB of the overall league: the imbalance of the championship race in Denmark dominates the balance of the overall league in regard to the assessment and behaviour of the fans.

5. Summary and Conclusion

In this chapter we try to better understand possible reasons for the gap between OCB and PCB as previously observed by *Pawlowski* (2013a; 2013b) as well as *Pawlowski & Budzinski* (2013). First, we recapitulate the findings of our previous studies and explain some observations by introducing and applying behavioural economic concepts. Based on these considerations, *framing effects* and *threshold effects* seem to occur which might be reasons for some divergences between OCB and PCB. Second, we provide preliminary evidence that suggests that the gap between PCB and OCB disappears when measures are employed that do not target the league as a whole but focus on relevant sub-competitions. Therefore, *attention level effects* seem to occur in this context as well: (for instance) a balanced championship race is more important to the fans than a high overall balance in the league.

There are two lines of important conclusions from this insight. Firstly, sports economics research into CB needs to focus on thoroughly analyzing mid-term UO in the future. Although *Szymanski* (2006) already mentioned some years ago that there "have been surprisingly few other papers that have examined empirically the effect of championship uncertainty", the mid-term dimension of CB has been rather neglected so far (in comparison to overall CB-analysis). Therefore, further research is necessary in order to develop and employ mid-term UO-measures along both of the lines that *Fort* and *Maxcy* (2003) emphasize, i.e. the analysis of competitive balance (ACB) (*Pawlowski* & *Bloching* 2013) and the analysis of uncertainty of outcome (UOH). Secondly, our analysis entails valuable implications for the management and governance of leagues: in order to make a league more attractive for fans, it is not so much relevant to improve overall OCB (i.e. the average CB of the league). Instead, it is more effective to ensure close competitions for outstanding position in the league ranking that receive high attention levels by the fans like the championship race, the fight against relegation or other relevant sub-competitions. In order to operationalize the management and policy implications, however, more research along the lines of our first conclusion is necessary, including research on the relative importance of different sub-competitions for the perception of the fans.

References

Benz, M.-A., Brandes, L. & Franck, E. (2009): Do Soccer Associations Really Spend on a Good Thing? Empirical Evidence on Heterogeneity in the Consumer Response to Match Uncertainty of Outcome, in: Contemporary Economic Policy, Vol. 27, 2, pp. 216–235.

Budzinski, O. (2003): Cognitive Rules, Institutions, and Competition, in: Constitutional Political Economy, Vol. 14, 3, pp. 215–235.

Buraimo, B. & Simmons, R. (2008): Do Sports Fans Really Value Uncertainty of Outcome? Evidence from the English Premier League, in: International Journal of Sport Finance, Vol. 3, 3, pp. 146–155.

Cairns, J. P., Jennett, N. & Sloane, P. (1986): The Economics of Professional Team Sports: A Survey of Theory and Evidence, in: Journal of Economic Studies, Vol. 13, 1, pp. 3–80.

Coates, D. & Humphreys, B. R. (2010): Week to Week Attendance and Competitive Balance in the National Football League, in: International Journal of Sport Finance, Vol. 5, 4, pp. 239–252.
Coates, D., Humphreys, B. R. & Zhou, L. (2014): Outcome Uncertainty, Reference-Dependent Preferences and Live Game Attendance, in: Economic Inquiry (forthcoming).
Denzau, A. T. & North, D. C. (1994): Shared Mental Models – Ideologies and Institutions, in: Kyklos, Vol. 47, 1, pp. 3–31.
Depken, C. A. (1999): Free Agency and the Competitiveness of MLB, in: Review of Industrial Organization, Vol. 14, 3, pp. 205–217.
Feddersen, A., Humphreys, B. R. & Soebbing, B. P. (2012): Contest Incentives in European Football, Working Paper No. 2012-13, University of Alberta.
Flores, R., Forrest, D. & Tena, J. D. (2010): Impact on Competitive Balance from Allowing Foreign Players in a Sports League: Evidence from European Soccer, in: Kyklos, 63, pp. 546–557.
Forrest, D. & Simmons, R. (2002): Outcome Uncertainty and Attendance Demand: The Case of English Soccer, in: Journal of the Royal Statistical Society, Series D (The Statistician), Vol. 51, pp. 229–241.
Forrest, D., Beaumont, J., Goddard, J. & Simmons, R. (2005): Home Advantage and the Debate about Competitive Balance in Professional Sports Leagues, in: Journal of Sports Sciences, Vol. 23, pp. 439–445.
Fort, R. & Maxcy, J. (2003): Competitive Balance in Sports Leagues: An Introduction, in: Journal of Sports Economics, Vol. 4, 2, pp. 154–160.
Humphreys, B. R. (2002): Alternative Measures of Competitive Balance in Sports Leagues, in: Journal of Sports Economics, Vol. 3, 2, pp. 133–148.
Jennett, N. (1984): Attendances, Uncertainty of Outcome and Policy in Scottish League Football, in: Scottish Journal of Political Economy, Vol. 31, pp. 176–198.
Kahneman, D. (2003a): A Psychological Perspective on Economics, in: The American Economic Review, Vol. 93, 2, pp. 162–168.
Kahneman, D. (2003b): Maps of Bounded Rationality: Psychology for Behavioral Economics, in: The American Economic Review, Vol. 93, 5, pp. 1449–1475.
Kahneman, D. & Tversky, A. (1979): Prospect Theory: An Analysis of Decision under Risk, in: Econometrica, Vol. 47, 2, pp. 263–292.
Pawlowski, T. (2013a): Wettbewerbsintensität im Profifußball – Eine empirische Untersuchung zur Bedeutung für die Zuschauer, Wiesbaden: Springer-Gabler.
Pawlowski, T. (2013b): Testing the Uncertainty of Outcome Hypothesis in European Professional Football: A Stated Preference Approach, in: Journal of Sports Economics, Vol. 14, 4, pp. 341–367.
Pawlowski, T. & Anders, C. (2012): Stadium Attendance in German Professional Football: The (Un)Importance of Uncertainty of Outcome Reconsidered, in: Applied Economics Letters, Vol. 19, pp. 1553–1556.
Pawlowski, T. & Bloching, B. (2013): How Exciting are the Major European Football Leagues? Main findings of a Study on the Competitive Balance within Football Leagues, http://www.rolandberger.com/media/pdf/Roland_Berger_Competitive_Balance_of_Football_Leagues_20130220.pdf (accessed 2013-12-02).
Pawlowski, T. & Budzinski, O. (2013): The (Monetary) Value of Competitive Balance for Sport Consumers – A Stated Preference Approach to European Professional Football, in: International Journal of Sport Finance, Vol. 8, 2, pp. 112–123.

Pawlowski, T., Breuer, C. & Hovemann, A. (2010): Top Clubs' Performance and the Competitive Situation in European Domestic Football Competitions, in: Journal of Sports Economics, Vol. 11, pp. 186–202.

Rottenberg, S. (1956): The Baseball Player's Labour Market, in: Journal of Political Economy, Vol. 64, 3, pp. 242–258.

Simon, H. A. (1955): A Behavioral Model of Rational Choice, in: The Quarterly Journal of Economics, Vol. 69, 1, pp. 99–118.

Stigler, G. J. (1961): The Economics of Information, in: Journal of Political Economy, Vol. 69, pp. 213–225.

Szymanski, S. (2006): Uncertainty of Outcome, Competitive Balance and the Theory of Team Sports, in: *Andreff, W. & Szymanski, S.* (eds.), Handbook on the Economics of Sport, Cheltenham: Elgar: pp. 597–600.

Theil, H. (1967): Economics and Information Theory, Amsterdam: North-Holland.

Vanberg, V. J. (2004): The Rationality Postulate in Economics: Its Ambiguity, Its Deficiency and Its Evolutionary Alternative, in: Journal of Economic Methodology, Vol. 11, 1, pp. 1–29.

Zimbalist, A. S. (2002): Competitive Balance in Sports Leagues: An Introduction, in: Journal of Sports Economics, Vol. 3, 2, pp. 111–121.

Spill-overs? Economic Progress, Football Facilities and the 2011 Asia Cup

Peter Ochieng

Abstract

Relative to poor nations, richer nations tend to develop (over time) the economic capacity to invest towards international football success by building massive football stadiums which later host economically draining mega football events. The aim of the study was to evaluate the possible combined effects of GDP per capita, football facility and hosting field advantage of nations that have qualified or not qualified for the Asian Cup. Binary logistic regression models indicated that the combined effects of stadiums and hosting ability and not purely GDP per capita explains football qualifications and achievements at the Asian Cup.

Keywords

Asia, economic progress, football facilities

1. Introduction

Since its inauguration in 1956, the Asia Cup has been held every four years. However, from 2004 its calendar changed strategically to 'accommodate' the FIFA World Cup and European calendars. To date there are 46 Asian nations eligible for the tournament. Of all nations that have qualified at least once, the most successful nations have been Japan and South Korea, while many other nations are yet to qualify! This study is based on selected national economic indicators and focuses on evaluating why some nations qualify while others don't.

Research into the economic contributors of national success or failure in sports is broad and growing. The national sports success has previously been attributed to GNP (*Grimes* et al. 1974; *Levine* 1974; *Condon* et al. 1999; *Van Bottenburg* 2000; *Hoffmann* et al. 2002a; *Tcha & Perchin* 2003), GNP per capita (*Jokl* 1964, *Novikov & Maximenko* 1972; *Kiviaho & Makela* 1978; *Gillis* 1980; *Condon* et al. 1999; *Tcha & Perchin* 2003), GNI (*De Koning & Olieman* 1996), GDP (*Shaw & Pooley* 1976; *Gartner* 1989; *Suen* 1992, 1994; *Den Butter & Van der Tak* 1995; *Bernard & Busse* 2000; *Morton* 2002; *Moosa & Smith* 2004).

However, although all the above articles used various economic indicators, they did not use GDP per capita which is a more accurate measure of a nation's economic potential to explain national sports success. Furthermore, the studies focused on identifying the reasons for success (after qualification and during a tournament) and not success in qualifying. This study aims to cover this gap by answering the 'first step' question of possible future football achievement – why do some nations qualify and others not?

As for the conceptual frame of the study, figure 1.1 illustrates the link between economic progress (as indicated by GDP per capita) and football sector progress (as indicated by hosting and football stadiums) against football achievements (as indicated by Asia Cup qualifications). The researcher postulates that the combined effects of GDP per capita, football facilities and home-field advantage may positively impact qualification for the Asia Cup. Strong economic capacity may enable football facility development and hosting. The combined effects of economic progress and football sector progress may boost Asia Cup qualifications and then later success.

Fig. 1.1: Linking economic progress, football sector progress & football achievements

2. Theory and Hypothesis Development

Several theoretical perspectives can be used to understand the link between success and failure in football. First, pioneering advantage also called first mover advantage is commonly applied to explain competitive advantage pertaining to product success or failures. The theory postulates that businesses that possess pioneering advantage tend to remain on top by -gaining control of resources and expertise that followers may not be able to have, deriving high profits as a result of a large market share and or a near monopolistic state and the accumulation of customer loyalty derived from a head start (*Lieberman & Montgomery* 1998). The possible disadvantages of pioneering advantage may involve uncertainty due to a riskier strategy, vulnerability to later entrants and lastly a culture of resistance especially when consumers are 'not ready' for novel ideas, services and goods. In the Asian football zone, indicators of pioneering advantage are evident in the fact that nations that became affiliated to both FIFA and AFC earlier such as Japan gradually (over the years) developed substantial pioneering advantage relative to late starters like Uzbekistan. Moreover, the earlier affiliates have qualified for the

Asia cup more than the latecomers and have accumulated more football resources through advanced professional football leagues in place (See Figure 2.1).

		# of Qualifications at the Asia Cup	Years since professional league began	FIFA affiliation	AFC Affiliation
1	Japan	7	8	1929	1954
2	South Korea	12	3	1948	1954
3	Saudi Arabia	8	3	1956	1956
4	China	10	5	1931	1974
5	Iraq	7	10	1950	1970
6	Iran	12	10	1948	1958
7	Uzbekistan	5	6	1994	1994
8	Vietnam	1	0	1964	1964
9	Lebanon	1	0	1936	1964
10	Turkmenistan	1	0	1994	1994
12	Yemen	1	0	1980	1962
12	Bangladesh	1	0	1976	1973
13	Cambodia	1	0	1954	1957

Fig. 2.1: Pioneering advantage at the Asia Cup

Sources: Various football websites, documentaries, reports; newspapers & www.FIFA.com, www.worldstadiums.com, www.the-afc.com

Secondly, resource-based theory postulated that sports organizations that strategically deploy competitive human resources (players, coaches and training staff), organizational resources (teams, clubs and professional leagues) and physical resources (stadiums, training camps and laboratories) do enhance their chances of succeeding (*Ochieng* 2012). In Asia, nations with high economic potential such as Japan and China and with massive investments in officials, clubs, teams and stadiums did better at the Asia Cup (See Figure 2.2).

	Team	Officials	# clubs	# Teams	# Stadiums
1	Japan	249,603	2,000	29,132	167
2	South Korea	4,648	100	864	251
3	Saudi Arabia	1,292	153	780	21
4	China	129,057	2,221	11,347	182
5	Iraq	2,900	110	170	45
6	Iran	25,800	120	270	105

	Team	Officials	# clubs	# Teams	# Stadiums
7	Uzbekistan	1,325	216	2,400	16
8	Vietnam	10,652	27	10,000	37
9	Lebanon	3,495	178	877	23
10	Turkmenistan	195	15	98	5
11	Yemen	502	110	220	5
13	Bangladesh	75,604	4100	8200	18
13	Cambodia	230	420	420	2

Fig. 2.2: Resource advantage at the Asia Cup

Sources: Various football websites, documentaries, reports; newspapers & www.FIFA.com, www.worldstadiums.com, www.the-afc.com

2.1 GDP per Capita and Sporting Success

A growing number of studies have looked into the combined effect of GDP per capita and other variables (*Levine* 1974; *Gartner* 1989; *Den Butter & Van der Tak* 1995; *Bernard & Busse* 2000; *Stamm & Lamprecht* 2000; *Hoffmann* et al. 2002b; *Johnson & Ali* 2002; *Kuper & Sterken* 2003; *De Bosscher* et al. 2003; *Johnson & Ali* 2000). Although the importance of all the above economic indicators is not in dispute the factors the researchers choose to analyse in addition are sometimes quite disputable. For instance Levine (1974) scrutinized the effects of GDP per capita controlling for population, urbanization and literacy. *Gartner* (1989) probed the impacts of GDP per capita and included the influence of population and political system. *Den Butter & Van der Tak* (1995) evaluated GDP per capita with population, human development index, quality of life index, and political system added to the model. *Bernard & Busse* (2000) explored the effects of GDP per capita and population, host, political system and past success in winning Olympic Medals. *Stamm & Lamprecht* (2000) investigated GDP per capita against politics, enrolments, population, and institutionalization of elite sports and years of membership at international associations. *Hoffmann* et al. (2002b) reviewed GDP per capita along with population, cultural influence, hosting and geography. *Johnson & Ali* (2002) considered GDP per capita, population, host, climate and political system. *Kuper & Sterken* (2003) vetted the effects of GDP per capita on population, host, political system, national culture and media. *De Bosscher* et al. (2003) examined GDP per capita on population, urbanization and religion. Lastly *Johnson & Ali* (2004) probed GDP per capita on population, host, climate and political system.

Economic progress as measured by GDP per capita reflects on the nation's ability to do the following – (a) afford, pay and sustain the costs necessary to fund football training and talent development, (b) afford football human capital such as coaches, players and medical staff, (c) develop organizational capacity exemplified by investing in football clubs, teams and professional football leagues, (d) invest in football infrastructure like stadiums, equipment, camps and laboratories, (e) host, sponsor and pay prize money during competitions and lastly, local people need the economic capability to be able to afford involvement in football. In this study, GDP per capita therefore represent capital. Bearing all this arguments for using GDP per capita to explain success, this study arrived at the following hypothesis.

H1: GDP per capita has a positive impact on Asia Cup qualification

2.2 GDP per Capita and Football Home Advantage

The benefits from hosting a football tournament may consist in a social, psychological, and physiological boost to the home team. Socially, playing amongst supportive friends and in a familiar environment familiarity may be an advantage to the home team. Secondly, the passionate crowd support may motivate the home team. Physiologically the short travel distances, familiar weather and climate effects put less strain on the home team as compared its the opponents.

These possible benefits have been highlighted by newspaper articles to have attributed the FIFA World Cup victories of Uruguay in 1930, Italy in 1934, England in 1966, Germany in 1974, Argentina in 1978 and France in 1998 to the fact that the tournament was held in the winners' country.

Additionally, home advantage has also been stated to exist in professional football clubs, as reported by *Armatas & Pollard* 2012; *Pollard & Gomez* 2009; *Poulter* 2009; *Seckin & Pollard* 2008; *Lago & Martin* 2007; *Carmichael & Thomas* 2005; *Neave & Wolfson* 2003; *Jacklin* 2005; *Tucker* et al. 2005; *Thomas* et al. 2004; *Bray* et al. 2003 – all in *Garcia* et al. 2013.

Data from Asia cup also indicates the presence of home advantage in 1960, 1964, 1968, 1976, 1980 and 1992.

Table 3.1: Home Advantage at the Asia Cup

Year	Host	1st Place
1960	South Korea	South Korea
1964	Israel	Israel
1968	Iran	Iran

Year	Host	1st Place
1976	Iran	Iran
1980	Kuwait	Kuwait
1992	Japan	Japan

Source: www. Fifa.com; www.the-afc.com

In line with the above arguments, the researcher sort to test the hypothesis that…

H_2: Home-field advantage has a positive impact on performance at the Asia Cup

2.3 GDP per Capita and Stadiums

In general terms, high GDP per capita nations such as Japan, South Korea and Australia, tend to possess more stadiums as illustrated in Figure 2.3.

	GDP per capita[1]	Stadiums[2]
South Korea	22,388	249
Australia	62,003	189
Japan	46,135	165
China	5,447	141
Iran	6,816	116
Indonesia	3,472	85
India	1,534	81
Pakistan	1,196	53
Thailand	5,193	50
Iraq	5,687	45
Philippines	2,365	34
Malaysia	10,012	30
Saudi Arabia	20,778	27
UAE	40,363	25
Lebanon	9,148	24

Fig. 2.3: GDP per capita and Stadiums in Asia

Notes: 2011 data[1] & Data as of jan-27-2011[2]

Sources: OECD Worldstadiums.com

Physical capital resources (PCR) consist of stadiums, training facilities, equipment, and sports technology such as information management systems for recruiting, training, monitoring and evaluating athletes (*Smart & Wolfe* 2003). PCR may therefore be viewed as a product that also encompasses sport finance, sport sponsorship, and event management. This is so because football finance may be sourced from football events themselves, or from sponsorships or directly from government and private financiers. In relation to national football performance, PCRs are usually found within training facilities with inbuilt technologically advanced sports equipment, supported by superior information management systems for coaching and training.

Economic policies that lead to the provision of dedicated training facilities and equipment enable footballers to train in high quality environment and therefore provide a link between football participation, talent development and excellence. Several studies have also demonstrated that availability of facilities in schools, parks and communities is associated with physical activity engagement which can be advantageous to talent development (*Huston* et al. 2003; *Humpel* et al. 2002; *Kahn* et al. 2002). The mere availability of facilities can therefore reinforce talent growth and development (*Cohen* et al. 2006). For instance, *De Bosscher & De Knop* (2002) showed that the number of tennis courts was highly correlated with international success of nations in tennis. Notable studies that demonstrate a positive relationship between training facilities/centres and national sporting performance include *Krüger* 1984; *Wells* 1991; *Clumpner* 1994; *Larose & Haggerty* 1996; *Green & Oakley* 2001; *Dufy* et al. 2001; *Nys* et al. 2002; *De Bosscher & De Knop* 2002; *Gibbons* et al. 2003; *van Bottenburg* 2003; *De Bosscher* et al. 2004; *Green & Houlihan* 2005 – all in *De Bosscher* et al. 2006.

3. Methods and Data

3.1 Data Sources

Football data was sourced from www.FIFA.com, Asia Football Confederation (www.the-afc.com), and world stadiums (www.worldstadiums.com) while economics data was derived from the Asian Development Bank (www.adb.org), the Organization for Economic Corporation & Development (www.oecd.org), and Economic Intelligence Unit (www.eiu.com). Content analysis of the various reports published by the above organizations were also reviewed.

3.2 Measurement Variables

Independent variables the two independent variables were; GDP per capita & number of stadiums. GDP per capita is gross domestic product divided by midyear population and given here in current US dollars (*OECD* 2013). GDP per capita has been used by other studies such as *Johnson & Ali* 2004; *Kuper & Sterken* (2003); *Hoffman* et al. 2002b.

Dependent variables was qualification measured as binary categorical variables such that 0=not qualified and 1=qualified for the Asia Cup in 2011.

Control variables Possible confounding factors that affect national football achievement were controlled for. Hosting history was measured as a binary categorical variable such that 0=never hosted and 1=hosted the Asia Cup tournament. Similar indicators have been previously used by *Johnson & Ali* 2002; *Kuper & Sterken* 2003. Data from the Asian tournament itself demonstrate that hosting tends to 'boost' potential success.

3.3 Logistic Regression Analysis

Logistic regression is useful in developing explanatory models for buying behaviour, fund performance, credit risk analysis, landslide susceptibility and financial/bankruptcy predictions. These models allow the assessment of how well a set of predictor variables predicts or explains a categorical dependent variable (outcome or target variable) by providing an indication of the relative importance of and interaction between predictor variable/s. The logistic regression can either be binary or multinomial. This study uses binary logistic regression analysis. According to *Verma* (2013), the advantage of binary logistic regression lies in its robustness as the independent variables do not have to be normally distributed or have equal variance in each group. Additionally, the independent variables are not required to be lineally related with the dependent variable nor need not follow normal distribution and the assumption of homoscedacity is not required.

Binary logistic regression is a useful statistical technique for developing a predictive model for events that are binary in nature (*Verma* 2013). It is used in situations when the dependent variable is categorical (e.g. win/lose; fail/pass; dead/alive). In this study, binary logistic regression was used to predict the presence or absence of the outcome (qualifying or not qualifying) based on valued of a set of predictor variables such as GDP per capita and number of stadiums while controlling for home advantage. Statistical explanations of Logit, Logistic function and logistic regression equation now follow:

The logit is a function which is equal to the log odds of a variable. If p is a probability that Y 1(occurrence of an event), then p/(1 p) is the corresponding odds. The logit of the probability p is given by,

$$\text{Logit}(p) \; \frac{p}{1-p} \qquad (3:3:1)$$

In logistic regression, logit is special case of a link function as it serves as a dependent variable which is estimated from the model (*Verma* 2013: 417).

In a logistic function, the shape of the curve is like a letter "S" with the argument z marked along horizontal axis and the value of the function f(z) along the vertical axis thus according to *Verma* (2013: 417):

$$p f(z) \frac{e^z}{1+e^z} \quad (3:3:2)$$

The main feature of this logistic function is that the variable Z can assume any value from minus ∞ to + ∞, but the outcome variable p can only have values in the 0–1 range. This function is used in logistic regression model to find the probability of occurring the target variable for a given value of independent variables.

Logistic regression equation is written as

$$\text{In}[p/(1- p)] = \beta_0 + \beta_1 X_1 + \beta_2 X_2 + \ldots\ldots \beta_k X_k \quad (3:3:3)$$

where β_0 is the intercept and β_1, β_2....β_n are the regression coefficients of X_1, X_2... X_n respectively. The dependent variable in the logistic regression is log odds, which is also known as logit.

4. Results

4.1 Descriptive Statistics

Table 4.1 represents descriptive statistics of the study variables. The results reveal that the average GDP per capita was 14,372.5 and a maximum of 90,523.5 with a standard deviation of 2171. The minimum number of stadiums was 1, maximum was 141 and a mean of 25. Number of times nations hosting was relatively evenly distributed with the most hosting 2 times, majority never hosting before (24 of the nations have never hosted while 13 have).

Table 4.1: Descriptive Statistics

	N	Minimum	Maximum	Mean	Std. Deviation
GDP per capita	37	6196	905235	143725	21712
Stadiums	37	10	1410	25649	324664
Hosting	37	0	20	25	4840

4.2 Regression Results

Direct Logistic regression was performed to assess the impact of GDP per capita, stadiums, and home field advantage on qualification for the 2011 Asia cup. The model contained 3 dependent variables (GDP per capita, number of stadiums, and whether or not the nation has hosted before). The full model contained all predictors and was statistically significant, c^2 (3, N = 37)= 76.02, P < .001, indicating that the model was able to predict who qualifies for the Asia Cup. The model as whole explained between 26% (Cox & Snell square) and 34.7% (Nagelkerke R squared) of the variance in qualification status, and correctly classified 75.7% of the cases. As shown in table 4.1, only 1 of the variables made a unique statistical significant contribution to the model (home-field advantage). The strongest predictor of qualifying was home-field advantage, recording an odds ratio of 13.021. This indicated that nations that hosted the Asia cup were 13 times more likely to qualify than those who didn't, controlling for all other factors in the model. The odds ratio for GDP per capita and stadiums was 1, indicating that every stadium and additional increase in GDP per capita, nations were less likely to qualify for the Asia Cup, controlling for other factors in the model.

Table 4.2: Logistic regression predicting likely hood of qualifying for Asia Cup

	B	S.E.	Wald	df	Sig.	Exp(B)	95% C.I. for EXP(B)	
							Lower	Upper
Hosting	2567	1144	5030	1	25	13021	1382	122657
Stadiums	2	16	12	1	912	1002	971	1034
GDP per capita	0	0	5	1	945	1000	1000	1000
Constant	-901	567	2524	1	112	406		

5. Discussions and Conclusions

The study explored how GDP per capita, stadiums and hosting influenced qualifying for the Asia Cup football tournament. In the analysis, of 37 Asian nations, the results showed that GDP per capita and stadiums were not significantly related to qualifying for the 2011 Asia Cup tournament. However, hosting was statistically significant in qualifying for the Asia cup. This could be explained by two factors: one – nations that host the Asia cup are usually accorded a direct qualification batch. Secondly, once a nation gets the hosting rights other advantages relating to hosting fall into place. These include social, psychological, and physiological benefits such as the performance boost of playing amongst friends, environmental familiarity and associated motivational crowd support (*Armatas & Pollard* 2012). Furthermore, hosting rights also generally boost stadium construction.

As highlighted by *Johnson & Ali* 2004, nations with high GDP per capita generally tend to succeed more at international sporting events as compared to economically disadvantaged ones. However, the link between GDP per capita can only be explained if individual nations take the concerted effort to choose to invest in football infrastructure such as stadiums and also host football tournaments. One example here is Qatar, who for the last decade have decided to invest heavily in football and has realized a slow increase in national football ranking and football tournament hosting.

Lastly, even with more stadiums, nations still have to organize competitive domestic tournaments in order to improve overall local quality of play. One example here is India which may have chosen to focus on Cricket facilities and not football as the latter is the national game. The results have important implications for understanding the combined link with football facilities and stadiums. For nations that have the economic capacity, a gradual local investment in stadiums followed by local football tournaments may go a long way to later qualifying for international football tournaments such as the Asia Cup.

References

Armatas, V. & Pollard, R. (2012): Home Advantage in Greek Football, in: European Journal of Sport Science, DOI: 10.1080/17461391.2012.736537.

Asia development bank (ADB): Various reports, http://www.adb.org/data/statistics (accessed 2014-2-04).

Asian Football Confederation (2013): http://www.the-afc.com/en/afc-asian-cup-home.html (accessed 2014-2-04).

Bernard, A. & Busse, M. (2000): Who wins the Olympic games? Economic Development and Medal Totals, in: The Review of Economics and Statistics, Vol. 86, 1, pp. 413–417.

Bray, S. R., Law, J. & Foyle, J. (2003): Team quality and game location in English professional soccer, in: Journal of Sport Behavior, Vol. 26, 4, pp. 319–334.

Carmichael, F. & Thomas, D. (2005): Home-field effect and team performance. Evidence from English premiership football, in: Journal of Sports Economics, Vol. 6, 3, pp. 264–281.

Clumpner, R. A. (1994): 21st century success in international competitions, in *Wilcox R.* (ed.): Sports in the global village, Morgantown: WV: FIT, pp. 298–303.

Cohen, D., Sehgal, A., Williamson, S., Strum, R., McKenzie, T. L., Lara, R., & Lurie, N. (2006): Park use and physical activity in a sample of public parks in the city of Loss Angeles, Santa Monica: RAND.

Condon, E., Golden, B. & Wasil, E. (1999): Predicting the success of nations at the summer Olympic using neural networks, in: Computer Operations Research, Vol. 26, pp. 1243–1265.

De Bosscher, V., De Knop, P. & Heyndels, B. (2003): Comparing relative sporting success among countries: create equal opportunity in sport, in: Journal of Comparative Physical Education & Sport, Vol. 3, 3, pp. 109–120.

De Bosscher, V., De Knop, P., van Bottenburg, M. & Leblicq, S. (2004): Why the Netherlands are successful and Belgium is not? A comparison of the elite sports climate and policies, Proceedings of the 12th congress of the European Association for Sport Management Belgium: Ghent, pp. 239–241.

De Bosscher, V., Knop, P., Bottenburg, M. & Shibli, S. (2006): A conceptual framework for analysing sports policy factors leading to international sporting success, in: European Sport Management Quarterly, Vol. 6, 2, pp. 185–215.

De Bosscher, V. & De Knop, P. (2002): Sport policy factors determining international success in tennis: the opinion of international tennis coaches, Working Paper No. 2002–09, Büssel: Vrije Universität Brüssel.

De Koning, J. & Olieman, R. (1996): Doubts about medal euphoria, in: Economische Statische Berichte, Vol. 2, pp. 813–815.

Den Butter, F. A. & Van der Tak, C. M. (1995): Olympic medals as an indicator of social welfare, in: Social Indicators Reasearch, Vol. 35, 1, pp. 27–37.

Duffy, P., Lyons, D., Moran, A., Warrington, G. & Macmanus, C. (2001): Factors promoting and inhibiting the success of high performance players and athletes in Ireland, Ireland: National Coaching and Training Centre.

FIFA (1980–2010): Various reports, www.FIFA.com (accessed 2014-2-04).

Garcia, M. S., Aguilar, O. Marques, P., Tobio, G. T. & Romero, J. F. (2013): Calculating home advantage in the first decade of the 21st century UEFA Soccer leagues, in: Journal of Human Kinetics, Vol. 30, 38, pp. 141–150.

Gartner, M. (1989): Socialist countries sporting success before perestroika-and after?, in: International Review for the Sociology of Sport, Vol. 24, 4, pp. 283–297.

Gibbons, T., McConnell, A., Forster, T., Riewald, S. & Peterson, K. (2003): Reflections on success. US Olympians describe the success factors and obstacles that most influenced their Olympic development, in: USOC report phase II, p. 48.

Gillis, J. (1980): Olympic success and national religious orientation, in: Review of Sport & Leisure, Vol. 5, pp. 1–20.

Green, M. & Houlihan, B. (2005): Elite sport development: Policy learning and political priorities, New York: Routledge.

Green, M. & Oakley, B. (2001): Elite sport development systems and playing to win: uniformity and diversity in international approaches, in: Leisure Studies, 20, 4, pp. 247–267.

Grimes, A., Kelly, W. & Rubin, P. (1974): A social-economic model of national Olympic performance, in: Social Science Quarterly, Vol. 55, pp. 777–782.

Hoffmann, R., Chew, L. & Ramasamy, B. (2002a): Public policy and Olympic success, in: Applied Economics Letters, Vol. 9, 8, pp. 545–548.

Hoffmann, R., Lee, C. & Ramasamy, B. (2002b): The socio-econmic determinants of international soccer performance, in: Journal of Applied Economics, Vol. 5, 2, pp. 253–72.

Humpel, N., Owen, N. & Leslie, E. (2002): Environmental factors associated with adult's participation in physical activity, in: American Journal of Preventative Medicine, Vol. 22, 3, pp. 188–199.

Huston, S. L., Evenson, K. R., Bors, P. & Gizlice, Z. (2003): Neighborhood environment, access to places for activity, and leisure-time physical activity in a diverse North Carolina population, in: American Journal of Health Promotion, Vol. 18, 1, pp. 58–69.

Jacklin, P. B. (2005): Temporal changes in home advantage in English football since the Second World War: What explains improved away performance?, in: Journal of Sports Sciences, Vol. 23, 7, pp. 669–679.

Johnson, D. K. N. & *Ali, A.* (2000): Coming to play or coming to win: participation and success at the Olympic games, Wellesley College Working Paper No. 2000–10, Colorado Springs: Colorado College – Department of Economics and Business.

Johnson, D. K.N. & Ali, A. (2004): A tale of two seasons: Participation and medal counts at the summer and Winter Olympic Games, in: Social Science Quarterly, Vol. 85, 4, pp. 976–993.

Johnson, D. K. N. & Ali, A. (2002): A tale of two seasons. Participation and medal counts at the summer and winter Olympic Games, Wellesley College Working Paper No. 2002–02, Colorado Springs: Colorado College – Department of Economics and Business.
Jokl, E. (1964): Health, wealth, and athletics, in: *Simin, E.* (ed.): International research in sports and physical education, Springfield: IL. Thomas, pp. 218–222.
Kahn, E. B., Ramsey, L. T., Brownson, R. C., Heath, G. W., Howze, E. H. & Powell, K. E., Stone, E. J., Rajab, M. W., Corso, P. & The Task Force on Community Preventive Services (2002): The effectiveness of interventions to increase physical activity. A systematic review, in: American Journal of Preventive Medicine, Vol. 22, 4, pp. 73–107.
Kiviaho, P. & Makela, P. (1978): Olympic success: A sum of non-material and material factors, in: International Review of Sport Sociology, Vol. 13, 2, pp. 5–17.
Krüger, A. (1984): To Moscow and back: international status of competitive research in regard to physical activity outside of schools, in: *Haag, H.* (ed.): Comparative Physical Education and Sport, Bd. 4, Champaign, Ill.: Human Kinetics, pp. 213–228.
Kuper, G. H. & Sterken, E. (2003): Olympic participation and performance since 1896, Research Report No. 03C19, Groningen: Graduate School: Research Institute Systems, Organisations and Management, University of Groningen.
Lago, C. & Martin, R. (2007): Determinants of possession of the ball in soccer, in: Journal of Sports Sciences, Vol. 25, 9, pp. 969–974.
Larose, K. & Haggerty, T. R. (1996): Factors associated with national Olympic success. An exploratory study. Unpublished Master's Thesis, Canada: University of Brunswick.
Levine, N (1974): Why do countries win Olympic medals – some structural correlates of Olympic Games success?, in: Sociology & Social Research, Vol. 58, 4, pp. 353–360.
Lieberman, M. & Montgomery, B. (1998): First-Mover (Dis)Advantages: Retrospective and Link with the Resource-Based View, in: Strategic Management Journal, Vol. 19, 12, pp. 1111–1125.
Moosa, I. & Smith, L. (2004): Economic development indicators as determinants of medal winning at the Sydney Olympics. An extreme bounded analysis, in: Australian Economic Papers, Vol. 43, 3, pp. 288–301.
Morton, H. (2002): Who won the Sydney Olympics? An allometric approach, in: The Statistician, Vol. 51, 2, pp. 147–155.
Neave, N. & Wolfson, S. (2003): Testosterone territoriality, and the 'home advantage', in: Physiological and Behavior, Vol. 78, 2, pp. 269–75.
Novikov, A. D. & Maximenko, A. M. (1972): The influence of selected socio-economic factors on the level of sports achievements in the various countries, in: International Review of Sports Sociology, Vol. 7, 1, 27–44.
Nys, K., De Knop, P. & De Bosscher, V. (2002): Factors determining international success in elite sports. Unpublished Masters Thesis, Belgium: Vrije University, Brüssel.
Ochieng, P. (2012): Rule of three. How resources separate winners from losses at the Africa Cup of Nations. Accepted at the World Football Conference II, Melbourne, Australia.
OECD (2013): Organization for Economic Corporation & development, www.econdata.com/databases/oecd/mei (accessed 2014-2-04).
Pollard, R. & Gomez, M. (2009): Home advantage in football in South-West Europe: Long-term trends, regional variation, and team differences, in: European Journal of Sport Science, Vol. 9, 6, pp. 341–352.
Poulter, D. R. (2009): Home advantage and player nationality in international club football, in: Journal of Sports Sciences, Vol. 27, 8, pp. 797–805.

Seckin, A. & Pollard, R. (2008): Home advantage in Turkish professional soccer, in: Perceptual and Motor Skills, Vol. 107, 1, pp. 51–54.
Shaw, S. & Pooley, J. (1976): National success at the Olympics: an explanation, in: *Lessard, C., Massicotte, J. P. & Leduc, E.* (eds.): Proceedings of the 6th international seminar: history of physical education and sport, Trois Rivieres: Quebec, pp. 1–27.
Smart, D. & Wolfe, R. (2000): Examining sustainable competitive advantage in intercollegiate athletics: a resource-based view, in: Journal of Sport Management, Vol. 14, 2, pp. 133–153.
Stamm, H. & Lamprecht, M. (2000): An international comparison of Swiss high level sport: an empirical analysis of the Olympic Games, 1964–1998. Zürich: Studendruckerei Uni Zürich.
Suen, W. (1992): Men, money and medals: an analysis of the Olympic Games, Discussion Paper, Hong Kong: University of Hong Kong.
Tcha, M. & Perchin, V. (2003): Reconsidering performance at the summer Olympic and revealed comparative advantage, in: Journal of Sports Economics, Vol. 4, 3, pp. 216–239.
Thomas, S., Reeves, C. & Davies, S. (2004): An analysis of home advantage in the English football premiership, in: Perceptual & Motor Skills, Vol. 99, pp. 1212–1216.
Tucker W, Mellalieu, D., James, N. & Taylor, J. B. (2005): Game location effects in professional soccer: a case study, in: International Journal of Performance Analysis in Sports, Vol. 5, 2, pp. 23–35.
Van Bottenburg, M. (2000): The elite sports climate in the Netherlands, Hertogenbosch: Dioper-Janssens and van Botternberg bv.
Verma, P. (2013): Data analysis in management with SPSS Software, New Delhi: Springer, pp. 413–442.
Wells, H. J. C. (1991): Developing sporting excellence in Hong Kong, in: Journal of Comparative Physical Education & Sport, Vol. 1, pp. 28–34.

The Economics of Sports Events

The Winner's Curse in Sports Economics

Wladimir Andreff

Abstract

A sports entity often maximizes its monopoly rent in creating an auction-like situation among competing agents for its exclusive product. The latter overbid up to the most optimistic bidder's price. Here comes the winner's curse whenever the market value of the auctioned object is unknown ex ante. The most optimistic bidder wins the bid and its actual net revenues will be lower than expected. A winner's curse occurs in bids for hosting a mega-sporting event, when several cities compete to host a team franchise, TV channels bid for a league's broadcasting rights, and teams overbid for recruiting a same free agent or superstar player.

Keywords

winner's curse, auction bid, cost overruns, asymmetric information, sports economics.

1. What Is the Winner's Curse All About?

In any auction-type setting where the value of the auctioned object is uncertain but will turn out to be the same for all bidders, the party that overestimates the value of the object is likely to outbid its competitors and win the contest. This defines a common value auction[1] where the item to be sold has a single objective value for all bidders, but this true value is unknown. Each bidder has to guess the item's true value at the time of bidding on basis of the information that is available, and without knowing the other's guesses. The items won are more often than not those whose value has been overestimated. The winner's curse occurs in common value auctions when bidders fail to account for the fact that the winner's valuation of the object is an upward-biased estimate of its true (unknown) value. The auction winner is cursed by having paid more for investing in an item than its true value. Thus, there is some adverse selection in this outcome, and the bidding process results in wins that produce below-normal or even negative returns, contrary to a

---

1 A common value auction must be distinguished from a private value auction where each player's valuation is independent of those of the other bidders. In such auctions, the bidder cannot extract any information about its own value from the valuations of the other players. At the time of the bidding, each bidder knows exactly what winning would be worth to him/her, but does not know what it would be worth to the others.

rational investment decision. *Thaler* (1994) stresses the asymmetric information across bidders, which leads to an extreme form of the winner's curse in which even any positive bid yields an expected financial loss to the winner. Moreover, an increase in the number of bidders implies that to win a common value auction, the bid must be more aggressive. The degree of a winner's overbid and hence the magnitude of its loss generally rises with the number of bidders. Yet the presence of more bidders also increases the chance that the winner will have overestimated the value of the auctioned object.

1.1 Four Variants of the Winner's Curse

The winner's curse hypothesis was first advanced by *Capen* et al. (1971) to explain the low returns on investments to companies engaged in competitive bidding for oil and gas leases. The impression was that winners had paid too high a price for oil and gas leases (*Gilley* et al. 1986); they had been cursed. Indeed, they paid an auction price higher than any likely market price and they bore too high a cost to be recouped by the revenues of their investment. This is the core example of the winner's curse.

A second variant, the most widespread in economic literature, is rooted in financial markets (*Kagel & Levin* 2002). For instance, the winner's curse assumption is utilised to explain the share value underestimation in initial public offerings and the positive initial returns earned by investors on newly issued equities (*Levis* 1990). When going alongside with non transparent information about the risks involved in the issuance of new financial products (derivatives, CDOs, CMOs, etc.), followed with securitisation, this second variant of the winner's curse combines with a third one – the sale of 'lemons' – in providing new insights about the current financial crisis (*Andreff* 2013). The second variant can hardly apply to sports objects.

A third variant of the winner's curse has been found in second-hand markets, primarily in the market for 'lemons'. *Akerlof* (1970) has demonstrated that in a context of information asymmetry the market mechanism leads to adverse selection and the purchaser is cursed. When information about quality is scarce and asymmetric, namely as regards a player's talent, this third variant of the winner's curse makes sense in sports economics.

A last variant of the winner's curse fits with a public choice approach. The winner is cursed after deliberately underestimating the cost – and/or overestimating the outcome – of a public investment decision. Winning the bid to get those resources allocated by a central body to decentralised operators or producers, the winner will pay the price of its initial cost underestimation with long-lasting cost overruns. Such typical overbidding processes have plagued for decades the former centrally planned economies (CPEs) that allocated a national centralised investment fund across state-owned enterprises (*Dyker* 1983). A central planning agency was standing in a monopoly position for supplying investment funds through an auction-like process while decentralised enterprises were overbidding each other for obtaining these funds.

Due to information asymmetry about investment projects – each project was well-known by the applying enterprise, not by the central planners -, the whole auctioning process regularly led to enterprise 'cheating' on information about their production capacity, overinvestment (excess fund allocation), adverse selection of investment projects and unexpectedly long completion duration of selected projects. Since information was asymmetric, enterprises applying for investment funds were incited to 'cheat' through underestimating their actual costs, and overestimating their actual returns. The winner's curse lies therein. The applicant enterprise that wins the bid due to overbidding based on such under/overestimation is cursed: due to informational cheating, it has submitted an infeasible project and, in practice, it will not be able to complete it within the deadline, and at ex ante announced costs/benefits.

For each investment project k a discounted net benefit (its social profitability) was calculated by the enterprise as:

$$B_k = \sum_{t=0}^{N} \frac{R_{kt} - c_{kt}}{(1+a)^t}$$

where R_{kt} stands for all revenues derived from the investment over its lifetime (from t = 0 to N), C_{kt} stands for all investment costs ($C_{kt} = C_0 + C_t + C_{ft}$ with C_0 the initial investment cost, C_t the cost of all further annual investment 'slices' in the case of a multiannual investment, and C_{ft} the operational cost of the equipment over its lifetime) and a is the national discount rate fixed by the central planners. Cheating on investment projects tended to be the rule rather than the exception in CPEs (*Kornaï* 1980; *Andreff* 1993) because:

- enterprises announced an investment cost c_k for project k and not the actual cost C_k, with $c_k < C_k$, in order to augment their chance of obtaining investment funding from the planners.
- enterprises declared very optimistic – often fully unrealistic – completion duration for project k; Soviet economies were famous for their unfinished investment building sites resulting from unattainable completion duration.
- enterprises anticipated overestimated revenue from investment: $r_k > R_k$, with r_k the ex ante announced revenues and R_k the actual ex post revenues.

A consequence of investment cost underestimation and investment revenue overestimation is that the social profitability of an investment project k sent by an enterprise to the planners was higher than its real social profitability: bk > Bk.

Since all enterprises adopted such strategic behaviour, the central planners were confused, and unable to make rational decisions about how and to whom to allocate the national investment fund. Facing a myriad of fabulous investment projects, planners had a tendency to inflate the number of financed projects. Indeed, all the projects submitted to planners were unrealistic, exhibiting an extraordinary social profitability, unbelievably low costs and a very short completion time. Adverse selection was the most common outcome and inefficient or low-efficiency investment projects were financed. Enterprises more often cheated by underestimating costs and completion duration than overestimating investment revenues.

Various sporting objects are allocated through auctions or an auction-like process in a context of information asymmetry across the bidders that face a sporting entity with a monopoly over these objects. In such circumstances, the winner's curse is likely to occur and materialise in financial loss.

1.2 The Winner's Curse Eventually Expresses the Monopoly Power of a Sports Entity

When the winner's curse is simply understood as resulting from irrational overbidding behaviour across the bidders, it is comprehended as a demand-side triggered phenomenon. In the sports industry, it happens that several TV channels are eager to broadcast a same sport event while just one sport team, league or federation is the only supplier. Then for TV channels there is no other way out than overbidding to obtain the broadcasting rights held by a monopoly; here the winner's curse is generated by a supply-side behaviour. If several sport teams are willing to recruit a same player, they have to trade off between abandoning any claim and overbidding the claims of competing teams. Again the winner's curse materialises a typical supply-side monopolistic behaviour. One implication of a monopolistic supply (which may even be a global monopoly, think of the IOC or FIFA) is that, on the demand side for an auctioned object, there must be more than one bidder for the winner's curse to occur. If there were only one candidate city applying to host the Olympics, the winner's curse could not occur; while as soon as there is more than one candidate, they have to overbid each other. In North American team sports leagues, if a team faced only one municipality eager to host its games, no way for the winner's curse; but if at least another one municipality would like to host the same team, then the latter is in a monopoly position and can fuel an overbidding process between the two cities.

In an auction or auction-like process, the interaction between two series of asymmetries is crucial for the occurrence of the winner's curse and its consequences such as overpricing, cost overruns, adverse selection, delayed project completion, and financial loss: first an asymmetry in the number of traders on both market sides with just one seller and several purchasers and, second, information asymmetry between the seller and purchasers as well as across the latter. At the end of the day, it is always a single sporting actor on the supply side which uses its monopoly power[2] to play demanders against each other, thus compelling them to overbid. Therefore, the winner's curse always ends up with an overpriced purchase for the winner since this price contains a monopoly rent[3] and is higher than equilibrium price in a free competitive market.

To sum up, to witness the winner's curse occurring in the sports industry requires: a/ a monopoly position of a sports entity over the supply of a sporting object[4]; b/ several rather aggressive demanders of this object, but not too many so that an auction(-like) process can easily be organised by the sporting monopoly (the demand side is oligopsonistic); c/ a common value auction where the true value of the sporting object is unknown to all bidders; d/ as a consequence of a and b, the market structure in which occurs the winner's curse is an oligopsonistic monopoly; e/ information and power asymmetries between the sporting monopoly and potential bidders; f/ information asymmetries across the bidders leading one of them to be the most optimistic and outbid the others; g/ information asymmetry across the bidders often pertains to the quality of the supplied sporting object even without a cheating behaviour of the sports entity – just like in a market for 'lemons'.

1.3 How to Verify the Very Existence of the Winner's Curse?

A major difficulty with the winner's curse concept is to test its very existence. The most common effect for a cursed winner is that it will actually pay ex post much more than expected ex ante, and lose money. Some sorts of cost overrun or

---

2 As *Vrooman* (1996) puts it: "Information asymmetries create the bias [the winner's curse] only because the auction process exists in a monopoly environment".

3 In an auction process with overbidding, bidders themselves determine the level of the monopoly rent through their repeatedly increased reservation prices, contrary to textbook monopoly behaviour where the monopolist shortens quantities in supply in view of raising its supply price.

4 *Vrooman* (2000) correctly stresses that, in the case of the winner's curse, information asymmetry is a necessary, but not a sufficient condition for the overbidding.

overpricing are always simple and general indices of the winner's curse: a city hosting the Olympics exhibits a local cost significantly higher than announced in the candidature file; a municipality subsidises a host team so much that this jeopardises its public finance, drifting toward an increase in local taxes; a TV company pays an excess price for broadcasting rights which undermines its financial balance or even its own existence; overpaying some players, a team loses control over its payroll, and its salary cost overruns drive its accounts into the red. One can infer from the different below-described cases of the winner's curse some indices that would enable to spot its existence resulting from the auction for hosting mega-sporting events, a professional sports team franchise, acquiring broadcasting rights, and those players in high demand.

In any case, the most convincing proof of the winner's curse would be to check that a significant negative difference is observed between ex ante and ex post net social outcome of a mega-sporting event (host team, TV rights, player) in comparing the results of an ex ante and an ex post cost–benefit analyses of a same sporting event (host team, etc.). Unexpectedly higher net social cost or lower net social benefit would confirm the winner's curse hypothesis that is if ex post net social cost is significantly higher than ex ante net social cost or if ex post net social benefit is significantly lower than ex ante net social benefit. A major difficulty with this criterion is that an ex post cost-benefit analysis usually is not available or published after hosting each mega-sporting event (hosting a team, paying TV rights fees, player recruitment). Hence, proxies are required; they are listed with the four types of the winner's curse surveyed below.

2. Bidding to Host a Mega-Sporting Event: the Winner's Cost Overruns

There is some similarities between a centralised auction for investment funds in a CPE and the functioning of the auction whereby the Olympics are allocated to a bidding city (*Andreff* 2012b). With the Olympics, the IOC publicises the task of hosting and organising the next Games within a precise deadline then it calls for projects proposals. These proposals are not applications for IOC funding; rather, cities are candidates for raising funds from different sources in order to cover the cost of those investments required to host the Games. At the end of an auction, which usually takes several years, the IOC allocates the right to host the Olympics to the most interesting city project. However, the fact that the object of such an auction is not to obtain finance allocated by the IOC but to win the status of being the next host city of the Olympics does not reduce the risk of a winner's curse. A city that wants to host the Games commits itself to a heavy investment over a six- to seven-year period and then hopes to benefit from the 'Olympics host city' label which provides a unique capacity for collecting and mobilising finance.

2.1 Candidate Cities Actually (though Inadvertently) Bid for Cost Overruns

The objective of the IOC, in a monopoly position to allocate the Games, is to elect every fourth year a host city for the Summer Olympics and the Winter Olympics with the expectation that bidding cities will provide projects including all the required facilities and commit themselves to adhering to an operational budget, which is a minimal precondition for a city to be selected. A complementary objective certainly is the best possible quality of the Games which consists of a guarantee of well-functioning and secure sports contests (quality of sporting equipment, distance between Olympic venues and the Olympic village, and so on), an excellent hosting quality (Olympic village, transportation, hotels), overall security, impressive opening and closing ceremonies, high-quality media and telecommunications and, nowadays, an environmental quality, all prerequisites according to the 20 chapters contained in a candidature file. Thus, if the IOC is maximising something, it is the overall quality of the project which must benefit from worldwide media coverage, leave a grandiose image of each Olympiad, and an unforgettable memory and indelible marks on the host city landscape. With a view to obtaining a grandiose project, it is in the IOC's interest to pave the way for or even fuel overbidding across bidding cities. This is what it clearly started to do after the single candidature of Los Angeles for the 1984 Olympics.

It is more than likely that the cost of the Olympics is not a decisive criterion in the voting of the 104 IOC members. Furthermore, the criterion of minimal cost to some extent clashes with maximising the desired extravagant quality of the Games. A proof of such a contention is that the IOC often selects the most expensive rather than the cheapest project (see Table 4.1 in *Andreff* 2012b), which means both adverse selection in terms of cost, and that the winner's curse is at work.

The objective function of bidding cities is crystal clear and consists in obtaining the right to host the Games. Therefore, each bidding city must promise fixed quantities of sporting facilities requested by the IOC and a variable quantity of non-sporting infrastructure, focusing on their excellent quality since it will be selected or not on these aspects of its candidature. Before Montreal 1976, investment cost and the LOOC[5] operational budget did not matter that much. Since then, and after Los Angeles 1984 demonstrated that the LOOC can end up in the black, the cost dimension of candidatures has become much more significant, though not the major decision criterion of IOC voters.

The primary interest of bidding cities is to maximise (and focus on) the qualitative components of their candidature, thereby encouraging ambitious project proposals. After 1984, bidding cities started to take an interest in also demonstrating reasonable or even low costs in parallel with the supposedly unbelievable quality of their candidature. The only way to reconcile an extravagant project with costs that are not exorbitant is, explicitly or implicitly, to cheat, that is, to communicate and to complete the candidature file on the basis of costs that are underestimated by different means (omitting the VAT, lowering the Paralympics budget, and so on). All in all, it is in the interest of the bidding cities to overbid upward with respect to the quality and downward with respect to the publicised cost of their project. Such a strategy compares with that of rival enterprises struggling for the allocation of investment funds in a CPE except that cities are seeking to be awarded the Games, because it is a precondition for mobilising the enormous financing necessary for hosting the Olympics. Thus, rival bidding cities are in sync with the principal objective of the IOC, which is to balance outward extravagance with the appearance of reasonable cost, but the host city is cursed.

The parallel with enterprises in CPEs cannot exactly be extended to the completion duration of investments since this was mandatory, but almost never met, in Soviet- type planning. Yet, the completion duration is mandatory and cannot be circumvented in hosting the Olympics – it is not feasible to hold Olympic sports contests if the stadium is not completed – but the IOC's recurrent worries about delayed Olympic building sites can be used as a control variable of the winner's curse. Building delays usually generate cost overruns when it comes to rushing in order to stick to the deadline. Revising building costs upwards (thus revealing the initial cost underestimation) or giving up some Olympic building to curb skyrocketing costs are also relevant signs of the winner's curse.

Another revealing factor is when the LOOC or the host city obtains extra finance or extra public subsidies, for instance, from the government. A financial deficit or an ex post lower financial surplus than expected by the LOOC provides further proof of the winner's curse while a sanction of the latter is a bidding city budget deficit which must be covered with a specific post-Olympics taxation.

5 Local Olympic organisation committee.

Information asymmetry is crucial in the genesis of the winner's curse. A bidding city knows its candidature project down to the tiniest detail, so it is able to communicate in such a way as to emphasise specific aspects of the file, in particular its supposedly extraordinary quality. In contrast, this in-depth knowledge of the candidature file allows the bidding city promoters to play down those less exciting characteristics of the project, namely excessive costs, stark security issues, negative externalities and a possible crowding-out effect. An economic impact study is instrumental in highlighting the best features and blurring the lesser ones. The IOC cannot have a similar in-depth knowledge (information) about each bidding city project and cannot control how accurate or fallacious is the information delivered in the application file, namely about actual costs, externalities, and so on. The Olympic site visits by the IOC representatives are not enough to compensate for information asymmetry between bidding city promoters and the IOC voters.

The allocation of the FIFA World Cup is also plagued with the winner's curse although *Sturgess & Brady* (2006) contend that evidence is rather mixed. However, *Preuss & Schnitzer* (2013) underline that the budgets of local organisation committees (LOC) are used as a strategic bidding tool; again given an asymmetrical availability of information, FIFA faces an adverse selection problem. The LOC conceals certain facts (the real costs of staging the World Cup) from FIFA until the hosting agreement is signed. Thus, the bidding committees strategically underestimate their LOC budgets and meet financial problems after being awarded the World Cup, as was the case in South Africa 2010. Bidding committees face a dilemma because they have to offer FIFA a good (often too low) LOC budget to look more attractive than other candidates. This dilemma translates into a winner's curse for the LOC that outbids the others.

2.2 Indices of the Winner's Curse in a Bid to Host a Mega-Sporting Event

A series of indices has been featured for verifying the existence of the winner's curse with regards to cities bidding to host a mega-sporting event (*Andreff* 2012b):

1. Cost overruns: A difference between ex ante cost in the candidature file and ex post cost reached on the sporting event's opening day or later exhibits the winner's curse. Given that over a period of six or seven years between the allocation and the opening of a mega-sporting event there is some inflation in any country and that upward cost revisions happen at a more or less clearly defined date and are usually published in current prices, one can accept as a proof consistent with an existing winner's curse a difference of at least 30 per cent between ex post actual and ex ante anticipated cost. The data to be found are the initial cost in the candidature file, the actual cost at the moment of the opening

ceremony and, if one can circumvent data paucity, the actual final cost overall. The example of cost overruns in all the Summer Olympics but one – Los Angeles 1984 when there was just one candidate city and thus neither overbidding nor a winner's curse – is exhibited in Appendix 1.

2. Ex post revisions in the mega sporting event's project: A second index can be used when some significant revisions occur in the project of a mega-sporting event between the dates of allocation and opening ceremony. For example, the appearance of a new building in the project which was not included in the candidature file is an explicit index of an initial cost underestimation. Similarly, an upward revision of expenditures linked to one sporting facility or non-sporting infrastructure project can also reveal the existence of the winner's curse. Or, when a building that was planned in the candidature file happens to be cancelled, this also reveals an initial cost underestimation: due to the latter the bill skyrocketed and the host city has no other way to curb cost overruns than by giving up some building described in the candidature file.
3. Delayed completion of a required investment: The completion dates of different sporting facilities required by the event which are mentioned in the candidature file simply cannot be missed. Thus, a delayed completion of such investment merely translates into a time lag between expected and actual completion dates, and in a subsequent final rush in the last weeks before the opening ceremony to complete the unfinished building. A final rush at the very last minute always inflates the actual investment cost.
4. Extra public subsidy or extra public finance: If the cost of hosting a mega-sporting event was initially underestimated, one way out for local organisers and the host city is to bargain and obtain additional public finance or an extra subsidy, for instance from the government or from some regional authority.
5. Host city fiscal deficit and debt: When the extra cost of the mega-sporting event project results in a heavy financial burden for the host city its budget plunges into a fiscal deficit and a public debt that has to be repaid over time. The same index may register the transformation of ex ante local organisers' surplus into ex post deficit.
6. A disappointing number of 'foreign' visitors: When the number of 'foreign' (that is, coming from outside the host city or region) visitors is lower than expected, then revenues will be lower than expected and, possibly, will increase financial losses.

3. Bidding to Attract a Sport Franchise: Is the Host City Worth off?

In North American professional team sports leagues, each time a franchise owner seeks a new location for its team several cities actually or potentially bid to be the host. Cities eager to promote economic development and image compete for hosting the team, and inadvertently find themselves victims of a bargaining process whereby all cities experience an auction-like bidding game (*Rosentraub & Swindell* 2002).

3.1 The Most Optimistic Bidding City Is Cursed

When looking for a location a team owner is in a monopoly position and may abuse of its power (*Quirk & Fort* 1999); cities are the bidders and the prize for the winner is to obtain the franchise being located in its municipal area. Bidders in such an auction-like bargaining process are played against one another by the team owner. Each competitor bases its bid on how much it expects the team to be worth, and submits the bid to the league. If a city overestimates the benefits the team will bring, it overbids for the franchise it would have been better off losing. The key of the winner' curse is that not all cities have the same expectations; only the most optimistic bidder wins the prize. When a city wins the bid this basically reflects its optimism about the unknown value of the team due to information asymmetry.

The team owners who control the process of bidding for teams place cities in sequential and simultaneous bargaining games (*Dixit & Nalebuff* 1991). This sequential game starts with a negotiation between a team and a single city, frequently the team's home city. The team puts demands on its host city for improved lease terms, stadium renovation, increased subsidies, and publicly funded new stadiums and arenas. The best strategy for a city is to simply add an increment to the previously accepted subsidy and thus overbid potentially competing cities. If its demands are not met, a team owner can point to other cities that may offer a large stadium subsidy as a potential to move if the incumbent host does not help. Conversations with other more cooperative or pliant municipalities will begin and here comes the simultaneous game. These combined games create an auction-like bidding for each city and trigger the likely winner's curse of providing a subsidy for the jurisdiction whose bid is accepted.

The bid for a franchise is conducted in a context of asymmetric information about the value of public investment and the bargaining strength of the team owner. Winning such a bidding game paves the way to the winner's curse when the returns on a municipality public investment for expected economic development opportunities fail to exceed the costs of the package that won.

Subsidies will not generate economic development if all they do is to keep an existing team from moving to another location. With asymmetric information, the outcome is a misrepresentation of the costs and benefits of the options available that leads to significant cost overruns (*Blair & Swindell* 1997): the winning city is cursed.

North American teams and leagues hold monopoly positions over entire cities. Cities compete over the right to host a franchise but do not participate in a formal market in which they directly pay for a good or a service. They pay the right to host teams by building facilities for them, providing them revenue guarantees, and allowing them to capture revenue from parking, concessions, and luxury boxes. Limiting the number of franchises enables a league to act as a franchise monopolist and maximise its members' monopoly rent. A league facilitates the monopoly power of team owners by restricting the number of teams in the league; this artificial restriction favours teams in their negotiations with host cities. In order for teams to exert their monopoly power over cities, the league should not place teams in every viable location. The size of the league relative to the number of cities that want to host teams plays a key role in the bargaining strength of the teams with cities. Restricting the number of available franchises, a league can drive up the price cities pay to attract a franchise or to retain one they already have. Because owners, acting as leagues, have controlled the location of teams so well, the cities are at a bargaining disadvantage and eventually are cursed.

As state and local governments are understandably reluctant to subsidise multimillion dollar sports enterprises, the teams threaten to leave for one of the viable locations its league has kept open. When a team contemplates a move, its owner usually cites the need for more skyboxes, lower lease payments, and better practice facilities. The implied threat in such statements is that some other city is offering such facilities. Given that leagues manage locations to keep teams the only game in town, a local government must deal with its current tenant or lose a team and hope that it can woo an unhappy owner or gain a team in the next expansion round. Hosts usually are unable to appeal some other team to replace their current team when it is gone. North American team sports leagues provide a number of famous stories of franchise relocation threats ending up with skyrocketing subsidies that materialise the winner's curse.

3.2 Indices of the Winner's Curse When Attracting a Sport Franchise

The winner's curse in attracting a sport franchise in North American team sports leagues may be checked with different indices, often mentioned in the literature, in particular:

1. The amount of subsidies for new sports facilities.
   Another index could be envisaged which is a team's relocation move since it always follows up preceding negotiations, bargaining and overbidding. However it is not a comprehensive index because such bargaining and overbidding may end up with a city keeping its franchise, and thus no move: remaining the host, a home city may be cursed as well.
2. An actually luxurious increase of the current subsidy devoted to a stadium or arena. Since subsidies are paid at taxpayer expenses, the host city is cursed but eventually local taxpayers have to pay the bill through the municipality budget whatever their willingness to pay for the stadium. They are cursed as well.
3. Cost overruns during the implementation of a blurred municipal project for stadium improvements, new parking places, the placement of hubs for airlines, and so on. The blurred municipal project misrepresents the real costs in order to have it accepted by local legislative bodies or voters. The magnitude of the winner's curse is in proportion to the cost underestimation.
   At the end of the day, a city is definitely cursed if, after attracting a franchise in its urban area:
4. Local economic growth slows down or stagnates instead of being boosted by municipal subsidies and/or a new stadium.
5. Urban development and restructuring is stagnant despite the forecast that a new stadium or stadium improvements would provide an opportunity for urban renovation.
6. Stadium attendance actually is lower than expected during the bargaining negotiations about the franchise location.

Some credibility is provided to the last three indices, though they are not so often calculated, by a number of studies (*Baade* et al. 2008; *Coates* 2007; *Johnson* & *Whitehead* 2000) which have exhibited that hosting a new franchise can create only a negligible positive net economic impact, when not negative, in North American urban areas.

4. Television Channels Bidding to Acquire Broadcasting Rights

In recent years the number of television (TV) channels involved in sports broadcasting has increased substantially. The process started in the 1970s in North America and in the 1980s in Europe. This development has triggered fierce competition between TV companies and dramatically increased the broadcasting rights on the most attractive sports. Here, the winner's curse results from staging an actual auction and not an auction-like mechanism as in the franchise location story.

4.1 When the Winner's Curse May Kill You

Competition between TV companies to broadcast the same sport event supplied by a single sports organisation (team, league, federation) – thus in a monopoly position – has inflated the broadcasting rights fees. English auction and sealed-first bid, or combinations of them, have been the most common procedures since sports broadcasting rights started to be auctioned (*Solberg* 2006).

In an English auction, the process starts with a low bid, which is then raised successively by just small amounts over the previous bid until one bidder wins. Meanwhile all other bidders give up when the bid rises higher than their own valuation and their maximum reservation price. The winner is the TV company with the highest bid which pays the last reservation price it has claimed to pay. The bidding procedure ends up when the price reaches just above the valuation of the bidder with the second-highest valuation. The narrower the difference between the last two bidders' valuations, the higher the final price. The risk of the winner's curse is very high since a TV company has no information about the actual maximum valuation of other competitors and thus must overbid to increase its information about rivals' valuation until the price reaches its own valuation.

In a sealed-first bid procedure, each bidder submits one bid without having any information on the rivals' bids. The highest bidder acquires the rights. A TV company's bid is a function of its own valuation and its prior beliefs about the rivals' valuations. Since the bids are kept secret, risk-averse bidders are not provided with increasing information to predict the value as during the process of an English auction. Information secrecy works to the seller's advantage, in particular when there is a wide gap between the highest and the second highest bids. The risk of the winner's curse is even higher than with an English auction since the winner never knows the (sealed) reservation prices of rival TV companies. Indeed, the bidder with the highest valuation faces two potential traps. Bidding too low a price, the bidder will be running the risk of missing out on a deal that could have been profitable. Countervailing this risk, each bidder is in danger of bidding more than necessary, and thus being cursed[6].

---

6 In some circumstances, some TV companies may enter the auction mainly to push the price up. The reason for this is to weaken the ability of the winner to submit bids on the next occasion a package of sports rights is being auctioned (*Gratton & Solberg* 2007).

With both auction procedures, the broadcasting rights have become extremely expensive and prices have increased so much that the TV company that acquires the rights is hit by the winner's curse. Quite a number of sports rights deals have ended up being unprofitable for the TV network (*Solberg & Hammervold* 2008) which translated into financial losses for the TV channel that won the bid. Several broadcasters have been hit by the winner's curse because they discovered too late they had overpaid for the rights and were thus unable to make the acquisition economically viable. In some cases, such as ITV Digital, the winning TV channel is so much cursed that it goes bankrupt (*Buraimo* 2006); a similar outcome occurred with the German Kirch Media. Take care, the winner's curse may kill you!

In both English auction and sealed-first bid the actual winner definitely is the monopolistic seller that is the sports organisation which offers its broadcasting rights. The higher the price of the rights, the larger the monopoly rent that falls to the seller. In general, the purpose of staging an auction is to maximise the seller's proportion of this rent. As in the two previous cases – bidding for a sporting event and a sport franchise – information and its distribution among the bidders is crucial. If there is not much information on which TV companies can build their subjective valuations of income (derived from fans, advertisers, etc.) to be earned from a sport broadcast, then the most optimistic – and therefore wrong – highest bidder will win and be cursed (*Fort* 2003).

Moreover there is a risk of excess supply if too many TV channels broadcast too many similar sport programmes simultaneously. Their uncoordinated actions can create severe financial problems. The demand may also fluctuate for those broadcast games after the bids are submitted[7]: it is impossible to estimate the income from broadcasting accurately when sports events will take place sometime in the future. Here, the winner's problem is that it realises this too late (*Gratton & Solberg* 2007). Income turns out to be lower than expected while it is impossible to reduce sunk costs. The winner's curse is more probable when the auction has to end before anyone knows when or where a sport event will occur and/or which are the sport teams that will qualify, as for instance with the FIFA World Cup final stage.

To countervail the risk of the winner's curse TV companies tacitly collude or openly merge in such a way as to balance the sporting seller's monopoly power

---

7 *Blair* (2012) stresses that the demand for advertising slots is far more unpredictable than broadcasting costs (including TV rights) since these slots cannot be sold before bidding on and being awarded the broadcasting rights. The winner's curse may be due to some cause reducing the demand for advertising in general (ex: an economic recession) or for a particular sporting event (*Gratton & Solberg* 2004).

with a monopsony power[8]. Such countervailing strategy curbs the inflation of broadcasting rights fees whereas its absence fuels a fee skyrocketing trend. For example, in the French market for football broadcast, the merger between Canal Satellite and TPS came out with moderating the rights fees inflation. But if a newcomer enters the market and thus increases the number of aggressive bidders, broadcasting rights fees and the monopoly rent of the sports organisation are likely to inflate. This is what occurred in the French market for football broadcast in 2012 with the entrance of Be In (an Al Jazeera subsidiary) outbidding Canal +.

Competition among TV companies can be cooled down with de-packaging the broadcasting rights on sale. After BSkyB obtained the whole package of the English Premier League football broadcasts for 2004–07, the European Commission started recommending that broadcasting rights on a single sporting event must be split and sold into different sets (live, highlights, first league games, second league games). This EU policy clearly aims at countervailing the sporting sellers' monopoly position and narrowing their rent through de-packaging. This is not to say that consequently the winner's curse would disappear, but the financial cost for cursed TV companies would be lower with de-packaged broadcast deals than with acquiring the whole package of TV rights. Any move back to re-packaging the rights would reinforce the seller's monopoly position and the impact of the winner's curse.

A last option for a TV company is to undertake a vertical integration (*Stotlar* 2000) with a sports team or a sports league[9] whose sporting events are targeted for broadcasting, in view of benefitting from a so-called toehold effect. A toehold is an asymmetry between the bidders in an auction, such as one bidder acquiring an ownership stake in the object being sold. One bidder toeholds work by multiplying up the potential of the winner's curse for other rival bidders. There is

8 If at the end of the day there is just one potential bidder facing a monopolistic seller then emerges a bilateral monopoly market structure (*Sandy* et al. 2004).

9 Some examples of partial or total share ownership by a TV company in a sports organisation are (or have been): TBS in Atlanta Braves (MLB), Atlanta Hawks (NBA) and Atlanta Thrashers (NHL), News Corporation in Los Angeles Dodgers, Walt Disney in Anaheim Mighty Ducks (NHL) and Anaheim Angels (MLB), Cablevision Systems in New York Kicks (NBA), New York Rangers (NHL) and New York Liberty (WBA), Comcast Corp in Philadelphia 76ers (NBA), Philadelphia Flyers (NHL) and Philadelphia Phantoms (WBA), UFA Sports in Borusia Dortmund, Hamburg SV and FC Nuremberg, Mediapartner in Milan AC, Granada in Arsenal and Liverpool, NTL in Aston Villa, Newcastle, Middleborough and Leicester City, M6 in Girondins de Bordeaux, Canal + in Paris-Saint-Germain and Servette de Genève.

strong evidence that acquiring a toehold – even a very small one – can confer a huge competitive advantage on a bidder in an auction (*Harbord & Binmore* 2000). In standard auctions, a bidder with a toehold is virtually guaranteed to win the auction, and at a lower price than it otherwise might have paid. This interacts in alleviating the winner's curse, causing other bidders without a toehold to reduce their bids for fear they have overbid in a contest with a competitor which already has an insider advantage.

A toehold is a TV company's attempt to divert a part of the monopoly rent from the sports organisation in lessening or expelling competition for TV broadcasting rights. A broadcaster ownership of a sports team or league is anti-competitive when it relies on a toehold effect (*Cave & Crandall* 2001) but it is a major hindrance against the most extreme impact of the winner's curse on a TV company benefitting from the toehold. Then a TV company would bid for a common value object of which it is already partial owner and would correspondingly reduce its outlay on the purchase of TV rights.

4.2 Indices of a Winner's Curse in a Bid for Broadcasting Rights

Bidding for broadcasting rights over a given sporting event is not an auction-like process but a genuine auctioning process. Indices that a winning TV channel is cursed are:

1. A very swift increase in TV rights fees on a same sporting event from one broadcasting contract to the next one.
2. Financial loss endured by a TV company on a broadcast deal: the income derived from televising a sporting event do not cover sunk costs of producing the broadcast, including those rights paid after outbidding competing TV channels.
3. A post-bid bankruptcy which exhibits ex post that a TV channel could not afford the bid which it won due to overoptimistic valuation.
4. Too many unknown and uncertain details about the date, the place and the participants (qualified teams and athletes) of a sporting event which falls adrift into unexpectedly low broadcast revenues and high costs ending up in a loss.
5. Outbidding newcomers which enter the broadcast market for a given sporting event, increase aggressive competition on the demand side and thus make the winner's curse more likely to happen.
6. TV rights re-packaging for a given sporting event, if any, in reducing the number of products on sale in the face of a given number of TV channels leads to increased competition that triggers TV rights fees inflation and thus a greater likelihood of the winner's curse.

5. Teams Bidding to Recruit Free Agent and Superstar Players

The former reserve clause in North American leagues and the former transfer system in European leagues effectively prevented a player from offering its services to another team in the league at any price. No auction-like mechanism could emerge. In the 1970s, veteran players obtained the status of a free agent in North American leagues while in the post-Bosman era (1996 on) players gained a free international mobility in European leagues. Then team owners started bidding in a free market for players, and often competition across teams for a same free agent or superstar[10] player drifted into overbidding.

In the labour market for talent, team owners are the bidders and free agent or superstar players are sellers of the right to use their talent. For each sale the free agent or superstar player is in a monopoly situation over its talent rights as soon as this player is not substitutable on the pitch[11] (*Andreff* 2014). The prize is for the winning team to recruit a player despite other teams' bids. The player auctions the right to use his talent and sells it to the highest bidder while the bids are determined by each team's estimate of the marginal revenue product associated with a given player after looking at his past performance and characteristics (points scored, age, height, experience, etc.). The team that expects the highest marginal contribution of a given player to its revenue offers the highest salary bid. If information about players' characteristics is limited, uncertain and asymmetric across teams, preconditions for the winner's curse are met. In the context of North American team sports leagues, the winner's curse pertains to trading free agent players whereas in European professional team sports leagues where there is no draft, all players being tradable, the issue is more with players in a monopoly position over their scarce (high quality) talent rights, i.e. superstars.

5.1 Recruiting a Free Agent ... who Reveals to Be a 'Lemon'

With regard to free agent players in North American leagues, overbidding is due to first an inherent element of uncertainty in evaluating a player's future

---

10 *Fort* (2003) even contends that rookies, untested at the professional level, are often paid more than established veterans and are not worth their huge bonuses and starting salaries. Teams are cursed with the rookies as well. Michael Jordan was one of the most obvious cases in point. Overpayment of NBA rookie salaries is successfully tested in *Eschker* et al. (2004).

11 A major aspect of a superstar player is precisely that its substitution elasticity is zero: it can only be substituted on the pitch by a 'superstar proxy' or a second best player having not the same impact on scoring, the sporting outcome, and drawing attendance.

marginal worth. Estimating a given player's marginal impact on team revenue entails estimating the player's contribution to team wins, hitting and pitching potential (in baseball), scoring, fan appeal, and so on. Presumably the bidders overestimate sometimes and underestimate sometimes. Given this uncertainty, the auction process necessarily biases the winning bid upwards when many bidders participate. Increasing the number of bidders magnifies the overestimation bias (*Cassing & Douglas* 1980). As a result free agents are likely to be overpaid, and the winning team is likely to be cursed. *Cassing & Douglas* argue that there will be a tendency to acquire a biased set of free agent players, those for which buying teams have overestimated the value and overpaid, thus the authors' contention of the winner's curse. The bids will not mirror the true worth of the player; a team that values it correctly has a poor chance of signing a player compared to a team that overestimates the player's value. Conclusion: free agents are really paid too much.

How to explain this since a sports league is a monopsony in the labour market for talent? A first assumption (*Fort* 2003) is that most owners are informed and experienced bidders in the free agent auction, but a few are not. Then most owners would only bid the true expected marginal revenue product of a player but the other inexperienced, uninformed bidders bid well below or well above it. Under a steep competitive free agent auction, the highest of these inexperienced/uninformed bids will win. The winner will be cursed and player salaries will be well above their actual marginal revenue product. Contrary to this hypothesis, the winner's curse has not vanished after some first years of free agency when all teams became experienced in bidding. Free agent wage overpayment[12] has not ceased (*Zimbalist* 1992; *Blecherman & Camerer* 1996) after years of free agency with experienced and well informed bidders, well aware of overpaying these players. Confirming *Cassing & Douglas* guesstimate, the winner's curse has been lasting in baseball though in a weaker form[13].

Another assumption is that the market for free agent players shares some features with a market for 'lemons'. *Lehn* (1984) found that owners lack all the information they need when they make bids and get stuck with injured players at a

---

12 Relatively to their marginal revenue product and to other players which are not free agents.

13 *Burger & Walters* (2007) distinguish a "strong form" curse when the team winning the bid actually loses money and a "weak form" curse when winning bidders fail to use available information in formulating efficient bids and their returns have proven disappointing. Econometric testing with data on MLB free agents shows a strong form during the early years of free agency in the late 1970s, and a weak form in the late 1990s.

high price; the market for talent is subject to self selection of 'lemons'. Then the winner's curse occurs in the same way as in Akerlof's market for 'lemons' and results in an adverse selection of recruited players.

Moreover, a player's talent may be team-specific (*Vrooman* 1996). Not only is the talent of the team-specific player asymmetrical or irreversible, but so is the knowledge about the team-specificity of the talent. The least incomplete information about the team-specificity of a player's talent resides with the owner (or general manager) of the team for which the player currently plays. The information about the team specificity of the player's talent is asymmetrically incomplete. Then the team for which the player has performed in the past seasons has more information about that player's future potential (or whether the player has health problems, is ill-natured or uneasy to coach for some reason) than other teams. The selling team is able to categorise its good and less good free agents while potential buying teams cannot. If buying teams fix their offer price on the expected value of the two types of players, then good players will never actually be sold, as the offer price will never reach the selling team's reservation price. The only players available in the market will be 'lemons': low quality players will drive good quality players out of the market. Only poor quality players will be traded at the reservation price.

However, in practice, one observes that good free agent players are traded but quite over the reservation price since potential buying teams have to bid one another for recruiting the best players. Eventually, systematic overbidding is due to free agent capacity of playing each bidding team against the others since each free agent player benefits from exclusivity rights over his talent and stands in a monopoly position in the market. This third assumption is in tune with the other explanations of the winner's curse (bidding for a sporting event, a sport franchise, or TV rights) but remains to be carefully tested.

A last question is to know whether the teams learned to behave in such a way as to eliminate the winner's curse. Econometric results (*Burger & Walters* 2007) show that the winner's curse lasts though in a weak form in MLB while it seems to have disappeared after two years in NBA with regards to international player transfers (*Eschker* et al. 2004). Mistakes have been made by NBA teams when evaluating foreign players in the first years when such international transfers started after 1989. Foreign players earned salaries nearly 150% higher – a 50% salary bonus – than players trained in the U.S., as tested in the 1996–97 and 1997–98 seasons. North American teams were suffering from a lack of information regarding the true talent of international players. From the 1998 season on, there is no longer any significant difference in salaries between the two groups of players. As more international players entered the league, NBA teams committed increasing resources to scouting and gathering information about the comparative talent in the international basketball leagues and became able to better assess the players value. Hence the winner's curse vanished. *Eschker* et al. (2004) also found for any player – not only international players – that changing teams between seasons has a large negative impact on salaries; this suggests that between season player move may represent a market for 'lemons' in which there is still a possibility for a team to be cursed. It is in view of alleviating this possible effect that mercato slots[14] have been introduced in European (football) leagues.

5.2 Overbidding in the Arms' Race for a Superstar Ends Up in the Red

Although we distinguish it from the winner's curse in a bid for free agents, overbidding for a superstar player can drive any team into the winner's curse as well. Free agency is specific to North American team sports leagues as compared to European leagues where all players older than 18 are free to negotiate their contract since the Bosman ruling and where overbidding pertains to superstar players. However, free agency and superstar may overlap as a cause of the winner's curse as illustrated in the case of an MLB superstar[15]. In MLB, all the teams paid an average \$2.8 million to attract one superstar in 2007, that is a 40% salary bonus, but they expected \$11 million of additional revenues from qualifying for the play offs (*Krautman & Ciecka* 2009). Most of them were obviously wrong since by definition not all teams can qualify for the play offs; and then were cursed.

The market for coaches in collegiate sports is also plagued with the winner's curse. The competitive process in which a superstar coach is hired is essentially auction-like; numerous bidders (universities) are vying against each other and no one wants to lose. The process clearly exhibits imperfect information about the future impact the superstar coach will have once he is hired and the additional revenue streams that will flow to the university (*Grant* et al. 2008).

14 Predefined periods of time (with a summer and a winter mercato) when player transfers (moves) are allowed and out of which transfers are forbidden.

15 "When Alex Rodriguez became a free agent while playing for the Seattle Mariners, several teams were interested in him. The Texas Rangers won the bidding, but it was widely reported that the \$252 million for ten years that the Rangers paid then the richest in team sports, was tens of millions of dollars more than they needed to pay in order to obtain Rodriguez's services" (*Staudohar* 2012: 110).

The ultimate cause of the winner's curse is the arms' race between teams to recruit a superstar player or coach. The arms' race is more intense between teams in post-Bosman European (football) leagues than in North American leagues (*Andreff* 2011), so that the winner's curse is more probable in the former than the latter market for superstars. The winner's curse has not been tested properly speaking for player movements in European (football) leagues. However, it is probably related to the so-called superstar effect empirically tested by *Lucifora & Simmons* (2003): a small number of players concentrate a disproportionate share of overall payroll in (Italian) football. Econometric testing shows that player salaries are convex in terms of performances exhibiting a superstar effect for players which are not perfectly substitutable when it comes to drawing attendances.

If one assumes that a superstar has a monopoly power over the rights on its scarce and imperfectly substitutable talent (*Rosen* 1981), then demand-side competition in a global market for talent[16] enables a superstar to capture a monopoly rent (*Borghans & Groot* 1998); the latter more than countervails the monopsony power and rent of sports leagues and owners. The uniqueness of a superstar talent or image adds an exclusivity right to the usual right of using talent which diverts a part of the team's monopsony rent to the superstar monopolist. Signing David Beckham in 2007 LA Galaxy was suspected to be cursed; signing him in 2012, was Paris-Saint-Germain better off? But there is just one Beckham in the world. Eventually he has spent a short time on the pitch over the past season and has not scored that much. Was it worth paying him a monopoly rent basically in view of earning higher commercial revenues?

Overbidding for superstar players jeopardises a team's budget and its financial balance (*Andreff* 2007) as it is witnessed with the current financial crisis of European professional football[17] and the data published by UEFA – 63% of European football clubs were in the red in 2011. A lasting and intense arms' race to recruit the best players has not faded away in European team sports leagues after 18 years of Bosman ruling. The bargaining power of a superstar is so high when facing the simultaneous demands of several competing teams that the bids' rise ends up with a salary higher than any credible and feasible level of marginal revenue product. Thus the superstar effect which is, on the team owner side, a

16 An alternative explanation for this non equilibrium solution is an excess demand for superstar talents in a lasting disequilibrium market for talent (*Andreff* 2014).

17 See the Journal of Sports Economics 7 (1) 2006 and 8 (6) 2007 issues.

"weak form" of the winner's curse turns out to be a "strong form" when, after transferring some superstars, the team budget falls in the red[18].

5.3 Indices of a Winner's Curse in a Bid for a Free Agent or Superstar Player

The winner's curse has a specific shape in team bids for scarce high quality talent. It is difficult to prove how much a league or team monopsony is countervailed by the exclusivity right of a player over its talent and which part of the monopsony rent is diverted to the player. A team is likely to be cursed when:

1. The number of bidding teams for a same player grows.
2. A player is significantly overpaid with a salary much higher than its marginal revenue product. This player has been able to bargain a salary overpayment or bonus through playing those teams that contemplate its recruitment against each other.
3. Acquiring a 'lemon' player who, after the bid, reveals to be in a bad shape, unhealthy, injured or has an unmanageable behaviour.
4. Disappointing returns on the bid, though the team does not lose money (the weak form of the winner's curse), or negative returns, i.e. financial loss after overbidding for a player (the strong form of the winner's curse).
5. A superstar effect that translates into a monopoly rent captured by a superstar player to the detriment of a team's budget is more often observed in the European than North American team sports leagues.
6. A team's financial deficit obviously due to an excess payroll, for instance a payroll/budget ratio higher than 100%, when it is linked to recruiting some superstars without generating performances and revenues that cover salary overpayment.

18 A unique experience of using an actual auction to allocate players across teams is the one of the new cricket Indian Premier League (IPL) in January 2008. The new franchises needed to acquire players. With no history for any team, the IPL hit upon a novel way of assigning players to teams with an English auction. It was a phenomenon which was probably not understood much by some franchises. The winner's curse was at the corner. *Parker* et al. (2008) show that bidding outcomes exhibited an overvaluation of the most experienced players, namely those with an international experience acquired in Twenty20 matches. The rules of the auction and the nature of the franchises triggered a salary bonus for Indian players. A greater bonus on younger Indian players was fuelled by the requirement that each team had four players under 22. The franchise owners were cursed.

Table 1: Indices of a winner's curse in sports auctions

Mega sporting event	Hosting a team franchise	Bidding for broadcasting rights	Overbidding for players
Cost overruns	Subsidies for new facilities	Swift TV rights fees increase	Growing number of bidders
Ex post project revisions	Luxurious increase in subsidies	TV company financial losses	Salary overpayment/ bonus**
Delayed completion	Stadium cost overruns	TV company post-bid bankruptcy	Acquiring a 'lemon' player
Extra public subsidy	Slow economic growth	Important properties of sports event* uncertain in advance	Bid returns systematically below expectations
Host city fiscal deficit / debt	Stagnating urban development	Outbidding newcomers	Superstar effect
Lower number of visitors	Lower attendance than expected	TV rights re-packaging	Team's deficit due to payroll

* The future date, place and qualified teams or athletes.

** A wage higher than marginal revenue product may have different causes, including a lasting excess demand for superstars.

6. Conclusion

The winner's curse appears to be a major concept in sports economics. It corresponds to various sporting objects allocated through an auction or auction-like process, namely hosting mega-sporting events, attracting a professional sports team franchise, negotiating TV broadcasting rights over a sporting event, recruiting free agent and superstar players. In all circumstances, the seven above-listed preconditions of the winner's curse are there. Possibly one can find additional circumstances, for example in the sport betting and wagering industry or in the sporting goods industry. Avenues for further research on imperfect sports markets with asymmetric information may reveal that an additional number of them do function on an auction-like basis so that the winner's curse is likely to occur. For the time being, we have listed some indices that may confirm the very existence of the winner's curse in the four aforementioned auctions or auction-like processes. A next step would be to define metrics for all these indices – it is already done for some of them such as players' overpayment.

The only way that has been found so far to countervail and alleviate the winner's curse is to restrict competition on the demand side: collusion between bidding TV companies, merger, vertical integration, and toeholds in the face of a league's or team's monopoly over its broadcasting rights, and a player's monopoly over its talent rights. It may be time to raise the alternative issue: why not make the supply side of the market for sporting objects more competitive in breaking up sport monopolies? This is a taboo issue for all mega sporting event organisers from the IOC to FIFA, from MLB to NBA, from the English Premier League to UEFA, from a major league team in Seattle to another one in Philadelphia, and so on. This also opens an avenue for further hypothesizing.

References

Akerlof, G. (1970): The Market for Lemons: Qualitative Uncertainty and the Market Mechanism, in: Quarterly Journal of Economics, Vol. 89, pp. 488–500.

Andreff, W. (1993): La crise des économies socialistes. La rupture d'un système, Grenoble: Presses Universitaires de Grenoble.

Andreff, W. (2007): French Football: A Financial Crisis Rooted in Weak Governance, in: Journal of Sports Economics, Vol. 8, 6, pp. 652–661.

Andreff, W. (2011): Some comparative economics of the organization of sports: Competition and regulation in north American vs. European professional team sports leagues, in: European Journal of Comparative Economics, Vol. 8, 1, pp. 3–27.

Andreff, W. (2012a): Mondialisation économique du sport. Manuel de référence en Economie du sport, Bruxelles: De Boeck.

Andreff, W. (2012b): The winner's curse: why is the cost of mega sporting events so often underestimated?, in: *Maennig, W. & Zimbalist, A.* (eds.): International Handbook on the Economics of Mega Sporting Events, Cheltenham: Edward Elgar, pp. 37–69.

Andreff, W. (2013): Crisis as Unexpected Transition … to a Greed-Based Economic System, in: *Zarembka, P.* (ed.): Contradictions: Finance, Greed, Labor Unequally Paid, Research in Political Economy, Vol. 28, Bingley: Emerald, pp. 1–48.

Andreff, W. (2014): Building Blocks for a Disequilibrium Model of a European Team Sports League, in: International Journal of Sport Finance, Vol. 9, 1, pp. 20–38.

Baade, R. A., Baumann, R. W. & Matheson, W. A. (2008): Assessing the Economic Impact of College Football Games on Local Economies, in: Journal of Sports Economics, Vol. 9, 6, pp. 628–643.

Blair, R. D. (2012): Sports Economics, Cambridge: Cambridge University Press.

Blair, J. & Swindell, D. (1997): Sports, politics, and economics: The Cincinnati story, in: *Noll, R. G. & Zimbalist, A.* (eds.): Sports, Jobs, and Taxes: The Economic Impact of Sports Teams and Stadiums, Washington D.C.: The Brookings Institution, pp. 282–323.

Blecherman, B. & Camerer, C.F. (1996): Is There a Winner's Curse in the Market for Baseball Players? Evidence from the Field, Social Science, Working paper No. 966, Pasadena: California Institute of Technology.

Borghans, L. & Groot, L. (1998): Superstardom and Monopoly Power: Why Media Stars Earn More than their Contribution to Welfare?, in: Journal of Institutional and Theoretical Economics, Vol. 154, pp. 546–571.

Buraimo, B. (2006): The Demand for Sports Broadcasting, in: *Andreff, W. & Szymanski, S.*, (eds.): The Handbook on the Economics of Sport, Cheltenham: Edward Elgar, pp. 100–111.

Burger, J. D. & Walters, S. J. K. (2007): The Existence and Persistence of a Winner's Curse: New Evidence from the (Baseball) Field, IASE-NAASE Working Paper No. 06-25, Baltimore: Loyola College in Maryland.

Capen, E., Clapp, R. & Campbell, W. (1971): Competitive bidding in high-risk situations, in: Journal of Petroleum Technology, Vol. 23, pp. 641–653.

Cassing, J. & Douglas, R. W. (1980): Implications of the Auction Mechanism in Baseball's Free Agent Draft, in: Southern Economic Journal, Vol. 47, pp. 110–121.

Cave, M. & Crandall, R. W. (2001): Sports Rights and the Broadcast Industry, in: Economic Journal, Vol. 111, pp. F4-F26.

Coates, D. (2007): Stadiums and Arenas: Economic Development or Economic Redistribution?, in: Contemporary Economic Policy, Vol. 25, 4, pp. 565–577.

Dixit, A. & Nalebuff, B. (1991): Thinking Strategically: The Competitive Edge in Business, Politics, and Everyday Life, New York: W.W. Norton.

Dyker, D. (1983): The Process of Investment in the Soviet Union, Cambridge: Cambridge University Press.

Eschker, E., Perez, S. J. & Siegler, M. V. (2004): The NBA and the Influx of International Basketball Players, in: Applied Economics, Vol. 36, 10, pp. 1009–1020.

Fort, R. (2003): Sports Economics, Upper Saddle River: Prentice Hall.

Gilley, O., Karels, G. & Leone, R. (1986): Uncertainty, experience and the winner's curse in OCS lease bidding, in: Management Science, Vol. 32, pp. 673–682.

Grant, R. R., Leadley, J. & Zygmont, Z. (2008): The Economics of Intercollegiate Sports, Singapore: World Scientific Publishing.

Gratton, C. & Solberg H. A. (2004): Sports and Broadcasting: Comparisons between the United States and Europe, in: *Fort, R. & Fizel, J.* (eds.): International Sports Economics Comparisons, Westport: Praeger, pp. 175–187.

Gratton, C. & Solberg, H. A. (2007): The Economics of Sports Broadcasting, Abingdon: Routledge.

Harbord, D. & Binmore, K. (2000): Toeholds, Takeovers and Football, in: European Competition Law Review, Vol. 21, 2, pp. 1–4.

Johnson, B. K. & Whitehead, J. C. (2000): Value of Public Goods from Sports Stadiums: The CVM Approach, in: Contemporary Economic Policy, Vol. 18, 1, pp. 48–58.

Kagel, J. H. & Levin, D. (2002): Common Value Auctions and the Winner's Curse, Princeton, NJ: Princeton University Press.

Kornaï, J. (1980): Economics of Shortage, Amsterdam: North Holland Publishing.

Krautmann, A. C. & Ciecka, J. (2009): The Postseason Value of an Elite Player to a Contending Team, in: Journal of Sports Economics, Vol. 10, 2, pp. 168–179.

Leeds, M. & von Allmen, P. (2002): The Economics of Sports, Boston, MA: Addison Wesley.

Lehn, K. (1984): Information Asymmetries in Baseball's Free Agent Market, in: Economic Inquiry, Vol. 22, pp. 37–44.

Levis, M. (1990): The winner's curse problem, interest costs and the underpricing of initial public offerings, in: Economic Journal, Vol. 100, pp. 76–89.

Lucifora, C. & Simmons, R. (2003): Superstar Effects in Sport: Evidence from Italian Soccer, in: Journal of Sports Economics, Vol. 4, 1, pp. 35–55.
Parker, D., Burn, P. & Natarajan, H. (2008): Player Valuations in the Indian Premier League, in: Frontier Economics, Vol. October, pp. 1–17.
Preuss, H. & Schnitzer, M. (2013): Organisation Costs for a FIFA World Cup and their Significance during a Bid, Working Paper Series Mainzer Papers on Sports Economics & Management No. 6, Mainz: Johannes Gutenberg-University Mainz.
Quirk, J. & Fort, R. D. (1999): Hard Ball: The Abuse of Power in Pro Team Sports, Princeton: Princeton University Press.
Rosen, S. (1981): The Economics of Superstars, in: American Economic Review, Vol.71, pp. 845–858.
Rosentraub, M. S. & Swindell, D. (2002): Negotiating Games: Cities, Sports, and the Winner's Curse, in: Journal of Sport Management, Vol. 16, pp. 18–35.
Sandy, R., Sloane, P. J. & Rosentraub, M.S. (2004): The Economics of Sports: An International Perspective, Basingstoke: Palgrave Macmillan.
Solberg, H. A. (2006): The Auctioning of TV Sports Rights, in: International Journal of Sport Finance, Vol. 1, 1, pp. 33–45.
Solberg, H. A. & Hammervold, R. (2008): TV Sports Viewers – Who Are They? A Norwegian Case Study, in: Nordicom Review, Vol. 29, 1, pp. 95–110.
Staudohar, P. (2012): The Reserve Clause and Labor Mobility, in: *Kahane, L. H & Shmanske, S.* (eds.): The Oxford Handbook of Sports Economics Volume 1: The Economics of Sport, Oxford: Oxford University Press, pp. 97–113.
Stotlar, D. K. (2000): Vertical Integration in Sport, in: Journal of Sport Management, Vol. 14, 1, pp. 1–7.
Sturgess, B. & Brady, C. (2006): Hosting the FIFA World Cup: Economic Boon or Winner's Curse, in: World Economics, Vol. 7, 4, pp. 145–164.
Thaler, R. H. (1994): The Winner's Curse: Paradoxes and Anomalies of Economic Life, Princeton, NJ: Princeton University Press.
Vrooman, J. (1996): The Baseball Players' Labor Market Reconsidered, in: Southern Economic Journal, Vol. 63, 2, pp. 339–360.
Vrooman, J. (2000): The Economics of American Sports Leagues, in: Scottish Journal of Political Economy, Vol. 47, 4, pp. 364–398.
Zimbalist, A. (1992): Salaries and Performance: Beyond the Scully Model, in: *P. Sommers,* (ed.): Diamonds Are for Ever: The Business of Baseball, Washington D.C.: Brookings Institution, pp. 109–133.

Appendix 1: Ex ante and ex post cost of Summer Olympics. Excerpt from Andreff (2012b)

Host city, year	ct-1: ex ante cost	Ct: ex post cost	After t cost
(Nb of bidders)			
Munich 1972	Overall cost: $2705m	Investment cost: $1757m00	
(4 bidders)		LOOC operation cost: $656m00	
Montreal 1976	Investment cost: $549.5m00	Investment cost: $3395.6m00	
(3 bidders)		LOOC operation cost: $476m00	Operation: $1592m
	Olympic stadium cost: $172m		Stadium: $1000m
Moscow 1980	Overall cost: $3.7bn	Overall cost: $9bn	
(2 bidders)	Operation cost: $2bn		
	Investment cost: $1,7bn		
Los Angeles 1984	No commitment	Overall cost: $1592m	
		LOOC operation cost: $546m	
Seoul 1988	Overall cost: $3.1bn	LOOC operation cost: $664m00	Extra cost: $2bn
(2 bidders)	Investment cost: $3450m	Investment cost: $4063m00	
Barcelona 1992	Investment cost in:	Investment cost: $10134m00	Debt: $6.1bn
(6 bidders)	1985: F13bn; 1988: F23,5bn	Overall cost: $9.3bn	
	1990: F35,5bn; 1992: F41,5bn		
	LOOC operation cost: $1670m	LOOC operation cost: $1793m00	
Atlanta 1996	Overall cost in 1990: $2021m	Investment cost: $1324m00	
(6 bidders)		LOOC operation cost: $1346m00	
Sydney 2000	Overall cost in 1994: $3428m		Overall cost: $6.6bn
(5bidders)	Investment cost. $2500m	Investment cost: $2601m00	
	LOOC operation cost: $1463m	LOOC operation cost: $2434m00	
	New South Wales Invt: $1220m	New South Wales Invt: $1249m	

Host city, year	ct-1: ex ante cost	Ct: ex post cost	After t cost
Athens 2004	LOOC operation cost: $2162m00	LOOC operation cost: $2404m00	
(5 bidders)	Overall cost: €4.6bn	Overall cost: €6.0bn (June 2004)	Overall: €9.6bn
Beijing 2008	Investment cost: $1600m00	Investment cost: $2170m00	Invt cost: €13.5bn
(5 bidders)	Invt. cost in 2006: $2800m		
	LOOC operation cost: $786m00	LOOC operation cost: $1458m00	
		Infrastructure cost: $35.6bn	Infrastr: €29bn
	Olympic stadium cost: €300m	Olympic stadium cost: €380m	
	Overall cost: €2.2bn ($bn1.9bn) 2004	Overall cost:$43 to 45bn	
	$2.4bn in 2006		
London 2012	Overall cost: £3.4bn in 2005;	Overall in 2011: $19bn (£11.6bn)	
(5 bidders)	£3.674bn end 2005; £9.3bn in 2007		
	£10.0bn in 2009		
	Investment in 2005: £2.664bn		
	in 2006: €15.0bn		
	LOOC operation 2005: £1010m		
	in 2006: €1900m		

m: million; bn: billion; $m00: in 2000 dollars; Australian dollars for Sydney;
F: French francs; t is the date of the opening ceremony.

Sports on the Air: A GARCH Examination of the Impact of Broadcasts of Live Sporting Events on Television Audience Sizes

José Baños, Levi Pérez, Víctor Puente, Plácido Rodríguez

Abstract

Television (TV) channels around the world are cognizant of the significant impact that broadcasts of sporting events, particularly soccer games, have on their audience. Using a unique data set that includes daily information about the audience of *Televisión del Principado de Asturias*, a Spanish public regional TV channel, this article examines different GARCH models to analyze whether the size of the TV audience increases when different live sports events are broadcast. Other seasonal and weather factors expected to affect audience figures are taken into account to address both strong habits in TV consumption and possible responses to climatic conditions.

Keywords

live sports, soccer, broadcasting, television audience, GARH model

1. Introduction

Currently, television (TV) broadcasts of live sporting events often draw large audiences, a phenomenon that can be observed for broadcasts of the Olympic Games, Formula One racing, or the FIFA (Fédération Internationale de Football Association) World Cup, among other events. The high potential viewership for sports broadcasts is most likely one of the primary motivations underlying the intense competition among the principal TV channels for the exclusive broadcasting rights to these events; this competition causes major TV channels to pay high prices for those broadcasting rights. As a short-term response to their investments in sports programming, the major TV channels often attempt to generate profits by reselling the exclusive rights for sports broadcasts to regional or local TV operators that seek to use those broadcasts to improve the size of their own audiences and differentiate themselves from their competitors. Therefore, a secondary market for sports broadcasting rights exists, given the aforementioned incentives for trading the rights in question.

Recent evidence has demonstrated that there has been an increase in the number of TV sports transmissions, as well as in the scheduled time devoted to these broadcasts. Most TV channels around the world appreciate the impact that broadcasts of sporting events may have on their audiences and therefore choose to participate in this global trend. However, although sports broadcasting is undoubtedly an important aspect of TV channel behavior that has been discussed in previously published economic literature, there is limited empirical evidence regarding the magnitude of the effect.

Building upon these considerations, this article analyzes the extent to which broadcasts of live sporting events positively impact the average daily number of viewers of a certain TV channel in a region of about one million inhabitants. The focus of this study is on the particular case of a Spanish public regional TV channel, Televisión del Principado de Asturias (TPA), and the aim of the research is to attempt to measure the primary effects of live sporting event broadcasts on audience size, distinguishing among different sports.

Thus, in the empirical exercise we employ GARCH models to explain TV audiences. We begin by using an autoregressive (AR) model with seasonality controls, including whether (or not) a sporting event is broadcast live on a particular day, to estimate the conditional mean of daily TPA audience. Then, the existence of the volatility is tested and some GARCH models are applied to estimate the conditional variance equation. Overall, the model analyzes which sports have the greatest impact on the general audience size of TPA. The studied sample size spans the period from January 1, 2007 to December 31, 2009. These estimates are expected to provide greater insight regarding whether the impact of sports broadcasts on audience size justifies TV channels' efforts to purchase the broadcasting rights.

The chapter is structured as follows. The next sections address the importance that sports transmissions have for TV viewership and review the findings of previous literature regarding the demand for sports on TV. Subsequently, the economic model that explains the variations in the TPA's average daily audience is presented, and the empirical findings of that model are discussed. Finally, certain concluding remarks are provided for consideration.

2. Selected Statistics Regarding the Broadcasting of Sporting Events

In Spain, there is evidence that the number of TV viewers is increased to a greater extent by broadcasts of live sporting events than by other types of TV programs. In accordance with this trend, Table 1, which displays the most watched programs in Spain in 2009, demonstrates that the fifteen most-viewed broadcasts were sporting events; in particular, all of these programs were soccer matches. In fact, only two of the programs in the entire table are unrelated to sporting events. The most watched TV program in Spain in 2009 was a soccer match from UEFA (Union of European Football Associations) Champions League, in which FC Barcelona played against Manchester United. This match had an average audience of more than eleven million viewers. It should be noted that soccer in Spain is so popular that no other sport appears among the twenty-five most-watched TV programs.

Table 1: The 25 most watched programs in Spain in 2009

	Description	Title	Channel	Date	Viewers (thousands)	Share
1	Soccer: Champions League	Barcelona-Manchester U.	A3	27/05/2009	11,310	61.7
2	Soccer: King's Cup	Ath. Bilbao-Barcelona	TVE1	13/05/2009	10,012	48.5
3	Soccer: Champions League	Olympique M.-R. Madrid	TVE1	08/12/2009	8,410	41.9
4	Soccer: Champions League	Barcelona-Inter	TVE1	24/11/2009	8,361	43.2
5	Soccer: Champions League	Milán-R. Madrid	TVE1	03/11/2009	8,287	42.4
6	Soccer: Champions League	Barcelona-Chelsea	A3	28/04/2009	8,282	46.1
7	Sports	Sports Magazine	TVE1	13/05/2009	8,238	44.2
8	After match: World Cup	Turkey-Spain	TVE1	01/04/2009	8,121	42.5
9	After match: Champions League	Barcelona-Chelsea	A3	28/04/2009	7,980	38.7
10	Soccer: Champions League	Liverpool-R. Madrid	A3	10/03/2009	7,968	41.8
11	Soccer: Confederations Cup	Spain-USA	T5	24/05/2009	7,776	55.1
12	After match: King's Cup	Ath. Bilbao-Barcelona	TVE1	13/05/2009	7,476	43.5
13	Soccer: Friendly match	Spain-England	TVE1	11/02/2009	7,385	36.9
14	Soccer: Friendly match	Spain-Argentina	TVE1	14/11/2009	7,073	43.9
15	Sports	*"Especial selección"*	TVE1	11/02/2009	7,050	35.7
16	TV Series	*"23F El día más difícil del Rey"*	TVE1	12/02/2009	6,920	35.5
17	Soccer: World Cup Qualification	Turkey-Spain	TVE1	01/04/2009	6,916	45.1
18	Soccer: World Cup Qualification	Spain-Turkey	TVE1	28/03/2009	6,891	39.9
19	Soccer: Champions League	Bayern Munich-Barcelona	A3	14/04/2009	6,832	38.1
20	Sports	*"Territorio Champions"*	A3	27/05/2009	6,793	44
21	Sports	Sports Magazine	TVE1	28/03/2009	6,665	39
22	Soccer: Friendly match	Austria-Spain	TVE1	18/11/2009	6,549	35.3

	Description	Title	Channel	Date	Viewers (thousands)	Share
23	After match: Champions League	Bayern M.-Barcelona	A3	14/04/2009	6,541	32.2
24	Soccer: Champions League	Barcelona-Chelsea	A3	28/04/2009	6,514	37.9
25	TV Series	*"23F El día más difícil del Rey"*	TVE1	10/02/2009	6,491	31.5

Source: www.vertele.com Los programas más vistos en España en 2009

The success of sports broadcasting in general and soccer's predominance in particular may explain why TV channels compete to obtain the exclusive rights for soccer broadcasts and, to a certain extent, why channels that do not obtain these rights decisively commit themselves to the broadcast of other sports. Table 2 presents the average audiences for the five most-watched TV programs in 2009 of each of the major national channels of Spain, which are TVE1, La 2, Antena 3, Cuatro, Telecinco and La Sexta. As mentioned above, it should be emphasized that channels that do not broadcast soccer may focus their interest on other sports, such as tennis and Formula One. In accordance with the trend observed for the national channels, it is expected that broadcasts of sporting events increase the average audience of TPA, the channel examined in this article's case study.

Table 2: The five most-watched programs by Spanish channels in 2009

Channel		Description	Title	Type	Viewers (thousands)	Share
	1	Soccer: King's Cup	Ath. Bilbao-Barcelona	Sports	10,012	48.5
	2	Soccer: Champions League	Olympiqyue M.-R. Madrid	Sports	8,410	41.9
TVE1	3	Soccer: Champions League	Barcelona-Inter	Sports	8,361	43.2
	4	Soccer: Champions League	Milan-R. Madrid	Sports	8,287	42.4
	5	Sports	Sports Magazine	Sports	8,238	44.2
	1	Tennis: Davis Cup	D. Ferrer-R. Stepanek	Sports	2,016	12.0
	2	Basketball: King's Cup	Unicaja-Tau Cerámica	Sports	1,886	12.8
La 2	3	English Premier League	Manchester U.-Liverpool	Sports	1,497	11.9

Channel		Description	Title	Type	Viewers (thousands)	Share
	4	*"Especial Informativo"*	*"Obama"*	News	1,441	7.2
	5		*"Saber y Ganar"*	Quiz	1,359	10.5
	1	Soccer: Confederations Cup	Spain-USA	Sports	7,776	55.1
	2	Soccer: *"Mundial de Clubes"*	Barcelona-Estudiantes LP	Sports	6,376	43.1
T5	3	Soccer: King's Cup		Sports	4,831	24.8
	4	Soccer: Confederations Cup	Spain-South Africa	Sports	4,497	36.8
	5	Soccer: *"Mundial de Clubes"*		Sports	4,368	31.9
	1	Soccer: Champions League	Barcelona-Manchester U.	Sports	11,310	61.7
	2	Soccer: Champions League	Barcelona-Chelsea	Sports	8,282	46.1
A3	3	Soccer: Champions League	Liverpool-R. Madrid	Sports	7,968	41.8
	4	Soccer: Champions League	Bayern M.-Barcelona	Sports	6,832	38.1
	5		*"Territorio Champions"*	Sports	6,793	44.0
	1		"House"	Drama	2,467	14.1
	2		*"Perdidos en la tribu"*	Others	2,134	13.5
CUATRO	3		*"Fama a bailar"*	Music	2,131	14.4
	4		"FlashForward"	Drama	2,088	10.6
	5	Tennis: Australian Open		Sports	2,005	29.7
	1	Soccer: King's Cup	Ath. Bilbao-Sevilla	Sports	5,827	28.3
	2	Formula One: GP Monaco		Sports	3,185	27.7
LA SEXTA	3	Formula One: GP Spain		Sports	3,116	23.3
	4	Formula One: GP Monaco		Sports	3,104	23.5
	5	Basketball: Eurobasket		Sports	2,979	18.8

Source: www.vertele.com – Los cinco programas más vistos en cada cadena en 2009

3. Previous Literature Review

There are few articles in the previous economic literature addressing the determinants of the number of TV viewers of a particular sporting event. However, certain American authors use Nielsen ratings, which are the audience measurement system developed by Nielsen Media Research to determine the audience size and composition for television programming in the United States, to study the TV audience of National Football League (NFL) games (*Carney & Fenn* 2004) or certain basketball games (*Kanazawa & Funk* 2001).

In the study by *Carney* and *Fenn* (2004), the determinants of TV audience size for NFL games from 2000 to 2001 are analyzed to ex ante estimate the number of viewers for each game and then efficiently set the price of advertisements during the examined games. The researchers in this investigation regress the Nielsen rating of the TV audience for a game on several demographic variables from the studied area and on statistical variables related to the teams involved in the game, among other factors. A fixed effects model is then estimated by the ordinary least squares procedure, producing the conclusions that the white population within the area, the income of the local population, the winning percentage of the team, the forecasted result of the game and the distribution of the games along the season (that is, the week during the season when the game is broadcast) are the most relevant factors for explaining the potential audience of an NFL game.

By contrast the study of *Kanazawa* and *Funk* (2001) attempts to test whether the patterns of TV consumption of National Basketball Association (NBA) viewers are systematically correlated with the racial composition of the teams. An examination of TV ratings corresponding to the second half of the 1996–1997 season reveals certain evidence of racism in the behavior of the viewers, as the TV ratings are positively correlated with the number of white players in the match, even if those players are on the bench. Furthermore, Kanazawa and Funk (2001) note that white players are better paid than black players of similar quality, most likely because the Marginal Revenue Product (MRP) of white basketball players would be based on the popularity of the live broadcasts of the games in which the players participate rather than on the success of the basketball team.

In Europe, *Kuypers* (1996) and *Buraimo* (2008) analyze the TV audience in the context of English soccer. *Kuypers* (1996) uses the number of subscribers that watch live matches during the 1993–1994 season as a dependent variable, whereas *Buraimo* (2008) focuses on explaining the TV ratings provided by the Broadcasters' Audience Research Board (BARB) from the 1997–1998 to the 2003–2004 seasons.

In his analysis of TV audiences, *Kuypers* (1996) investigates whether the subscribers of the channel that broadcast the soccer match choose to watch soccer instead of participating in any other activity. Ordinary least squares estimates from a TV audience model show that the relevance of the match for the competition, the number of international players playing in the match, the average attendance at the stadium in the last three years, the weather (proxied by a dummy variable that assumes a value of 1 for rainy days, as is also specified in our model) and the number of goals scored by the visiting team in the last three matches, among other factors, were statistically significant in explaining the proportion of Sky Sports subscribers watching English Premier League matches during the 1993–1994 season.

Furthermore, both *Kuypers* (1996) and *Carney* and *Fenn* (2004) suggest that TV grids should be flexibly planned to include matches that are of particular interest over the course of the championship season because of the performances of the teams that are involved.

Buraimo (2008) conducts an analysis of the TV demand for English Premier League soccer matches through seven consecutive seasons (1997–2004). In his empirical examination, he follows a two-stage ordinary least squares procedure where the TV audience level is analyzed. *Buraimo* (2008) considers a number of covariates, including several variables reflecting the distinctions between the considered teams (such as the differences in table position and in talent, among other factors), dummy variables accounting for derbies, seasonal variables and a variable representing the outcome uncertainty for the match. (Note that certain of the seasonal factors considered by *Buraimo*, 2008, such as months and the days of the week, are also considered in this article's empirical exercise; however, he only examines the months belonging to the soccer season, from September to May, whereas in this article, all of the months of the year are considered because we examine every sporting event rather than only assessing soccer games.) The empirical results of the study by *Buraimo* (2008) indicate that when the most talented teams play against each other and the event is broadcast live, the TV audience may be increased. However, matches televised on weekdays other than Thursday have lower audience levels than matches that are shown during the weekend. In addition, the months with the largest shares of the TV audience are January and February.

Apart from the studies discussed above, a different branch of the literature conducts more specific analyses regarding the particular topic of why the channels that hold the TV rights to particular sports events decide to broadcast those events. This approach can be observed in the papers of both *Forrest*, *Simmons* and *Buraimo* (2005) and *García* and *Rodríguez* (2006), who estimate a demand model for the TV audiences for English and Spanish soccer, respectively.

Finally, there are other studies that attempt to measure the impact of broadcasting a particular sports event on the attendance at the event in question (*García & Rodríguez* 2002; *Putsis & Sen* 2000; *Zuber & Gandar* 1988); these studies analyze how the audience is influenced by the outcome uncertainty of the broadcast sporting event (*Alavy* et al. 2006) or by patriotic sentiment (*Nuesch & Franck* 2009).

4. The Determinants of the TV Audience

Based on a case study of TPA, this article focuses on whether broadcasts of live sporting events affect TV ratings; if an effect is detected, this article examines the direction and magnitude of this effect. In the empirical exercise, the dependent variable that is examined is the average daily audience of TPA between 2007 and 2009, which indicates the average number of people watching TPA per day for all of the days within the time period under consideration.

With respect to the definition of the dependent variable, it is relevant to note that there exist several metrics that measure the number of people in an audience. In particular, the most commonly cited Nielsen results in the previous literature are reported either as ratings points, which measure the average percentage of viewers watching a program at a given time period relative to the total number of households with TVs in a certain geographical area, or as share, the percentage of viewers watching a program during a given time period relative to the total number of viewers watching TV at that time. The difference between these measurements is that rating reflects the percentage of the total population of televisions that are tuned to a particular program, whereas share reflects the percentage of televisions that are actually in use.

It should be noted that Nielsen Media Research is not the only source for audience data. In the United Kingdom, for example, the TV audience is measured by BARB and the Kantar Media network (including TNS) currently measures TV audiences in several countries around the world. In fact, in Spain, there are two companies supplying TV audience size data: the Estudio General de Medios (EGM) and the aforementioned Kantar Media. The former obtains audience information from different national surveys, whereas the latter uses the people meter, which provides information regarding the number of viewers watching a certain TV program. According to Kantar Media (http://www.kantarmedia-audiences.com/television/peoplemeter.aspx), "…these meters are attached to television sets within the homes of a representative demographic group or 'panel'", so "… panel members indicate their presence in the room using a remote control, creating audience data that is reported overnight using both telephone lines and GPRS".

In addition to the two measurements discussed above, in the case of Spain, Kantar Media offers additional measures, such as the cumulative rating (which measures the total number of viewers that tuned in to a program for at least one minute of time, relative to the total reference population) and the average number of viewers watching a certain program at any given time, computed as the mean size of the audience on a minute-by-minute basis throughout the length of the program.

However, this type of information has traditionally been bought by media companies at high prices to assess audience demands. These steep prices may provide an explanation for the dearth of broader empirical economic literature in this field.

As mentioned above, the daily average number of viewers watching the TPA is employed as the dependent variable in this study. Kantar Media uses a minute-by-minute system for measuring audiences that provides the number of viewers tuning in to a channel each minute through the day. Calculating the mean out of all the minutes broadcasted a day leads to the daily average number of viewers. For the purposes of this study, the use of this absolute rating is preferable to the use of audience share because (all else being equal) the latter metric simply captures the quality of the programming that has been scheduled against the sporting event in question, whereas the former metric measures the pure attractiveness of the sports broadcast. In particular, the logarithm of the dependent variable is considered in estimations to obtain quantitative results in terms of either elasticities or rates. Time series regression is used to explain the variation of the dependent variable in terms of a set of explanatory variables that have commonly been used in the previously published literature.

To conduct the regressions, a day-by-day time series data set for the period from 2007 to 2009 (1096 observations) is employed to identify both the determinants of the average daily audience of the TPA and the impact of live sports events broadcasting on the audience size.

5. Empirical Facts and Discussion

The summary statistics for the logarithm of the TV audience are shown in Table 3. The large difference between its maximum and minimum values as well as its high standard deviation in relation to the number of observations is highlighted, indicating a high level of fluctuation of the daily TV audience. Besides, the time series exhibits skewness and excess kurtosis. Figure 1 shows the graph of the log TV audience, which evidences seasonal and cyclical patterns, an upward trend, some jumps and an apparent large volatility.

Table 3: Summary statistics for Log(TV audience)

Mean	2.270
Median	2.347
Max	3.401
Min	0.966
Standard deviation	0.391
Skewness	-0.795
Kurtosis	3.536

The first step of the empirical analysis is to determine whether the daily TV audience is stationary. In this sense, Augmented Dickey-Fuller (ADF) and Phillips-Perron (PP) tests were made to identify the presence of a unit root for the variable in logarithmic terms. Table 4 reports the results from ADF and PP unit root tests with an intercept and a deterministic trend, required to capture the increase in average audience that took place since 2008. In order to correct for serial correlation, the number of lagged difference terms in the ADF regressions was chosen according to the Schwartz Information Criteria (SIC). The Phillips-Perron test uses the same models as the Dickey-Fuller tests, but rather than using lagged variables for serial correlation, it employs a non-parametric correction (*Newey & West* 1987). In this case, we have chosen the lag truncation for this nonparametric correction using an automated bandwidth estimator, the Bartlett kernel.

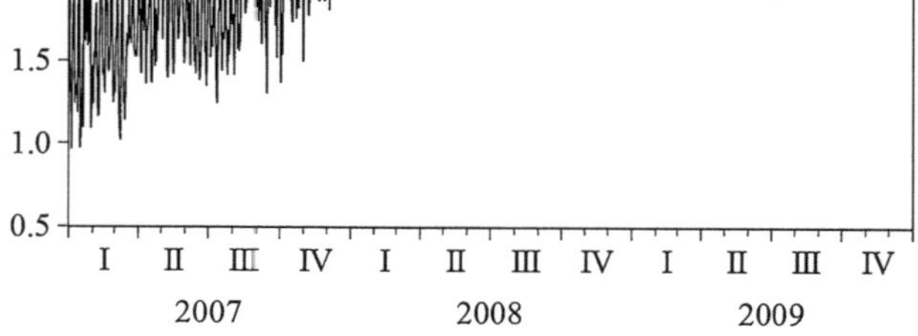

Fig. 1: Log(TV audience)

Table 4: Unit root tests, Log(TV audience)

	Test statistic	*d*	5% Critical Value (McKinnon Critical Values)
ADF	-3.14*	13	-3.41
Arranz et al. (2000) ADF	-3.70**	11	-3.41
PP	-23.47***	16	-3.41

Note: d shows lagged differences of log of TV audience in the ADF test and truncation lags in the PP test. ***, ** and * indicate rejection of the null-unit root hypothesis at 1%, 5% and 10 % level of significance, respectively.

The PP test rejects the null hypothesis of a unit root at the 1% level of significance, whereas the ADF test only does it at the 10%. However, the existence of outliers or jumps in the data of daily television audience would bias the ADF unit root inference. Thus, we also perform the complementary ADF test proposed by *Arranz* et al. (2006) in order to deal with this problem. Essentially, this procedure consists of applying Dickey-Fuller tests on the series previously filtered with the median filter. This method is robust to the presence of additive outliers and, as *Escribano* et al. (2011) stress, it is easier to apply than other tests proposed for the same purpose, as for example *Lucas* (1995) or *Vogelsang* (1999).

Now the results of the complementary ADF contrast and the PP test suggest that TV audience can be treated as an integrated of order zero variable. In other words, TV audience is a stationary time series and, in a second stage of our analysis, this allows estimating a conditional mean equation for the variable in levels, to identify both daily and seasonal effects as well as serial correlation.

Conditional Mean Equation

As discussed above, TV audience appears to have a strong seasonal behavior, either intra-daily, weekly or intra-year. Since it is usual in time series literature, we try to capture weekly seasonality by means of daily dummies (D_i) and monthly seasonality by monthly dummies (M_i)[1]. In this study, January and Monday are used as the respective reference values for these two categories.

Furthermore, we consider the possibility of stochastic seasonality by incorporating lags in the mean equation, in an attempt to model the persistence of the data. Thus, as suggested in *Becker* and *Murphy* (1988), lags of the dependent variable are considered to control for a possible inertia effect in TV consumption.

1 Trigonometric functions as an alternative specification to dummy variables, that captures the curvature of the series by applying sines and cosines, were also estimated but the results are no presented to save space.

More specifically, we allow for weekly stochastic seasonality by including up to fourteen lags in the TV audience variable conforming an autoregressive process of order fourteen, AR(14), sufficient to remove all the correlations from the series [2].

The selection of these lags and the other deterministic seasonal factors are made by estimating a general to specific equation based on tests for serial correlation of the residuals and the Akaike information criteria (AIC), according to the model in equation 1:

$$y_t = \phi_0 + \phi_1 \text{Trend} + \phi_2 (\text{Trend})^2 + \sum_{i=1} \varphi_i y_{t-i} + \sum_{i=1} \delta_i D_i + \sum_{i=1} \eta_i M_i + \mu_i H_i + \zeta_i R_i + \lambda_i \text{Sport}_i + \varepsilon_t \quad (1)$$

where we also consider whether a day is a holiday (H_i) and we include a trend (day number) and its square to account for any secular changes in the preferences of individuals for watching TV. The latter means that the interest of many participants in certain leisure activities fades over time as issues such as boredom arise.

Moreover, as discussed by *Buraimo* (2008), weather is expected to influence TV audience size. In particular, it is assumed that unfavorable weather conditions may cause individuals to remain at home, likely increasing TV audience levels. Therefore, a dummy variable for rainy days (R_i) is also considered in this investigation (this variable has been computed according to the data provided by www.tutiempo.net which registers whether it rained on a certain day).

In the empirical exercise, in addition to the variables described above, a dummy variable taking a value of one in the day when a sport event is broadcast live is included in the conditional mean equation for the TV audience.

Besides, the model analyzes whether different types of sports have a distinct impact on TV audience size. In this case, a set of dummy variables is defined for each of the following types of sporting events broadcast by the TPA within the sample period; these include soccer, cycling, basketball, motor sports, canoeing, roller hockey, the equestrian sports of horse jumping and horse races, handball, tennis and Asturian bowling. Furthermore, we differentiate among the various soccer broadcasts available nowadays. These include UEFA Champions League games, Real Sporting de Gijón [3] and Real Oviedo matches (being these two teams

2 We used the autocorrelation and partial autocorrelation functions for selecting the AR model. Other specifications, such as multiplicative seasonality or MA terms were considered as well.

3 Real Sporting de Gijón had been 10 years in Spanish Second Division of soccer until season 2007/08 when they achieved the promotion to First Division (the top professional league

the most important ones in the region of Asturias) among others. Thus, these different dummy variables are considered in the specification.

The summary statistics for the dependent variables included in the models of TV demand are reported in Table 5, while Table 6 reports the ordinary least squares parameter estimates of equation (1). We start by estimating the general AR(14) model and progressively eliminate the insignificant parameters to obtain a more reasonable specification. The preferred model is shown in the last column of Table 6.

Table 5: Key summary statistics

	Mean	Std.Dev.	Min.	Max.
Average daily audience (number of viewers)	10,375.33	3,635.028	2,630	30,010

	Frequency (Total # of programs)	Percentage
Broadcast live sports events	**225**	**20.529**
Soccer	110	10.04
Cycling	35	3.19
Basketball	7	0.64
Motor sports	14	1.28
Hockey	1	0.09
Canoeing	2	0.18
Equestrian	3	0.27
Handball	1	0.09
Tennis	4	0.36
Bowling	19	1.73
Rainy days	**518**	**47.26**
Total days (sample size)	**1096**	**100**

in Spain). Some of the decisive games were broadcast by TPA during the studied period obtaining high audience levels. It is also relevant to remark that Sporting de Gijón can be considered the most important soccer team in the region taking into account the number of fans, its legacy, the news generated and its social importance in general.

Table 6: The ordinary least squares estimation results

	Model 1	Model 2	Model 3	Model 4
Log(TV audience)$_{-1}$	0.231***	0.234***	0.237***	0.233***
Log(TV audience)$_{-2}$	0.028*	0.022*	0.031*	0.035*
Log(TV audience)$_{-6}$	0.094***	0.082***	0.079***	0.081***
Log(TV audience)$_{-7}$	0.177***	0.172***	0.186***	0.182***
Log(TV audience)$_{-10}$	-0.094***	-0.078***	-0.084***	-0.085***
Log(TV audience)$_{-14}$	0.122***	0.103***	0.078***	0.076***
Trend	0.001***	0.001***	0.001***	0.001***
Trend^2	-7.21E-07***	-7.99E-07***	-8.14E-07***	-8.20E-07***
February	-0.004	-0.004	0.001	0.001
March	-0.031	-0.045	-0.036	-0.034
April	-0.035	-0.048	-0.033	-0.034
May	-0.039	-0.086**	-0.080*	-0.075
June	-0.092***	-0.103***	-0.099***	-0.097***
July	-0.090***	-0.092***	-0.087***	-0.088***
August	-0.052	-0.096***	-0.110***	-0.104***
September	-0.057*	-0.074***	-0.076**	-0.074***
October	-0.034	-0.046	-0.047	-0.046
November	-0.008	-0.017	-0.018	-0.017
December	0.031	0.028	0.032	0.035
Tuesday	-0.010	-0.014	-0.014	-0.015
Wednesday	0.051**	0.024	0.008	0.007
Thursday	0.026	0.023	0.027	0.025
Friday	0.037	0.039	0.047**	0.046*
Saturday	0.102***	0.055**	0.056**	0.052***
Sunday	0.163***	0.139***	0.164***	0.172***
National holiday	0.096**	0.078**	0.082**	0.092***
Rainy day	0.030***	0.032***	0.037***	0.037***
Sport	0.426***			
Soccer		0.147***		
Champions League			0.452***	0.450***
Sporting			0.306***	0.308***
Oviedo			0.023	
Other soccer			-0.009	
Cycling		0.096**	0.090**	0.086**
Basketball		-0.025	-0.041	
Motor		0.001	-0.001	
Hockey		-0.008	-0.020	

	Model 1	Model 2	Model 3	Model 4
Canoeing		0.039	0.052	
Equestrian		-0.064	-0.066	
Handball		0.113	0.100	
Tennis		0.016	0.013	
Bowling		0.081**	0.056	
Constant	0.632***	0.669***	0.669***	0.675***
Adjusted R^2	0.725	0.734	0.756	0.758
Q(1)	0.103	0.134	0.161	0.196
Q(4)	1.726	2.304	6.433	6.515
Q(7)	3.223	3.694	7.243	7.426
Q(20)	23.545	23.115	24.757	24.800
Skewness	0.451	0.323	0.237	0.262
Kurtosis	4.653	4.593	4.563	4.631
F-statistic	2.055***	2.281***	2.029***	2.007***
TR^2	40.348***	44.549***	39.849***	39.448***
N	1,095	1,095	1,095	1,095

Notes: Coefficient estimates are shown to three decimal places. ***, ** and * indicate statistical significance at the 1%, 5% and 10% levels, respectively. Q represents the Ljung-Box statistics for autocorrelation in the residuals. F and TR^2 indicate ARCH tests for 20 lags. The dependent variable is (the log of) the average daily audience.

A strong effect on TV consumption habits is demonstrated by the highly significant coefficient of the lagged dependent variable. Indeed, the results indicate that the lagged TV audience coefficients of order 1, 2, 6, 7, 10 and 14 are significant at the 5% level. The sum of the AR coefficients, close to 0.5, highlights a strong persistence in the TV audience. However, the average daily audience of the TPA appears to follow an inverted U-shaped trend from 2007 to 2009, reflecting an initial increase in audience size, followed by an incipient drop.

With respect to seasonal patterns in the evolution of the audience of the TPA, calendar effects appear to be quite relevant for explaining the average number of TPA viewers. In particular, the average daily audience increases during the weekend, including on Fridays, relative to weekdays. This phenomenon could be explained by the fact that the opportunity cost of watching TV diminishes during weekends. This finding is similar to the results obtained by *Buraimo* (2008); however, one major difference between this study and the earlier investigation is that Thursdays do not significantly differ from Mondays in our estimates. The fact that more than one sport is examined could be an explanation for this difference, given that various sports do not have the same broadcast schedule as soccer matches. An increase in average daily audience that appears to be similar to the weekend effect also occurs during national holidays that are celebrated in Spain. Furthermore, estimates reveal that spring and summer months have lower audience levels than January, whereas December and February have audience sizes that are similar to or higher than the January levels, a result that closely corresponds to the findings of *Forrest* et al. (2005) and *Buraimo* (2008). Moreover, we also find that bad weather conditions have a positive effect on TV ratings.

As mentioned in the introduction, the main objective of this article is to evaluate the impact of broadcasts of live sporting events on the average daily audience of TPA. The evidence suggests that only soccer and cycling broadcasts have a positive effect on the number of TPA viewers. Given the functional form chosen for the model specification, the estimated coefficient of the dummy variables could be interpreted as short-term rates. Long-term rates are calculated by dividing these coefficients by one minus the lagged coefficient of the dependent variable. As a consequence, the broadcasts of live UEFA Champions League matches as well as Real Sporting de Gijón games and cycling events increase the audience by approximately 45%, 31% and 8.6% in the short term in comparison to days where there is no live broadcast,. Over the long term, these percentages increase to 94%, 64% and 18%, respectively. The live broadcasting of other sport events does not appear to produce a significant effect on audience size.

These results imply that it seems to be profitable for TPA to broadcast live sporting events, as the increased audience sizes that the channel obtains from these broadcasts may justify the huge investment it initially made to obtain the broadcasting rights for sporting events. It should also be emphasized that, even when the TPA competed for its sports-related audience with other TV channels, its broadcasts of live sporting events were nonetheless hugely successful for the size of its audience.

Finally, for these results to be consistent there must be no serial correlation in the error terms. The Ljung-Box Q-statistic performed indicates that the residuals are serially uncorrelated. Additionally, the coefficient of determination (R^2) obtained was approximately 0.76, indicating that the proposed model specifications explain a considerable portion of the variance in the average daily audience of TPA. The remaining unexplained variance may be attributed to viewer preferences, unemployment-related effects, and the presence of cable television or similar alternatives in households, among other factors. These determinants of TV viewing are highly complicated to quantify but obviously influence audience size. Nevertheless, the adjusted R^2 obtained in this article appears to be higher than the R^2 value calculated in previously published literature.

Compared to the findings of the previously published economic literature, the results of this study indicate that the coefficients of the considered covariates have the expected signs and that the goodness of fit measures are quite reasonable.

GARCH Models

The third step of our empirical study analyzes the residuals of the mean equation (1) for time varying volatility. A general view of ε_t shows the existence of volatility of daily TV audience (Figure 2), and specifically, it appears to exhibit the volatility clustering property, that is to say, large changes tend to be followed by other large changes, of either sign, and small changes tend to be followed by small changes. Another piece of evidence for the volatility of ε_t (see Table 6) is the high value of kurtosis (4.63). In any case, more formally, we apply the Lagrange Multiplier test proposed by *Engle* (1982) about the existence of conditional heteroskedasticity in the residual series.

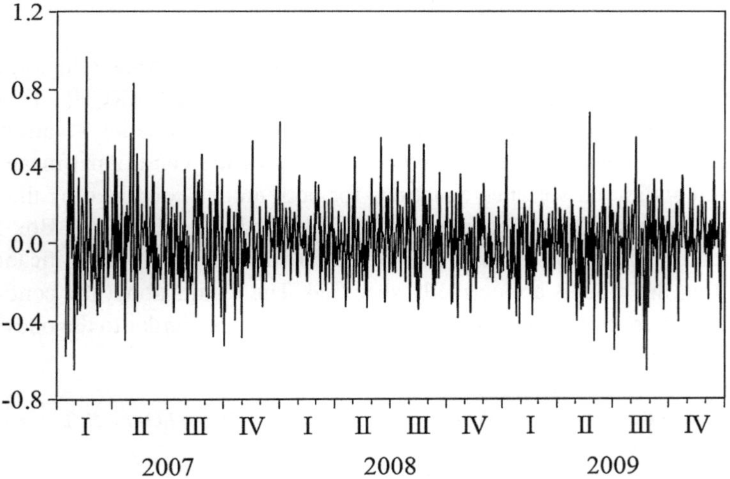

Fig. 2: Time series plot of ε_t

The results reported in Table 6 for the F and TR^2 test statistics indicate that the null hypothesis of homoskedasticity is rejected at the 1% significant level and hence, in the fourth step we study the TV audience using a Generalized Autoregressive Conditional Heteroskedasticity error model (GARCH). Unlike classical regression models which assume that volatility is time invariant and constant, a GARCH model considers that one period ahead variances are dependent on current available information. Therefore, the GARCH model requires joint estimation of the conditional mean and variance process, where the former is represented in this paper by the above autoregressive process for TV audience shown in equation (1).

The GARCH model, proposed by *Bollerslev* (1986), is an extension of the Autoregressive Conditional Heteroskedasticity model (ARCH) of *Engle* (1982). The ARCH(p) model, on the assumption that the conditional mean error (ε_t) is distributed with zero mean and time-varying conditional variance (σ_t^2), describes this conditional variance as a linear function on the past p squared innovations (ε_{t-i}^2). Besides, the GARCH model specifies that the current conditional volatility is a function of the first q past conditioned volatilities as well as the p past squared error terms considered by ARCH(p) models. Thus, the GARCH(p,q) procedure is given by equation 2:

$$\sigma_t^2 = \omega + \sum_{i=1}^{p} \alpha_i \varepsilon_{t-i}^2 + \sum_{j=1}^{q} \beta_i \sigma_{t-i}^2 \quad (2)$$

We compare several symmetric GARCH models at different p and q lags applying the standard Akaike information criterion. Accordingly, the GARCH(1,1) and the GARCH(1,3) have been chosen as the best processes for modeling volatility.

Table 7 summarizes the estimated coefficients of the conditional mean equations and conditional variance equations for both models, obtained by the maximum likelihood method[4]. Diagnostic statistics based upon the Ljung-Box test of the standardized and the squared standardized residuals are all insignificant, suggesting that the models are correctly specified. The results about the conditional mean parameters estimated in these GARCH models are similar to the ones previously reported under AR(14) estimation alone.

Table 7: Estimation results of the GARCH (1, 1), GARCH (1, 3) and EGARCH (1, 1) for the log of the average daily audience

	GARCH(1,1)	GARCH(1,3)	EGARCH(1,1)
Conditional mean			
Log(TV audience)$_{-1}$	0.230***	0.222***	0.224***
Log(TV audience)$_{-2}$	0.065**	0.053*	0.052*
Log(TV audience)$_{-6}$	0.086***	0.075***	0.072***
Log(TV audience)$_{-7}$	0.160***	0.152***	0.151***
Log(TV audience)$_{-10}$	-0.081***	-0.092***	-0.090***
Log(TV audience)$_{-14}$	0.078***	0.097***	0.090***

4 *Doornik* and *Ooms* (2008) point out that including a dummy variable as a regressor into mean equation can lead to a multimodality problem, but this depends on the data, being more likely when there are large interventions or for large outliers.

	GARCH(1,1)	GARCH(1,3)	EGARCH(1,1)
Conditional mean			
Trend	0.001***	0.001***	0.001***
Trend^2	-7.85E-07***	-8.23E-07	-8.42E-07
February	-0.002	-0.005	-0.010
March	-0.019	-0.013	-0.023
April	-0.039	-0.034	-0.034
May	-0.074**	-0.104***	-0.095***
June	-0.088***	-0.097***	-0.095***
July	-0.081***	-0.088***	-0.086***
August	-0.102***	-0.104***	-0.096***
September	-0.072**	-0.083***	-0.088***
October	-0.042	-0.038	-0.043
November	-0.014	-0.019	-0.029
December	0.034	0.037	0.034
Tuesday	-0.017	-0.021	-0.023
Wednesday	0.016	0.008	0.008
Thursday	0.032	0.032	0.027
Friday	0.051**	0.047**	0.045***
Saturday	0.049**	0.037*	0.043***
Sunday	0.178***	0.157***	0.158***
National holiday	0.078***	0.058**	0.047**
Rainy day	0.030***	0.025***	0.025***
Champions League	0.462***	0.509***	0.513***
Sporting	0.315***	0.301***	0.296***
Cycling	0.084***	0.077***	0.079***
Constant	0.648***	0.707***	0.719***
Conditional variance Parameters			
ω	0.001***	0.001***	-0.065***
α	0.015**	0.018**	0.022
β_1	0.965***	-0.019***	0.986***
β_2		-0.027***	
β_3		0.977***	
γ			-0.017*
Adjusted R^2	0.756	0.761	0.752
Q(1)	0.332	0.387	6.234
Q(4)	4.608	6.797	6.550
Q(7)	5.479	6.965	14.176

	GARCH(1,1)	GARCH(1,3)	EGARCH(1,1)
Conditional variance Parameters			
Q(20)	19.066	20.898	19.277
$Q^2(20)$	17.213	20.548	15.436
F-statistic	0.806	0.977	0.723
TR^2	16.205	19.571	14.547
N	1,095	1,095	1,095

Notes: Coefficient estimates are shown to three decimal places. ***, ** and * indicate statistical significance at the 1%, 5% and 10% levels, respectively. Q and Q^2 represent the Ljung-Box statistics for autocorrelation in the residuals. F and TR^2 indicate ARCH tests for 20 lags.

Overall, the results suggest that there is significant time varying volatility in the TV audience during the sample period. However, the estimated β_1 coefficient in the GARCH(1,3) model was negative and significant, violating the conditions, so the conditional variance is always nonnegative (*Nelson & Cao* 1992; *Doornik & Ooms* 2008). Therefore the model of choice for this study is the GARCH(1,1), for which all the estimated coefficients are positive and statistically significant at the 5% level, with values of 0.015 and 0.965 for the α and β parameters, respectively. The measure of persistence of volatility shocks ($\alpha + \beta$) is quite close to one, which indicates a near long memory process.

Finally, in order to capture a possible asymmetry response to shocks in the TV audience volatility, we estimate the Exponential GARCH model (EGARCH) introduced by *Nelson* (1991). In the EGARCH (p, q) model, the logarithm of the conditional variance depends on both the size and the sign of lagged shocks as follows in equation 3:

$$\log(\sigma_t^2) = \omega + \sum_{j=1} \beta_i \log(\sigma_{t-i}^2) + \sum_{i=1} \alpha_i \left|\frac{\varepsilon_{t-i}}{\sigma_{t-i}}\right| + \sum_{k=1} \gamma_k \frac{\varepsilon_{t-k}}{\sigma_{t-k}}$$

In this specification, conditional volatility is always positive even if the parameter values are negative. This means that the non-negativity restrictions for parameter imposed in the GARCH model are not necessary. Moreover, the existence of asymmetric impacts and the leverage effect can be tested by the hypothesis that γ_k is not equal to zero while γ_k is less than zero. The latter refers to the characteristic of time series that "bad news" tends to increase volatility more than "good news".

In Table 7, we also report the estimation results for an EGARCH(1,1) model. In this case, the parameter γ_k is negative but statistically significant only at the 10% level, implying a weak evidence of asymmetric impacts and leverage effect.

6. Concluding Remarks

The objective of this study has been to apply some of the most important volatility models to estimate a TV audience size demand and to measure the impact of broadcasts of live sporting events on the number of viewers of TPA, a Spanish public regional TV channel.

We have modeled the conditional variance using symmetric GARCH and asymmetric EGARCH models and our results show that a GARCH(1,1) is the best specification to describe the process. The findings indicate that the impact of new shocks on TV audience is highly persistent and suggest, however, that there is no strong evidence of asymmetric effects on its volatility.

The results also indicate that the process followed by the conditional mean of TV daily audience can be represented by an AR(14) model with deterministic seasonal factors, in order to capture the nature of the data that we use.

Evidence regarding the positive impact of broadcasts of live sports events on audience size is demonstrated. In the specific case that was analyzed for this study, the empirical findings are robust enough to conclude that broadcasts of live sporting events produce a significant positive impact on the long-term audience size. In particular, the broadcasts of live UEFA Champions League matches, Sporting de Gijón games and cycling events significantly increase the audience in the long run.

In conclusion, seasonal patterns appear to be important determinants of TV audience size. However, the nature and degree of seasonal effects are not easy to identify. We find that there is a "natural seasonality" of TV audiences that is caused by seasonal variations in climate; in particular, in accordance with previous studies, we find that the average daily audience of TPA is significantly higher on those days with bad weather conditions (rain). In addition, we conclude that an "institutionalized seasonality" related to holidays and other factors appears to matter. This type of seasonality would arise from the variance in individuals' preferences that is caused by time and opportunity cost issues.

A possible extension of this paper could be to consider jointly a GARCH model with jumps and other types of asymmetric GARCH behavior. Another important line of research would be to examine the ability of the GARCH models to forecast the volatility of TV audience.

References

Alavy, K., Gaskell, A., Leach, S. & Szymanski, S. (2006): On The Edge of Your Seat: Demand for Football on Television and the Uncertainty of Outcome Hypothesis, Working Paper No. 631, International Association of Sport Economists.

Arranz, M. A., Escribano, A. & Mármol, F. (2006): Effects of Applying Linear and Nonlinear Filters on Tests for Unit Roots with Additive Outliers, Working Paper No. 00-86, Madrid: Universidad Carlos III de Madrid.

Becker, G. & Murphy, K. (1988): A Theory of Rational Addiction, in: Journal of Political Economy, Vol. 96, 4, pp. 675–700.

Bollerslev, T. (1986): Generalised Autoregressive Conditional Heteroskedasticity, in: Journal of Econometrics, Vol. 31, 3, pp. 307–327.

Buraimo, B. (2008): Stadium Attendance and Television Audience Demand in English League Football, in: Managerial and Decision Economics, Vol. 29, 6, pp. 513–23.

Carney, S. & Fenn, A. (2004): The Determinants of NFL Viewership: Evidence from Nielsen Ratings, Working Paper No. 2004–02, Colorado Springs: Department of Economics and Business – Colorado College.

Doornik, J. & Ooms, M. (2008): Multimodality in GARCH Regression Models, in: International Journal of Forecasting, Vol. 24, 3, pp. 432–448.

Engle, R. (1982): Autoregressive Conditional Heteroscedasticity with Estimates of the Variance of UK Inflation, in: Econometrica, Vol. 50, 4, pp. 987–1008.

Escribano, A., Peña, J. I. & Villaplana, P. (2011): Modelling Electricity Prices: International Evidence, in: Oxford Bulletin of Economics and Statistics, Vol. 73, 5, pp. 622–650.

Forrest, D., Simmons, R. & Buraimo, B. (2005): Outcome Uncertainty and the Couch Potato Audience, in: Scottish Journal of Political Economy, Vol. 52, 4, pp. 641–661.

García, J. & Rodríguez, P. (2002): The Determinants of Football Match Attendance Revisited: Empirical Evidence from the Spanish Football League, in: Journal of Sports Economics, Vol. 3, 1, pp. 18–38.

García, J. & Rodríguez, P. (2006): The Determinants of TV Audience for Spanish Football: A First Approach, in: *Rodriguez, P., Kesenne, S. & García, J.* (eds.): Sports Economics after Fifty Years. Essays in Honour of Simon Rottenberg. Oviedo: Ediciones Universidad de Oviedo, pp. 147–167.

Lucas, A. (1995): An Outlier Robust Unit Root Test with an Application to the Extended Nelson-Plosser Data, in: Journal of Econometrics, Vol. 66, 1–2, pp. 153–173.

Kanazawa, M. & Funk, J. (2001): Racial Discrimination in Professional Basketball: Evidence from Nielsen Ratings, in: Economic Enquiry, Vol. 39, 4, pp. 599–608.

Kuypers, T. (1996): The Beautiful Game? An Econometric Study of Why People Watch English Football, Discussion Paper in Economics No. 1996–01, London: University College London.

Nelson, D. B. (1991): Conditional Heteroscedasticity in Asset Returns: A New Approach, in: Econometrica, Vol. 59, 2, pp. 347–370.

Nelson, D. B. & Cao C. Q. (1992): Inequality Constraints in the Univariate GARCH Model, in: Journal of Business and Economic Statistics, Vol. 10, 2, pp. 229–235.

Newey, W. K. & West, K. D. (1987): A Simple Positive Semi-definite Heteroskedasticity and Autocorrelation Consistent Covariance Matrix, in: Econometrica, Vol. 55, 3, pp. 1029–1054.

Nuesch, S. & Franck, E. (2009): The Role of Patriotism in Explaining the TV Audience of National Team Games – Evidence from Four International Tournaments, in: Journal of Media Economics, Vol. 22, 1, pp. 6–19.
Putsis, W. & Sen, S. (2000): Should NFL Blackouts be Banned?, in: Applied Economics, Vol. 32, 12, pp. 1495–1507.
Vogelsang, T. J. (1999): Two Simple Procedures for Testing for a Unit Root when there are Additive Outliers, in: Journal of Time Series Analysis, Vol. 20, 2, pp. 173–192.
Zuber, R. & Gandar, J. (1988): Lifting the Television Blackout on No-Shows at Football Games, in: Atlantic Economic Journal, Vol. 16, 2, pp. 63–73.

Gridiron Games: A Case Analysis of Turf War Issues and the Economic, Social, Cultural, and Political Incentives for Government Subsidization

Christopher M. Keshock, Brooke Forester, Shelley Holden

Abstract

The purpose of this report was to examine the economic, social, and cultural support of three different amateur college level football "American Gridiron" contests. Results examine how politicians use exaggerated monetary values to garner community support of the events they propagandize.

Keywords

athletic events, subsidization, reciprocal value, economic impact, politics

1. Introduction

Public spending reciprocal value is a complex matter and casual scrutiny of how tax-payer dollars are distributed during the recent United States economic crisis has ostensibly provoked fiscal transparency concerns in the country. Government proration becomes even more concerning when funds are distributed toward leisure initiatives rather than more gripping educational, infrastructure, and law enforcement based public entities. When public officials do invest tax dollars to support recreational facilities or host sports contests economic impact figures are typically publicized to reassure community residents it is money well spent. However, other considerations are often purported to support sport facility and event yields beyond economic growth in the form of social, cultural, and quality of life opportunities gained by a community and its residents. Unfortunately these benefits may succumb to surreptitious biased agendas of sports officials, promoters, and political figures when decisions are made regarding which athletic events get funded and the amounts dispensed. Even though professional sports receive the majority of attention and financial support amateur sporting events may also receive public seed money to build a community venue or host a contest, thus prompting a similar review of their own sport benefit underpinnings.

2. Purpose

As previously mentioned conversations relating to the value of community sports events are especially timely in the current economy, which contains the charge of "Do better with less," in contrast to that of a surplus economy and more liberal spending patterns. This raises the question of whether hosting sports events and the high cost to run these contests are worth the financial effort. Consequently, turf war issues escalate between community event planners fighting over limited public resources with each publicizing their own attributes, both genuine and exaggerated. Debate toward the legitimacy of findings has subsequently created the need to examine the independent worth of each publicly sponsored event relative to others. Therefore, the purpose of this report was to examine the economic benefit (tourist direct spending), economic impact (multiplier effect), social benefits, and cultural support of three different college level football "American Gridiron" contests: an end of season All-Star game (Senior Bowl) comprised of the best intercollegiate football players in the country; a Post-Season Bowl game (GoDaddy.com Bowl) between two National Collegiate Athletic Association (NCAA) Division I institutions; and, a regular season contest (Gulf Coast Classic) between two southeastern Division I Historically Black College and University schools. All three games were played in the same stadium located in a Gulf Coast United States city and each received subsidization from the host city to help cover contest operational costs. Also, a comparison of the event impact calculations and propagandized economic impact results from each of the three football contests are discussed in an attempt to assess turf warfare for public seed money distributed to community events in the host city. A final aim of this case analysis was to unearth possible economic, social, cultural or political motives of community stakeholders who advocated the financial subsidization of one specific football contest over the others.

3. Review of Literature

Numerous studies exist examining the economic benefits and impacts of sporting events. Calculations of economic impact by modern sport economists have the potential to suggest losses from building public venues and hosting events, a condition described by *Szymanski* (2009) as "sporting money illusion", which brings debates concerning the current recession into sharper focus especially in times of staggering national debt in the United States. Likewise, sport business and research textbooks (*Rosner & Shropshire* 2011; *Gratton & Jones* 2008; *Noll*

1997) and contemporary writers in the field of sport such as *Baade, Quirk, Fort, Crompton* and *Zimbalist* and luminaries in the world of economics such as Adam Smith and the Nobel Prize winners John Nash and John Maynard Keynes are often revisited to assess the relevance of their theories to the burgeoning field of sport economics. However, when it comes to the economic impact of sports events careful attention to the source and calculations used for event impact estimation must be paid. This is especially true when community events are to be compared to one another and subsidizations are paid based on how they may add new money to the local economy that would not exists if the events were held in another location.

Economic impact studies carried out by paid consultants in comparison to theoretically grounded research performed by academics vary in methodologies, applications, and assumptions resulting in different conclusions. This discourse has led to other methods used to determine the value of sport contests such as cost/benefit analyses and the Contingent Valuation Method (CVM), especially when referendum voting or tax increases to pay for new public facilities or to host community events in an area are deliberated. Typically, civic events, expositions, fairs and festivals, cultural experiences, entertainment, and sporting contests all compete for taxpayer dollars in a community with each asserting their own event as a mechanism to boost or revitalize an economy. While the competition between different community events and positioning for budget earmarks is habitually an ongoing debate a review of relative worth amongst similarly related events in their attempts to establish superior attributes to garner public funds is less researched. Juxtaposing of like events held in a specific location provides an opportunity to further probe the true economic worth of and reciprocal value of events congruent in nature, style, and purpose. In an attempt then to add to the literature of sport economic impact applications three college football sporting events held in the same destination were examined in this study.

4. College Football in the United States

Without question, college football is a major part of the American sports landscape where rivalry games, league championships and post season bowl games are closely watched and deeply woven into the fabric of many American households. Millions of dollars are spent each year on broadcasting rights, team apparel, ticket sales, state-of-the-art facilities, and weekend tailgates. But how and why has one sport played by 18–22 year old men impacted the lives of so many

Americans? To answer these questions, one must ultimately understand the fans of collegiate football, the economic and social impacts of the game and the role the media have played in a quest to fulfill society's insatiable desire for anything college football.

The first intercollegiate football game was played between Rutgers and Princeton in 1869. Since that game, the student-athlete participation in college football has reached nearly 100,000 participants (*Brown* 2012). Likewise, the fan base has grown exponentially. In 2011, approximately 49,699,419 fans attended college football games nationwide (*National Football Foundation* 2013). This number represents an all-time high in attendance since the collection of attendance figures by the NCAA began in 1948. The University of Michigan alone has an average of 112,252 fans per football game, the highest attendance figure in the nation for any collegiate athletic program (*Chambers* 2013).

In addition to high attendance figures, college football as a whole enjoys even higher television viewership ratings. The 2012 Discover Bowl Championship Series (*BCS* 2013) National Championship Game on ESPN between Alabama and Notre Dame garnered the second-most viewed program rating in television history. Approximately 26.4 million viewers tuned in to view the game (*National Football Foundation* 2013). Interestingly, the game is second in viewership only to the 2011 BCS Championship Game. Based on the Senior Bowl College All-Star game NFL Network broadcasting 2.5 million watched the roughly 34 hours of Senior Bowl practices, game day coverage, and re-broadcasts of coverage after the event which was televised on the day of the NFL draft show (*Keshock* 2008). The GMAC Bowl (now called the *GoDaddy.com Bowl*) recorded a viewer audience of over 4 million households in the last quarter and overtime period making it one of the most watched FBS bowl games of 2010. Such statistics highlight America's passion for college football and the large popularity of post-season bowl games.

While the media, universities, and fans are primarily interested in the major bowl games, there are many noteworthy "minor" bowl games or non-BCS bowl games. These non-BCS bowl games also have hefty payouts, although they are but a fraction of the major BCS bowl games payouts. The 2014 Capital One Bowl has a payout of $8.5 million representing the highest non-BCS bowl payout while The Famous Idaho Potato Bowl only pays $650,000, representing the lowest payout ("2013–2014 Bowl,").

Much like the revenue distribution for BCS bowl games, the minor bowl game revenue distribution is based on formulae created by conferences. Some conferences choose to give each school within the conference an equal share of the payout while others have a performance based distribution system. Individual bowl game organizers are responsible for providing participants with payout money which is subsequently used by the invited schools to pay for team travel costs and school travel parties visiting the bowl game location. In return for their bowl payout distributions schools are required to sell an allotment of game tickets to the bowl contest. In some instances selling bowl game tickets can create financial concerns for institutions that are located far away from the bowl game destination and those who do not have a large fan base interested in attending a bowl contest at the end of the season.

5. Economic and Social Impact of College Football

It has become a common practice to use economic impact analyses/studies to measure the benefits a locality may realize as a result of hosting a sport event. *Howard* and *Crompton* (2004: 105) define economic impacts as, "the net economic change in the incomes of host residents that results from spending attributed to a sports event or facility". The authors further emphasize the main purpose of economic impact analyses should be to examine what residents receive as a result of a sport event or facility in the local community. Unfortunately, many economic analyses are conducted to legitimize certain positions rather than seeking a true and accurate assessment of the impact of an event or facility (*Mondello* & *Rishe* 2004). Consequently, those studying the economic impact of major sport events, such as collegiate football games, must have a discerning eye able to recognize flaws or inconsistencies in economic impact reports.

There are several key components to a solid, well executed economic impact study. First, visitor purchases from those attending a sporting event must be estimated. In doing so, those conducting the analysis should include only certain individuals' spending within a selected geographic area. It is important to establish the geographic parameters of the area to be included in the study with the main purpose of determining those who will be considered "visitors" to the area and those who are considered as "locals." Time switchers, those visitors who would have come to town at some point but switched their travel time to coincide with a sport event, should not be included the in the study (*Brown* et al. 2010). Similarly, casual visitors' spending should not be included. Casual visitors are those who are in town for a reason other than the sport event but decided to attend the event simply because it happened to be available (*Brown* et al. 2010). The most important group of individuals included in an economic impact study are incremental or non-local visitors who are in a community or city as a direct result of a sport event.

There are three types of spending analyzed in most economic impact studies, direct, indirect, and induced impacts. The dollar amount spent as a result of the sport event such as ticket purchases, hotel/motel purchases, and rental car fees is considered direct spending. Direct spending may be calculated by determining the total number non-local visitors to the sport event, the average length of their stay, and the approximate dollar amount spent to attend the event. Typically this data is collected through primary research methods such as on-site surveying. Another component of economic impact studies is indirect economic impacts defined as "impacts that occur in the area of impact that represent the circulation of initial visitor expenditures (direct impacts)" (*Brown* et al. 2010: 308–309).

Further, the impact of indirect spending termed induced impact is calculated. Induced economic impact is the combined effect of direct and indirect impacts on factors such as earning and employment levels (*Irwin & Rascher* 2013). Both indirect and induced impacts are calculated by using a multiplier and it is at this junction of an economic impact analysis where results may be most skewed. It is imperative a correct multiplier is used for the size of the city included in the study. Again, discerning readers will be able to determine where potential flaws in a study may lie.

While there are many published studies focusing on the economic impact of sports, most of the studies are concerned with professional sports. In the current literature there are a limited number of studies with a primary focus on the economic impact of intercollegiate sports and even fewer on intercollegiate football. There are however several noteworthy studies. *Coates* and *Depken* (2006) for example, studied the effects of college football games, in addition to other sport-related variables, on the taxable sales in selected Texas counties. Based on their analysis they found an increase in tax revenues in the range of $20,000 and $34,000. These figures were based on the total number of taxable sales. Interestingly, this effect was only significant in the smallest counties in their study. Larger cities such as Dallas and Houston had no statistically significant evidence indicating college football positively impacted tax revenues. *Baade* et al. (2011) examined the impact of college sports on local economies. Of the two sports included in the study, college basketball and football, only home football games had a statistically significant impact on the local economy. The researchers found for each home football game, the host cities in the study (Tallahassee, Florida and Gainesville, Florida) enjoyed a taxable sales increase of approximately $2 million.

Likewise, *Baade* et al. (2008) found no statistically significant impact on a host community from collegiate football games. With this particular study the researchers analyzed 63 metropolitan areas from 1970–2004 which hosted major college football programs. Much like other studies, the researchers found no statistically significant impact on the local economies. While many boosters, politicians, and high ranking city officials across the nation love to purport college football makes a significant impact to the local economy, this is often not the case.

6. Mobile, Alabama

Mobile is the oldest settlement and the second largest city in the state of Alabama with a population of 194,822 residents comprised mostly of African Americans (50.6%) and Whites (45%) according to the *United States Census Bureau* (2012). Mobile presently operates under a Mayor/Council form of government with bi-annual public elections to determine the mayor and seven council members representing various city districts. Located at the junction of the Mobile River and Mobile Bay on the northern Gulf of Mexico, the city is the only seaport in Alabama. The Port of Mobile has always played a key role in the economic health of the city beginning with the city as a key trading center between the French and Native Americans down to its current role as the 12th-largest port in the United States (*City of Mobile* 2013). As one of the Gulf Coast's cultural centers, Mobile has several art museums, a symphony orchestra, a professional opera, a professional ballet company, and a large concentration of historic architecture.

Mobile is best known for having the oldest organized Carnival celebrations in the United States, "Mardi Gras" celebrated in the first decade of the 18th century. Mobile annually hosts the BayFest Music Festival drawing crowds of over 200,000 visitors during the first weekend in October, American Junior Miss Pageant, LPGA Golf Classic, and the largest Outdoor Fishing Rodeo in the nation. It is the home of the publicly owned Ladd-Peebles Stadium which opened in 1948 and has a current capacity of 40,646 where the Senior Bowl, GoDaddy.com Bowl, Gulf Coast Classic, University of South Alabama Jaguar football program and local high school football contests take place. Mobile, Alabama is in the heart of the tradition rich pigskin cult area of the United States where football is a prominent social activity.

7. Senior Bowl History

The inaugural Senior Bowl Game was played in Jacksonville, Florida on January 7, 1950. Jimmie Pearre, a Nashville, Tennessee businessman created the bowl game as a way to showcase the nation's top college football seniors. Only 16,487 fans showed up for the first game, a new tradition was created which still lives today. Just one Senior Bowl game was played in Jacksonville, Florida. Due to the low fan attendance, the event coordinators decided to move the game to Mobile, Alabama where it has been played ever since enjoying sell-out crowds in 11 of the last 13 years. In 1952 the game was played under the sponsorship of the Mobile Arts and Sports Association (MASA). MASA is a non-profit association that still runs the Senior Bowl today. The game has become known as a pre-draft spectacle event for the National Football League (NFL) where NFL coaches and scouts are in attendance to evaluate players during the weeklong practice sessions leading up to the game and with sports agents and sporting goods manufacturing representatives looking to secure soon to be NFL players as professional clients.

8. GoDaddy.com Bowl History

GoDaddy.com became the official sponsor of the former GMAC (General Motors Acceptance Corporation) Bowl in 2011. Since 1999 the game has been played in Mobile, Alabama at Ladd Peebles Stadium, although with different title sponsors. In 1999, the game was simply titled the Mobile Alabama Bowl and then from 2000–2010 GMAC became the title sponsor of the bowl game. The GoDaddy.com bowl payout to each team has traditionally been $750,000 ("2013–2014 Bowl").

9. Gulf Coast Classic History

Although not considered a "bowl" game, The Gulf Coast Classic was held every year in Mobile, Alabama at Ladd Peebles Stadium. Now defunct, the annual game was presented as the Home Coming game for Alabama State University, which is classified as a Historically Black College and University (HBCU) (*Staff Reports* 2010). From 1974 to 2009 the game was played in Mobile, with Alabama State competing against another team from the Southwestern Athletic Conference. After the financial rift among the Mobile City Council, a non-profit organization who provided funds for the game, and Alabama State, the game was discontinued after the 2009 football season (*Staff Reports* 2010).

10. Methodology

Validity and reliability issues appear in the assessment of sports events relative to their worth. Spurious results and the increasingly important role of government leaders who may use sports contests as a means to promote political positioning also create controversy. In an attempt to showcase inflated estimates of economic impact and the different approaches used by stakeholders of the three different football games empirical survey research results, a meta-analysis of like football game impacts, and aggregate based tourism applications (average group spending and hotel bed night assumptions) were used for the purposes of this paper. Policy implications and controversial evidence used by football officials and certain members of the local council to advance the support of one football game over others were examined.

11. Findings

Primary research data and secondary sources were used to evaluate and compare the community value of the Senior Bowl, GoDaddy.com Bowl, and Gulf Coast Classic football games hosted in Mobile, Alabama. Secondary data such as organizational spending, sponsorship revenue, city subsidies, and game day attendance were provided by the event organizers of all three games. Results taken from an empirical study (*Keshock* 2008) where spectator data was collected from fans attending the Senior Bowl and careful attention to Crompton's-Eleven sources of misapplication (1995) for sport event economic impact were recognized and accounted for. Further, the Senior Bowl study did not use secondary data such as hotel occupancy rates during the time of the Senior Bowl or other extrapolations readily used by destination tourism marketers to determine the direct spending of Senior Bowl visitors. For example, it has been a common practice in the assessment of other Mobile events to adopt the Destination Marketing Association International (DMAI) formula with the number of participants and estimated visitors. Per DMAI, the average expenditure is based on accommodations, food, retail, fuel and miscellaneous totaling $250 per day. The Mobile Bay Convention and Visitors Bureau then use a standard of 2.5 as the number of dollar turns (*Mobile Business View 2012*). This cavalier approach has been the mechanism in which other events in the city are awarded public monies: LPGA- $350,000, American Junior Miss Pageant- $108,000, Mobile Tennis Center- $722,040, US Boxing Trials- $135,000, and the MoonPie New Year's Eve Celebration- $123,000.

In the Senior Bowl study visitor direct spending was calculated from survey responses collected on-site before the contest in a random sample questionnaire format of "true economic tourists" -non-local resident survey responses or those returning a home zip code response outside the study impact zone; time switchers and casuals were not included in the results. In addition, other dubious methodological approaches were not a part of the study such as the assumption that all fans spent the night in Mobile, bought a souvenir at the event and ate a meal while in town. Instead subjects were asked specific questions in the survey to determine where they were staying, the number of days and nights in town and how much they spent on food and beverage, retail shopping, entertainment, transportation, and other purchases while in the area specifically to attend the Senior Bowl. In addition to surveying spectators a separate survey was created and given to business travelers attending the Senior Bowl. This group included NFL coaches, professional scouts, media personnel reporting and broadcasting the game, sponsors and sporting goods manufacturing personnel. Participants in the game (105 players) represented numerous schools from across the nation. Since all of their travel and accommodations were paid by the Senior Bowl this spending was included in the organizational direct spending category. Last, and most important the survey response directing spending data of true economic tourists was applied to a RIMS II multiplier (1.75) appropriate for the Mobile, Alabama impact region rather than the spurious 2.5 multiplier adopted by many travel industry professionals in town (*Kirby & Murtaugh* 2009).

Due to time constraints efforts to collect on-site data for the GoDaddy.com Bowl game were not possible. Instead a meta-analysis (*Keshock* 2010) was conducted where the aggregated results of NCAA football games and bowl contests held in similar size cities (39 football game economic impact reports) and local Mobile, Alabama event data (15 reports) were used to illustrate and approximate dimensions of economic impact. GoDaddy.com Bowl visitor estimates included the two opponent schools participating in the game and their players, coaches, support staff, cheerleaders, band members, and official travel parties; spectators following their individual schools and general fans at the game; Bowl sponsors, league officials, sport industry specialists, media personnel, and traveling workers.

For the Gulf Coast Classic game efforts to conduct on-site surveying or a meta-analysis report were not petitioned for and thus only rough best guess estimates of game worth existed. As with the Senior Bowl and GoDaddy.com bowl contests estimates for game attendance (ticket sales) were reported by event organizers and then verified by Ladd-Peebles Stadium officials tracking actual turnstile count attendance. Economic impact figures for the Gulf Coast Classic game were based on ambivalent estimations provided by the sport event management company hired to plan the game and other local stakeholders interviewed by the local newspaper media.

The following table depicts important aspects of each of the three football games held in Mobile, Alabama. Of particular interest is disproportionate government subsidization of the three football games relative to economic impact findings and reported game attendance. The Senior Bowl received $115,000 from the city for the first time in 2009 and then $135,000 thereafter. Many believe it was the Senior Bowl office administrators' threat to leave Mobile and relocate to another city that prompted public fund allocations to the Senior Bowl and contract renewal to keep the game in Mobile till 2016. The economic impact report findings were used as part of the negotiations during the process. The GoDaddy.com Bowl game has traditionally been awarded $150,000 of city funds on a yearly basis. The agreement with the city required the city of Mobile to provide game organizers with $1.15 M and then $1M was later to be paid back to the city budget from the game title sponsorship revenue. However, during the US economic crisis and government bailout of the major automotive industries, title sponsor GMAC was pressured into discontinuing its sports sponsorships and did not provide the entire reimbursable amount owed to the city for the game ultimately leading to a change in title sponsorship to GoDaddy.com. Therefore in and around about the same time the meta-analysis report was conducted a reduction in sponsor repayment to the city resulted in the city subsidizing the event by nearly $500,000, which was a drain on the budget but highly atypical and more of a result of the turbulent economic circumstances throughout the nation. Of all three games surprisingly the Gulf Coast Classic received a $250,000 city subsidization and $25,000 from the discretionary funds of a city councilmember. The game was scheduled to be earmarked for $450,000 out of the city budget for the next year until the local media ran articles insinuating misappropriation of taxpayer funds relative to the unconfirmed economic impact values and a closer look at the actual attendance for the game being near 10,000 fans rather than the nearly 27,000 attendance figure provided by the game administrators.

Table 1: Senior Bowl, GoDaddy.com Bowl, Gulf Coast Classic overview

	Senior Bowl	**GoDaddy.com Bowl**	**Gulf City Classic**
Background	1951-Present	1999-Present	1974–2009 Discontinued
Ownership	Mobile Arts and Sport Association Non-profit	Mobile Alabama Bowl Incorporated	Gulf Coast Scholar and Sports Foundation
Participants	North and South squads comprised of 105 top college players	One team each from Mid-American Conference and SunBelt Conference	Alabama State vs HBCU school regular season game
Broadcast	ESPN, NFL Network	ESPN	None
Events	Week long practices, NFL Combine, Meet the Players, Tailgate Challenge, Fun Run, Fan Fest, etc.	Hospital visit, team bowling challenge, Mayor's luncheon, City parade, Fireworks, Pep-rally, etc.	Battle of the Bands, Mayor's luncheon, Step show
City Subsidization	$115,000 first time in 2009 $135,000 thereafter	$1,150,000 then portion repaid to city from game sponsor, typically $150,000 ($250,000 when sponsorship shortfall)	$275,000 plus $25,000 from councilmember's discretionary funds, $450,000 earmarked
Attendance	Sellout crowd (40,646), true economic tourists (33,452), Plus 1,560 business travelers	34,486 attendance, true economic tourists (27,588), Plus 800 business travelers	26,819 reported, 10,732 turnstile count for game, true economic tourists?
Study	On-site data collection, $128.11 average spend per day visitors, 1.75 multiplier	Meta-analysis (54 studies) $196.11 average spend per day visitors, 1.75 multiplier	None
Reported Economic Impact	$19.4 Million	$18.2 Million	"Millions and Millions of dollars" newspaper quote of local politician.

12. Discussion

As previously mentioned many boosters, politicians, and high ranking city officials across the nation love to purport college football makes a significant impact to the local economy, and as illustrated in this report this is often not the case. Numerous revenue sources are available from the marketing, sponsorship, and television rights fees to cover some of the administrative costs, however public monies are still needed for most intercollegiate competitions and especially football where traditionally only a select few major football programs and contests reap the benefits of sport commercialization. Sports organizations rely on public dollars to improve or build sports venues and to provide resources needed to run contests. In the case of the three intercollegiate football games hosted in the same city with each purporting different economic values it becomes clear some of the football game spokespersons are using exaggerated monetary values to garner community support of government subsidizations. A case analysis of the events resulted in one of the football contests providing no theoretical substance of economic impact and financial return to area taxpayers one year and ironically being scheduled for a two-fold increase in public monies for the next year's event. Befittingly, city officials denied added subsidization to this football contest based on propagandized economic impact guesstimates. An effort then to create and implement government policies toward a more uniform examination of community event impact values to dismiss embellished findings is recommended. Secondly, so as not to hoodwink local citizens' quality of life, social, and cultural support may be a better alternative or at least a more plausible course used by politicians when theoretically grounded economic impact studies are not possible to garner public funds for football games in Mobile, around the country, and for any community events public officials endorse for tax payer dollar payouts.

References

Baade, R. A., Baumann, R. W. & Matheson, V. A. (2008): Assessing the Economic Impact of College Football Games on Local Economies, in: Journal of Sports Economics, Vol. 9, 6, pp. 628–643.

Baade, R. A., Baumann, R. W. & Matheson, V. A. (2011): Big Men on Campus: Estimating the Economic Impact of College Sports on Local Economies, in: Regional Studies, Vol. 45, 3, pp. 371–380.

BCS (2013): Alliance and Coalition Games Year-by-year, http://www.bcsfootball.org/news/story?id=4809942#1999 (accessed 2014-1-27).

Brown, G. (2012): NCAA Student Athlete Participation Hits 450,000, http://www.ncaa.org/about/resources/media-center/news/ncaa-student-athlete-participation-hits-450000 (accessed 2014-2-04).

Brown, M. T., Rascher, D. A., Nagel, M. S. & McEvoy, C. D. (2010): Financial Management in the Sport Industry, Scottsdale, AZ: Holcomb Hathaway.

Chambers, R. (2013): New Study Names Michigan as College Football's Most Engaged Fans, http://bleacherreport.com/articles/1712099-new-study-names-michigan-as-college-footballs-most-engaged-fans (accessed 2014-1-27).

City of Mobile (2013): http://www.cityofmobile.org/(accessed 2014-1-27).

Coates, D. & Depken, C. (2006): Mega-Events: Is the Texas-Baylor Game to Waco What the Super Bowl Is to Houston? International Association of Sports Economists, Working Paper No. 06-06, Limoges: International Association of Sport Economists.

Crompton, J. L. (1995): Economic Impact Analysis of Sport Facilities and Events: Eleven Sources of Misapplication, in: Journal of Sport Management, Vol. 9, 1, pp. 14–35.

Gratton, C. & Jones, I. (2008): Research Methods for Sports Studies, London: Routledge.

Howard, D. R. & Crompton, J. L. (2004): Financing Sport, Morgantown: Fitness Information Technology.

Irwin, R. & Rascher, D. (2013): 2012 Valero Alamo Bowl Economic and Fiscal Impact Analysis, http://www.valeroalamobowl.com.php5-2.dfw1-1.websitetestlink.com/pdf/Valero%20Alamo%20Bowl%20Economic%20Impact%20Report-12-29-12.pdf (accessed 2014-1-27).

Keshock, C. M. (2008): Estimating the Economic Impact of the Senior Bowl on the Local Mobile Economy, unpublished manuscript.

Keshock, C. M. (2010): The Impact of the 2010 GMAC Bowl on Mobile Alabama, unpublished manuscript.

Kirby, B. & Murtaugh, D. (2009): Mini Mardi Gras: Senior Bowl Has Major But Hard-to-measure Impact on Business in Mobile, http://blog.al.com/live/2009/10/senior_bowl_has_major_but_hard.html (accessed 2014-1-27).

Mobile Business View (2012): A Big Hit! How Sports Impact Mobile's Economy, in: The Business View, Vol. XLIII, 6, pp. 15–18.

Mondello, M. J. & Rishe, P. (2004): Comparative Economic Analyses: Differences across Cities, Events, Demographics, in: Economic Development Quarterly, Vol. 18, 4, pp. 331–342.

National Football Foundation (2013): Passion for College Football Remains Robust, http://www.footballfoundation.org/tabid/567/Article/53380/Passion-for-College-Football-Remains-Robust.aspx (accessed 2014-1-27).

Noll, R. G. (1997): Sports, Jobs, and Taxes: the Economic Impact of Sport Teams and Stadiums, Washington, DC: Brookings Institute Press.

Rosner, S. R. & Shropshire, K. L. (2011): The Business of Sports, Sudbury: Jones & Bartlett Publishers.

Staff Reports (2010): Alabama State Backs Out of Gulf Coast Classic, 2010 Game in Limbo, http://hbcudigest.com/alabama-state-backs-out-of-gulf-coast-classic-2010-game-in-limbo/ (accessed 2014-1-27).

Szymanski, S. (2009): Playbooks and Checkbooks: An Introduction to the Economics of Modern Sports, Princeton: Princeton University Press.

Tucker, I. B. (2004): A Reexamination of the Effect of Big-time Football and Basketball Success on Graduation Rates and Alumni Giving Rates, in: Economics of Education Review, Vol. 23, 6, pp. 655–661.

United States Census Bureau (2012): State & County QuickFacts, http://quickfacts.census.gov/qfd/states/01/0150000.html (accessed 2014-1-27).

New Research on Individual Sports

Public Opinion on Doping in Cycling: Differences among Population Groups

Daam Van Reeth, Wim Lagae[1]

Abstract

Despite the vast amount of literature available on doping in sports, little is known about how the general public actually thinks about doping. It is even more unclear how public opinion on doping differs within the population. Our questionnaire-based study for Flanders (Belgium), with a focus on doping in cycling, shows a strong disapproval of doping use by all respondents. There are statistically significant differences, though, among population groups. Cycling fans tend to be less negative towards doping in cycling than non-cycling fans. Cycling fans also express a clear feeling of their sport being treated unfairly compared to other sports. Furthermore, we observe some clear gender-based and age-based differences in opinion: women and older people are much more opposed to doping than men and younger people.

Keywords

doping, cycling, public opinion, anti-doping policy, drugs

1. Introduction

Understanding public opinion on doping is highly relevant for an effective and well-supported anti-doping policy. Still, despite the enormous amount of public discussion that goes on about anti-doping policies and the vast amount of literature available on doping in sports, little is known about how the general public actually thinks about doping. It is even more unclear how public opinion on doping differs within the population among groups of people.

The aim of this study is therefore to gain insight into popular belief on doping in sports. Our work is complementary to the research by *Stamm* et al. (2008), *Solberg, Hanstad & Thöring* (2010), *Vangrunderbeek & Tolleneer* (2011) and *Moston, Skinner & Engelberg* (2012) who all focus on the question to what extent economic, moral or health considerations regarding doping use find support in society. Our approach differs in two ways. First, while the aforementioned

1 We are grateful to the participants in the 5th ESEA Conferences on Sports Economics (Esbjerg), the 16th Annual Congress of the Arbeitskreis Sportökonomie (Magglingen) and the DESport seminar (Paris) for their helpful comments on earlier drafts of this text. Remaining errors are, of course, our own.

authors analyse doping in general across all sports, we focus on doping in one sport only: i.e. professional road cycling. Cycling is a very popular spectator sport in Flanders.[2] Consequently, many people are quite familiar with the sport. This generates more valid responses since it is well documented that the more people are interested in a topic, the more willing they are to be questioned about it (*Solberg* et al. 2010). However, whether justified or not, the sport has since long explicitly been associated with doping too. Road cycling is one of the physically hardest sports. Professional riders easily cover 35,000 kilometres in competition and training a year, and face up to 100 competition days, which is extremely high in comparison to other endurance sports like marathon or triathlon. These characteristics make cycling vulnerable to doping (*Rebeggiani & Tondani* 2008). In fact, cycling recently went through a turbulent doping period because of the *USADA* (2012) investigation and the doping confessions by Lance Armstrong, a global cycling icon.[3]

Second, rather than focussing on overall popular belief, we compare public opinion across clearly defined population groups which make this study different from most of the aforementioned papers. Our study raises questions such as: are cycling fans more lenient towards doping than non-cycling fans? Do cycling-active people have a different opinion on anti-doping measures than cycling-inactive people? And does doping knowledge play a role in one's opinion on doping?

Popular belief on doping in cycling was analysed with a two-part questionnaire. The first series of questions measures attitudes and opinions on doping through a number of statements respondents had to evaluate. The second series of questions was used to identify the population group a respondent belonged to. Through the responses of almost 2,000 persons a clear view on the attitudes and opinions on doping of people in Flanders was created.

The rest of the paper proceeds as follows. First, in section 2 we discuss the basic principles that explain the decision of athletes to use doping. Next, a short survey of literature is introduced in section 3. We describe the details of our research methodology and the distribution of the respondents that participated in the questionnaire in section 4. In sections 5 and 6 our results are presented. First, we briefly consider general public opinion on doping in cycling. Next, the differences in opinion among well-defined groups of people are discussed in detail. Conclusions follow in section 7.

2 For practical purposes, our research focused on Flanders, the Northern part of Belgium, only.

3 Interestingly, a previous important doping crisis in cycling, the 'Festina' Tour de France of 1998, lead to the creation of the World Anti-Doping Authority (WADA) in 1999.

2. Why Athletes Use Doping

Two types of reasoning are generally used to explain the use of doping in sport. The first theory is derived from the economics of crime (*Becker* 1968). It basically assumes that whether athletes use doping or not is the result of a well-thought assessment in which costs and benefits are rationally weighed. As long as the benefits (e.g. glory, higher prize money, etc.) sufficiently outweigh the costs (e.g. punishment if caught, health costs, etc.) athletes will continue to use doping. The testimony of *Bobby Julich*, 3rd in the 1998 Tour de France, is illustrative of this theory: "During the 1998 Tour, my fiancé found out what was going on from another rider's wife. She confronted me on it and it was one of the most dreadful experiences of my life. She told me right then and there that if it ever happened again, our relationship would be over. That was motivation enough and I knew I had to stop" (*Cycling News* 2012). When his wife found out, the costs of using doping became so high it was no longer a rational choice for *Bobby Julich* to continue using EPO. Note also that a mere net benefit is not good enough since the benefit has to be sufficiently high to compensate the athlete for the ethic standard he breaches. Consequently, all else being equal, the higher the ethic standard of an athlete, the more difficult an athlete will find it to use doping and vice versa. A well-known example of a cyclist whose ethic standards were so high that he preferred to end his career as a professional cyclist rather than to use doping is two-times Tour of Flanders winner *Edwig Van Hooydonck*. At the other end, we find cyclists like *Danilo Di Luca* or *Riccardo Ricco* who, knowing that a second doping offense could lead to a lifetime ban, still took the risk of using doping after they were caught already a first time.

The second theory is based on game theoretic principles. In this analysis, doping use is the result of a 'prisoner's dilemma'-situation athletes are facing. All athletes would be better off if nobody used doping because in that case athletes incur neither health costs nor any other doping costs. However, in this ideal situation when nobody uses doping, the advantage of being the sole user of doping is enormous. If all athletes reason like this, they all will resort to doping and incur the associated costs while the sporting result is likely to be very similar. The net benefit thus clearly is lower than in a no-doping situation since in spite of using doping, benefits are the same while costs are now higher. This is, of course, under the assumption that doping helps to increase performance and that it increases performance for all athletes to the same degree. Game theory predicts the only stable outcome will be that all athletes use doping. In this reasoning, if they want to be successful, athletes do not really have a choice and just have to follow the others to maintain a level-playing field. As a result, they do not feel like being cheaters either, as is clearly obvious from the statement by 1997 Tour de France winner *Jan Ullrich*: "Almost everyone at the time was taking performance-enhancing substances. I didn't take anything that was not taken by the others. It would only have been cheating for me if I had gotten an advantage which was not the case. I just wanted to ensure I had an equal opportunity" (*Cycling News* 2013). In his book on doping, former cyclist *Tyler Hamilton* clearly explains the sentiment among cyclists in the second half of the nineties, when it was still impossible to detect EPO-use. During those years, trying to ride 'clean' was considered by many to be an unprofessional attitude for a cyclist. In fact, it signalled a lack of motivation (*Hamilton & Coyle* 2012).

3. Survey of Literature

There exists a substantial body of literature in sports economics on the problem of doping. We refer, for instance, to excellent papers by *Maennig* (2002), *Haugen* (2004), *Kräkel* (2007) and *Eber* (2009). Like many of the texts that discuss doping in a general sense, these papers focus on the pros and cons of fighting or admitting doping use from a theoretical point of view with economic, ethical or health arguments often being part of the reasoning.

Doping has also been discussed in the specific context of professional road cycling. *Brewer* (2002) presents a historical analysis. He links commercialization and transformations in professional cycling in the second half of the previous century to the rationalization of doping. Complementary to this study is *Lentillon-Kaestner, Hagger & Hardcastle* (2012), discussing the change in the organization of doping from team-based doping practices to individual cyclist behaviour in the last decade. *Wagner* (2010) and *Coupé & Gergaud* (2012) both analyse aspects of the anti-doping policy of the International Cycling Union (UCI). *Wagner* (2010) describes the number of difficulties the International Cycling Union faces when implementing rigorous anti-doping measures like the biological passport, while *Coupé & Gergaud* (2012) test rather unconvincingly the correlation between the UCI's "Index of Suspicion" and Tour de France performance.

The analysis of public opinion on doping, by contrast, has received little research interest so far. A literature study for WADA by *Backhouse* et al. (2007) identified only 4 published studies that examined attitudes towards doping amongst non-athletic adults. Three studies were conducted in the United States and one in Australia. All surveys used students in relatively small samples (100 to 400) and the majority of the research focused upon attitudes towards anabolic steroids use in particular. This limits significantly their research relevance.

Research on popular belief on doping has recently gained some more interest. We identified a handful of relevant studies that have been published worldwide since 2007. The basic characteristics of their methodology and the most relevant findings are summarized in table 1.

Four studies favour a questionnaire approach. When public opinion is the focus of the analysis, usually between about 1,000 and 2,500 responses are collected. The number of respondents is considerably lower when specific population groups are analysed. Two studies use another methodology. In their research on student's perception on doping, *Vangrunderbeek & Tolleneer* (2011) make use of a discourse analysis while *Stewart & Smith* (2012) conducted twelve in-depth interviews to analyse differences in elite and non-elite athlete's attitudes to drugs in sport.

Table 1: Literature on popular belief on doping

Study (country)	**Methodology (year)**	**Respondents (number)**	**Findings**
Stamm, Lamprecht, Kamber, Marti & Mahler (2008) (Switzerland)	Questionnaires (1995/98/01/04) (2006)	All population (1201/800/1535/2114) Top-level athletes (369)	The vast majority of the Swiss population and top-level athletes are strongly against doping and support a strategy that combines strict prohibition and sanctioning with informational and educational efforts. The views stated by the public are largely in line with the current anti-doping strategy followed by the Swiss authorities.
Solberg, Hanstad & Thöring (2010) (Norway)	Questionnaire	Sports consumers (925)	Consumers show no tolerance for pure doping substances. The majority were in favour of tough responses to athletes involved in doping. Those who were strongly interested in sport were more willing than others to accept doping.
Vangrunderbeek & Tolleneer (2011) (Belgium)	Discourse analysis (1998–2006)	Students (155)	Over the years students seem to have developed a more diffuse ethical attitude on the doping issue. A shift from the zero tolerance principle towards a more lenient attitude towards doping in elite sports is observed and discussed.

Study (country)	Methodology (year)	Respondents (number)	Findings
Moston, Skinner & Engelberg (2012) (Australia)	Questionnaire	All population (2520)	Clubs should be penalized if athletes were found to use drugs and companies and government should stop sponsoring athletes who have been using drugs. Opinion was split on the issue of whether performance-enhancing drug use should be criminalized. These results show that the Australian public support anti-doping measures.
Petróczi (2007) (United States)	Questionnaire	College athletes (199)	Athletes' win and goal orientation and competitiveness do not play a statistically significant role in doping behaviour, but win orientation has an effect on doping attitude. The analysis provides empirical evidence that sport orientation and doping behaviour is not directly related.
Stewart & Smith (2010) (Australia)	In-dept interviews	Elite and non-elite athletes (12)	Athlete's attitudes are contingent upon the legality of the substance, its performance impact and its social impact. Substance use in sport is neither a matter of linear and logical decision-making nor one of fundamental morality. Drug-management policies which are underpinned by punitive models or moral certitude and deterrence do not match with prevailing attitudes.

Most studies show no tolerance for clear doping substances and a solid support for strict anti-doping measures with the general public. Still, when looking at certain population groups, a more diverse picture emerges. Sports consumers are more willing than others to accept doping, while older people turned out to be more negative towards doping (*Solberg* et al. 2010). The latter result is in line with the findings in a longitudinal study by *Vangrunderbeek & Tolleneer* (2011) that students have developed a more lenient attitude towards doping throughout the years. Regarding the views of the athletes themselves, evidence is mixed. A Swiss study by *Stamm* et al. (2008) shows no difference between top-level athletes and the general public while *Petróczi* (2007) and *Stewart & Smith* (2010) detect a more pragmatic attitude with U.S. and Australian athletes. Using performance enhancing substances is often a more rational, outcome optimizing, behaviour than deviance and athlete's attitudes are very much contingent upon the legality of the substance. Basically, when athletes balance the costs and benefits of substance use they do so logically. If a substance is not illegal, providing performance support, expediting recovery, or making the user feel better, then it is considered legitimate (*Stewart & Smith* 2010: 65).

4. Methodology and Respondents

Our main research question goes as follows: how does public opinion on doping in cycling differ among population groups? To this goal, our methodology specifically allows to separate cycling fans from non-cycling fans, cycling active people from cycling inactive people, and doping-informed from doping-uninformed persons. In addition, differences in opinion based on gender and age will also be analysed. Data were collected using a two-part questionnaire. The first part of the survey consisted of a number of opinion questions. Each respondent could express his (dis)agreement on 26 doping-related statements through the use of a 5-point Likert scale from totally disagree to totally agree. We refer to table A1 in the appendix for a survey of these statements. The statements formulated clear opinions along six dimensions: the acceptability, under certain conditions, of doping use (5 statements, A1 to A5), the reasons why doping use should be fought (4 statements, F1 to F4), the impact of doping use on the image of cycling (4 statements, I1 to I4), the motives of why cyclists use doping (4 statements, M1 to M4), the sanctions that should be imposed for doping use (7 statements, S1 to S7) and the perceived different treatment of doping in cycling versus doping in other sports (2 statements, D1 to D2).

The second part of the survey was used to determine the profile of the respondent and consisted of 10 questions. These questions generate the necessary information to successfully classify respondents in different population groups. In our analysis, we define different population groups based on 5 characteristics: gender, age, cycling activity, cycling interest and doping knowledge. For cycling interest and doping knowledge, a number of behavioural and knowledge questions were used to identify the population segments a respondent belongs to. We thus work with "revealed" population segments, avoiding the problems associated with self-selection. For instance, questions like "If you are at home during the Tour de France, how many stages of the Tour de France do you watch?" or "to what team did the winner of the Tour of Flanders last year belong to?" give a much more valid indication of the cycling interest of a respondent than a straightforward question asking the respondent to declare whether or not he is a cycling fan. To measure doping knowledge, similar questions (e.g. "Which product is not a prohibited substance for a cyclist?") were included in the questionnaire.

For the design of the online survey the *Qualtrics* software was used. Respondents were contacted by the authors and their contacts through different channels. The survey period was from August 2011 until February 2012. This survey period predates the turbulent times cycling went through after the Armstrong revelations. Care was taken to have a sufficiently diversified panel of respondents, geographically, demographically as well as socially.

The questionnaire was started by 2,045 respondents but only 1,968 (96.2%) completed the survey. Subsequently, a quality check was performed. Erroneous and invalid questionnaires were deleted. Finally, 1,949 responses were kept for our analysis representing 95.3% of all initial respondents.

Table 2 shows the distribution of the respondents over the distinctive population groups. Compared to the overall population we have an overrepresentation of young and male people in our dataset. Still, our dataset is sufficiently large to also generate statistically sound results for the underrepresented groups.

Seven out of ten of our respondents said to be cycling inactive. About 9% performed cycling at the competitive level while just over 20% were cycling recreationally. The behavioural and knowledge questions on cycling interest and doping knowledge allowed us to separate cycling-oriented people and doping-informed people from their counterparts. Based on their personal answers, over 43% of our respondents were classified as cycling-oriented and almost 37% as well informed on doping.

Table 2: Distribution of respondents over population groups

Gender	Male		Female			
	1,266	65.0%	683	35.0%		
Age	Young		Middle-aged		Old	
	845	43.4%	631	32.4%	473	24.2%
Cycling activity	Competitive		Recreational		Inactive	
	174	8.9%	423	21.7%	1,352	69.4%
Cycling interest	Yes		No			
	846	43.4%	1,103	56.6%		
Doping knowledge	High		Low			
	714	36.6%	1,235	63.4%		

5. Overall Public Opinion on Doping in Cycling

Figure 1 shows the strength of overall public opinion on the 26 doping statements. The vertical axis measures the percentage of respondents that agree with a given statement. It is defined as the ratio of the sum of the respondents that completely agree and rather agree (a score of 4 and 5 on the Likert scale) over the sum of all the respondents that expressed a clear opinion (a score of 1, 2, 4 or 5 on the Likert scale). The horizontal axis measures the percentage of respondents that expressed no clear opinion. It is defined as the percentage of respondents that answered neutral (a score of 3 on the Likert scale) or gave no opinion at all. Suppose, for example, we have a distribution of answers as follows: completely disagree (20%), rather disagree (20%), neutral (10%), rather agree (20%), completely agree (20%) and no opinion (10%). The % agree (vertical analysis) for this question would consequently be 50% (40/80) while the % neutral would be 20% (20/100). Statements that are situated in the right upper and right lower corner of the figure indicate statements with a broad and pronounced consensus across the whole of the population. The more statements are situated to the left and to the middle the more opinions are divided.

As explained above, each of the 26 statements falls into one of 6 categories. In figure 1, all statements are coded with a letter, indicating the category the statements belongs to, and a reference number, corresponding to the information provided in table A1 in the appendix. The combined score of the questions for each category is marked with a circle.

Our results show a clear consensus on the reasons why doping in cycling has to be fought. The strongest arguments against doping are the fact that it contradicts the principle of fair play (F1) and that it produces bad role models to young riders (F4). For both arguments there is over 95% of agreement and less than 10% of neutral opinion. The health argument (F2) and the financial argument (F3) also have over 90% of agreement, but for these statements a larger part of the respondents feel indifferent. The same consensus is found on the disagreement to accept doping. Almost nobody favours free use of doping (A1, A3). People also prefer a clean performance to an exceptional doping-prone performance, as can be seen from the strong disagreement score on question A4. Although a bit less outspoken, there is also little support to allow doping under strict medical supervision (A2).

Fig. 1: Strength of opinion on doping statements

There is a strong belief that cyclists use doping because of the pressure put upon them (M2, M3). Often cited reasons for doping use like races that are too hard or the necessity of doping use to deliver top results (M1, M4) find less support with the general public in Flanders.

Flemish public opinion seems to be quite pragmatic about the doping problem in cycling. According to our respondents, doping damages cycling's credibility (I2) but at the same time they feel it will never disappear from cycling (I1) and therefore they are not convinced it really harms cycling's popularity (I4). This confirms research on TV viewing behaviour for cycling in Flanders that showed doping has only a minor negative impact on Tour de France TV viewing (*Van Reeth* 2013). We acknowledge these findings are probably heavily influenced by the huge popularity of cycling in Flanders and therefore cannot simply be generalized at the international level. In spite of this pragmatic view, about 75% think doping makes it harder to find sponsors willing to invest in cycling (I3). It should be noted, though, that over 30% of the respondents found it difficult to express an opinion on this statement.

There was generally less agreement on statements related to the sanctions and control mechanisms that should be used to fight doping. Highest support, but with only about 60% of agreement and 20% of the respondents expressing no clear opinion, was found for the statements that doping belongs in criminal law (S2) and that anti-doping policy can violate cyclist's privacy (S3). Our results signal that anti-doping measures could not be imposed at any cost. Only 20% of our respondents found it acceptable that, as a result of a strict policy, from time to time innocent cyclists are sanctioned (S7). With almost 40% of our respondents not expressing a clear opinion, it is rather unclear if Flemish people think too much money is being spent on anti-doping policy (S4). Still, amongst the persons who expressed an opinion there is a clear sentiment this is not the case.

A final remarkable result is the shared feeling that, when it comes to doping, cyclists are being treated differently. Between 70 and 80% of our respondents agree with the statements that cyclists are controlled more often and sanctioned harder than athletes in other sports (D1, D2). We think this view is partly the result of the huge attention doping cases in cycling receive in Belgian media. For instance: about 50% of the doping-related articles in Belgian newspapers in 2010 and 2011 mention "cycling" while in reality only 15% of all doping-cases were cycling-related (*Lagae* et al. 2012).

6. Differences in Public Opinion among Population Groups

6.1 Comparative Analysis

The different scores per population group on the 26 doping statements are presented in table A1 in the appendix. Scores that are at the 1% level significantly different between groups are highlighted. Because a complete analysis of the table would lead us too far, we will limit the discussion to some of the main findings.

There are some notable differences in doping attitude between men versus women and younger versus older people. In general, our results show that women and older people are much more opposed to doping than men and younger people. This last result is in line with the observation by *Vangrunderbeek & Tolleneer* (2011) of a more lenient doping attitude among students. The reason for this stronger opposition towards doping use can be seen from the statement that doping should be fought because it is unhealthy (F2). The older people are, the more they agree with this view and there is also a marked difference between women and men on this statement. This leads to a similar difference in their view on acceptable doping measures. Older people and women much more support strong anti-doping measures, even if this violates cyclist's privacy rights (S3) or creates innocent victims (S7). Still, women appear to be more forgiving than older people. There is no significant difference in opinion on a life time ban for doping offence between men and women, while this difference does exist between younger an older people.

Differences in opinion based on cycling activity are especially prominent statements that relate to the motives to use doping and on statements that h some aspect of fairness of anti-doping policy. Compared to recreational cy and non-cyclists, competitive cyclists show significantly less agreement with the statements that doping use is the result of races that are too hard (M1) or of pressure put upon them (M2, M3). Together with the recreational cyclists, they signal a strong sentiment of unfair treatment compared to other sports (D1, D2). The importance of the fairness element is also illustrated by the fact that competitive cyclists, more than other respondents, claim doping should be fought because it financially harms cyclists that ride clean (F3). They also express a clear fear of being wrongfully accused (S7) or of wealthy cyclists having better chances of defending themselves (S6). Another remarkable result is that competitive cyclists, together with cycling-inactive people, are much less willing to accept doping, than recreational cyclists are (A1, A2).

Differences in opinion based on cycling interest are for an important part similar to what is discussed for cycling activity. This comes, of course, as no surprise since most cycling-active people probably also show a significant interest in cycling. The most important findings are that cycling-interested people are less convinced that doping use should be considered a criminal offence (S2) or that anti-doping policy can violate cyclist's privacy rights (S3). Consequently, it is not surprising to see that they are a bit more willing to accept doping than the other respondents too (A1, A2).

A better understanding of what doping entails does have an impact on one's opinion on doping. We find especially significant results for statements related to the acceptance of doping, the sanctions for doping use and the different treatment of doping in cycling versus doping in other sports. Our data very much support the idea that the more people know about doping, the more willing they are to accept doping (A1), especially under strict medical supervision (A2). In the same vein, they are less supportive of severe sanctions for doping use (S2, S3, S7). Finally, people who are better informed on doping matters indicate very strongly that they feel cyclists are treated worse under the current anti-doping policy than ...her sportsmen (D1, D2).

... figure 2 the impact of doping knowledge is analysed more in detail. To this ...r three dimensions of the questionnaire (acceptance of doping, agreement ...ctions and reasons to fight doping) an average overall score was calculated ... different population groups, subdivided each time in people with high ...vledge (full line in the figure) and people with low doping knowledge ... We see that being well-informed on doping does not really make a ... the reasons to fight doping are looked at. The views between well ... informed people differ, however, on the acceptance of doping ... that should be imposed for doping use. In general, persons with a better doping knowledge are a bit more liberal towards doping. They are less convinced of the fact that strict sanction s are an important part of any anti-doping policy (purple dotted line is above the purple full line) and they are slightly more open to some sort of controlled acceptance of doping (blue dotted line is below the blue full line).

The figure also shows that doping knowledge does not affect the intolerance of male and old respondents towards the use of doping, but it does affect their view on how severe doping sanctions should be. In addition, we find that the views on doping by young people and by persons with limited interest in cycling are largely unaffected by differences in doping knowledge amongst them. Conversely, views on doping by cyclists active at the competitive level are the most influenced by mutual differences in doping knowledge. The interpretation of this last observation is not straightforward. One could argue that this shows that the better informed athletes are on doping, the more cautious they become in their views. However, more cynically, one could also conclude from this that a better doping knowledge by some competitive cyclists is proof of their (past or current) use of doping which would, logically, imply that they have a more tolerant attitude towards doping.

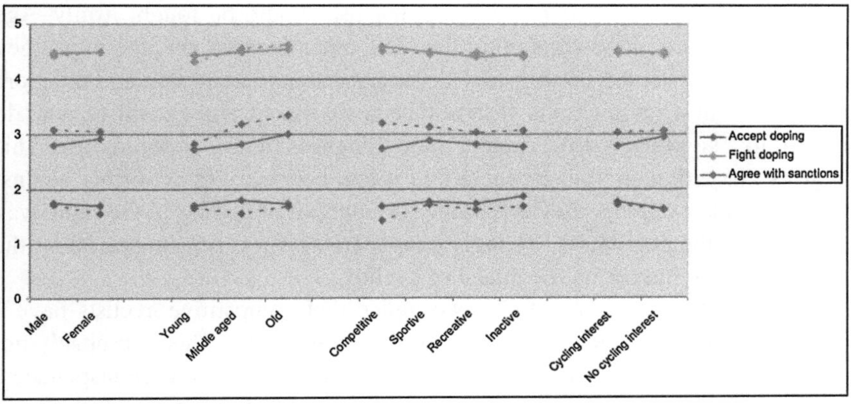

Fig. 2: Impact of doping knowledge for different population groups

6.2 Multivariate Analysis

In the previous section, the differences in public opinion on doping have been analysed in a disaggregated way only. Overall average scores for all groups were calculated and compared with each other. In this section, we use a multivariate regression analysis to look at the combined impact of all the characteristics of a respondent. To this end, aggregate scores for a respondent were used for each of the 6 dimensions present in the survey questions. The dimension-specific aggregate scores were computed as the average respondent score on all the questions attributed to that dimension. This procedure, validated by a principal component analysis (Varimax with Kaiser normalization), enabled us to regroup the 26 answer scores from a respondent into 6 new meaningful scores, each capturing one aspect of the respondent's opinion on doping in cycling. Six versions of the same regression model were consequently run, with the aggregated scores for the 6 dimensions as the changing dependent variable from one regression to another. The independent variables are dummy variables that define the gender and the age of the respondent, as well as his/her cycling activity, his/her cycling interest and his/her doping knowledge. The reference respondent is a young inactive male person with low doping knowledge and low cycling interest.

The regression results are presented in table 3. When all respondents' characteristics are considered, we see that gender differences are a bit less outspoken than thought at first sight. Only for two dimensions, women have a significantly different view than men. They are less willing to accept doping use and they have stronger sentiments about why doping use should be fought firmly. Age clearly affects the views on doping too. The older persons are, the more they are convinced about the reasons why doping use should be fought and the more they agree with strict sanctions. It should be noted though that age differences do not lead to a significant difference in the willingness to accept doping use. This suggests that although young people find it less necessary to act firmly against cyclists who use doping, they essentially disapprove of doping in the same way as the rest of the population. Younger people are also less pessimistic about the negative doping impact on the image of cycling.

With respect to cycling activity, we notice that competitive cyclists have a significantly different view on doping in all 6 dimensions. This is probably not so surprising since, after all, in this study they are at the same time respondents and research objects. We can conclude that in general competitive cyclists have a stricter view on doping than other people. The results show a lower willingness to accept doping use, a stronger willingness to fight doping and a higher agreement with strict sanctions. Competitive cyclists also clearly indicate they feel their sport is treated differently in a negative way compared to other sports. To our surprise, sportive cyclists or recreational cyclists do not have very different views on doping in comparison to the reference group of the cycling inactive people.

Table 3: Multivariate analysis

	(A)	(D)	(F)	(I)	(M)	(S)
Constant	1.76 (35.96)	3.14 (43.33)	4.22 (105.78)	3.62 (67.21)	3.34 (66.88)	2.85 (51.86)
Female (reference category: male)	-0.12 (-2.92)	-0.05 (-0.92)	0.11 (3.44)	0.08 (1.72)	0.04 (0.87)	0.03 (0.67)
Middle-aged	-0.05 (-1.40)	-0.07 (-1.23)	0.21 (6.66)	0.15 (3.54)	0.14 (3.43)	0.28 (6.54)
Old (reference category: young)	-0.02 (-0.43)	0.11 (1.73)	0.29 (8.44)	0.27 (5.85)	0.13 (2.90)	0.47 (9.73)
Competitive	-0.23 (-3.16)	0.44 (4.27)	0.26 (4.43)	0.20 (2.51)	-0.28 (-3.88)	0.19 (2.32)
Sportive	-0.07 (-1.35)	0.25 (3.07)	0.07 (1.52)	0.10 (1.59)	-0.01 (-0.09)	0.10 (1.65)
Recreational (reference category: inactive)	-0.08 (-1.87)	0.02 (0.30)	0.06 (1.74)	0.01 (0.26)	-0.02 (-0.52)	0.02 (0.44)
Rather high doping knowledge (reference category: low knowledge)	0.03 (0.80)	0.33 (5.25)	0.00 (-0.12)	0.00 (-0.09)	0.02 (0.35)	-0.21 (-4.26)
Rather high cycling interest (reference category: low interest)	0.10 (2.37)	0.41 (6.46)	0.02 (0.58)	-0.02 (-0.37)	-0.11 (-2.37)	-0.14 (-2.89)
N	1949	1824	1948	1945	1948	1947
R^2_a	0.02	0.15	0.05	0.02	0.03	0.07
F-statistic	4.89	39.72	12.46	5.24	7.44	19.04

(A): average score of the questions on the acceptability of doping
(D): average score of the questions on the different treatment of cycling versus other sports
(F): average score of the questions on the reasons to fight doping
(I): average score of the questions on the image of cycling
(M): average score of the questions on the motives of why cyclists use doping
(S): average score of the questions on the sanctions for doping use
(t-values between brackets. grey-shaded coefficients are significant at the 5% level)

A difference in doping knowledge only has a limited impact. People with a high doping knowledge are, compared to less informed persons, in favour of softer sanctions and they do find cycling is treated differently. There is much more difference in opinion on doping, though, between persons with high cycling interest and persons with low or no cycling interest. Cycling interested people are a bit more willing to accept some level of doping, are less in favour of firm sanctions and feel like their sport is treated unfairly compared to other sports. They also differ in their views on the motives of why cyclists use doping.

In a final analysis we regrouped all our respondents into 14 different types, based on gender, age, cycling activity and cycling interest. Note that in contrast to the analysis above, not 4 but only 2 levels of cycling activity were now used. Cycling active people were defined as persons who cycle in a sportive way or at a competitive level. Respondents who cycle at the recreational level only were grouped together with inactive persons. Care was taken to create sufficiently large groups to get reliable results. The smallest male group ('Middle aged inactive men with no cycling interest') counts 100 respondents, the largest one ('Middle aged cycling active men') 209. The smallest female group ('Young inactive women with cycling interest') consists of 45 respondents, the largest one ('Young inactive women with no cycling interest') 299.

For all 14 types of respondents, the average scores on the acceptability of doping use (horizontal axis) and the agreement on the reasons to fight doping (vertical axis) are plotted in figure 3. The inverted vertical axis makes it possible to visualize the doping aversion of different types of respondents. The closer a group is situated to the origin (low agreement to allow doping, high agreement to fight doping), the higher the doping aversion of this group. From the figure we can see that especially women have a high doping aversion while inactive men with a high cycling interest have the lowest doping aversion.

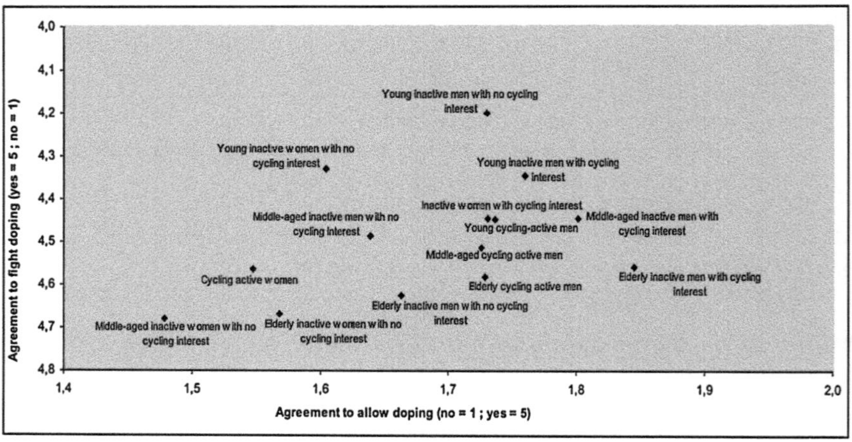

Fig. 3: Doping aversion for types of respondents

Figure 4 positions the types of respondents according to their views on doping sanctions. The average scores on the different treatment of cycling (horizontal axis) and the agreement with strict sanctions (vertical axis) are shown. The inverted vertical axis implicates that the further a group is situated from the origin (strong belief that cycling is treated differently and low agreement with strict sanctions), the stronger this group of respondents is convinced that cyclists who are caught using doping are sanctioned too hard. The figure shows that especially cycling interest and cycling activity are of great importance in this respect while gender and age are unimportant. There is a clear separation visible between the six types of respondents that combine inactivity with no cycling interest and the eight types of respondents that are cycling active and/or express a high cycling interest.

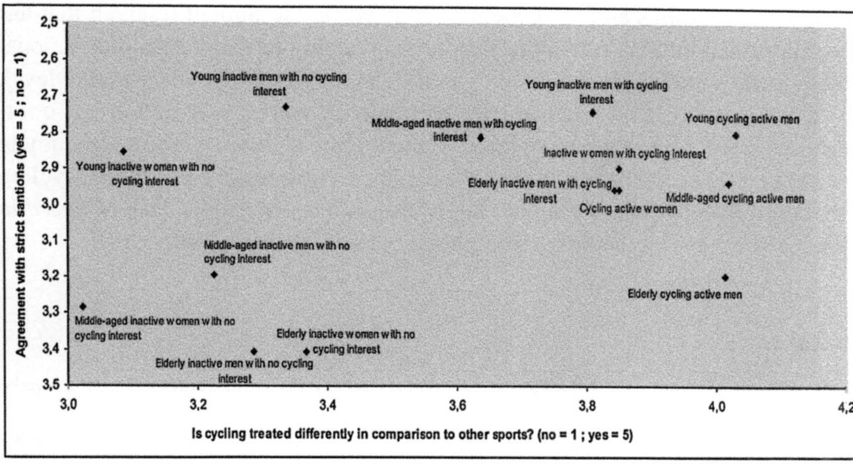

Fig. 4: Opinion on sanctions for types of respondents

7. Conclusion

This study analyses public opinion on doping in Flanders, with a focus on the endurance sport of professional road cycling. Our results, based on a survey that was completed by almost 2,000 respondents, show a strong disapproval of doping use by all respondents. There are statistically significant differences, though, between distinct population groups. Women and older people attach greater value to health issues and consequently have a much more outspoken anti-doping attitude than men and younger people. In general, cycling fans tend to be less negative towards doping in cycling than non-cycling fans. Cycling fans and cycling active people, on the competitive as well as on the recreational level, also express a clear feeling of their sport being treated unfairly compared to other sports. Furthermore, competitive cyclists provide some evidence that, contrary to popular belief, doping use is not primarily caused by the severity of the race or the pressure put upon them. We also show that doping knowledge does create a more liberal view on doping reflected in a somewhat greater willingness to accept doping and in less support for strong doping sanctions.

Of course, the (international) generalization of our results is limited by the applied methodology. We only made use of Flemish respondents and all statements were related to the sport of cycling. Still, we notice some remarkable similarities between our findings and the conclusions drawn in the limited research that has been published in this field so far. Because the doping problem is an international problem and an effective anti-doping policy can only be applied on a global level, we strongly advocate a comparative international survey with equivalent questions to further explore public opinion on doping. In addition, a follow-up study in Flanders could reveal to what extent the doping revelations in professional cycling regarding Lance Armstrong in late 2012 and, among others, *Michael Boogerd* in March 2013, have had an impact on public opinion on doping in cycling.

References

Backhouse, S., McKenna, J., Robinson, S. & Atkin, A. (2007): WADA Literature Review, Leeds: Leeds Metropolitan University.

Becker, G. (1968): Crime and Punishment: an Economic Approach, in: Journal of Political Economy, Vol. 76, pp. 169–217.

Brewer, B. (2002): Commercialization in Professional Cycling 1950–2001: Institutional Transformations and the Rationalization of "Doping", in: Sociology of Sport Journal, Vol. 19, pp. 276–301.

Coupé, T. & Gergaud, O. (2012): Suspicious Blood and Performance in Professional Cycling, in: Journal of Sports Economics, Vol. 14, pp. 546–559.

Cycling News (2012): Exclusive: Bobby Julich Doping Confession, http://www.cyclingnews.com/news/exclusive-bobby-julich-doping-confession (accessed 2013-10-25).

Cycling News (2013): Ullrich Refuses to Hand Over Olympic Medals, http://www.cyclingnews.com/news/ullrich-refuses-to-hand-over-olympic-medals (accessed 2013-10-05).

Eber, N. (2009): Doping and Fair Play, in: Economic Analysis & Policy, Vol. 39, 3, pp. 345–347.

Hamilton, T. & Coyle, D. (2012): The Secret Race: Inside the Hidden World of the Tour de France – Doping, Cover-ups and Winning at all Costs, New York: Bantam.

Haugen, K. (2004): The Performance-Enhancing Drug Game, in: Journal of Sports Economics, Vol. 5, 1, pp. 67–86.

Kräkel, M. (2007): Doping and Cheating in Contest-like Situations, in: European Journal of Political Economy, Vol. 23, pp. 988–1006.
Lagae, W., Van Reeth, D., Benijts, T. & Vanclooster, B. (2012): Het professionele wegwielrennen: een economische en marketingdoorlichting, in: Praktijkgids Sportmanagement, pp. 103–166.
Lentillon-Kaestner, V., Hagger, M. & Hardcastle, S. (2012): Health and Doping in Elite-level Cycling, in: Scandinavian Journal of Medicine & Science in Sports, Vol. 22, pp. 596–606.
Maennig, W. (2002): On the Economics of Doping and Corruption in International Sports, in: Journal of Sports Economics, Vol. 3, 1, pp. 61–89.
Moston, S., Skinner, J. & Engelberg, T. (2012): Perceived Incidence of Drug Use in Australian Sport: a Survey of Public Opinion, in: Sport in Society, Vol. 15, 1, pp. 64–77.
Petróczi, A. (2007): Attitudes and Doping: a Structural Equation Analysis of the Relationship between Athletes' Attitudes, Sport Orientation and Doping Behaviour, in: Substance Abuse Treatment, Prevention, and Policy, Vol. 2, 34.
Rebeggiani, L. & Tondani, D. (2008): Organizational Forms in Professional Cycling – an Examination of the Efficiency of the UCI Pro Tour, in: International Journal of Sport Finance, Vol. 3, 1, pp. 19–41.
Solberg, H. A., Hanstad, D. V., & Thöring, T. A. (2010): Doping in Elite Sport, Do the Fans Care? Public Opinion on the Consequences of Doping Scandals, in: International Journal of Sports Marketing & Sponsorship, Vol. 11, 3, pp. 185–199.
Stamm, H., Lamprecht, M., Kamber, M., Marti, B. & Mahler, N. (2008): The Public Perception of Doping in Sport in Switzerland, 1995–2004, in: Journal of Sports Sciences, Vol. 26, 3, pp. 235–242.
Stewart, B. & Smith, A. (2010): Player and Athlete Attitudes to Drugs in Australian Sport: Implications for Policy Development, in: International Journal of Sport Policy, Vol. 2, 1, pp. 65–84.
USADA (2012): Reasoned Decision of the United States Anti-doping Agency on Disqualification and Ineligibility, Colorado: United States Anti-Doping Agency.
Vangrunderbeek, H. & Tolleneer, J. (2011): Student Attitudes Towards Doping in Sport: Shifting from Repression to Tolerance? in: International Review for the Sociology of Sport, Vol. 46, 3, pp. 346–357.
Van Reeth, D. (2013): TV Demand for the Tour de France: the Importance of Stage Characteristics versus Outcome Uncertainty, Patriotism and Doping, in: International Journal of Sport Finance, Vol. 8, 1, pp. 39–60.
Wagner, U. (2010): The International Cycling Union under Siege – Anti-doping and the Biological Passport as a Mission Impossible? in: European Sport Management Quarterly, Vol. 10, 3, pp. 321–342.

Table A1: Mean scores on doping statements over population groups

Statement		Gender		Age			Cycling activity			Cycling interest		Doping knowledge	
		Male	Female	Young	Middle aged	Old	Competitive	Recreational	Inactive	No	Yes	Low	High
Doping use should be admitted freely.	A1	**1.4**	**1.3**	1.3	1.4	1.4	**1.3**	**1.5**	**1.4**	**1.3**	**1.5**	**1.3**	**1.5**
Doping use is acceptable under strict medical supervision, so that health risks are limited.	A2	**2.1**	**1.7**	1.9	2.0	2.1	**1.8**	**2.2**	**1.9**	**1.8**	**2.2**	**1.8**	**2.2**
Doping use is not a problem if everybody else is doing it.	A3	**1.4**	**1.3**	1.4	1.3	1.3	1.3	1.4	1.4	1.3	1.4	1.3	1.4
Only the sporting result is of importance, not the way this result is achieved.	A4	1.7	1.6	1.6	1.6	1.7	1.6	1.6	1.7	1.6	1.7	1.6	1.7
Cyclists are adults and can therefore decide themselves on what substances to use, bearing in mind the impact doping use might have on their health.	A5	2.1	2.1	**2.2**	**1.9**	**2.0**	2.1	2.0	2.1	2.1	2.1	2.1	2.1
Cyclists are sanctioned harder than other athletes when found guilty of a doping offense.	D1	**3.6**	**3.1**	3.4	3.4	3.5	**4.1**	**3.8**	**3.2**	**3.1**	**3.8**	**3.1**	**3.8**
Cyclists are controlled more often on doping use than other athletes.	D2	**3.9**	**3.4**	3.7	3.8	3.8	**4.3**	**4.1**	**3.6**	**3.4**	**4.1**	**3.5**	**4.2**
The fight against doping is necessary because doping contradicts the principle of fair play.	F1	**4.6**	**4.7**	4.6	4.6	4.6	4.7	4.6	4.6	4.6	4.6	4.6	4.6
The fight against doping is necessary because doping damages a cyclist's health.	F2	**4.3**	**4.5**	**4.2**	**4.4**	**4.5**	4.4	4.3	4.3	4.3	4.3	4.3	4.3

Statement		Gender		Age			Cycling activity			Cycling interest		Doping knowledge	
		Male	Female	Young	Middle aged	Old	Competitive	Recreational	Inactive	No	Yes	Low	High
The fight against doping is necessary because doping harms financially cyclists that ride clean.	F3	**4.4**	**4.3**	**4.2**	**4.5**	**4.6**	**4.5**	**4.5**	**4.3**	**4.3**	**4.5**	**4.3**	**4.5**
The fight against doping is necessary because doping produces bad role models to young riders.	F4	4.6	4.6	**4.4**	**4.7**	**4.7**	4.7	4.6	4.6	4.5	4.6	4.6	4.6
Doping use will never disappear completely from cycling.	I1	**4.2**	**4.1**	4.2	4.2	4.2	4.1	4.3	4.2	4.2	4.3	**4.1**	**4.3**
The doping problem damages cycling's credibility.	I2	4.3	4.4	4.3	4.4	4.4	4.3	4.3	4.3	**4.4**	**4.3**	**4.4**	**4.2**
The doping problem makes it more difficult to find sponsors interested in cycling.	I3	**3.7**	**3.4**	**3.5**	**3.7**	**3.7**	**3.7**	**3.8**	**3.5**	**3.3**	**3.9**	**3.4**	**3.9**
The doping problem damages cycling's popularity.	I4	3.3	3.4	**3.2**	**3.4**	**3.7**	3.4	3.4	3.4	**3.5**	**3.3**	**3.4**	**3.3**
Cyclists use doping because races are too hard.	M1	**2.7**	**3.0**	2.8	2.8	2.9	**2.3**	**2.7**	**3.0**	**3.0**	**2.6**	**3.0**	**2.7**
Cyclists use doping as a result of the pressure to perform put upon them.	M2	**4.0**	**4.2**	4.1	4.2	4.1	**3.8**	**4.1**	**4.1**	**4.2**	**4.0**	4.1	4.0
Cyclists use doping to create a level playing field with the other riders.	M3	4.1	4.1	**4.0**	**4.2**	**4.2**	**3.9**	**4.2**	**4.1**	4.1	4.0	4.1	4.1
Doping use is necessary to deliver top results in cycling.	M4	**2.4**	**2.2**	**2.2**	**2.5**	**2.4**	2.2	2.5	2.3	2.3	2.4	2.3	2.4

Statement		Gender		Age			Cycling activity			Cycling interest		Doping knowledge	
		Male	Female	Young	Middle aged	Old	Competitive	Recreational	Inactive	No	Yes	Low	High
Riders found guilty on the use of doping should be banned for life.	S1	3.1	3.0	**2.9**	**3.2**	**3.1**	3.1	3.1	3.0	3.1	3.0	3.1	3.0
Doping is a problem that concerns society as a whole and therefore belongs in criminal law.	S2	**3.3**	**3.5**	**3.1**	**3.3**	**3.7**	3.2	3.3	3.4	**3.5**	**3.2**	**3.5**	**3.1**
To be effective, anti-doping measures may violate privacy rights from cyclists.	S3	**3.1**	**3.3**	**2.9**	**3.2**	**3.5**	3.0	3.2	3.2	**3.3**	**3.0**	**3.3**	**3.0**
Doping is a mere sporting problem and society therefore uses too much money fighting it.	S4	2.5	2.6	2.6	2.5	2.5	**2.2**	**2.5**	**2.6**	2.6	2.5	**2.6**	**2.4**
Regular health controls with short suspension periods are preferable to strict doping controls with two-year suspensions.	S5	**2.4**	**2.7**	**2.4**	**2.5**	**2.7**	**2.2**	**2.3**	**2.6**	**2.6**	**2.3**	**2.6**	**2.3**
The fight against doping is unfair because it privileges wealthy cyclists who have themselves defended better and more easily escape prosecution.	S6	**2.8**	**2.6**	2.7	2.7	2.8	**3.1**	**2.9**	**2.7**	**2.6**	**2.9**	**2.7**	**2.9**
Anti-doping measures should be strict, even if this results in an innocent rider being suspended every now and then.	S7	**2.3**	**2.5**	**2.3**	**2.5**	**2.6**	**2.1**	**2.4**	**2.5**	**2.5**	**2.3**	**2.5**	**2.2**

Scores that are significantly different (at the 1% level) between groups are underlined and put in bold (one-way ANOVA test).

Analysis of Event Visitors' Expenditure Patterns: The Case of Three Fis Ski Jumping World Cup Events 2013

Grzegorz Kwiatkowski, Ove Oklevik[1]

Abstract

The aim of this study is to analyze the socio-demographic, psychographic and trip-related factors that determine the sport event visitors' expenditure behavior. The quantitative analysis is based on primary data collected by means of self-administered questionnaires at three FIS Ski Jumping World Cup events staged in Norway in 2013.

Keywords

sport events, determinants of spending, Tobit model, FIS Ski Jumping World Cup events

1. Introduction

Acknowledging the event visitors' expenditure behavior and the underling determinants affecting such behavior have been recognized as valuable by planners, marketers and event organizers (*Mok & Iverson* 2000; *Taks* et al. 2013). First of all, the improved knowledge of how socio-demographic, trip-related and psychographic determinants influence the individuals' expenditure might help to identify the market segments that provide higher incomes for local businesses (*Brida* et al. 2011). This, in turn, allows for more effective and efficient marketing strategy construction (*Shani* et al. 2010; *Saayman* et al. 2005). Secondly, accurate information on visitors' expenditure patterns leads to more reliable *ex-ante* economic impact assessments.

However, although studies on the expenditure patterns of regular tourists have received much attention to date, studies on special-interest tourists, of which sport event visitors are an example, remain limited (*Boo* et al. 2009; *Shani* et al. 2010). This is particularly surprising, since event visitors who attend special events are inherently different in their behavior from regular tourists as they display different expectations and posses different needs. Among others, *Kaplanidou* (2009), *Kim* and *Chalip* (2004), and *Wann* et al. (2001) have provided relevant contributions that directly support this view. Moreover, based

---

1 We have benefited greatly from comments by participants of the 5th ESEA conference and Arne Feddersen to the previous versions of this chapter.

on a consistent methodology, so far, scholars have rarely attempted to analyze if and how individuals' expenditure behavior varies between events. Indeed, the major part of the existing literature is based on single cases and individual or rather isolated research designs. This means that, normally these analyses might provide insightful knowledge on single event outcomes and, thus, it is hard to draw broader cross-event comparisons. In fact, to date only the papers written by *Saayman* et al. (2005), *Brida* et al. (2011) and *Barquet* et al. (2011) have attempted to close the gap, providing event studies focusing on more than single cases.

Given that, the purpose of this study is to extend the literature by examining factors that determine event visitors' expenditure behavior during three FIS (Fédération Internationale de Ski) Ski Jumping World Cup events staged in Vikersund, Trondheim and Oslo (all Norway) in 2013. Thereby, the core research questions that guide this study can be stated as follows: (a) Which factors influence (and to what extent) event visitors' expenditure behavior significantly? (b) How does expenditure behavior vary among the considered events?

To achieve the purpose of the current study, this chapter is organized in the following way. Section 2 briefly reviews existing research on the determinants of event visitors' expenditure behavior. Section 3 presents methodology and data used in the empirical analysis. Section 4 presents the results and discussion. Finally, Section 5 concludes the study.

2. Literature Review

To date, numerous empirical studies on tourists' expenditure behavior have been undertaken. Among others, the papers of *Crouch* (1994), *Li* et al. (2005), *Song* and *Li* (2008), *Wang* and *Davidson* (2010) and *Brida* and *Scuderi* (2013) provide comprehensive and critical reviews of these studies. Nevertheless, as stated above the assessment of the literature indicates that only a small part of the tourist demand literature has dealt with primary purpose event tourists as the main focus of interest. This review section provides a more targeted review of special event studies as they have not recieved their due attetion previeously.

The current review has two objectives. First of all, the review seeks to identify the principal research areas within studies on the economic impact of special events (festivals). Secondly, throughout the review special attention is given to methodological aspects of examining the determinants of event visitors' expenditure.

A review of the literature reveals two inherently different areas within special events' economic impact studies. The first area contains a significant body of contributions which seek to estimate the primary economic impact of special events. Within this area special attention was placed to define a set of principles central to the integrity of the economic impact analyses (*Crompton* et al. 2001). Given that, researchers made an effort to define which behaviour of residents and people from outside the region causes crowding-out, re-distribution, and deterrence effects and why this behaviour does not lead to a primary economic impact. Moreover, these studies highlight which behaviour leads to an injection of money into the host region and why only this amount of money can be regarded as a primary impact (*Burgan & Mules* 1992; *Crompton* 1999; *Crompton* et al. 2001; *Crompton & McKay* 1994; *Frechtling* 2006; *Késenne* 2005; *Preuss* 2006; *Preuss* et al. 2007; *Tyrrell & Johnston* 2001).

The second area of interest is the estimation of the expenditure that visitors make during the event. Among these papers, the majority scrutinized the size and determinants influencing such behavior. However, regardless of this overarching purpose, the great variance in terms of the problem formulation, guiding research questions, contextual settings and employed econometric method have been exposed. These studies are central to the current review. Table 1 provides a reference in relation to the research purpose, sample size, contextual settings, models, and variables used in the past event studies.

Table 1: Past event-related studies on determinants of spending

Author (year)	Aim	Sample			Context		Method	Dependent and independent variables																									
		No. of questionnaires			Type	Loc.																											
		Coll.	Used	%				D1	D2	D3	Inc	Opi	Mot	Age	Edu	Gen	Hou	Mar	Lan	Ocu	Nat	Acc	Act	Des	Inf	Len	Tra	Par	Pla	Rea	Dis	Typ	Oth
Tang and Turco (2001)	P1	–	472	–	C	USA	OLS		+															○		○		○		○	○		
Thrane (2002)	P1	1061	957	90.2	M	Norway	Multiple log. reg.		+		○	○		○		○	○			○						○			○	○		○	○
Kim et al. (2008)	P1	550	534	97.0	C	South Korea	Tobit model			+	○		○	○	○			○		○						○	○	○				○	
Kruger et al. (2010)	P1	495	151	30.5	C	South Africa	Stepwise reg.		+					○						○			○		○	○		○		○		○	
Wicker et al. (2012)	P1	1967	1156	58.8	S	Germany	Multiple reg.	+	+		○			○	○	○					○			○								○	
Chhabra et al. (2002)	P1	1437	850	591	C	UK	Multivariate reg.		+	+		○		○						○	○										○	○	○
Barquet et al (2011)	P2a	353	344	97.5	S	Italy	Tobit model			+	○							○	○									○		○			
Dixon et al. (2011)	P2a	895	620	69.3	S	USA	Descriptive stat.	+		+	○			○	○	○						○	○			○		○	○	○		○	○
Kruger et al. (2012)	P2a	507	207	40.8	S	South Africa	Stepwise linear reg.		+				○		○	○			○	○		○	○			○	○	○		○		○	○
Taks et al. (2013)	P2a	1546	1379	89.1	S	Canada	Logistic reg.	+		+				○		○																○	

Author (year)	Aim	Sample: No. of questionnaires			Context		Method	Dependent and independent variables																									
		Coll.	Used	%	Type	Loc.		D1	D2	D3	Inc	Opi	Mot	Age	Edu	Gen	Hou	Mar	Lan	Ocu	Nat	Acc	Act	Des	Inf	Len	Tra	Par	Pla	Rea	Dis	Typ	Oth
Boo et al. (2009)	P2b	_	369	_	O	USA	Factor analysis	+		+																							
Wang and Lee (2011)	P2b	240	211	87.9	O	Taiwan	OLS	+		+	○			○	○	○		○		○												○	○
Saayman et al. (2005)	P3a	_	965	_	S	South Africa	Descriptive stat.		+	+				○									○										○
Brida et al. (2012)	P3a	1288	1240	96.3	C	Italy	Double-hurdle	+		+	○		○				○	○			○					○				○			○
Cannon and Ford (2002)	P3b	3572	2488	69.6	S	USA	OLS	+			○				○			○	○		○					○		○					
Kruger et al. (2009)	P3b	1972	1840	93.3	C	South Africa	OLS		+				○	○		○			○	○	○	○	○				○	○		○			
Downward et al. (2009)	P4	3104	373	12.0	S	UK	OLS, Tobit		○		○	○																○					
Kim et al. (2010)	P4	600	583	97.2	C	South Korea	Logit, OLS, Tobit	+		+	○		○	○	○	○										○	○	○		○		○	○

Notes: Aim: P1, P2, … P4 – explained in the main text; Dependent variables: D1, D2, D3 – explained in the main text; Type of the event: C – Cultural event, M – Music event; S – Sport event; O – Other; independent variables: Inc – income; Opi – opinions about trip; Mot – motivation; Age – age; Edu – education; Hou – household numerousness; Mar – Marital status; Lan – Language; Ocu – occupation; Nat – nationality; Acc – accommodation; Act – activities; Des – destination; Inf – information source; Len – length of stay; Tra – transport mode; Par – party size/structure; Pla – planning horizon; Rea – repeat visitor; Dis – distance travel ; Typ – type of the visitor; Oth – other

Referring to the primary purpose of the reviewed literature, four groups of research were identified.[2] The first (P1) focuses on the examination of the expenditure that visitors spend during one event and the determinants explaining such behavior (*Kim* et al. 2008; *Kruger* et al. 2010; *Tang & Turco* 2001; *Thrane* 2002; *Wicker* et al. 2012). The second group (P2) gravitates towards the examination of the differences in the expenditure behavior between different segments of visitors attending the same event. Among these studies, two distinct angles of investigation evolved. The first line (P2a) encompasses econometric analysis of the expenditure behaviour which is preceded by a market segmentation (*Barquet* et al. 2011; *Dixon* et al. 2011; *Kruger* et al. 2012; *Taks* et al. 2013) and in the second line (P2b) emphasis is placed to trace out differences in the expenditure behaviour between primary purpose event visitors and regular tourists (*Boo* et al. 2009; *Wang & Lee* 2011). The third group (L3) considers whether there is any significant difference in the expenditure behavior between (L3a) visitors attending different events (*Brida* et al. 2012; *Saayman* et al. 2005) or (L3b) visitors attending the same event across time (*Cannon & Ford* 2002; *Kruger* et al. 2009). Finally, the fourth group (L4) assesses whether determinantes of visitors' expenditure and their power vary from one econometric technique to another (*Downward* et al. 2009; *Kim* et al. 2010).

The sample sizes used in the reviewed studies ranged from 151 to 2488 observations, yet almost half of the reviewed studies were based on sample size containing less than 600 usable observations. In the majority of these studies the target population was limited to event spectators. Only recent studies of *Kruger* et al. (2012) and *Wicker* et al. (2012) took both groups of event attendees, i.e. spectators and participants, into consideration in an effort to expose variation in their expenditure. Almost half of the reviewed literature was based on sport and cultural events staged in South Africa (six out of nineteen reviewed studies), the US (three papers) and South Korea (two papers). Other events (music, conferences) have rarely been investigated. All reviewed studies were published after 2000.

The assessment of the literature revealed three major types of expenditure-dependent variables adopted: (D1) total expenditures per day per person, (D2) total expenditures per trip per person and (D3) disaggregated expenditures in several categories. Again, nearly half of the studies were based on more than one dependent variable. For instance, *Wicker* et al. (2012) used (D1) and (D2), *Wang* and *Lee* (2011) adopted (D1) and (D3), while *Barquet* et al. (2011) as well as *Saayman* and

2 It has to be clarified that some papers have several objectives.

Saayman (2012) employed (D2) and (D3). Another important observation is that the disaggregation of the dependent variable into particular categories was conducted in a twofold manner. The first approach is based on the disaggregation of expenditure according to the category of goods and services on which money was spend (e.g. transport, lodging, shopping, entertainment, etc.). The second is based on the place where the good or service was purchased (at the event venue or outside).

Further, the reviewed studies employed a wide range of econometrical methods of which Ordinary Least Squares (OLS) regression was the most common approach (employed in six studies). Moreover, the researchers frequently used Tobit models (four contributions). However, it is worth mentioning that contrary to what is the case for general tourism studies, more sophisticated methods such as the double hurdle model (only one paper) or Hackman model (no paper) were adopted very rarely if at all.

Regarding the selection of the independent variables, the current review indicates that there is high heterogeneity and case-study peculiarity with respect to the selection of potential determinants of expenditures. Specifically, the current assessment pointed out more than twenty exploratory variables of which seven were applied in almost half of the reviewed papers (i.e. income, age, gender, length of stay, party size and/or structure, previous attendance, type of the visitors).

3. Methodology

3.1 Sampling and Data

The target population for this study consisted of spectators who were attending three FIS Ski Jumping World Cup events staged in Vikersund (January 26–27), Trondheim (March 14–15), and Oslo (March 16–17) in 2013.

The three FIS Ski Jumping Word Cup events were chosen because, to date, little research has been carried out in the area of economic impact of non-mega sporting events, notably determinants of ski jumping event visitors spending. Moreover, the chosen events represent a typical winter sport attraction which also has not received the adequate scholars' attention.

The data for this study was collected by means of a self-administered questionnaire. Data has been collected on (a) trip-related characteristics (origin, previous attendance, planning horizon, composition of an immediate group, transport mode, accommodation, length of stay), (b) consumption patterns (expenditure per day), (c) psychographic characteristics (fan motivation, identity) and (d) socio-demographic information (age, gender, education, employment status, household status, income). Altogether, the collected data provides a relatively complete picture of the respondents' event related behavior.

Two language versions (English and Norwegian) of the questionnaire were created and, prior to the fieldwork, tested to identify and eliminate potential shortcomings. The team of interviewers consisted of four bachelor- and two PhD students. In a preceding meeting the interviewers were instructed about the purpose, scope, target group, and technique of the data collection. The interviewers approached as many individuals as possible in the breaks during the ongoing competition and asked them to fill in the questionnaire. As an incentive for participation, the information that the survey has a purely scientific character was given to the participants. The data collection took place exclusively within the ski jumping arenas.

Overall, 870 questionnaires were returned of which 461 are from Vikersund, 105 from Trondheim and 304 from Oslo. Due to missing answers for some of the questions, the number of usable observations for the analysis was reduced to 528 (60.7%). This sample size is consistent with the average sample size used in corresponding event related studies (*Barquet* et al. 2011; *Boo* et al. 2009; *Downward* et al. 2009; Kim et al. 2008; *Kim* et al. 2010; *Kruger* et al. 2010).

3.2 Determinants of visitors' expenditure

The dependent variable of the study is expenditure per person per day, measured in Euro. Moreover, the current study scrutinizes the influence of ten explanatory variables on event visitors' expenditure. The selection of the most relevant exploratory variables has been based on the review of both events related- and general tourism studies. The independent variables included trip-related, psychographic and socio-demographic characteristics. A more detailed description of the variables and the expected sign of the coefficients are given in Table 2.

Table 2: Measurement of variables and research hypotheses

Variable	Description	Expected sign
	DEPENDENT VARIABLE	
Expenditure	Euro amount of expenditures per person.	
	INDEPENDENT VARIABLES	
Trip planned ahead	Continuous variable. Number of days the trip was planned in advance.	-
Repeat visitor	Dummy variable with value 1 if respondent attended the event in the past, 0 otherwise.	-
Children in a party	Dummy variable with value 1 if there are children in an immediate group, 0 otherwise.	-
Travel time[a]	Continuous variable. An average journey time (expressed in minutes) from a given postal code area to the event venue.	+

Variable	Description	Expected sign
Fan motive[b]	Dummy variable with value 1 if a ski jumping fan, 0 otherwise.	+
Age	Continuous variable. Age measured in years.	+/-
Gender	Dummy variable with value 1 if man, 0 if woman.	+/-
Education		
Middle school	Dummy variable with value 1 if middle school level of education, 0 otherwise.	-
High school	Dummy variable with value 1 if high school level of education, 0 otherwise.	-
Undergraduate and graduate	Dummy variable with value 1 if undergraduate or graduate level of education, 0 otherwise.	+
Postgraduate	Dummy variable with value 1 if postgraduate level of education, 0 otherwise.	+
Household status		
Single without children	Dummy variable with value 1 if single without children, 0 otherwise.	+/-
Married/ partner without children	Dummy variable with value 1 if married/partner without children, 0 otherwise.	+/-
Single with children	Dummy variable with value 1 if single with children, 0 otherwise.	+/-
Married/ partner with children	Dummy variable with value 1 if married/partner with children, 0 otherwise.	+/-
Income		
Low income	Dummy variable with value 1 if monthly family income before tax is between 0€ and 3300€.	-
Middle income	Dummy variable with value 1 if monthly family income before tax is between 3300€ and 5500€.	+
High income	Dummy variable with value 1 if monthly family income before tax is greater than 5500€.	+

Notes: + positive; – negative i; +/- inconclusive. [(a)] Existing studies analyzing determinats of tourist spending mostly use a measure of distance travel (expressed in km or miles) (*Brida & Scuderi* 2013). However, because of many geographical barriers in Norway such as mountains and fiords which highly condition travel time, the application of the traditional regressor of distance travel seems to be unsuitable. Given that, distance travel was replaced in a favor of travel time. To measure an estimated travel time between the event venue and a given postal code area the rout planning software (Google maps) was adopted.

[(b)] To gauge a fan motivation one item of *Shamir's* (1992) scale of a self-identity was measured. The item was adjusted to the sport context according to *Snelgrove* et al. (2008) study. Respondents were asked to rate how much they agree with the statement "being a ski jumping fan describes me". The item was rated on a six-point Likert scale ranging from strongly disagree (1) to strongly agree (6). Respondents who agreed (5) or strongly agreed (6) with the statement were classified as the ski jumping fans.

3.3 Data Analyses

A common feature of survey data on tourists' expenditures is the presence of values equal to zero (*Alegre* et al. 2013), which is shared by the dataset collected for this analysis. This, in turn, leads to a situation in which the distributional assumptions underlying OLS regression methods are not fulfilled. More significantly, in this case, the estimated parameters in OLS regressions are inconsistent (*Humphreys* et al. 2010). In this context, one critical issue is to ascertain why the zeros are present in the data since their source affects the choice of an appropriate estimator (*Humphreys* 2013). In general, according to Humphreys et al. (2010, p. 166) zeros can be present in survey data for three reasons: (1) "the respondent did not purchase the good or undertake the activity in question during the sampling period for the survey because the good is purchased infrequently" (non-observable response); (2) "the respondent would never purchase the good or undertake the activity in question under any circumstance or at any price" (abstention); (3) "the respondent would be interested in purchasing the good or participating in the activity in question, but the cost of purchase or participation is currently too high to elicit purchase or participation given the respondent's preferences and level of income" (corner solution).

Given that, under scenario (1) the Heckman sample selection model applies, while in case of scenarios (2) and (3) the Tobit and double hurdle model are more appropriate (*Humphreys* 2013). The main difference between the recent two models is that throughout the estimation of the double hurdle model two different sets of relevant independent variables for two different hurdles are obtained (i.e. first, whether or not a person decides to participate in the activity in question and second, if so, how much the person spends on it), while in the Tobit model the first hurdle is irrelevant to the consumer's decision about how much to spend (*Brida* et al. 2011).

Since it is assumed that all "zero spending" in the current data represent the standard corner solutions and that negative values are unobservable and bunched at zero, standard censored Tobit analysis was selected as an appropriate technique for the final model estimation. The Tobit model was previously adopted to investigate event visitors' as well as regular tourists' determinants of spending by *Barquet* et al. (2011), *Brida* et al. (2012), *Downward* et al. (2009), *Kim* et al. (2008), *Kim* et al. (2010) and *Zheng* and *Zhang* (2013).

The general formulation of the Tobit model (*Tobin* 1958) is:

$$\begin{aligned} &y^* = x_i\beta+u_i && i=1,2,\ldots,n \\ &y = y^* && if\, y^* > 0 \\ &y = 0 && if\, y^* \leq 0, \end{aligned} \qquad (1)$$

where represents the expenditure made by tourist, is a vector of independent covariates that explain the individuals' decisions about how much to spend, is an unobserved random variable capturing all factors other than that influence the decision about the intensity of spending.

4. Results and Discussion

4.1 Descriptive Statistics

Table 3 displays descriptive statistics (minimum and maximum values, mean as well as standard deviation) for all variables. The statistics are presented both for the whole sample as well as separately for each sub-sample (Vikersund, Tondheim, and Oslo).

Table 3: Summary statistics

Variable	Whole sample				Vikersund				Trondheim				Oslo			
	Min[a]	Max[b]	Mean[c]	SD[d]	Min	Max	Mean	SD	Min	Max	Mean	SD	Min	Max	Mean	SD
Expenditure	0	500	38.85	55.24	0	370.37	51.03	65.17	0	246.91	31.60	43.22	0	500	25.47	38.92
Trip planned ahead	1	365	51.92	91.85	0	365	67.21	108.85	0	365	58.77	103.09	1	365	31.19	54.34
Repeat visitor	0	1	0.52	0.50	0	1	0.71	0.45	0	1	0.25	0.44	0	1	0.37	0.48
Children in a party	0	1	0.17	0.38	0	1	0.17	0.38	0	1	0.18	0.38	0	1	0.17	0.38
Travel time	1	711	107.15	124.43	11	711	112.16	116.12	1	448	71.89	119.14	8	688	111.68	134.41
Fan motive	0	1	0.34	0.47	0	1	0.44	0.50	0	1	0.29	0.45	0	1	0.24	0.43
Age	16	93	41.70	16.49	16	92	45.30	16.01	18	77	37.21	16.38	17	93	38.62	16.20
Gender	0	1	0.43	0.45	0	1	0.32	0.42	0	1	0.51	0.50	0	1	0.52	0.50
Education																
Middle school	0	1	0.14	0.34	0	1	0.18	0.38	0	1	0.10	0.31	0	1	0.09	0.29
High school	0	1	0.24	0.43	0	1	0.29	0.45	0	1	0.13	0.34	0	1	0.22	0.41
Undergraduate and graduate	0	1	0.60	0.49	0	1	0.51	0.50	0	1	0.75	0.43	0	1	0.66	0.48
Postgraduate	0	1	0.03	0.16	0	1	0.02	0.15	0	1	0.01	0.11	0	1	0.03	0.18

Variable	Whole sample				Vikersund				Trondheim				Oslo			
	Min[a]	Max[b]	Mean[c]	SD[d]	Min	Max	Mean	SD	Min	Max	Mean	SD	Min	Max	Mean	SD
Household status																
Single without children	0	1	0.25	0.43	0	1	0.19	0.39	0	1	0.34	0.48	0	1	0.30	0.46
Married/ partner without children	0	1	0.21	0.41	0	1	0.17	0.38	0	1	0.23	0.43	0	1	0.25	0.43
Single with children	0	1	0.06	0.23	0	1	0.06	0.24	0	1	0.04	0.19	0	1	0.05	0.22
Married/ partner with children	0	1	0.48	0.50	0	1	0.57	0.50	0	1	0.40	0.49	0	1	0.40	0.49
Income																
Low income	0	1	0.29	0.45	0	1	0.22	0.42	0	1	0.51	0.50	0	1	0.31	0.46
Middle income	0	1	0.32	0.47	0	1	0.34	0.47	0	1	0.30	0.46	0	1	0.29	0.46
High income	0	1	0.39	0.49	0	1	0.43	0.50	0	1	0.19	0.39	0	1	0.40	0.49

Notes: [a] minimum value; [b] maximum value; [c] mean value; [d] standard deviation.

For the sake of simplicity, the description of summary statistics focuses exclusively on the whole sample. Spectators of the three FIS Ski Jumping World Cup events spend on average 38.85€, while the minimum spending was zero euro and the maximum 500€. The standard deviation is 55.24€. The advance in planning to attend the event ranged from 1 to 365 days, with mean of 51 days and standard deviation of 91 days. 52% of the respondents attended the events in the past. About 16% of the respondents attend the event with children. On average, spectators travel to the event 107 minutes. However, the majority of respondents travel less than one hour (Median = 58 minutes). Figure 1 shows the inverse cumulated travel time density (expressed in minutes), whereas the individual travel times are calculated between the geographical centroid of the individual's postal code area as stated in the questionnaire and the event venue.

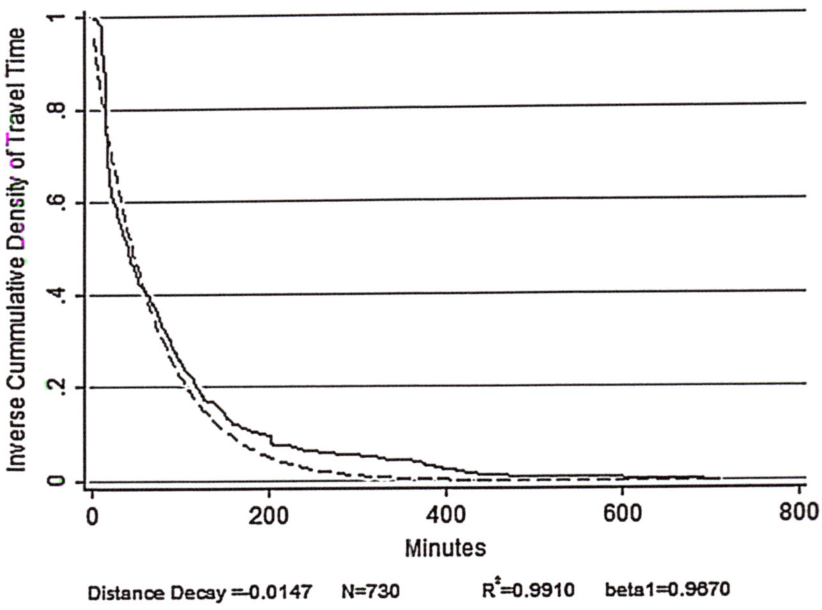

Fig. 1: Inverse cumulated travel time density to the event venue

Further, about 34% of the respondents claimed that they are ski jumping fans. The average age of the individuals in the sample is 41 years, ranging from 16 to 93 years. About 43% of the respondents are male. The majority of individuals (60%) are educated to a university degree level (undergraduate or graduate level). For another 24% the high school degree is their highest level of education, while 14% state that they have a middle school degree. Finally, 3% hold a postgraduate degree. With respect to the marital status, married/partner households with children (48%) are dominating. The group of couples without children is represented by 21% of the individuals, while single households without children are represented by 25% of respondents. Only a minority of respondents can be classified as a single household with children (6%). With respect to the income, 29% of respondents have a monthly household income before tax lower than 3,300€, another 32% of respondents between 3,300€ and 5,500€, while the remaining 39% of respondents have a monthly household income before tax greater than 5,500€.

4.2 Tobit Model Estimation

Table 4 features the results of the Tobit regression model (column A) and the marginal effects for the respective truncated sample (column B). Both outcomes are presented for the whole sample (referred to as full model) and separately for the three sub-samples (Vikersund, Trondheim, and Oslo). Based on the likelihood-ratio test, all estimations are significant at least at the 5% level: model ($p < 0.001$), Vikersund ($p = 0.029$), Trondheim ($p = 0.052$), and Oslo ($p = 0.013$).

Prior to reporting the final results it is necessary to clarify that the Tobit coefficients cannot be interpreted in the same manner as OLS coefficients (*Gujarati* 2011). In fact, the Tobit model estimates the effects of the vector of independent variables upon the "latent" variable, and not the linear effect on the observed outcome as it occurs in a case of OLS regression (*Downward* et al. 2009; *Gujarati* 2011). This is because "the ordinary output from a tobit analysis provides only one (unstandardized) coefficient for each independent variable, despite the presence of two "types" of cases in the analysis – those with zero on the dependent variable and those with nonzero values" (*Roncek* 1992). This, in turn, makes it impossible to describe these two different effects by a single coefficient, and as McDonald and Moffitt (1980 cited from *Roncek* 1992) noted, researchers often misinterpreted these coefficients.

There are, however, at least two common approaches with respect to the interpretation of coefficients from Tobit estimations present in the existing literature. In the first approach, researchers limit the presentation of results to scant information about the statistical significance and the sign of the obtained coefficients. As a result, these studies provide the insight into which factors (e.g. gender, travel distance, etc.) significantly influence spending and whether these factors have positive or negative impact on the expenditures.

Besides information about significance and the sign of coefficients, the second approach provides additional insight about the magnitude of these effects. To obtain this information it requires computing the marginal effects of each independent variable for the so-called truncated sample (i.e. all cases with positive expenditures). Interpreting the marginal effects of the truncated sample, in turn, seems to be more useful for policy makers and event marketers, since the effects are represented as monetary values. Previously, similar approaches have been adopted in event-related studies conducted by *Kim* et al. (2008) and *Downward* et al. (2009).

Consequently, the marginal effects for truncated sample are presented and discussed in the following.

Table 4: Attributes associated with event-related expenditures

Variables	Full model		Vikersund		Trondheim		Oslo	
	A Coef. (Std. Err.)	B dy/dx (Std. Err.)	A Coef. (Std. Err.)	B dy/dx (Std. Err.)	A Coef. (Std. Err.)	B dy/dx (Std. Err.)	A Coef. (Std. Err.)	B dy/dx (Std. Err.)
Trip planned ahead	-0.001 (0.026)	-0.001 (0.014)	0.011 (0.037)	0.006 (0.0214)	-0.112* (0.059)	-0.071* (0.038)	-0.124*** (0.043)	-0.072*** (0.025)
Repeat visitor *(ref. no)*	4.804 (5.029)	2.602 (2.717)	-1.930 (10.229)	-1.106 (5.881)	14.227 (9.669)	9.400 (6.704)	-1.370 (3.940)	-0.791 (2.272)
Children in a party *(ref. no)*	-20.712*** (6.116)	-10.516*** (2.912)	-33.325*** (10.510)	-17.440*** 5.057	-18.174 (15.441)	-10.443 (8.064)	-0.425 (5.156)	-0.245 (2.970)
Travel time	0.052*** (0.019)	0.028*** (0.010)	0.049 (0.038)	0.028 (0.022)	0.112*** (0.038)	0.071*** (0.024)	0.044*** (0.016)	0.025*** (0.009)
Fan motive *(ref. no)*	4.234 (5.039)	2.314 (2.773)	-2.326 (8.409)	-1.327 (4.793)	30.061** (12.476)	21.048** 9.672	8.362* (4.517)	5.054* (2.849)
Age	0.271 (0.179)	0.147 0.097	0.408 (0.302)	0.233 (0.173)	0.130 (0.616)	0.082 (0.389)	-0.042 (0.152)	-0.024 (0.088)
Gender *(ref. female)*	-13.053*** (4.850)	-6.992*** (2.568)	-18.151** (9.037)	-10.036** 4.847	9.959 (8.808)	6.258 (5.520)	-3.742 (3.924)	-2.167 (2.274)
Education (ref.: middle school)								
High school	-15.665* (8.505)	-8.816* (4.966)	-15.950 (12.745)	-8.991 (7.378)	-11.881 (20.281)	-9.604 16.671	-4.668 (9.028)	-2.768 (5.499)
Undergraduate and graduate	-10.952 (7.752)	-6.311 (4.651)	-2.340 (11.863)	-1.395 (7.111)	-30.069* (17.604)	-21.811* (14.642)	-3.519 (8.296)	-2.110 (5.120)
Postgraduate	-22.400 (17.270)	-12.182 (8.729)	-19.812 (30.148)	-10.989 (15.707)	-14.880 (36.363)	-11.836 27.592	-2.804 (15.000)	-1.693 8.957

Variables	Full model		Vikersund		Trondheim		Oslo	
	A Coef. (Std. Err.)	B dy/dx (Std. Err.)	A Coef. (Std. Err.)	B dy/dx (Std. Err.)	A Coef. (Std. Err.)	B dy/dx (Std. Err.)	A Coef. (Std. Err.)	B dy/dx (Std. Err.)
Household type (ref.: single without children)								
Married without children	-5.967 (6.861)	-3.054 (3.529)	-21.565 (13.502)	-11.811 (7.537)	20.703* (11.328)	13.061* (7.382)	6.140 (5.376)	3.361 (2.931)
Single with children	4.568 (11.942)	2.473 (6.546)	0.449 (20.675)	0.269 (12.410)	5.882 (28.230)	3.285 16.207	17.539* (10.101)	10.749* (6.848)
Married with children	7.442 (7.444)	4.090 (4.044)	-3.086 (12.713)	-1.825 (7.566)	12.920 (19.408)	7.659 (11.612)	8.069 (6.380)	4.505 (3.533)
Income (ref.: Low-income)								
Mid-income	2.533 (6.281)	1.312 (3.249)	2.321 (11.574)	1.232 (6.127)	-6.435 (11.519)	-3.847 (6.809)	2.479 (5.147)	1.413 (2.932)
High-income	12.117* (6.346)	6.606* (3.427)	19.759* (11.295)	11.299* (6.286)	14.209 (13.522)	9.924 (9.921)	3.140 (5.255)	1.802 (3.005)
Constant	26.615** (11.171)		40.361** (19.162)		22.960 (29.096)		18.235* (10.921)	
Sigma	50.421*** (1.646)		61.222*** (2.785)		29.994*** (2.870)		25.435*** (1.375)	
Observations	528	528	264	264	62	62	202	202

Notes: Standard errors in parentheses *** $p<0.01$, ** $p<0.05$, * $p<0.1$; A – tobit model estimation; B – marginal effects for truncated sample

The results of the full model estimations indicate that the presence of children in an immediate group, gender, and high-school level of education have a significant and negative effect on the expenditure-dependent variable. The first two of the mentioned variables are highly significant on the 1%-level, while the last one is significant only on the 10%-level. Referring the obtained results to the relative values it can be sated that attending the event with children entails a decrease in spending on average 10.52€. Similarly, individuals who possess a high school degree spend on average 8.82€ less than those from the reference group (middle school education). Again, being male decreases spending on average 6.99€ compared to being female.

Comparing these findings with previous research, it is apparent that, first, the significant negative effect of children in the immediate group is consistent with studies conducted by *Agarwal* and *Yochum* (1999), *Cannon* and *Ford* (2002) and *Saayman* and *Saayman* (2012) who pointed out that the presence of children in the travel party leads to a decrease in expenditure. Second, the significant negative effect of being male is coherent with the result presented by *Craggs* and *Schofield* (2009). Nevertheless, it is worth mentioning that the majority of studies found a gender variable as well as other socio-demographic variables to be insignificant.

In contrast, two covariates in the full model (travel time and income) have a significant positive influence on expenditure. The significance level for these variables is 1% and 10% respectively. For example, one minute of extra travel time to the event increases spending by about 0.03€, while respondents with high income spend on average 6.61€ more than those with low income. Here, as it was expected, the variable travel time has a significant and positive effect on the respondents' expenditure since travel costs are assumed to be larger if travel time increases. The current result confirms previous empirical findings obtained by *Prideaux* (2000), *Lee* (2001), *Chhabra* et al. (2002), *Nicolau* and *Más* (2005), *Pouta* et al. (2006) as well as *Wang* et al. (2006). Regarding the effect of income, again, the current findings confirm expectations and previous research of, e.g., *Cannon* and *Ford* (2002), *Thrane* (2002) and *Kruger* et al. (2009). Finally, it should be noted that remaining covariates ("trip planned ahead", "repeat visitor", "fan motive", "age", level of education: "undergraduate and graduate", "postgraduate", all considered "household types", level of income: "mid-income") appear to have no significant effect on the dependent variable.

The results obtained for the Vikersund model are similar to the full model with respect to three covariates "children in a party", "gender" and "level of income" (high income). Here, the signs of the estimated coefficients are exactly the same for the two models. Also some clear evidence can be found in terms of the level of significance of variables and their magnitude. In line with the findings related to the full model, "children in a party" and "gender" have a significant negative effect on the dependent variable. Bringing children to the event reduces spending by 17.44€ compared to attending without children and being male decrease spending by 10.04€ compared to being female. As in the whole sample, high income has a positive and significant effect on the dependent variable which is found to be equal to an extra spending of 11.30€ compared to participants having a low income. However, in contrast to the full model estimation, the explanatory variables "travel time" and "high school education" do not reveal any significant impact on the expenditure.

The results of the Trondheim model are considerably different from the two previously discussed models. First, the variable "plan the trip in advance" shows a negative significant effect on the expenditure which is equal to a reduction of spending by 0.07€ for each day the trip was planned ahead. Here, this result confirms once again the preliminary assumption and previous empirical findings presented by *Oppermann* (1997) and *Pouta* et al. (2006). Second, being a ski jumping fan significantly increases expenditure in the Trondheim model. Visitors with a fan motive have higher expenditures of 21.05€ compared to the reference group (regular visitors), which is in line with the preliminary assumption that the higher one's fan motivation, the more likely it is that one will spend more at the event venue. This result corresponds to earlier research of *Snelgrove* et al. (2008). Third, possessing a graduate or undergraduate degree reduces expenditures by 21.81€ compared to the reference group (middle school degree). Fourth, being married without children has a significant and negative effect on expenditures (minus 13.06€). Unlike the results from the full model, time traveling to the event increments expenditures significantly: One extra minute of travelling increases spending on average by 0.07€.

Finally, the results from Oslo have the same magnitude as those from Trondheim when it comes to the effect of planning the trip in advance, travel time, and fan motive. Planning the trip in advance has a negative significant effect on the expenditures. That is, spending is reduced by 0.07€ for each day the trip has been planned in advance. Further, one extra traveling minute increases spending by 0.03€. Respondents with a fan motive have 5.05€ higher expenditures than those who are not ski jumping fans. Despite some similarities with the previously presented models, the results from Oslo contain also several deviations. While there are significant and negative effects of variables capturing the level of education at the 10% level in both the Trondheim and the full model, these variables are not significant in the Oslo model. The variable couple without children was significant at the 10%-level and positive in Trondheim but not in the other two models. Furthermore, the variable capturing respondents being categorized as single with children is only significant (at the 10% level) in the Oslo model.

5. Conclusion

The study showed that even though sport event tourism has recently gained in importance, the knowledge about the expenditure behaviour of sport event visitors is yet limited. In many aspects the existing contributions are heterogeneous which renders generalization of results difficult or even impossible. The literature review clearly identified a research gap and highlighted an avenue towards further research on determinantes of event visitors' expenditure. Here, a few aspects come to the fore. First, there is a need for more methodologically consistent approaches that allow comparisons between different sporting events. Second, when zero-censored data is analysed more attention should be given to the selection of a reliable econometric method, since traditional OLS regression might provide inconsistent results. Finally, more consideration should be given to non-mega sporting events located in a wide range of geographical areas which, to date, both have not received adequate scholarly attention.

Accordingly, the current study sought to bridge the aforementioned research gaps by examining various determinants of three FIS Ski Jumping World Cup event visitors' expenditures. Methodologically, the study adopted Tobit model as a reliable method to analyse the left-censored data.

As a result, the current study confirmed that there are meaningful differences in terms of expenditure behavior and underlying determinants influencing such behavior among the three considered events. Furthermore, it can be stated that focusing on the aggregated dataset might camouflage significant effects occurring at more disaggregated levels. For instance, by looking only into the results from the aggregated dataset, it could lead to a situation when fan motivation and planning horizon of attending the event would not have any impact on the expenditure behavior. However, studying subsamples in more detail allow exposing significant effects in both the Oslo and the Trondheim sample. An opposite pattern has been found among other independent variables: significant effects at aggregated level but not at disaggregated, exemplified by the variable capturing respondents with children in a party. Thus, the examination of determinants of sport event visitors' expenditure should have a more complex approach focusing on both effects across single events and at aggregated level in order to get a more complete picture.

References

Agarwal, V. B. & Yochum, G. R. (1999): Tourist Spending and Race of Visitors, in: Journal of Travel Research, Vol. 38, 2, pp. 173–176.

Alegre, J., Mateo, S. & Pou, L. (2013): Tourism participation and expenditure by Spanish households: The effects of the economic crisis and unemployment, in: Tourism Management, Vol. 39, pp. 37–49.

Barquet, A., Brida, J. G., Osti, L. & Schubert, S. (2011): An analysis of tourists' expenditure on winter sports events through the Tobit censorate model, in: Tourism Economics, Vol. 17, 6, pp. 1197–1217.

Boo, S., Kim, M. & Jones, D. L. (2009): Comparative Analysis of Travel-Related Characteristics Between Special Event Attendees and Non-Attendees in a Metropolitan City, in: Journal of Convention & Event Tourism, Vol. 10, 1, pp. 50–71.

Brida, J. G. & Scuderi, R. (2013): Determinants of tourist expenditure: A review of microeconometric models, in: Tourism Management Perspectives, Vol. 6, pp. 28–40.

Brida, J. G., Bukstein, D., Garrido, N. & Tealde, E. (2012): Cruise passengers' expenditure in the Caribbean port of call of Cartagena de Indias: a cross-section data analysis, in: Tourism Economics, Vol. 18, 2, pp. 431–447.

Brida, J. G., Disegna, M. & Osti, L. (2011): Visitors' Expenditure Behaviour at Cultural Events, Working Paper, Bolzano: Free University of Bolzano.

Brida, J. G., Disegna, M. & Osti, L. (2012): The effect of authenticity on visitors' expenditure at cultural events, in: Current Issues in Tourism, Vol. 16, 3, pp. 266–285.

Burgan, B. & Mules, T. (1992): Economic impact of sporting events, in: Annals of Tourism Research, Vol. 19, 4, pp. 700–710.

Cannon, T. F. & Ford, J. (2002): Relationship of demographic and trip characteristics to visitor spending: an analysis of sports travel visitors across time, in: Tourism Economics, Vol. 8, 3, pp. 263–271.

Chhabra, D., Sills, E. & Rea, P. (2002): Tourist Expenditures at Heritage Festivals, in: Event Management, Vol. 7, 4, pp. 221–230.

Craggs, R. & Schofield, P. (2009): Expenditure-based segmentation and visitor profiling at The Quays in Salford, UK, in: Tourism Economics, Vol. 15, 1, pp. 243–260.

Crompton, J. L. & McKay, S. L. (1994): Measuring the Economic Impact of Festivals and Events: Some Myths, Misapplications and Ethical Dilemmas, in: Festival Management & Event Tourism, Vol. 2, pp. 33–43.

Crompton, J. L. (1999): Measuring the Economic Impact of Visitors to Sport Tournaments and Special Events, Ashburn/VA: National Recreation and Park Association.

Crompton, J. L., Lee, S. B. & Shuster, T. (2001): A Guide for Undertaking Economic Impact Studies: The Springfest Example, in: Journal of Travel Research, Vol. 40, 1, pp. 79–87.

Crouch, G. I. (1994): The Study of International Tourism Demand: A Survey of Practice, in: Journal of Travel Research, Vol. 32, 4, pp. 41–55.

Dixon, A. W., Backman, S., Backman, K. & Norman, W. (2011): Expenditure-based segmentation of sport tourists, in: Journal of Sport & Tourism, Vol. 17, 1, pp. 5–21.

Downward, P., Lumsdon, L. & Weston, R. (2009): Visitor Expenditure: The Case of Cycle Recreation and Tourism, in: Journal of Sport & Tourism, Vol. 14, 1, pp. 25–42.

Frechtling, D. C. (2006): An Assessment of Visitor Expenditure Methods and Models, in: Journal of Travel Research, Vol. 45, 1, pp. 26–35.

Gujarati, D. (2011): Econometrics by Example, London: Palgrave Macmillan.

Humphreys, B. R. (2013): Dealing With Zeros in Economic Data, Working paper, Edmonto: University of Alberta, Department of Economics.

Humphreys, B. R., Lee, Y. S, & Soebbing, B. P. (2010): Consumer behaviour in lottery: the double hurdle approach and zeros in gambling survey data, in: International Gambling Studies, Vol. 10, 2, pp. 165–176.

Kaplanidou, K. (2009): Relationships among Behavioral Intentions, Cognitive Event and Destination Images among Different Geographic Regions of Olympic Games Spectators, in: Journal of Sport & Tourism, Vol. 14, 4, pp. 249–272.

Késenne, S. (2005): Do We Need an Economic Impact Study or a Cost-Benefit Analysis of a Sports Event?, in: European Sport Management Quarterly, Vol. 5, 2, pp. 133–142.

Kim, N.-S & Chalip, L. (2004): Why travel to the FIFA World Cup? Effects of motives, background, interest, and constraints, in: Tourism Management, Vol. 25, 6, pp. 695–707.

Kim, S. S., Han, H. & Chon, K. (2008): Estimation of the Determinants of Expenditures by Festival Visitors, in: Tourism Analysis, Vol. 13, 4, pp. 387–400.

Kim, S. S., Prideaux, B. & Chon, K. (2010): A comparison of results of three statistical methods to understand the determinants of festival participants' expenditures, in: International Journal of Hospitality Management, Vol. 29, 2, pp. 297–307.

Kruger, M., Saayman, M. & Ellis, S. (2012): Determinants of visitor spending: an evaluation of participants and spectators at the Two Oceans Marathon, in: Tourism Economics, Vol. 18, 6, pp. 1203–1227.

Kruger, M., Saayman, M. & Ellis, S. M. (2010): Determinants of Visitor Expenditure at the Aardklop National Arts Festival, in: Event Management, Vol. 14, 2, pp. 137–148.

Kruger, M., Saayman, M. & Saayman, A. (2009): Sociodemographic and Behavioral Determinants of Visitor Spending at the Klein Karoo National Arts Festival, in: Event Management, Vol. 13, 1, pp. 53–68.

Lee, H.-C. (2001): Determinants of recreational boater expenditures on trips, in: Tourism Management, Vol. 22, 6, pp. 659–667.

Li, G., Song, H. & Witt, S. F. (2005): Recent Developments in Econometric Modeling and Forecasting, in: Journal of Travel Research, Vol. 44, 1, pp. 82–99.

Mok, C. & Iverson, T. (2000): Expenditure-based segmentation: Taiwanese tourists to Guam, in: Tourism Management, Vol. 21, pp. 299–305.

Nicolau, J. L. & Más, F. J. (2005): Heckit modelling of tourist expenditure: evidence from Spain, in: International Journal of Service Industry Management, Vol. 16, 3, pp. 271–293.

Oppermann, M. (1997): First-time and repeat visitors to New Zealand, in: Tourism Management, Vol. 18, 3, pp. 177–181.

Pouta, E., Neuvonen, M. & Sievänen, T. (2006): Determinants of Nature Trip Expenditures in Southern Finland – Implications for Nature Tourism Development, in: Scandinavian Journal of Hospitality and Tourism, Vol. 6, 2, pp. 118–135.

Preuss, H. (2006): Impact and Evaluation of Major Sporting Events, in: European Sport Management Quarterly, Vol. 6, 4, pp. 313–316.

Preuss, H., Seguin, B. & O'Reilly, N. (2007): Profiling Major Sport Event Visitors: The 2002 Commonwealth Games, in: Journal of Sport & Tourism, Vol. 12, 1, pp. 5–23.

Prideaux, B. (2000): The role of the transport system in destination development, in: Tourism Management, Vol. 21, 1, pp. 53–63.

Roncek, D. W. (1992): Learning More From Tobit Coefficients: Extending a Comparative Analysis of Political Protest, in: American Sociological Review, Vol. 57, 4, pp. 503–507.

Saayman, M. & Saayman, A. (2012): Determinants of Spending: an Evaluation of Three Major Sporting Events, in: International Journal of Tourism Research, Vol. 14, 2, pp. 124–138.

Saayman, M., Saayman, A. & du Plessis, C. (2005): Analysis of spending patterns of visitors of three World Cup Cricket matches in Potchefstroom, South Africa, in: Journal of Sport & Tourism, Vol. 10, 3, pp. 211–221.

Shamir, B. (1992): Some correlates of leisure identity salience: three exploratory studies, in: Journal of Leisure Research, Vol. 24, pp. 301.

Shani, A., Wang, Y., Hutchinson, J. & Lai, F. (2010): Applying expenditure-based segmentation on special-interest tourists: The case of golf travelers, in: Journal of Travel Research, Vol. 49, 3, pp. 337–350.

Snelgrove, R., Taks, M., Chalip, L. & Green, B. C. (2008): How Visitors and Locals at a Sport Event Differ in Motives and Identity, in: Journal of Sport & Tourism, Vol. 13, 3, pp. 165–180.

Song, H. & Li, G. (2008): Tourism demand modelling and forecasting – A review of recent research, in: Tourism Management, Vol. 29, 2, pp. 203–220.

Taks, M., Green, B. C., Chalip, L., Kesenne, S. & Martyn, S. G. (2013): Visitor composition and event-related spending, in: International Journal of Culture, Tourism and Hospitality Research, Vol. 7, 2, pp. 133–147.

Tang, Q. & Turco, D. M. (2001): Spending Behaviors of Event Tourists, in: Journal of Convention & Exhibition Management, Vol. 3, 2, pp. 33–40.

Thrane, C. (2002): Jazz Festival Visitors and Their Expenditures: Linking Spending Patterns to Musical Interest, in: Journal of Travel Research, Vol. 40, 3, pp. 281–286.

Tobin, J. (1958): Estimation of Relationships for Limited Dependent Variables, in: Econometrica, Vol. 26, 1, pp. 24–36.

Tyrrell, T. J. & Johnston, R. J. (2001): A Framework for Assessing Direct Economic Impacts of Tourist Events: Distinguishing Origins, Destinations, and Causes of Expenditures, in: Journal of Travel Research, Vol. 40, 1, pp. 94–100.

Wang, S.-T. & Lee, Y.-S. (2011): Expenditure Differences Among Conference and Regular Tourists in Taiwan: The Role of Situational Factors, in: Journal of Convention & Event Tourism, Vol. 12, 4, pp. 290–312.

Wang, Y. & Davidson, M. C. G. (2010): A review of micro-analyses of tourist expenditure, in: Current Issues in Tourism, Vol. 13, 6, pp. 507–524.

Wang, Y., Rompf, P., Severt, D. & Peerapatdit, N. (2006): Examining and identifying the determinants of travel expenditure patterns, in: International Journal of Tourism Research, Vol. 8, 5, pp. 333–346.

Wann, D. L., Melnick, M. J., Russell, G. W. & Pease, D. G. (2001): Sport fans: The psychology and social impact of spectators, New York: Routledge.

Wicker, P., Hallmann, K. & Zhang, J. J. (2012): What is influencing consumer expenditure and intention to revisit? An investigation of marathon events, in: Journal of Sport & Tourism, Vol. 17, 3, pp. 165–182.

Zheng, B. & Zhang, Y. (2013): Household Expenditures for Leisure Tourism in the USA, 1996 and 2006, in: International Journal of Tourism Research, Vol. 15, 2, pp. 197–208.

The Economics of Motorsport Centers

Anika Müller, Oliver Budzinski

Abstract

This paper presents a systematic economic analysis of motorsport centers, including their description and categorization. Furthermore, the economic theory of motorsport centers is explored and motorsport centers are viewed to be platforms.

Keywords

motor racing, motorsport centers, platform competition, multisided markets, sports economics

1. Introduction

Sports facilities represent an important element of professional sports markets. Most professional and high-level amateur sports disciplines require specialized and sophisticated facilities like arenas for athletics, tennis and others, stadiums for football, baseball and others, halls for basketball, handball, swimming, hockey, judo and others, or tracks for horse or motor racing. Building and managing such a professional facility represents serious business, and markets for sports facilities possess several interesting characteristics from an economic point of view. Sports economic literature has addressed sports facilities topics with an emphasis on cost-benefit analyses (inter alia, *Crompton* 1995; *Noll & Zimbalist* 1997; *Siegfried & Zimbalist* 2000, 2006; *Sanderson* 2000; *Chapin* 2002), often including the problem of subsidizing them with taxpayer money (inter alia, *Irani* 1997; *Coates & Humphreys 2003, Grieve & Sherry 2012*), but also addressing questions like the economics of specialized versus generalized facilities (*Feddersen & Maennig* 2009). In doing so, different types of sports facilities as well as different sports disciplines' facilities have been subject to economic analyses (*Coates & Humphreys 2003*). Race tracks, however, have been neglected in the literature so far, in particular tracks for professional motor racing. This is surprising given the high economic importance of professional motor racing with the FIA Formula One World Championship (in the following just F1) alone representing the worldwide second biggest sport in economic terms. This flagship championship of monoposto race cars is accompanied by professional sports and touring car racing (e.g. NASCAR, FIA World Touring Car Championship, DTM), rallying (e.g. FIA World Rally Championship), motor bike racing (e.g. FIM Road Racing World Championship Grand Prix), motocross racing (e.g. FIM Motocross World Championship) and many more. These millions of dollars businesses take place on different race tracks around the world including such famous facilities as the Indianapolis Motor Speedway (U.S.), Le Mans' Circuit de la Sarthe (France), the Silverstone Circuit (Great Britain), the Circuit de Monaco as well as the Monte Carlo Rally street and off-road track (Monaco), the Suzuka International Racing Course (Japan), the Dutch TT Circuit Assen (the Netherlands), the Autodromo Nazionale Monza (Italy), the Mount Panorama Motor Racing Circuit Bathurst (Australia), the Daytona International Speedway (U.S.), the Autódromo José Carlos Pace in Interlagos (Brazil), the Macau Grand Prix Guia Circuit (China), or the Nürburgring (Germany).

The latter venue further demonstrates the importance of economic knowledge about motor racing facilities. Following heavy investment into modernization of the facility including a business center, a shopping mall, and an amusement park, this famous facility has now run into insolvency with an estimated debt of € 413 million (*Seiwert* 2012). The pure costs of hosting a F1 race, the hosting fee, currently is around € 20 to 25 million – and contracts furthermore contain an in-built price acceleration of up to 10 per cent per year (*Sylt & Reid* 2013). The city of Singapore pays an estimated € 110 million per year for its F1 night race (*Harjani* 2011), which does not include building a track since they use the city streets of Singapore. Building a new race track cost approximately a minimum of € 58 million and that would only include the track and no other needed facilities like a media centre or grand stands, etc.

Against this background, the virtual complete lack of academic literature and analyses of motor racing facilities and their markets represents a serious research gap. This gap is part of a larger research gap regarding motor racing in general since the economics of motorsports is significantly under-researched compared to its relative economic importance within professional sports. Even Formula One has only been addressed by few papers like *Jenkins & Floyd* (2001) and *Jenkins* (2010), tracing technological trajectories and discontinuities from 1967 to 1982, *Cygan* (2007) and *Budzinski* (2012), discussing the antitrust implications of the so-called FIA abuse of dominance case from the late 1990s, *Stadelmann & Eichenberger* (2008), employing econometric methods in order to identify the best driver in F1 history, *Bekker & Lotz* (2009) simulating race-strategy choices for three 2005 F1 races, *Solitander & Solitander* (2010), presenting a case study on sharing and the thievery of intellectual property in F1, as well as *Kipker* (2003), *Mastromarco & Runkel* (2009), *Krauskopf* et al. (2010), *Judde* et al. (2013) and *Budzinski & Feddersen* (2014), analyzing competitive balance issues. The latter has also been done for the US tin top racing series NASCAR (*Berkowitz* et al. 2011). Eventually *Baade & Matheson* (2000) present an economic impact study of Florida's famous Daytona 500 sports car race and *Connaughton & Madsen* (2007) analyze the motorsport industry of North Carolina.

None of these contributions addresses motor racing facilities. To the best of our knowledge, *Müller* (2012) represents the first economic take on this relevant topic. Based upon her insights, we present a deeper and enriched economic analysis of the basic elements of motor racing facilities and related markets. Due to the lack of prior research, this paper needs to dwell into definition and classification issues first (chapter 2) before employing the economic theory of platform competition in order to describe the special characteristics of markets for motor racing facilities.

2. What Is a Motorsport Center?

2.1 Basic Definitions

Motorsports refers to competitions that are performed with a motor-powered vehicle and run over a defined distance.[1] Originally, the races were run as reliability contests over long distances from city to city on public roads. For instance, in the first motorsports event in history in July 1894, the participants were required to manage the distance between Paris and Rouen on public roads (approx. 126 km) within eight and a half hours and the winner was chosen by a jury according to criteria such as safety, economy and ease of handling (*Cimarosti* 1997: 16).[2] During the 1920s, it became customary to run races on purpose-built tracks, in particular in order to enhance safety and prevent accidents with 'innocent' people not involved in the racing event – with the notable exception of off-road races.[3] Also, in the course of time, the reliability element lost weight compared to the racing element, i.e. who is faster and who finishes first. Both elements have been an essential part of motorsports from the beginning, though, and mark a special characteristic of motorsports: unlike most other disciplines, it is not only about the athlete, it is also about the technology of the vehicle he or she drives. In the early days, there was a wide range of technologies[4] and motorsports was a tool to

1 A widely acknowledged definition does not exist yet and still needs to be discussed (*Budzinski* 2012: 57). For a definition that, however, merely covers combustion engine-powered vehicles, see *Hainz* (1999).

2 Jules-Albert Comte De Dion was fastest to Rouen in his steam powered De Dion-Bouton car. However, the jury awarded the win to the slower Peugeot and Panhard & Levassor cars since the De Dion was considered to be too cumbersome in handling (*Cimarosti* 1997: 17).

3 Off-road races, labeled "rallys", run on public streets and in nature. However, nowadays – and in distinct contrast to the origins – these roads are shut for normal travelling during the event.

4 The first motorsport event in 1894 was entered by cars with engine systems powered by steam, electricity, kerosene as well as petrol (*Cimarosti* 1997: 16).

test innovation of engines and vehicles and to market those to customers. In the course of time, combustion engines have become the standard in motorsports (so that some older definitions even declared this to be a defining element; see *Hainz* 1999), but recently hybrid engine systems like the FROGREEN team within the German ADAC GT Masters series (www.frogreen.de) or the Audi Team at Le Mans with the first hybrid car to win Le Mans in 2012 have enjoyed increasing popularity. Amidst an increasing importance of environmental protection and a tendency towards greener racing, electrically powered engines will race in an own championship, the FIA Formula E, from 2014 on. Furthermore, a number of technological innovations used in today's customer cars originates from the competitive desire to be successful in motorsports, for instance, ceramic disk brakes, carbon fiber as construction material, the four-wheel drive, electronic clutches or active wheel suspension (*Heublein* 2008). Consequently, motorsports has always thrived on their close interaction with the motor car and motor bike manufacturing industries.

As mentioned in the preceding paragraph, most contemporary races take place on purpose-built tracks, which more often than not are run as professional businesses. We will call them motorsport centers because – as the discussion in section 3 will show – they comprise more activities than 'just' the odd race. Generally speaking, a *motorsport center* is a facility where races within motor racing series can be held. There is a wide range of different motor-racing series that take place in such motorsport centers. On the one side, there is a vertical differentiation which refers to the level of internationalization. When looking at the vertical range of race series we can find races on intercontinental level like the F1 or MotoGP, often labeled world championships, as well as continental championships like the FIA European Formula Three Championship or the Indycar racing series in North America. Moreover, all sorts of national races like motocross or autocross championships are held either on national levels like the German championships or even on regional level like the "Norddeutsche Motocross Meisterschaft" (= motocross championship of Northern Germany).

On the other side, there is a horizontal differentiation. The most obvious one relates to the number of wheels: four-wheel racing (motor cars) can be distinguished from two-wheel racing (motorbike) – and there is even three-wheel racing (e.g. sidecar racing[5]). Very special variants of motor-racing are powerboat racing, a racing series with engine-powered boats, or air racing with airplanes (zero-wheel

---

5 A sidecar is added to a motorbike and a second person in that side car is helping to steer the bike by leaning to either side of the bike depending on what kind of corner is coming up.

racing).[6] Within four-wheel racing, further distinctions can be made according to the placement of the wheels inside or outside the cars' main body:

- wheels outside the main body (open-wheel racing): monoposto racing, quad racing, kart racing,
- wheels inside the main body: sports car racing, rally car racing, street car racing, saloon car racing.

Alternative differentiations refer to the existence of a roof or whether the racing cars are prototypes or adapted street cars. Furthermore, racing series can be one-make cups (every driver drives the same car, like for instance in the ADAC Mini challenge or the Volkswagen Scirocco R Cup) or competitions with different constructions. Eventually, racing series may be differentiated by the age of the contestants, be it driver or machinery. For instance, Kart races differentiate according to the drivers' age. The German ADAC for example distinguishes between Bambini, aged 10 to 14, the KF3, aged 12 to 16 (with extra license), and the KF2 that is for all drivers older than 15 and with extra licenses. When it comes to the age of the machinery, racing series with historical race cars enjoy an increasing popularity, especially in Great Britain. In summary, racing series may be differentiated according to several criteria (the examples above are certainly not exhaustive). This is particularly true given that every racing series is run according to a technical regulation that defines and limits the technical specifications of the machinery that may be used. Consequently, even within the categories described in this paragraph, there can be different and competing racing series. For example, when it comes to feeder series to F1, i.e. series in which young drivers may qualify for becoming a F1 driver, the GP2 series competes with Renault's FR 3.5 series or the Auto GP series. All of them are open-wheel monoposto one-make series with comparable cars, just differentiated by rather detailed technical specifications. And they compete in providing the better 'ladder' towards F1.

However, for the purpose of our paper, a relevant categorization should follow criteria that allow a subsequent differentiation of racing facilities. While many of the racing series mentioned in the preceding paragraph can be run on the same race track, this does not hold for all types of racing series. Therefore, we focus on two criteria that represent ways to differentiate and classify motorsport centers: track surface and permanency of the track.

6 Whether powerboat racing and air races (like the Red Bull Air Race World Championship) is part of motorsports may not be that uncontroversial within the racing community. According to our definition, however, it belongs into this category of sports.

2.2 *Track Surface*

When we look at the German Motocross Open and the IDM (International German Motorbike Championships), then these races are never held on the same track because these races require different track surfaces. Cross series are held on off-road race tracks whereas racing series like the IDM or the ADAC Masters GT are held 'on-road' on tarmac tracks. In total, the following basic track surfaces for motorracing can be distinguished:

(i) tarmac tracks (tarmac, asphalt, concrete, etc.),
(ii) dirt tracks (sand, dust, shale, gravel, grass, etc.),
(iii) frozen surface tracks (ice, snow),
(iv) water tracks,
(v) air tracks.

Firstly, one of the most commonly found track surface is tarmac. Most major racing series like F1 or Moto GP on international level or the IDM and the ADAC GT Masters on national level are held on tarmac tracks. These races include the biggest racing events with the largest numbers of viewers. Due to the attraction of big events with large crowds, some tarmac tracks are fairly well-known, some of them enjoy worldwide popularity. Examples of well-known tarmac motorsport centers include the German Hockenheimring, the Silverstone circuit in Great Britain, or the Indianapolis Motor Speedway in the US.

Secondly, another widely found type of track is the off-road tracks, sometimes also called dirt tracks. They are characterized by a loose surface like sand, grass, earth, shale or gravel. These venues host races within the so-called cross series like moto- and autocross or U.S. dirt track racing as well as motorcycle speedway and grasstrack racing. Races within the cross-series are generally shorter and the public appeal is smaller compared to tarmac races. This leads to the fact that these off-road tracks are usually smaller in scale than asphalt tracks. Due to the smaller scale, these centers are also less popular with the public than the tarmac tracks which can also be attributed to the fact that off-road tracks often host local, regional or national events. Examples include the American Capeway Rovers or the Dutch Lelystad. Motorcycle speedway and related races are usually held on stadium-like oval tracks in specialized arenas and are very popular in regions like the UK, Scandinavia and Eastern Europe. Examples of specialized centers include the Millennium Stadium in Cardiff, Great Britain, or the Stadion Polonii Bydgoszcz in Poland.

Some venues offer both tarmac as well as off-road tracks. This enables especially small to medium sized venues to be suitable for more race series and thus attract more events which in turn would also attract more viewers.[7] The Swedish Linköping Motorstadion and the Norwegian Vålerbanen are two examples of medium sized courses which offer both coverings. Furthermore, also rallying often includes both tarmac elements (public roads) and dirt track elements (gravel and forest tracks).

Thirdly, another example of race surfaces is ice. Ice racing can take place on temporarily frozen lakes or rivers like the popular Trophée Andros car racing series in France. But there are not only just temporary tracks with ice as surface. Dirt tracks are also used in regard to the ice covering. The operator plows off the snow or sprays the surface with water at times when the temperature is below freezing thus making the water freeze and the track becomes suited for ice racing. For instance, ice speedway motorcycle races are usually held in stadium-like ovals. Eventually, rallying may include racing on snow or ice as well, like the French national ice racing championship or the Team Ice Racing World Championships.

Fourthly, boat racing series are obviously held on water tracks, i.e. circuits that are marked on lakes, rivers or in coastal ocean areas. For instance, the Class 1 World Powerboat Championship and the F1 Powerboat World Championship (sanctioned under the helmet of the Union Internationale Motonautique (UIM)) are international offshore motorboat racing series including feeder categories.[8] Furthermore, jetsprint boat racing or drag boat racing may also take place in rivers or on lakes.

Air racing is the fifth component and it involves airplanes racing over a marked course. There are different ways of determining the winner: the one who returns in the shortest time, the plane completing the track with the most points collected or the one coming closest to a time that is set prior to the race. Today there are different active air races series: the Aero GP, European Air Racing Championship or the Red Bull Air Race World Championship with the latter most likely being the one best known.

2.3 Permanency of Track Setup

When we want to categorize motorsport centers we can also do so by the time of setup of the track. The main distinction to be made here is between (i) permanent and (ii) temporary tracks.

Permanent race tracks are built with motor racing as the main purpose. These kinds of purpose-built motorsport centers exist all year and their circuits are

7 The correlations and connections between the individual players in this market will be explained later in the discourse.

8 The UIM also organized aquabike and jet-ski championships with boats that somewhat resemble bikes.

clearly separated from non-racing related use, for instance from the public road system. Although the main purpose is racing, most permanent motorsport centers also offer other activities at the track. The renting out to racing teams for testing or the opening of the track for private people and their cars are very famous concepts and widely spread amongst these kinds of tracks. Permanent tracks are amongst others, the Australian Phillip Island Grand Prix Circuit, the American Indianapolis Motor Speedway or the German Hockenheimring. They can have a tarmac surface like the mentioned ones or an off-road surface like the Talkkessel in Teutschenthal, Germany, or the Valkenswaard track in the Netherlands. Ice racing can be included also, when a dirt track arena is sprayed with water and frozen.

Temporary tracks are set up for only a certain period of time, often only for the duration of a specific racing event once a year. They use roads (or other surfaces), which are built and maintained with a different purpose than racing as their main area of business. The main purpose of temporary tracks depends on the area and what the area is used for during the rest of the year when there are no races being held at the location. We can distinguish further between city streets, public country roads, and airfields.

- City circuits are normally set up for big races like F1. For these kinds of races, usually the entire city or at least large parts of it are closed down for all other traffic during the time of racing. This is a major task, especially if F1 races are held in larger cities like Monaco or Singapore. City circuits are a very distinct set of tracks and have a special appeal to spectators as the races take place within a city which makes the track narrower and harder to drive for the drivers but at the same time makes it more exciting for the fans. As far as we know, all temporary city circuits are tarmac tracks.
- Temporary tracks being set up on country roads are referred to as temporary street circuits. For races on these tracks, public roads are being shut for civil traffic and race equipment is being set up. Street circuits are found widely around the world and often consist of tarmac tracks, running on tarmac country roads such as the Argentinean Gran Primo de Santa Fe or the Chinese Beijing International Street Circuit. A very popular variant of (predominantly) grassroots races run on temporary tarmac tracks are hill-climbing races where the participants do a time trial competition up the roads of a mountain like the Mount Pikes Peak, the Wiscombe Park in Great Britain or Rossfeld in Germany. However, they may also run on gravel, grass or sand roads through nature like the famous rallying events – and sometimes even outside any road or defined way, for instance through the desert (e.g. the Rally Dakar who originally led through the Sahara but is nowadays run in South America).

- Another possible track form that can be temporarily used is civil or military airfields. Some of the used airfields are still in use when races are not on. Others have already closed down as an airfield such as the English Abingdon Airfield which is now home to track days as a non permanent race track. The German Airfield Diepholz Racetrack on the other hand is still in use by the German Air force whilst also being host to car races. Obviously, the surface of airfield tracks is always tarmac.

Water and air tracks are always temporarily established on public lakes, rivers or coastal ocean regions (water tracks) as well as up in the air over former airfields like Berlin Tempelhof or even above race tracks like the Texas Motor Speedway (air tracks).

2.4 A Classification System

When we take all these various points together, we can make main distinctions like permanent vs. temporary or asphalt vs. offroad. The other various forms can be summarized in figure 1.

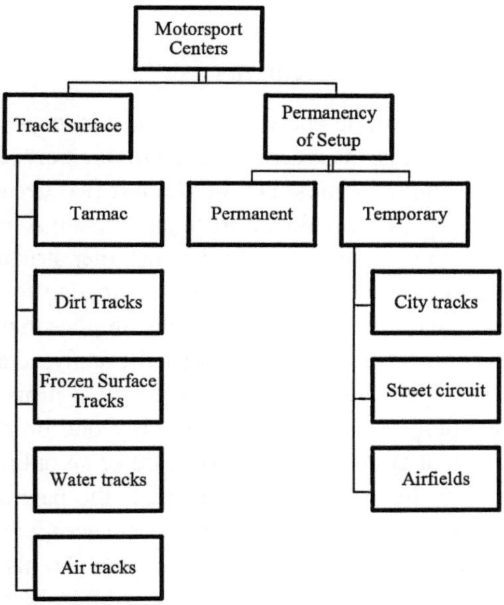

Fig. 1: Overview of distinction options for Motorsport Centers

In fig. 1 we summarize the above described possibilities to differentiate between tracks. When we look at the various characteristics and think about a possible definition, we would include only certain characteristics. The first distinction should be made between facilities which have the main purpose of hosting race events and venues which have their main purpose within another line of business like for example the airfields which host races only as a side business. Mainly, only facilities which mainly serve as a race venue should be included in the definition of a motorsport center. The tracks which do not have their main business in racing have it in another area. Therefore they also fall within another market and not in the one of motorsport centers. Moreover they do not face the challenge of compiling a race calendar which is a major aspect for motorsport centers. Taking this into consideration, we exclude temporary tracks from the definition. Frozen lakes and rivers belonging to the group of frozen surface tracks are questionable in this regard as they might serve as a race track in summer as well as opposed to lakes whose main purpose is not races and which thus should be excluded from the definition.

Summing up these various aspects we define a motorsport center as a venue that is set up permanently and whose main purpose it is to host motorsport races. The track surface itself can vary and, thus, the kinds of races that are being held.

3. Motorsport Centers as Platforms

In order to deepen the economic analysis of motorsport centers, we employ the economic theory of platforms, thus reconstructing motorsport centers as platforms facing multisided demand structures. During the last two decades, the theory of platform economics has been developed in order to analyse markets that differ from 'ordinary' goods markets in regard to the customer structure. An 'ordinary' goods market is generally modelled as suppliers competing for a definable group of customers. In the case of multiproduct firms, this implies that these firms act on more than one relevant market, each of which can be analysed as a distinct (product) market. However, there are some markets in which firms deal with distinct groups of customers despite basically offering only one product. For instance, the supplier of a payment system (e.g. a credit card or an online payment system like PayPal) deals with 'buyer' customers who use the payment system to buy goods in shops as well as with 'seller' customers who accept the payment system as compensation for trading their goods. In order to make his product (the payment system) work, the platform supplier needs to bring both sides of demand together. Indeed, the genesis of the theory of platform economics[9] was inspired

9 The original name was "theory of two-sided markets", implicitly referring to two demand sides. However, many researchers view this name to be somewhat misleading because (i) all

by economic expert analysis into the market for payment cards in the course of antitrust proceedings challenging the business behaviour of VISA and MasterCard (*Rochet & Tirole* 2002; *Schmalensee* 2002; *Evans* 2003). *Evans* and *Schmalensee* (2007) specify three constitutional elements of platforms:

- the existence of at least two *distinct* (i.e. clearly distinguishable) customer groups,
- which are indirectly connected by indirect network effects (*indirect network externalities*), and
- these externalities cannot be sufficiently internalised (for instance, through side-payments and arbitrage) because of prohibitive *transaction costs*.

The framework of multi-sided markets has been applied to the sports market with special regard to European Football (*Hartwich* 2007; *Bae & Kwon* 2008; *Budzinski & Satzer* 2011; *Dietl & Duschl* 2012; *Dietl* et al. 2012), whereas to our best knowledge there is no literature applying this framework to motorsport in general or to motorsport centers in particular. However, *Lyons* (2009) has used the platform economics framework to analyze horse racing, which comes closest to our analysis among the existing body of literature.

3.1 Distinct Customer Groups

The first characteristic of multi-sided markets, as mentioned above, is the existence of distinct customer groups. The following discussion of potential customer groups of motorsport centers closely draws upon *Budzinski* and *Satzer* (2011) who have provided a similar analysis for sports business in general. We adjust the discussion to the special characteristics of motorsport centers and, accordingly, distinguish the following customer groups[10]:

- fans who buy tickets to attend the races at the venue (*attendees*),
- racing series officials who represent the different motorsport series holding races at the venue (*promoters*),
- various types of media (e.g. TV channels) that buy broadcasting rights (*media*),

---

markets have two sides (demand and supply) and (ii) some markets actually serve more than two demand sides. Therefore, platform economics is increasingly becoming the dominant label.

10 *Budzinski* and *Satzer* (2011) additionally include the group of "merchandise demand" in their article. As they come to the conclusion that this is not a clearly distinguishable group, however, we do not include it in our discussion.

- advertisers and sponsors who buy advertisement space around the circuit or on the car/bike (*sponsors*), as well as
- companies and other actors that rent the facility for other purposes than motorsport races (*different facility users*; DFU).

Having identified these different demand groups, the next question is whether they are indeed distinctive groups of customers or not. The attendees of a motorsport race are the fans that buy tickets to experience the race live at the venue. They want to enjoy the cars/ bikes, their sound and speed in real life instead of just in front of the TV. They can therefore be clearly separated from the other customer groups.

The next demand group is the one of the promoters. These officials manage the races from the side of the racing series like the officials from the Formula 1, the IDM or the smaller series like Motocross or Autocross. Their main goal is to attract as many fans as possible and to offer them a spectacular and memorable racing event. Moreover they are also interested in attracting sponsors for financing the racing series and their own financial gain. One of their tasks in regard to the motorsport centers is to find the right date to hold the event at the respective motorsport center and to organize their schedule so that it fits in with all the other racing series and other big events. When we look at the vast number of different racing events and the fact that they also have to consider events like the Olympics or Soccer World Championships, then it becomes clear that this is not an easy task. It further should be noted that the relationship between motorsport venues and promoters can be different. For big series like the F1, the center actually pays for having them at the location which would make them a customer of the promoter. But with smaller series it is the other way around. Here, promoters pay to have their race in the schedule of the center. These different relationships make it rather hard to analyze this group and all its interactions in the scope of this work.

The next mentioned group is "media". This group is made up of different parts of media, mainly TV channels but also newspapers or magazines writing about the event as well as internet sites and radio channels. The TV channels can also be subdivided into pay TV vs. free TV and free TV into private channels and public ones (*Budzinski & Satzer* 2011). But no matter which type of channel we look at, all of them have the main goal of attracting viewers thus they want to maximize their viewer numbers in order to maximize their revenues.

The sponsors are a profit-maximizing group like the media. They come from all sorts of industries and aim at maximizing their presence in the media and the public which they try to achieve via the advertisement around the tracks, via TV advertisements in connection with the broadcasting of the event or even by placements on the racing cars/ bikes themselves. By connecting the image of their product to the image of the sport and its different brands, the advertisers try to push the demand for their own products. Yet again this group can be clearly distinguished from the others. Advertisement that is clearly visible on TV can become very expensive especially in the case of Formula 1. Being a team's main sponsor can cost several million dollars per year. Ferrari's main sponsor, Marlboro, pays an estimated $ 125 Mio per year (*Wood* 2008). Smaller sponsors like Nescafé or FedEx who pay for little spaces on the cars, pay an amount between $ 1.5 Mio and $ 4.6 Mio. A special contract like the one Lewis Hamilton has with TAG (watches)[11] can cost around $ 23 Mio per year depending on the details of the contract and the success of the driver (*Wood* 2008).

The group of DFUs adds another important aspect to the picture. Most motorsport centers do not only use their venues for motorsport racing. If they would do so, most would quickly face financial problems. Most centers also rent out their track to other (and often non-professional) events. One of the other aspects these tracks are used for are so called track days where private people use the track to drive on them with their own cars against payment towards the venue. Another often seen possibility are test days when professional racing teams rent the circuit for testing their cars/ bikes often before a new season or within a season break. But there are also events at these centers which do not concern racing at all. Concerts and music festivals are also being hosted at race venues. The German Nürburgring for example is used as a venue for one of Germany's biggest rock festivals, the "Rock am Ring". Most motorsport centers also have a business area which they rent out to companies for meetings and congresses. Here the special event characteristic of the facility plays an important role in the attractiveness for firms.

After having identified the various groups as being clearly distinguishable, we will now look at the existing externalities as they play another important role in the concept of multi-sided markets.

3.2 Externalities between the Customer Groups

In order to fulfill the necessities for being defined as a multi-sided market, there have to be indirect connections between the individual players in the market. These externalities can be either positive or negative. How the interrelations work in the market for motorsport centers will be analyzed in the following:

11 Lewis Hamilton is supposed to wear a TAG Heuer watch at every public event thus also at the presentation ceremony at Formula 1 races which attracts a lot of media attention.

(1) Attendees & promoters: The first possible externality to look at is the effect of attendees on promoters. The more attendees visit a race the better it is for the racing series as revenues go up and it can also increase the attractiveness of the series, which in turn would mean increased revenues again. If a motorsport center can attract large numbers of fans, it also gets more interesting for a promoter to hold one of its races at this location as apparently a large number of fans will attend and thus the before described effect sets in. Thus we conclude that the more fans can be attracted, the more races (represented through the promoters) are attracted to the venue as well. The other way to look at the interrelations is the effect of promoters on attendees. If the platform, i.e. the motorsport center, can convince many promoters to bring their race to the venue, the calendar of the center is filled and this will in turn also attract more fans. It is also positive to attract many races as the variance of races offered at the venues can be broadened which will make the venue also more interesting to a wider fan base. The more races are held at the center, the more fans will be attracted throughout the year.

(2) Attendees & Media: The connections between these two groups are very complex and rather difficult to describe. What seems rather clear is that the more attendees there are at the race, the better it is for the TV channel or the media in general. The more fans attend a race the higher the popularity of that sport is and the more interesting it becomes for the TV channel to broadcast the race or that series as it will attract more viewers in front of the TV thus increasing revenues. Moreover, the number of attendees has a positive effect on the broadcast itself. A larger crowd and enthusiastic fans enhance the atmosphere and the experience of watching for the viewer (*Budzinski & Satzer* 2011).

When we look at the connections the other way around, the analysis becomes more difficult. Live broadcasting can be viewed as a direct substitute by attendees as opposed to attending a race.[12] If this holds true for racing fans, it would in turn mean that the availability of direct and live broadcasting would decrease the fan attendance at races thus lowering ticket sales. Therefore this would constitute a negative externality from TV channels to fans. Although this effect might be straight forward, there are other ways of broadcasting that make the picture a little less easy to analyze. There is also the case of time delayed broadcasting like it is apparent in soccer. Here it is argued that time delayed broadcasting does not necessarily imply a negative effect as the fan can see interesting sequences again and mostly also in slow motion. Whether this holds up for motorsport is rather

12 *Allan* and *Roy* (2008) observe this for soccer fans. There is no evidence yet to support this view for motorsports fans.

questionable. On the one side there are not many, if any, time delayed broadcasts. Almost all broadcasts are directly live from the race and even if there is a repetition of the race on TV, they are mostly re-live thus not offering any different angles. On the other side though, live broadcasts might be even more interesting as a fan who is live at the race cannot see every part of the track thus missing a potentially important moment of the race if it happens on the other side of the circuit. Here the TV channel can offer more for the viewer.

In soccer, there are also TV shows which summarize all matches of the day. These are generally regarded as posing a positive network effect on the attendees as they see it as a complement to going to the match. Thus it might be that a higher participation of the media group will positively influence the attendance of fans. Yet again it is hard to say whether this is also the case for motorsport. Summarizing TV shows are rather rare (an example is Eurosport's *Motorsports Weekend* magazine). It is difficult to assess whether such a show will be interesting for every motorsport fan since different motorsport races from different series would be summarized – and games from the same league as in football.

(3) Attendees & Sponsors: As opposed to the connections between attendees and media, this relation seems clearer. From a sponsor's point of view a platform that can attract more visitors is more interesting than one which attracts low numbers of visitors. The more fans attend a race, the more people see the advertisement. This is clearly a positive network externality as the higher the number of attendees, the higher the number of sponsors. Now when we look at the effect of sponsors on attendees, the positive effect is not apparent anymore. A small level of advertisement may not have considerable effect on the utility of the fans. However, an increasing level of advertisement is likely to be increasingly perceived as a disturbance. Empirical evidence for other commercial sports indicates that fans strongly disfavour advertisement when its intensity of rises beyond certain perception thresholds (inter alia, *Turco* 1996; *Manaï* 2008). Therefore, we can observe a negative network externality between advertisers and attendees. For soccer stadiums there is a special dislike towards the electronic boards (*Hartwich* 2007). These electronic boards can also be found along the tracks of big racing events but not around small ones. Generally speaking, there is not necessarily a negative effect within the lower racing series as the advertisement level is rather low there. But the evidence from the soccer case might be well applicable to bigger and more popular racing series like the Formula 1 or the MotoGP.

(4) Attendees & DFUs: With a high number of attendees a location becomes better known and for one might attract more firms to hold their events there. Also there could be a positive effect of high visitor numbers in the regard that the money from the ticket sales can possibly improve the surrounding infrastructure or the

technical equipment which in turn might attract more DFUs. But this effect seems to be of rather small scale or even negligible.

For the other side of the relationship between these groups there is evidence from Feddersen & Maennig (2009) that a multi-functional soccer stadium means a reduced demand for tickets by 10% as opposed to pure soccer stadiums. Therefore there is a negative externality between these two groups. Motorsport centers on the other hand are mostly built for racing and the existence of a business area does not change the layout of the course in most cases. Therefore, there is considerable doubt that this negative effect is very apparent in motorsport arenas. However, since there is no evidence for this suspicion the question of whether there is a negative effect of DFUs on attendees in motorsport centers remains unanswered at this stage.

(5) Promoters & Media: The topic of promoters is rather complicated to analyze in detail as the promoters are basically a platform on their own. When it comes to the media, there are two options. When we look at a high racing series like the Formula 1, the media is handled directly through the promoter and therefore is not of primary concern to the motorsport center. In smaller series there is also the option that the centers handle the media contracts on their own or in coordination with the promoters. If we take that case, it can be said that the more races a center can attract the more media attention it gets. The other way around it could also work that the more media attention a motorsport center gains, the more races it might attract due to its increased popularity.

(6) Promoters & Sponsors: In the analysis of the interrelation between these two groups we yet again face the problem that most racing series have their own sponsors so that the platform itself, i.e. the motorsport center, is not included in this process. If a center has its own sponsors, these advertisement displays sometimes have to be covered or taken down for some races as the promoters of that series insist that only their own sponsors will be shown. In case the center manages to negotiate that their sponsors can be shown as well, the attendance of more racing series at the venue increases the interest of sponsors as they would in turn get a higher number of people seeing their advertisement with more races being held there. The influence of sponsors on promoters is rather questionable as it is doubtful that more sponsors would increase the number of races being held. The higher income that can be generated through more races could be put into better features of the track and thus attract more promoters, but how high this influence really is, remains questionable.

(7) Promoters & DFUs: The connections between the promoters of racing series and other facility users could be described as follows: the more promoters bring their races to a venue, the more interesting it gets for the DFUs as the awareness

level of awareness rises. Thus the higher attractiveness generated through many races can be used to attract more DFUs. Whether this is really the case might be hard to say as more races also limit the times of availability of the venue for other users. More DFUs would also limit the availability of days for racing. But it is questionable whether a motorsport center would turn down a racing series promoter for a DFU. This does not belong to the core business of such venues. Therefore, we can again conclude that the externalities between promoters and DFUs are fairly weak and hard to analyze at this stage.

(8) Media & Sponsors: Media attendance has a positive effect on sponsors. The more widely and more often a race is shown on TV or featured in magazines or newspapers, the more the advertisements will be shown as well. Moreover, there is the effect of the better perception of advertisement via TV. Thus if the sponsor knows about a high media presence it might also invest more in the sponsoring.

The other way around, meaning the influence of sponsors on media, the picture is a bit different. Sponsors might pull back from advertising both on track and on TV – they might be regarded as substitutes- and chose the possibly cheaper alternative of the track advertisement, the TV loses money. As this influences the refinancing of the media, the TV channels willingness to pay would decrease. Therefore the motorsport center faces a negative externality of sponsors towards media.

(9) Media & DFUs: The basic principle is the same as mentioned for attendees and DFUs. The higher the participation of the media the higher the interest of DFUs might be. The higher income from the media might result in better infrastructure or better technical equipment. Also the increased popularity of the center could result in more interest from the side of DFUs. This also works the other way around as an increased usage through DFUs might increase media attention. However, yet again the question arises whether these effects really are strong enough to be further considered.

(10) Sponsors & DFUs: A high usage of the motorsport center through other users will also increase the attention the advertisements will get always provided that the advertisements are not taken off for these events. Therefore the higher the usage through DFUs is the higher is the attention the sponsors get, meaning that a positive externality can be observed. Trying to find a connection in the other direction is rather difficult. There could be the same effect as between sponsors and attendees meaning that maybe high sponsoring and advertisement activity lead to a dislike from the side of DFUs.

Summing all the above statements together, it is shown that the market for motorsport centers is indeed a multi-sided one with clearly distinguishable customers groups and indirect network effects between them. Thus the theory of multi-sided markets is well suited for analyzing the market of motorsport centers.

4. Challenges of the Economic Analysis of Motorsport Centers

Understanding motorsport centers as platforms coordinating different demand sides reveals the multi-faceted character of this market but also poses challenges for delineating the market. In terms of the relevant product market, the main research questions revolve around the competitive relations among different racing series. It is part of the special character of commercial sports markets that there is an inherent tendency towards having only one championship per category in one geographical area. For instance, there is only one four-wheel monoposto world championship (F1) or one rallying world championship (just like there is only one top-level league in most ball sports in each jurisdiction). This inherent tendency towards organizing the competition in one single championship is motivated by the benefits of bringing the best talent together in this one championship. This increases consumer welfare because witnessing the best talent competing with each other is an important element of the demand factors of commercial sports. However, having one single championship per category does not automatically imply that each championship constitutes its own product market. Even though different motor racing championships are certainly not perfect substitutes, they may represent imperfect substitutes to varying degrees and as such they exert competitive pressure on each other, i.e. consumers may be willing to substitute visiting or viewing one racing series with another.

Among the many different racing series, the degrees of substitution will likely differ. While F1 probably enjoys quite a monopoly-like position with other racing series being only very weak substitutes, the many existing four-wheel feeder monoposto racing series like GP2, GP3, Renault World Series, AutoGP, Formula 3 European Championship, etc., appear to represent rather close substitutes. However, instead of more anecdotic plausibility considerations like in the preceding sentence, a systematic analysis would be helpful. Do consumers find four-wheel racing more interchangeable with other types of four-wheel racing and less with two-wheel racing? Or is racing on tarmac a closer substitute to other races on tarmac than to off-road racing? Does it matter whether the cars have roofs or wheels are open? Knowledge about the competitive closeness of different racing series would represent a precondition for a product market delineation of motorsport centers. Does a permanent tarmac track center compete only with other permanent tarmac track centers or also with centers with gravel surfaces? What about bike-suitable tracks versus car-suitable tracks? This research is still to be done (but see for first approaches: *Müller* 2012; *Budzinski & Müller* 2014).

Moreover, the geographical market delineation represents an important field. Here, the multisided character entails relevant implications. In terms of getting a track on the calendar of a racing series, the geographical market may be different and determined by different factors than in terms of attracting audience. For instance, for the former factors like an even presence in different parts of the world, a continent or a country or agglomeration benefits like the volume of transportation costs (for teams) between two racing events may point to wider or narrower markets respectively. With respect to the audience, knowledge about how far fans are willing to travel to attend specific racing events is relevant. Again, these issues represent open research questions (see for first approaches *Müller* 2013).

Altogether, a better understanding of the market for motorsport centers is necessary for assessments of (i) whether to build a new motorsport center in a given region, more often than not with some involvement of public subsidies, (ii) what to build in order to fill market niches or provide competent competitors to existing venues, (iii) how to manage existing motorsport centers facing a multisided demand structure, and (iv) how to deal from a policy perspective with cooperation and concentration processes among motorsport centers. Regarding the latter, for instance, the U.S. market has recently witnessed considerable concentration processes. Today, the *International Speedway Corporation* (ISC) owns 13 race tracks across the USA, among them two high-profile tracks in Florida (Daytona and Homestead). ISC-owned race tracks are host to 19 out of 36 NASCAR racing events – a figure that has given rise to controversy and even antitrust law suits against the background of commercial interrelations among the owners of NASCAR, ISC and Penske Motorsports (a top team in U.S. motorsports). One of ISC's main competitors in the North-American market for motorsport centers is *Speedway Motorsports, Inc.* (SMI), a company that owns 9 motorsport centers across the U.S. So far, such concentration processes remain a North-American phenomenon, however, they further corroborate why economic research on motorsport centers is gaining in importance.

References

Allan, G. & Roy, G. (2008): Does Television Crowd Out Spectators?, in: Journal of Sports Economics, Vol. 9, 6, pp. 592–605.

Baade, R.A. & Matheson, V. (2000): High Octane? Grading the Economic Impact of the Daytona 500, in: Marquette Sports Law Review, Vol. 10, 2, pp. 401–415.

Bae, S. H. & Kwon, J. (2008): Two-sided Network Effects and Competitive Balance in Professional Team Sports, http://ssrn.com/abstract=1094821 (accessed 2014-03-28).

Bekker, J. & Lotz, W. (2009): Planning Formula One Race Strategies Using Discrete-event Simulation, in: Journal of the Operational Research Society, Vol. 60, 7, pp. 952–961.

Berkowitz, J. P., Depken, C. A. & Wilson, D. P. (2011): When Going in Circles Is Going Backward: Outcome Uncertainty in NASCAR, in: Journal of Sports Economics, Vol. 12, 3, pp. 253–283.

Budzinski, O. (2012): The Institutional Framework for Doing Sports Business: Principles of EU Competition Policy in Sports Markets, in: International Journal for Sport Management and Marketing, Vol. 11, 1–2, pp. 44–72.

Budzinski, O. & Feddersen, A. (2014): Measuring Competitive Balance in Formula One Racing, Discussion Paper.

Budzinski, O. & Müller, A. (2014): The Market for Motorsport Centers, Conference Manuscript, Discussion Paper, forthcoming.

Budzinski, O. & Satzer, J. (2011): Sports Business and Multisided Markets: Towards a New Analytical Framework?, in: Sport, Business and Management: An International Journal, Vol. 1, 2, pp. 124–137.

Chapin, T. (2002): Identifying the Real Costs and Benefits of Sports Facilities, Working Paper, Cambridge: Lincoln Institute of Land Policy.

Cimarosti, A. (1997): The Complete History of Grand Prix Motor Racing, London: Aurum.

Coates, D. & Humphreys, B. R. (2003): Professional Sports Facilities, Franchises and Urban Economic Development, in: Public Finance and Management, Vol. 3, 3, pp. 335–257.

Connaughton, J. E. & Madsen, R.A. (2007): The Economic Impact of the North Carolina Motorsports Industry, in Economic Development Quarterly, Vol. 21, 2, pp. 185–197.

Crompton, J. (1995): Economic Impact Analysis of Sports Facilities and Events: Eleven Sources of Misapplication, in: Journal of Sports Management, Vol. 9, pp. 14–35.

Cygan, A. (2007): Are All Sports Special? Legal Issues in the Regulation of Formula One Motor Racing, in: European Business Law Review, Vol. 18, 6, pp. 1327–1352.

Dietl, H. M. & Duschl, T. (2012): The Organization of Professional Sports Leagues: A Comparison of European and North-American Leagues from the Perspective of Platform Organization, in: *Büch, M.-P., Maennig, W. & Schulke, H.-J.* (eds.): Sport und Sportgroßveranstaltungen in Europa zwischen Zentralstaat und Regionen, Hamburg: Hamburg University Press, pp. 111–126.

Dietl, H. M., Duschl, T., Franck, E. P. & Lang, M. (2012): A Contest Model of a Professional Sports League with Two-Sided Markets, in: Journal of Economics and Statistics, Vol. 232, 3, pp. 336–359.

Evans, D. S. & Schmalensee, R. (2007): The Industrial Organization of Markets with Two-Sided Platforms, in: Competition Policy International, Vol. 3, 1, pp. 151–179.

Evans, D. S. (2003): The Antitrust Economics of Multi-Sided Platform Markets, in: Yale Journal of Regulation, Vol. 20, 2, pp. 325–382.

Feddersen, A. & Maennig, W. (2009): Arenas versus Multifunctional Stadiums, in: Journal of Sport Economics, Vol. 10, 2, pp. 180–191.

Grieve, J. & Sherry, E. (2012): Community Benefit of Major Sporting Facilities: The Darebin International Sports Centre, in: Sport Management Review, Vol. 15, 1, pp. 218–229.

Hainz, E. (1999): Emissionsdaten von Motorsportanlagen, http://www.lfu.bayern.de/laerm/doc/sport_motorsport.pdf (accessed 2014-03-18).

Harjani, A. (2011): Singapore's F1 Excitement Rubs Off on the Economy, http://www.cnbc.com/id/44635128 (accessed 2014-02-24).

Hartwich, T. (2007): It's coming home: die Fußball Bundesliga und zweiseitige Märkte, in: Medienwirtschaft, Vol. 4, 1, pp. 15–25.

Heublein, S. (2008): Technologietransfer, http://www.motorsport-magazin.com/formel1/news-62298-aus-der-f1-in-die-serie-technologietransfer.html (accessed 2014-03-18).

Irani, D. (1997): Public Subsidies to Stadiums: Do the Costs Outweigh the Benefits?, in: Public Finance Review, Vol. 25, 2, pp. 238–253.

Jenkins, M. & Floyd, S. (2001): Trajectories in the Evolution of Technology: A Multi-Level Study of Competition in Formula 1 Racing, in: Organization Studies, Vol. 22, 6, pp. 945–969.

Jenkins, M. (2010): Technological Discontinuities and Competitive Advantage: A Historical Perspective on Formula 1 Motor Racing 1950–2006, in: Journal of Management Studies, Vol. 47, 5, pp. 884–910.

Judde, C., Booth, R. & Brooks, R. (2013): Second Place Is First of the Losers An Analysis of Competitive Balance in Formula One, in: Journal of Sports Economics, Vol. 14, 4, pp. 411–439.

Kipker, I. (2003): Determinanten der TV-Nachfrage in der Formel 1 – Superstar- vs. Spannungseffekte und Implikationen für die Wettbewerbspolitik, in: *Dietl, H.* (ed.): Globalisierung des wirtschaftlichen Wettbewerbs im Sport, Schorndorf: Verlag Karl Hofmann, pp. 85–103.

Krauskopf, T., Langen, M. & Bünger, B. (2010): The Search for Optimal Competitive Balance in Formula One, CAWM Discussion Paper No. 38, Münster: University of Münster.

Lyons, B. R. (2009): The Orders and Rules of British Horseracing: Anticompetitive Agreements or Good Governance of a Multi-Sided Sport?, in: *Lyons, B. R.* (ed.): Cases in European Competition Policy: The Economic Analysis, Cambridge: Cambridge University Press, pp. 230–262.

Manaï, S. (2008): Les Attributs de la Personnalité du Sportif et leur Commercialisation dans le Contexte du Contrat de Sponsoring Individuel, thèse de licence et de doctorat, University of Lausanne.

Mastromarco, C. & Runkel, M. (2009): Rule Changes and Competitive Balance in Formula One Motor Racing, in: Applied Economics, Vol. 41, 23, pp. 3003–3014.

Müller, A. (2012): The Market for Motorsport Centers: An Empirical Analysis of the Competition Structure, Unpublished Master Thesis, University of Southern Denmark.

Müller, A. (2013): Influences on Willingness-to-pay at Motorsport Events in Germany, Manuscript.

Noll, R. & Zimbalist, A. (1997): The Economic Impact of Sports Teams and Facilities, in: *Noll, R. & Zimbalist's, A.* (eds.): Sports, Jobs, and Taxes: The Economic Impact of Sports Teams and Stadiums, Washington, DC: Brookings Institution Press, pp. 55–91.

Rochet, J.-C. & Tirole, J. (2002): Cooperation among Competitors: The Economics of Payment Card Associations, in: Rand Journal of Economics, Vol. 33, 4, pp. 549–570.

Sanderson, A. (2000): In Defense of New Sports Stadiums, Ballparks and Arenas, in: Marquette Sports Law Journal, Vol. 10, 2, pp. 173–192.

Schmalensee, R. (2002): Payment Systems and Interchange Fees, in: Journal of Industrial Economics, Vol. 50, 2, pp. 103–122.

Seiwert, R. (2012): 413 Millionen Schulden, http://www.motorsport-magazin.com/formel1/news-147652-nuerburgring-steht-vor-der-insolvenz-413-millionen-schulden.html (accessed 2014-02-24).

Siegfried, J. & Zimbalist, A. (2000): The Economics of Sports Facilities and Their Communities, in: Journal of Economic Perspectives, Vol. 14, 3, pp. 95–114.

Siegfried, J. & Zimbalist, A. (2006): The Economic Impact of Sports Facilities, Teams and Mega-Events, in: The Australian Economic Review, Vol. 39, 4, pp. 420–427.

Solitander, M. & Solitander, N. (2010): The Sharing, Protection and Thievery of Intellectual Assets: The Case of the Formula 1 Industry, in: Management Decision, Vol. 48, 1, pp. 37–57.

Stadelmann, D. & Eichenberger, R. (2008): Wer ist der beste Formel 1 Fahrer? Eine ökonometrische Talentbewertung, in: Perspektiven der Wirtschaftspolitik, Vol. 9, 4, pp. 486–512.

Sylt, C. & Reid, C. (2013): The Cost of Hosting a Formula 1 Grand Prix, http://businesslife.ba.com/Ideas/Features/The-cost-of-hosting-a-Formula-1-Grand-Prix.html (accessed 2014-02-24).

Turco, D. M. (1996): The Effects of Courtside Advertising on Product Recognition and Attitude Change, in: Sport Marketing Quarterly, Vol. 5, 4, pp. 11–15.

Wood, R. (2008): Formula One Information Guide Part 2: Money, Money, Money (Making a Profit), http://bleacherreport.com/articles/41459-formula-one-information-guide-part-2-money-money-money-making-a-profit (accessed 2014-02-24).

Epilogue

A Survey of 5 Years of ESEA Conferences

Daam Van Reeth

Abstract

On September 19–20 2013, the 5th ESEA conference was held in Esbjerg, Denmark. This lustrum edition proved to be an excellent opportunity to make a first round-up of a new but promising tradition of European sports economics conferences that started in Paris in 2009. This paper presents an overview of the conference participants and the nature of the research that has been presented at the first 5 conferences. It focuses on elements such as international diversity and gender of the participants and research contents and methodology of the papers. Some important observations are that two thirds of the participants originate from 4 countries only (Germany, France, the United States and the United Kingdom), that about 80% of the research is empirical and that although soccer research still has a prominent share of about one third of all presentations, there is a clear trend towards more diversified conferences.

Keywords

European Sports Economics Association, annual conference, sports economics

1. Introduction

Because of its growing importance over the last couple of decades, the sports industry has gained substantial research interest by professional economists. Sports economics has therefore become a widely recognized sub-discipline of economics with an active research agenda (*Sánchez Santos & Castellanos García* 2011: 222). One of the most significant indicators of this recognition of the discipline was the creation of two specialized journals: the *Journal of Sports Economics* (2000) and the *International Journal of Sport Finance* (2006).

It was *Wladimir Andreff* who realised that a conference devoted entirely to sports economics would constitute another important milestone in the promotion of sports economics as a distinct research field. On September 14th and 15th, 2009, a first European conference in sports economics was organised at the *Centre d'Economie de la Sorbonne* of the University of Paris (*Andreff* 2010). This turned out to be a landmark date for European sports economics research. It was the start of a yearly tradition that has since then brought together sports economics researchers from all over the world in Cologne (2010), Prague (2011), London (2012) and Esbjerg (2013), respectively.

At the second conference in Cologne another important decision was made. On October 4th, 2010, the *European Sport Economics Association* (ESEA) was founded. This association "pursues the goal of promoting communications between scientists as well as between scientists and practitioners working in the field of sports economics, and of demonstrating to the fields of science, day-to-day practice, politics and the general public the benefits that are derived from appropriate research and academic education in Europe. The purpose is predominantly realized by holding an annual conference and publishing documents in the field of sports economics".[1]

This paper presents an overview of the first 5 ESEA conferences. It focuses on two basic questions: who are the participants at the ESEA conferences and what is the nature of the research that has so far been presented? The purpose of the paper is to contribute to a better understanding of the role and importance of the ESEA conferences in the global development of sports economics research. The raw data for the research were collected from two primary sources. The analysis of the attendees in section 2 is based on the lists of conference participants that were provided by *Wladimir Andreff* (Paris), *Christoph Breuer* (Cologne, Prague and London) and *Arne Feddersen* (Esbjerg). The publicly available detailed conference programs were used as a second input. The content analysis presented in section 3 is mainly based on these programs.

It is important, though, to note that we encountered some difficulties with the analysis of the data. First, due to the fact that information on late registrations or cancellations was not available for all conferences, it is not guaranteed that all attendee lists are 100% correct. Furthermore, it was not clear if the lists of participants always included all (doctoral) students that attended the conferences. Second, for the analysis of the presentations, often an abstract or a (working) paper was searched on the internet to complement the contents information that was already obvious from the title. However, as these efforts proved to be unsuccessful in some cases, a small number of presentations were excluded from the analysis because of lack of precise information. Bearing these complications in mind, it is wiser to focus on the general trends and the global observations rather than on precise numbers.

The second section provides a global overview of the 5 conferences. Section 3 delivers an insight into the participants over the years by looking at such elements as international diversity and gender balance. The fourth section focuses on the research that has been discussed at the conferences. A content analysis as well as an author analysis is presented. Conclusions follow in section 5.

---

1 http://sporteconomics.eu.

2. From Paris to Esbjerg

After 5 editions it seems to be a good moment to make a first round-up on the participants and the research contents of the ESEA conferences. As a start, table 1 brings together the key data of the 5 conferences. With the exception of the Prague conference, all the conferences took place in September or early October. The number of participants ranges from a minimum of 62 in Prague to a maximum of 89 in Esbjerg. So far, 228 different persons attended an ESEA conference. The total number of presentations is 296, with a big difference between the first and the last conference: from 42 up to 78 presentations. This increase was realized by moving from two to three parallel sessions from the Cologne conference on, and by increasing the number of sessions from 16 in Paris over 18 (Cologne, Prague, London) to 21 in Esbjerg.

Table 1: Key data of the 5 ESEA conferences

Venue	Date	Participants	Presentations	Ratio	Countries
Paris, France	September 14–15, 2009	81	42	52	18
Cologne, Germany	October 5–6, 2010	77	64	83	18
Prague, Czech Republic	May 17–18, 2011	62	55	89	14
London, United Kingdom	September 6–7, 2012	70	57	81	17
Esbjerg, Denmark	September 19–20, 2013	89	78	88	21
	UNIQUE TOTAL :	228	296	1.30	26

Source: Own calculations based on information provided by the conference organizers.

The relatively low number of presentations in Paris, due to capacity constraints rather than to the quality of the submitted abstracts[2], in relationship with the high number of attendees makes the Paris conference the only one with a low presentations-to-participants ratio of 0.52. For the other conferences, the ratio is stable between 0.80 and 0.90. The 5-year ratio (total presentations over unique participants) amounts to 1.30, indicating that, on average, for every two people that presented one paper there was a third person presenting two papers.

Over the years, the ESEA conferences have welcomed sports economics researchers from 26 different countries.[3] At the conference in Esbjerg, researchers

2 There is no analysis of the number of submitted and the number of accepted abstracts because precise data were unavailable.

3 Note that since affiliation or residency can change from year to year, for practical purposes nationalities of the participants were used to measure international diversity.

from 21 countries were present, making it the most international conference so far. International diversity was the lowest in Prague with only 14 countries represented at the conference.

3. The Participants

Figure 1 illustrates the breakdown by nationality of the 228 conference participants. They represent 26 different countries in total, including four non-European countries: the United States, Canada, Australia and Chile. When we ignore small states like Luxembourg, Monaco or Malta, we can conclude that all Western, Northern and Southern European countries have at least been present once at the ESEA conferences. The only blind spots on the European map are in Central and Eastern Europe. Slovakia, Romania, Bulgaria, the Baltic states and Hungary are just a few of the missing countries from that region.

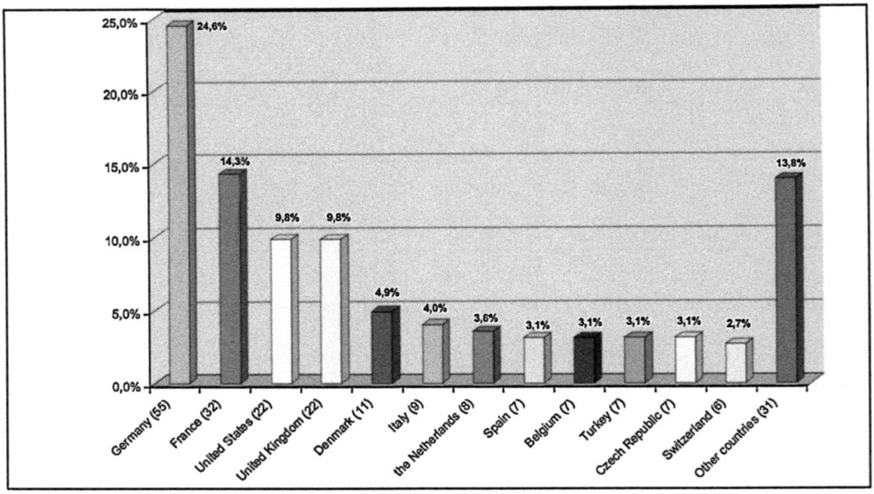

Fig. 1: Nationalities of the ESEA conference participants

Source: Own calculations based on information provided by the conference organizers.

Germany is the best represented country. No less than 55 German researchers have taken part in at least one of the ESEA conferences, representing about a quarter of all conference participants. France comes in second with 32 participants (14.3%) and the United States and the U.K. are joint third with 22 (9.8%). The 'big 4' thus record a share of about 60% of all participants. Just like at the Olympics, there exists a 'host nation' effect because smaller countries that organized a conference rank relatively high in this list: Denmark had 11 conference participants in total (4.9%), the Czech Republic 7 (3.1%). Note as well that relatively small countries like Belgium and the Netherlands have about the same number of conference attendees as big Southern European countries like Italy and Spain. The 14 countries included in the 'other' category in figure 1 are: Norway, Canada, Austria, Australia, Poland and Russia (all with 3 attendees), Greece, Portugal, Finland, Ireland and Chile (2 attendees), and Serbia, Ukraine and Sweden (1 attendee only).

When we look at historical trends in international representation, especially the French share of researchers at the conferences shows a remarkable evolution. At the first conference in Paris, quite logically, a very high 'home' share of almost 40% (31 persons) was recorded. One year later, in Cologne, the share went down to 14% (11 persons), which is still acceptable. At the last 3 conferences, however, the French share fell below 10% with an absolute low in Esbjerg where only two French sports economists were present. A closer look at the data reveals that there is little or no 'fresh' inflow from France. In fact, since the Paris conference only one new French researcher has joined the conference, bringing the French 5 year total to 32 from already 31 after the first conference. As a comparison: the total number of German attendees went up from 9 in Paris to 55 in Esbjerg, the Belgian total number went from 2 to 7 over the same period of time.

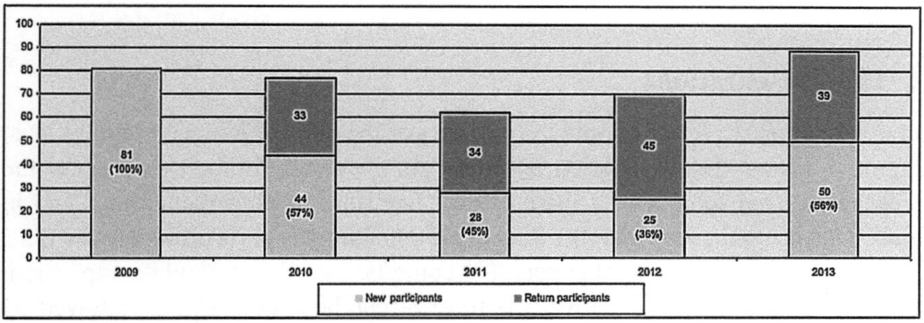

Fig. 2: New participants versus returnees

Source: Own calculations based on information provided by the conference organizers.

Figure 2 shows that while the number of new participants varies considerably from year to year, with a solid increase in Esbjerg, there is a rather stable number of returnees each year. We could conclude from this that the beating heart of the conference consists of about 40 sports economics researchers. This also becomes evident when the participation frequency is analyzed. Of the 228 conference participants, 42 persons have attended at least three conferences, 22 attended at least four conferences and 12 of them were present at all 5 conferences: *Christoph Breuer*, *Tim*

Pawlowski & Markus Kurscheidt (Germany), *Stefan Szymanski & Paul Downward* (United Kingdom), *Stefan Késenne & Thomas Peeters* (Belgium), *Wladimir Andreff* (France), *Placído Rodriguez* (Spain), *Joel Maxcy* (United States), *Ross Booth* (Australia) and *Mario Lackner* (Austria). In contrast, two thirds of the conference participants (153 persons) have been present only once. Consequently, the average participation frequency is only 1.66 per researcher. There exists a significant gender difference though: the average number of participations for men is 1.75 while for women it is 1.31.

Women are strongly under-represented at the ESEA conferences. Female participation was highest at the first conference in Paris (18 female attendees, a share of 22%) and lowest in Prague and London (less than 10 female attendees and a share of about 10%). The conference in Esbjerg was about as women-friendly as the conference in Cologne with the presence of 14 women and a 16% share. When we look at all the participants over the years, the global women share is 19.7% (45 out of 228) and thus higher than the average of the yearly shares. This difference is the result from a lower participation frequency of female sports economics researchers. While 36% of all male researchers attended at least two conferences, for female researchers this is only 20% (9 out of 45). It is unclear what could be the reason for this observation and whether or not it is conference related or a general gender phenomenon observed also at other conferences.

4. The Presentations

In this section, we first examine the contents of the 296 conference presentations. Figure 3 shows the distribution by sport. As expected, football (soccer) is the most researched sport with a share of over one third of all presentations, 103 in total. This is much more than the total of all other single sports presentations (75). Within the subset of football papers that could be traced to a single competition, the UK Premier League (12) was the most researched competition, followed by the German Bundesliga (10), the World Cup (6), the Italian Serie A and the Turkish first division (both 5). Relatively little research was presented on the Spanish Primera División and the Champions League (both 4) and the French Ligue 1 (1). Although still very prominent, the importance of football at the ESEA conferences shows a decreasing trend. While in Paris football related research had a share of 42%, in Prague this had already decreased to 38%, to finally record an all-time low of 31% in Esbjerg.

Apart from soccer, the 4 main American professional sports, basketball (14), American football (10), baseball (9) and ice hockey (7), received most attention, although not all of the research on these sports was related to the North American competitions. Only two more sports scored significant research interest with at least 5 papers: cycling (8) and athletics (5). One of the more striking results of this survey is the fact that economically important sports like car racing and tennis have gathered only minor academic interest at ESEA conferences so far. There were only 4 papers on NASCAR or Formula One and just one paper was dedicated to tennis.

Overall, there is a clear trend towards more diversified conferences with an increasing number of sports being researched. At the first conference, only 7 sports were discussed (soccer, basketball, American football, baseball, ice hockey, Australian football and rugby). At each subsequent conference, a number of new sports became part of the conference program. Cycling, athletics and equestrian sport were introduced in Cologne where in total 9 different sports were on the program. Car racing and motor racing first appeared on the program in Prague, with now already 10 different sports on the program. In London, the number of sports discussed increased to 12 as ski, surfing and tennis were introduced. There was only one new sport in Esbjerg (triathlon). Nevertheless, research on a record total of 13 sports was presented in Denmark making in the most diversified conference so far. Overall, 16 sports have been the subject of a presentation at a ESEA conference.

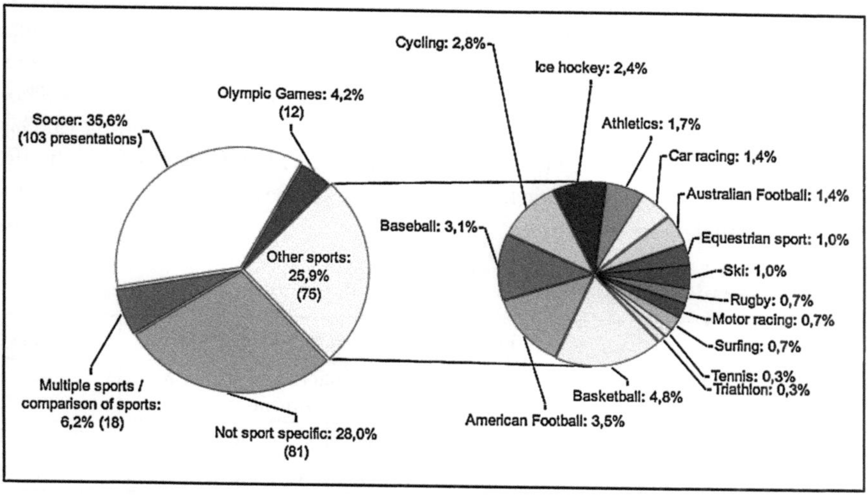

Fig. 3: Presentations at the ESEA conferences, distribution by sport

Source: Own calculations based on the official conference programs.

Figure 3 also shows that over 80 presentations were not linked to a specific sport. This mainly refers to papers on sports participation and theoretical papers on e.g.

optimal league formats. Another 18 presentations analyzed multiple sports, for instance, papers in which American and European league formats are compared. Finally, the Olympic Games was the focus of attention in 12 papers. Not visible from the figure is the dominant focus on professional sports: only about 15% of the conference papers dealt with amateur sports.

Table 2 shows the distribution of the conference presentations over a number of typical sports economics research areas. A distinction was made between 9 main categories and 21 more detailed sub-categories. The main categories largely correspond with thematical sessions at the conferences while the sub-categories provide a better insight into the different aspects of some broadly defined research areas.

Roughly one paper out of three (31.9%) dealt with 'the economics of sports leagues', making it the most popular research domain at the conferences. Almost one presentation out of 4 was related to regulation, governance & organisation of sports leagues, the most popular sub-category, and almost one presentation out of 10 dealt with the issue of competitive balance. The analysis of socio-economic aspects of sport is the second most important research domain, present in 28% of all presentations. Economic impact / cost benefit studies and participation studies both have a share of about 10%, while gender & discrimination is the subject of 5% of all research presented at the ESEA conferences. Three other relatively important research categories are the evaluation of sport and referee performances (17%), consumer demand for sport (16%) and labour aspects of sport (14.9%). Research domains that got less attention at the conferences were betting (5.3%) and marketing & sponsorship (2.1%). Especially for the latter category this should not be considered a problem, since there are other conferences where this kind of research is much more at its place.

Table 2: Presentations at the ESEA conferences, distribution by research area

Main category	Percentage[i]	Sub-category	Percentage
The economics of sports leagues	31.9%	Regulation, governance & organisation	23.0%
		Competitive balance	8.9%
		Valuation of teams & leagues	2.8%
Socio-economic aspects of sport	28.0%	Economic impact / cost benefit	11.3%
		Participation	9.2%
		Gender & discrimination	5.0%
		Volunteerism	2.5%

Main category	Percentage[i]	Sub-category	Percentage
Performance analysis	17.0%	Sport performance	15.2%
		Referee performance	1.8%
Consumer demand	16.0%	Live attendance	7.1%
		Media consumption	6.0%
		Sport consumption expenditures	3.2%
Labour aspects of sport	14.9%	Recruitment, agents & coaching	9.2%
		Wages, pay & prizes	6.0%
Mega-events	8.9%	Mega-events	8.9%
Dysfunctions in sport	8.2%	Financial fairplay	2.8%
		Violence	1.8%
		Doping	1.8%
		Match-fixing / corruption	1.8%
Betting	5.3%	Betting	5.3%
Marketing & sponsorship	2.1%	Marketing & sponsorship	2.1%

Source: Own calculations based on the official conference programs.

[i]*The percentages do not add up to 100 because a research paper can have a multiple research focus, e.g. 'The economic impact of mega-events' or 'The impact of competitive balance on game attendance'.*

There is a clear imbalance in the gender focus of the research presented at the conferences. Over half of the papers (152 in total, or 52%) had an exclusive focus on men's sports. This is in sharp contrast to the mere 5 papers that were devoted exclusively to women's sports (2%). The remaining papers either were gender neutral (27%), often the case with theoretical papers, or were implicitly (e.g. Olympic Games) or explicitly (e.g. gender discrimination) combining men's and women's sports in the analysis (19%). This gender imbalance is in line with the observations made by *Mondello & Pedersen* (2003) in their content analysis of the Journal of Sports Economics in 2003. In the first 10 editions of the journal, there was not a single article that focused exclusively on women's sports and only 14% of the articles focused on a combination of male and female athletes.

There is some encouraging evidence though of a growing importance of women's sports at the ESEA conferences. While in the first three conferences only one paper was presented on women's sports (i.e. on the FIFA Women's World Cup in Germany), the last two conferences saw four of such papers (three on women's football and one on women's tennis). Also the share of the combined male-female research has grown during the same periods from 18% to 24%.

Research presented at the ESEA conferences was predominantly empirically based. Only 19% of the papers had a clear theoretical focus while 79% were essentially empirically inspired. A small number of the presentations (2%) were non-academic testimonies from practice. The 80/20 distribution of empirical versus theoretical research was present at all conferences, except for the first one in Paris when almost 40% of the research was theoretic. Maybe much more than at later conferences, in Paris the aim was also to offer a state-of-the-art of sports economics theory.

Research presented at the ESEA conferences has clearly found its way into (sports) economics literature. Of the 218 papers that were discussed at the first four conferences, at least 48 (22%) had been published (or were accepted for publishing) in peer-reviewed international journals (44) or international handbooks (4) by the summer of 2013. This is, of course, an underestimation since some papers might have witnessed significant changes in the title before getting published and, as a result, were not identified as former ESEA presentations in our scan of the literature.[4]

The percentage of papers published is rather stable from one conference to another: Paris (23.8%), Cologne (23.4%) and Prague (21.8%) all record very similar percentages. Of the papers presented in London, 12% had already been published after one year. The bulk of the articles, 17 in total, were published in the official journal of the association, the *International Journal of Sport Finance* (table 3). Other sports-oriented journals in the list are *Journal of Sports Economics* (7), *European Sport Management Quarterly* (3), *European Journal of Sport Science* (1), *International Journal of Sport Management and Marketing* (1), *Journal of Sport Management* (1) and *Sport Management Review* (1). But the recognition of sports economics as a valuable sub-discipline of economics becomes most obvious from the fact that 13 papers have been published in more than 10 different non-sports economics journals, such as *Labour Economics*, *Economic Inquiry* and *Review of Economics and Statistics*.

Table 3: ESEA conference research published in peer-reviewed international journals

Journal	**Number of articles**
International Journal of Sport Finance	17
Journal of Sports Economics	7
European Sport Management Quarterly	3

4 We should also note that this survey does not include papers published in the conference books.

Journal	Number of articles
Labour Economics	2
Applied Economic Letters	1
Applied Economics	1
Bulletin of Economic Research	1
Economic Inquiry	1
Economics & Finance Research	1
Economics Letters	1
European Journal of Sport Science	1
European Review of Physical Activity and Aging	1
International Journal of Industrial Organization	1
International Journal of Sport Management and Marketing	1
Journal of Sport Management	1
Review of Economics and Statistics	1
Southern Economic Journal	1
Sport Management Review	1
The Journal of Socio-Economics	1

Source: Own calculations.

There is a trend towards more multi-authored conference papers. At the first three conferences, single-author papers had a share of 45%. At the last two conferences, this share had decreased to 32%, which means that over two thirds of all papers are now multi-authored. For the same time period, the share of the papers with a least three authors has increased from 21% to 30%. In principle, an increased collaboration leads to qualitatively better research, which is potentially even more true in the case of international collaboration. The international diversity of the conference papers is therefore illustrated in table 4. Only 48 (16%) of all papers were the result of an international collaboration with 3 of these papers a collaboration between researchers from 3 different countries. There are important differences between the conferences though, and we find evidence of a trend towards more international collaborations. While at the first three conferences on average only 14% of all research was the result of an international collaboration, for the last two conferences this increased to 19% with an all-time maximum of 21.8% in Esbjerg.[5] German researchers are the most involved in international collaboration: they are part of 48% of all such collaborations. The U.K. (35%) and the United

5 Note that if only the multi-author papers are taken into account, the only ones in which in fact international collaboration is possible, the share of the international collaborations rises to 27%.

States (31%) come second and third. With only 15%, the French share is remarkably low.

Table 4: International diversity of conference papers

Authors from...	All papers (296)	Multi-author papers (180)
One country	248 (84%)	132 (73%)
Two countries	45 (15%)	45 (25%)
Three countries	3 (1%)	3 (2%)

Source: Own calculations based on the official conference programs.

Brad Humphreys was the most prolific conference attendee with 12 contributions in total (table 5). He is closely followed by *Christoph Breuer* and *Bernd Frick* with 11 contributions each. Note that for this list we count all the papers in which a conference participant is mentioned as an author or co-author, it does not necessarily imply that the person also presented the paper. The top 10 consists of researchers from only 3 countries and includes 4 American, 4 German and 2 British sports economists. Absent in this list are the French. Not surprisingly, Wladimir Andreff is the most prolific French researcher with 6 contributions.

Table 5: Top ten of most prolific conference contributors

Rank	Researcher	Number of papers
1.	Humphreys, Brad	12
2.	Breuer, Christoph	11
	Frick, Bernd	
4.	Downward, Paul	9
	Ruseski, Jane E.	
6.	Paul, Rodney	8
7.	Dawson, Peter	7
	Feddersen, Arne	
	Maxcy, Joel	
	Pawlowski, Tim	

Source: Own calculations based on the official conference programs.

5. Conclusion

This survey shows how ESEA conferences have evolved from the first edition in Paris in 2009 to the fifth edition in Esbjerg in 2013. Over the years, 228 participants originating from 26 countries gave almost 300 presentations on sports economics. Little by little the conference seems to gather more international appeal. In Esbjerg a record total of 21 countries were represented. France and Germany have been the main contributors to the conferences, but while the German share of sports economics researchers present at the conference has gradually increased over the years, the French share has drastically fallen. The ESEA conferences are attended mainly by male researchers, but the gender imbalance has been slightly reduced recently.

The conference became more diversified over the years as the number of sports discussed at the conference increased from 7 in Paris to 13 in Esbjerg. The dominant research areas are regulation, governance & organisation of sports leagues, economic impact and/or cost-benefit analyses and sport performance analyses. Research is mainly empirically based and heavily oriented towards men's sports. The ESEA conferences also seem to have stimulated (international) collaboration. A growing number of presentations is multi-authored with sports economics researchers from different countries involved. From a quick scan of the economics literature, the solid standard of the research presented at the conferences became clear. About a quarter of all the papers were published in quality publications within two years after presentation. The recognition of sports economics as a valuable sub-discipline of economics is illustrated by the fact that also at least a dozen papers have been published in reputable non-sports economics journals.

It would be interesting to replicate this analysis in five years time, to examine whether the observations made in this initial survey hold over a longer period of time. Such a replication study would also allow to check if the ESEA conferences keep the pivotal role they play in stimulating sports economics research, as established in this paper.

References

Andreff, W. (2010): An Introduction to Papers from the European Conference in Sports Economics, in: International Journal of Sport Finance, Vol. 5, p. 107.

Mondello, M. J. & Pedersen, P. M. (2003): A Content Analysis of the Journal of Sports Economics, in: Journal of Sports Economics, Vol. 4, pp. 64–73.

Sánchez Santos, J. M & Castellanos García, P. (2011): A Bibliometric Analysis of Sports Economics Research, in: International Journal of Sport Finance, Vol. 6, pp. 222–244.

List of Contributors

Andreff, Wladimir, Dr.
Professor Emeritus, Honorary President of the International Association of Sports Economists and European Sports Economics Association, University Paris 1 Panthéon Sorbonne, Paris, France.

Baños-Pino, José, Dr.
Professor, Department of Economics, Fundación Observatorio Económico del Deporte, University of Oviedo, Gijón, Spain.

Beck, Nikolaus, Dr.
Associate Professor, Faculty of Economics, University of Lugano, Lugano, Switzerland.

Budzinski, Oliver, Dr.
Professor, Economic Theory, Institute of Economics, Ilmenau University of Technology, Germany.

Feddersen, Arne, Dr.
Professor (MSO), Department of Environmental and Business Economics, University of Southern Denmark, Campus Esbjerg, Denmark.

Forester, Brooke, Ph.D.
Assistant Professor, Department of Health, Physical Education and Leisure Studies, University of South Alabama, Mobile, Alabama, USA.

Hamil, Sean, Mr.
Lecturer, Departement of Management, Birkbeck College, University of London, and Director, Birkbeck Sport Business Centre, England.

Holden, Shelley, Ed.D.
Assistant Professor, Department of Health, Physical Education and Leisure Studies, University of South Alabama, Mobile, Alabama, USA.

Keshock, Christopher Michael, Ph.D.
Assistant Professor of Sport and Recreation Administration, Department of Health, Physical Education and Leisure Studies, University of South Alabama, Mobile, Alabama, USA.

Könecke, Thomas, Dipl.-Hdl.
Research Assistant, Department of Sport Economics and Sport Sociology, Johannes Gutenberg University, Mainz, Germany.

Kwiatkowski, Grzegorz, M.Sc.
Ph.D. Student, Department of Environmental and Business Economics, University of Southern Denmark, Campus Esbjerg, Denmark.

Lagae, Wim, Dr.
Associate Professor, Faculty of Economics and Business, Campus Antwerp, and Faculty of Movement and Rehabilitation Sciences, KU Leuven; Part-time Guest Lecturer, Department of Sport and Movement Sciences, University Ghent, Belgium.

Maxcy, Joel, Ph.D.
Associate Professor, School of Tourism and Hospitality Management, Temple University, Philadelphia, Pennsylvania, USA.

Meyer, Mark, Dipl.-Vw.
Senior Researcher, Institute for Economic Structures Research, Osnabrück, Germany.

Müller, Anika, M.Sc.
Ph.D. Student, Chair for Economic Theory, Institute of Economics, Ilmenau University of Technology, Germany.

Ochieng, Peter, Ph.D.
Professor, School of Sports & Exercise Science, Victoria University of Technology, Melbourne, Australia.

Oklevik, Ove, Ph.D.
Associate Professor, Faculty of Social Science, Sogn and Fjordane University College, Sogndal, Norway.

Pawlowski, Tim, Dr.
Professor of Sport Economics, Institute of Sports Science, Faculty of Economics and Social Science, University of Tübingen, Germany.

Peeters, Thomas, M.Sc.
Ph.D. Student, Department of Economics, University of Antwerp, Antwerpen, Belgium and Flanders Research Foundation, Brussel, Belgium.

Pérez, Levi, Dr.
Associate Professor, Department of Economics, University of Oviedo, Spain, and Fundación Observatorio Económico del Deporte, Gijón, Spain.

Puente, Víctor, M.Sc.
Ph.D. Student, Department of Economics, University of Oviedo, Spain, and Fundación Observatorio Económico del Deporte, Gijón, Spain.

Rodríguez, Plácido, Dr.
Professor, Department of Economics, University of Oviedo, Spain, and Fundación Observatorio Económico del Deporte, Gijón, Spain.

Schubert, Mathias, M.Sc.
Research Assistant, Department of Sport Economics and Sport Sociology, Johannes Gutenberg University, Mainz, Germany.

Szymanski, Stefan, Ph.D.
Stephen J. Galetti Professor of Sport Management, Department of Kinesiology, University of Michigan, Ann Arbor, USA.

Van Reeth, Daam, Dr.
Associate Professor, Faculty of Economics and Business, Center for Research on Economic Markets and their Environments, Campus Brussel, KU Leuven, Belgium.

Schriften zur Politischen Ökonomik
Evolutorische und ökologische Aspekte

Political Economics, Competition and Regulation

Herausgegeben von / Edited by Udo Müller, Oliver Budzinski, Yücel Calbay, Jörg Jasper und Torsten Sundmacher

- Band 1 Jörg Jasper/Torsten Sundmacher (Hrsg.): Ökologische Kompatibilität und technologischer Wandel. 2000.
- Band 2 Torsten Sundmacher: Das Umweltinformationsinstrument Ökobilanz (LCA). Anwendungsbezug und instrumentelle Ausgestaltungsmöglichkeiten. 2002.
- Band 3 Oliver Budzinski/Jörg Jasper (Hrsg.): Wettbewerb, Wirtschaftsordnung und Umwelt. Festschrift für Udo Müller. 2004.
- Band 4 Robert König: Die Elementarschadenversicherung in der Bundesrepublik Deutschland als Element der finanziellen Risikovorsorge gegen Naturereignisse. Diskussion staatlicher Regulierungsoptionen am Fallbeispiel der Hochwasser 2002 unter Berücksichtigung versicherungswirtschaftlicher Präferenzen. 2006.
- Band 5 Sven Twelemann: Stromwirtschaft im Spannungsfeld zwischen Wettbewerb und Klimapolitik. Eine Untersuchung am Beispiel des deutschen Strommarktes. 2006.
- Band 6 Shin-Yuan Tsai: Globalization Effects on China's Influence on Taiwan Economy. 2007.
- Vol. 7 Marina Gruševaja / Christoph Wonke / Ulrike Hösel / Malcolm H. Dunn (Hrsg.): Quo vadis Wirtschaftspolitik? Ausgewählte Aspekte der aktuellen Diskussion. Festschrift für Norbert Eickhof. 2008.
- Band 8 Ann Kathrin Buchs: Schutz der Biodiversität durch Benefit-sharing? Das Beispiel pharmazeutischer Bioprospektierung. 2009.
- Band 9 Susanna Hübner: Wettbewerbsanalyse des Fernsehsektors. Anforderungen an eine neue Rundfunkordnung aus ordnungspolitischer Sicht. 2009.
- Band 10 Arndt Christiansen: Der "More Economic Approach" in der EU-Fusionskontrolle. Entwicklung, konzeptionelle Grundlagen und kritische Analyse. 2010.
- Vol. 11 Claudia Schmidt: Refusal to License Intellectual Property Rights as Abuse of Dominance. 2010.
- Band 12 Ninja Mariette Lehnert: Möglichkeiten und Grenzen der ökologischen Innovationspolitik im Pkw-Verkehr. 2013.
- Band 13 Dirk-Christof Stüdemann: Europäische Politik aus einem Guss? Energiepolitik zwischen europäischen Visionen und nationalen Realitäten am Beispiel von Deutschland und Frankreich. 2014.
- Band 14 Oliver Budzinski / Arne Feddersen (eds.): Contemporary Research in Sports Economics. Proceedings of the 5th ESEA Conference. 2014.

www.peterlang.com

www.ingramcontent.com/pod-product-compliance
Ingram Content Group UK Ltd.
Pitfield, Milton Keynes, MK11 3LW, UK
UKHW021831100926
8556IPUK00004B/272

9 783631 646571